PUGET'S SOUND

Murray Morgan

PUGET'S SOUND

A Narrative
of Early Tacoma and
the Southern Sound

University of Washington Press

Seattle & London

Library of Congress Cataloging in Publication Data

Morgan, Murray Cromwell, 1916–
    Puget's Sound : a narrative of early Tacoma and the
southern Sound.

    Bibliography: p.
    Includes index.
    1. Tacoma—History.   2. Puget Sound area—History.
I. Title.
F899.T2M67   979.7'78   79-4844
ISBN 0-295-95680-1 (cloth)
ISBN 0-295-95842-1 (paper)

For Rags

Contents

Illustrations

ix

PUGET'S SOUND

The Eyes
of Discovery . . .

LATE on the sunny afternoon of Saturday, May 19, 1792, His Britannic Majesty's sloop-of-war *Discovery* dropped anchor in 210 feet of water over sandy bottom in mid-channel between Blake and Bainbridge islands three miles west of Alki Point. Three hundred years after the European discovery of America, white men had reached the area of Tacoma and Seattle.

From the deck of the three-year-old ship, George Vancouver studied his surroundings. He was a dour man of Dutch descent, little given to poetic expression, but he was moved by the splendor of the sea in the forest, which he was first to describe. The waterway lay cradled between mountain ranges. To the east, the Cascades "in various rugged and grotesque shapes rear their heads above the lofty pine trees that appear to compose one uninterrupted forest between us and the snow range." To the west lay "the ridge of mountains on which mount Olympus is situated, whose rugged summits are seen no less fancifully towering over the forest."

The land nearest the *Discovery* was a finger of sandstone pointing eastward, its surface "a beautiful meadow covered with luxurient herbage." Indian women were digging bulbs with fire-hardened sticks. At the far edge of the meadow, against the dark forest, dimly seen from the ship, were scattered make-shift shelters formed by covering a loose frame of poles with rush mats.

This was a summer encampment. The Indians—Suquamish—had come to gather food. They paid remarkably little attention to the *Discovery*, the first ship to visit their area. Although several canoes were drawn up on the rocky beach below a low bluff, only one was launched. Two naked men paddled the blunt-nosed dugout as it circled the hundred-foot-long, copper-sheathed warship, slowly and at a most respectful distance. For a long time the paddlers ignored the calls of greeting, the beckoning gestures, and the displays of

3

trinkets by the English sailors. Then, suddenly, they turned toward the warship paddling swiftly, threw on deck the pelt of a small animal, and dug hard for shore.

Late in the afternoon Vancouver had himself rowed ashore. He landed in "a small cove about half a mile in width, encircled by compact shores, with a cluster of rocks nearly in its center, little worthy of further notice." No Indians approached the landing party, nor did the Englishmen climb the low bluff to visit the natives. The setting sun haloed the crest of the Olympics and washed the Cascades with afterglow as Vancouver returned to his ship.

The thirty-four-year-old captain retired to his cabin at the stern of the vessel to plan the next day's activities. The general mission of his expedition was to fill in the blank spaces in the chart of the coast of Northwest America begun by Captain James Cook in 1778, a voyage Vancouver had accompanied as a midshipman. The formal instructions given him by the Office of the High Admiral of Great Britain and Ireland defined Vancouver's first task as "acquiring accurate information with respect to the nature & extent of water communication which may tend in any considerable degree to facilitate an intercourse, for the purpose of commerce, between the North West Coast of America and the country on the opposite side of the continent occupied by his Majesty's subjects."

This was the last flicker of Europe's centuries-old vision of a Northwest Passage, a navigable waterway connecting the Atlantic and Pacific through the inconvenient bulk of North America. The Admiralty had long since despaired of discovering such a route for ships south of Bering Strait but still hoped to find a system of rivers and lakes by which the canoe fleets of the Hudson's Bay Company and the North West Company could carry trade goods and furs across the continent.

British merchant captains who visited Northwest America in the sea otter trade that commenced after Cook's voyage had reported the existence of the Strait of Juan de Fuca leading toward the interior. The Admiralty instructed Vancouver to explore it, reminding him that "the discovery of a new communication between any such sea or strait and any river running into or from the Lake of the Woods [in northern Minnesota] would be particularly useful."

These orders had brought Vancouver to the Sound. His hope was that this inland sea might swing eastward through the Cascades or at least be fed by a river that did. But there were complications to exploring it. The waterway just ahead was split by a headland: a broad channel to port slanting southeast, a narrow arm to starboard leading south. These were constricted waters and the 330-ton *Discovery* drew fifteen feet. Vancouver decided it would be prudent to leave the ship at anchor awaiting the arrival of its small consort, the *Chatham*, which was making a reconnaissance along the eastern shore. He would send a party to explore the southern Sound in small boats "although the execution of such a service in open boats would necessarily be extremely laborious, and expose those so employed to numerous dangerous and unpleasant situations."

Having made his decision, Vancouver seated himself on a chest that doubled as chair, laid paper on the slanted surface of his writing box, and took up a quill pen. I like to imagine the scene: the ship rocking gently, rigging creaking, small waves slapping, gulls mewing as they wheeled on steady wings. Somewhere out in the darkness a loon laughed. In the cabin, the soft light of the whale oil lamp; ashore, the flare of the Indian fires.

Memo (to Lieutenant Peter Puget)

Concerning a further Examination of the Inlet we are in Necessary and capable of being executed by the Boats. You are at 4 o'Clock tomorrow Morning to proceed with the Launch accompanied by Mr. Whidbey in the Cutter (whose Directions You will follow in such points as appertain to the Surveying of the Shore etc) & being provided with a Weeks Provision you will proceed up the said Inlet keeping the Starboard or Continental shore on board. Having proceeded three Days up the Inlet, should it then appear to you of that Extent that you cannot finally determine its limits and return to the Ship by Thursday next, You are then to return on board, reporting to me an account of your Proceedings and also noticing the appearance of the country, its Productions and Inhabitants, if varying from what we have already seen.

> Given on board his Britannic
> Majesty's Sloop Discovery
>
> GEO VANCOUVER

In the pre-dawn darkness of Sunday, May 20, the longboats were stowed with muskets, pistols, cutlasses, powder and ball, presents and trading goods, tents, navigating equipment, survey equipment, food, and wine for the officers. The launch was clinker built, twenty feet long and broad enough to seat five pairs of oarsmen, two abreast; it had two demountable masts which, when in place, carried lug-sails. The cutter was smaller, eighteen feet, with six oars and a single mast. Neither had cabin or decking, though a canvas awning astern gave the officers some protection from the weather.

They were a young lot, accustomed to hardship. Nearly all of the enlisted men were in their teens or early twenties. Second Lieutenant Peter Puget was twenty-seven or twenty-eight—his exact birthday is unknown—and had spent half his life in the Navy, having entered service as a midshipman in 1778. Puget had attracted Vancouver's attention while serving under Captain James Vashon in the West Indies after the Revolutionary War. Joseph Whidbey, master on the *Discovery*, was about Puget's age, had served under Vancouver in the West Indies, and was the best man with instruments on the expedition. A fine mathematician, Whidbey had perfected the method of surveying from small boats. His system was to land on conspicuous points, take compass bearings of other prominent landmarks, and, whenever possible, make observations of the sun at noon to determine latitude. As the boats cruised between landings, the officers sketched and took notes. On return to the *Discovery*, the data were put down on a smooth map and tied into the charts already drawn.

The oldest man in the longboat party was Archibald Menzies, thirty-eight, a spare, craggy Scot who had visited the Northwest Coast in 1787 as physician aboard the sea otter vessel *Prince of Wales* and now represented the Royal Society, Britain's leading scientific organization, as botanist. He had asked to accompany the Puget party "though their mode of procedure in surveying Cruizes was not very favorable for my pursuits as it afforded me so little time on shore . . . yet it was the most eligible I could at this time adopt in obtaining a general knowledge of the Country."

It was still dark when the longboats pulled away from the *Discovery*, heading south. A small island (Blake) loomed dim, ragged with fir, against the eastern sky. By the time they entered the chute of Colvos Passage, the Cascades were silhouetted black against an orange sunrise. The tide was against the oarsmen. Squadrons of coots flipped below the surface as the boats approached with thrashing oars. Gulls circled, crying warnings to their nesting young. Seals surveyed them with round, blank eyes, leaned back, and disappeared, the memory of their closing nostrils lingering like the smile of the Cheshire. Herons lifted from the surf-line on somber wings and, with cries like tearing canvas, settled into the tree tops.

The English were not alone. A small, dark dugout followed them, its two paddlers holding close to the western shore, responding neither to waved handkerchiefs nor to the flourish of fir branches, a sign of peace among Indians farther north.

About eight o'clock the canoe spurted ahead and turned into a narrow cove (Olalla, "the place of many berries"). It was time for breakfast. Perhaps the natives would join them. Puget gave orders to enter the inlet. They found the canoe "hauled up close to the trees" among the salal and huckleberry, but the Indians had disappeared. "Some Beads, Medals and Trinkets were put among their other articles in the Canoe as a Proof that our Intentions were Friendly."

The tide was slack when they again took to the water, but a fair

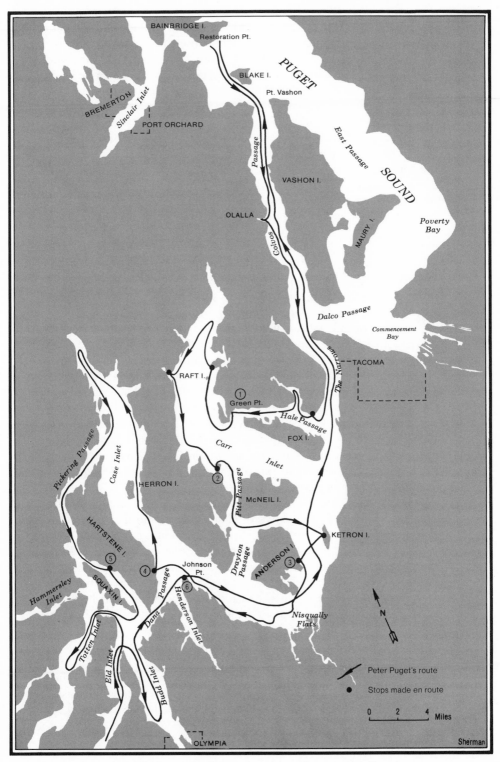

Peter Puget's route (circled numbers mark where each night was spent)

north wind helped them down a channel two miles wide and so deep that though "soundings were frequently tried no Bottom could be reached with 40 fthms of line." The sky was clear, the sun hot. About noon, the shore on their left curved away to the east. They found themselves looking up Dalco Passage into Commencement Bay where Tacoma now stands.

Ah, to have been with those first Europeans to see the bay, see it unimproved, the cone of the slumbering volcano heavy with winter's snow sweeping up from green tideflat and dark forest to dominate the Cascade barrier. They had sighted the Mountain before—Vancouver first noted it from Marrowstone Point up by Port Townsend on May 8 and named it in honor of an old friend, the myopic Rear Admiral Peter Rainier—but no view of Mount Rainier surpasses this one.

"A most charming prospect," wrote the scientist Menzies. The Mountain "appeared close to us though at least 10 to 12 leagues off. The low land at the head of the Bay swelled out very gradually to form a most beautiful and Majestic Mountain of great elevation whose line of ascent appeared equally smooth & gradual on every side with a round obtuse summit covered two thirds of its height down with perpetual Snow as were also the summits of a rugged ridge of Mountains that proceed from it to the Northward."

From the poor vantage of sea level, they puzzled out the pattern of waterways and guessed correctly that the land they had coasted on the port side was an island (which Vancouver later named for Puget's old commanding officer, James Vashon). Their instructions were clear; they were to follow the shore to starboard, so they did not inspect Commencement Bay, instead entering the Narrows where "a most Rapid Tide from the northward hurried us so fast past the shore that we could scarce land."

For five miles the rowboat flotilla rode the tidal stream south. Then an arm opened to westward, Hale Passage, and they entered it only to find to their surprise the current so strong against them they could make little progress. (It sweeps clockwise around Fox Island, the southern shore of the passage.) So Puget's party put ashore on Point Fosdick to take their noon meal and wait a change of tide. As they dined, two canoes which had followed them through the Narrows passed the picnic spot and disappeared into an inlet farther west.

The Puget party reached the inlet about three in the afternoon. Wollochet Bay, the place of squirting clams, is narrow but about two miles in length. The evergreen forest was interspersed with the cinnamon boles of madronas and the rounded crowns of mountain ash, the first ash they had seen on the Sound. "The Soil appeared good &

produced a quantity of Gooseberry, Raspberry and Current Berries now highly in Blossom which intermixed with Roses, exhibited a Strange Varigation of Flowers but by no Means unpleasant to the Eye."

Just inside the eastern entrance they detected the house frames of a deserted village, but not until they were leaving the cove did they see Indians. Then they heard a shout from the western shore and saw a party digging clams. When it became clear the English intended to land, the women and children gathered their baskets and "scudded into the woods loaded with parcels." The men came out in two canoes to meet the strangers. They were all naked. "In their Persons these People are slenderly made. They wear their Hair long which is quite Black and exceeding Dirty. Both Nose and Ears are perforated, to which were affixed Copper Ornaments & Beads." This first meeting of the Puyallup-Nisqually people with the whites went well.

"We made them some little presents to convince them of our amicable intentions, on which they invited us by signs to land," says Menzies. "The only one we found remaining on the Beach was an old woman without either hut or shelter, setting near their baskets of provisions & stores. The former consisted chiefly of Clams, some of which were dried and smoked and strung up for the convenience of carrying them about their Necks, but a great number of them were still fresh in the shell, which they readily parted with to our people for buttons, beads & bits of Copper." The women and children who had hidden in the forest were lured from the woods and were also presented with beads and bits of metal.

When the explorers set out, the Indian men followed in their canoes. Puget made camp about eight o'clock on Green Point, where Hale Passage merges into Carr Inlet. As the seamen erected the marquee, a large field tent, for the officers and smaller shelters for themselves, the Indians "lay on their Paddles about one Hundred Yards from the Beach attentively viewing our operations."

The presence of the Indians presented Puget with a bit of a problem. It was customary when making camp to discharge the firearms that had been carried primed and shotted in the boats during the day. But Puget was afraid the shots would alarm the natives. "Finding however they kept hovering about the Boats & being apprehensive they would be endeavouring to commit Depredations during the night, I ordered a Musquet fired but so far was it from intimidating or alarming them they remained stationary, only exclaiming *Poh* at every report, in way of Derision." Whether the Indians were mocking the whites or merely mimicking the sound remains in doubt. No matter. They soon withdrew and made camp on Fox Island. The night passed without incident.

The Englishmen awoke Monday morning in light rain and set off without breakfast. The tide ran against them but the rain soon stopped. Flocks of pigeon guillemots cruised the heavy green waters; some dived as the longboats approached but most skittered across the surface in long take-off runs, trailing hoarse whispers of protest as they curved toward land to fire themselves point blank into nest holes in the clay cliffs.

When the English landed on a small island off the mouth of Horsehead Bay (the journals do not make clear whether it was Raft Island or tiny Cutts), a host of crows voiced objection. In vain: the explorers shot some fledglings and breakfasted on young crow cooked on spits over a beach fire. Puget was pleased. He jotted a note that his men's willingness to eat crow meant the provender in the boats could, if necessary, be stretched across extra days of exploration.

Puget thought the inlet led nowhere, but

. . . more clearly to ascertain what appeared almost a Certainty, we continued pulling up for its head till near Eleven, when the Beach was close to the Boats. [They were in Burley Lagoon.] In the SW Corner of the Cove was a Small Village among the Pines, and beyond the termination the country had the appearance of a Level Forest, but close to the water it was covered with small Green Bushes. We pulled in toward the Village but seeing a Canoe paddling from it towards us induced us to lay on our Oars to wait their Approach, but neither Copper nor any Article in our Possession had sufficient allurement to get them close to the Boats.

They lay about twenty yards from us and kept continually pointing to the Eastward, expressing of a Wish that our Departure would be more agreeable than our Visit. Knowing all our Solicitations would not bring on a Reciprocal Friendship, & we were only losing time, therefore we left Those Surly Gentlemen and Kept along the Opposite or Southern Shore of this Western Branch. However I did not like to quit these Indians altogether without giving some evident Proof that our Intention was perfectly friendly, & an Expedient was hit on that soon answered our Purpose. Some Copper, Medals, Looking Glasses & other Articles were tied on a Peece of Wood & left floating on the water. We then pulled away to a Small Distance. The Indians immediately Picked them up. Eventually they ventured alongside the Boat but not with that Confidence I could have wished.

These Indians were "more Stout than any we have hitherto seen," and two of the three in the canoe had lost their right eyes and were pitted with smallpox. "During the time they were alongside the Boats they appeared exceeding shy and distrustful, notwithstanding our Liberality towards them. . . . Though they wanted Copper from us they would not part with their Bows or Arrows in Exchange."

The English rowed southward along the western shore of the inlet.

The day had cleared; it was hot and muggy, Puget's thermometer registering 90 degrees, very warm for May. Early in the afternoon they put into a small cove, probably the lagoon at the mouth of Minter Creek, to dine. "Here," says Menzies' journal, "we found two or three small runs of water & was going to haul a small Seine we had in the Launch, but the appearance of six Canoes with about 20 people in them which our shy followers had collected by their voiciferous noise prevented it."

The first confrontation between whites and Indians on Puget Sound occurred in a dispute over fishing. The Salish peoples were not greatly concerned with material possessions but were jealous of songs, prayers, insignia of rank and kinship, and of places where a man had the right to hunt or fish, first or exclusively. Such rights were sacred possessions passed between generations; they could not be sold or traded, though they might in desperation be risked in gambling. Their protection was integral to the Indians' web of culture, a basic strand in the fabric of society. For someone to violate such rights was stealing; worse than stealing, it was insult, implying a master-slave relationship: "I am so much above you I need not even ask." And here were these strangers beside the stream with a net.

Puget knew none of this. What he did know was that his party was confronted by men, hostile and armed. He knew, too, that five years earlier a landing party from the British sea otter vessel *Imperial Eagle* had simply disappeared at the mouth of the Hoh River on the western side of the Olympic Mountains. He need not be an anthropologist to recognize danger. Quietly he told his men to fold up the net but to act unconcerned. He drew a line in the beach gravel and by gestures "the intent of which they perfectly understood" asked the Indians to stay on the far side.

Several of the landing party had brought their muskets ashore. Puget reasoned that to go back to the boats for more weapons might precipitate trouble. Instead he led the party up the bank and settled down nonchalantly to eat, keeping unobtrusive watch. The Indians got back in their canoes and began a lively discussion among themselves, pointing sometimes to the boats, sometimes at the shore party, gesturing as if planning tactics. Some canoes began to move toward the launch and cutter. Puget's group shouted and pointed their guns. The Indians paddled back to the mouth of the stream.

At this point, a seventh canoe carrying four men entered the cove. As it approached, the Indians already present splashed ashore and began stringing their bows, but whether for an attack on the newcomers or the whites Puget could not be sure. He found his position "most awkward, being unwilling to fire on these poor People, who might have been unacquainted with the advantage we had over them, and not wishing to run the Risk of having my People wounded by the first discharge of their Arrows, I absolutely felt at a Loss how to Act." Doubts about the Indians' intentions were quickly resolved: the men from the new canoe joined the party on the beach and strung their bows.

For a moment they formed an ancient frieze, motionless under the mid-day sun, red confronting white, native facing invader, stone age man resisting the intrusion of change. No one spoke. The very crows were quiet. Then a lone warrior edged up the bank, bow in hand, quiver bristling, and moved toward the protection of a tree only fifteen feet from Puget's party. The English arose, muskets ready. The men in the launch and cutter swung the small cannon mounted on swivels at the prow of each craft to menace the Indians by the stream. One of Puget's men approached the young man who had climbed the bank, put a musket to his chest and marched him, unresisting, back to the beach.

On the bank the seamen quickly gathered the equipment they had brought ashore and made ready to leave. The Indians remained on their side of the line in the gravel, shouting, gesturing, sharpening their arrowheads on the beach rocks. Puget ordered one of the swivel guns to be fired across the water as a demonstration of the power of cannon. Neither the explosion and smoke nor the distant splash of grapeshot seemed at first to impress the Indians. *Poh,* they exclaimed, more loudly than before.

Abruptly, unexpectedly, the confrontation ended. The Indians "now offered for Sale those Bows and Arrows which had shortly before been strung for the worst of Purposes." They even sold the garments from their backs, and, as the explorers rowed away, offered what remaining articles they had to trade. At last "finding we were drawing fast from their Habitations they began to leave us. In half an hour we were again left to ourselves but we had the Satisfaction of having convinced them of our Friendship before their Departure." The weather, too, had changed. Clouds drawn from the ocean by the unseasonable heat released "a perfect deluge of rain" and about five miles from Alarm Cove, Puget landed at South Head and made camp.

For the next five days in weather that ranged from rain to fog "so thick we could not see the boats from the tents" to a thunder storm, then back to brilliant sunshine, the survey party traced the outlines of the inland sea, circling its islands, probing its inlets. They noted flora and fauna. They found delicious small oysters, abundant clams, "luxuriant ferns that grow over head." They reported few streams, failing to locate the mouth of the Nisqually among the cattails.

Everywhere they found the Indians friendly. Indians brought them presents of wild raspberry shoots, arrow grass, and (on request) salmon while the party camped on Anderson Island; happily traded from their canoes in the shoals off Nisqually Reach; taught Menzies how to count from one to ten in Salish; gave navigating directions by sign language; and on the last day of the survey entertained the English ashore in a village on Eld Inlet.

"We landed for a short time and were received by the Inhabitants with all the Friendship and Hospitality we could have expected," said Puget:

These people I should suppose were about Sixty in Numbers of all Ages and Descriptions. They lived under a kind of Shed open at the Front and Sides. The women appeared employed in the Domestic Duties such as curing Clams & Fish, making baskets of various reeds, so neatly woven that they were perfectly water tight. The occupations of the men I believe consist chiefly in Fishing, constructing Canoes and performing all the laborious work of the Village. . . .

The only Difference I perceived between our present companions and former visitors were the Extravagance with which their Faces were ornamented. Streaks of Red Ochre & Black Glimmer were on some, others entirely with the Former, and a few gave the Preferences to the latter. Every person had a fashion of his own, and to us who were Strangers to Indians this Sight conveyed a Stronger Force of the Savageness of the Native Inhabitants than any other Circumstance we had hitherto met with; not but their Conduct, friendly and inoffensive had already merited our warmest Approbation, but their *Appearance* was absolutely terrific.

It will frequently occur that the Imagination receives a much greater Shock by such unusual Objects than it would was that object divested of its Exterior Ornaments or Dress, or the Sight was more familiarized to People in a State of Nature. Though we could not behold these Ornaments with the same satisfactory Eye as themselves, yet in receiving the Looking Glasses, each native appeared well satisfied with his own Fashion; at least the Paint was not at all Altered. They likewise had the Hair covered with the Down of Birds, which certainly was a good substitute for Powder. Their Paint only differed in the Colour and not the Quantity used by our own Fair Countrywomen. In these two Instances we meet with some Resemblance to our Customs and I believe the above mentioned Ornaments were of a Ceremonious Nature for our Reception at the Village. . . .

They appear much attached to the Women and hold Chastity as one of the Cardinal Virtues, and not like our friends at the Sandwich Islands make Prostitution a Trade. Immense Presents would not tempt these Girls, though coaxed with Rage to violate the Marriage Bed and much to their Credit be it Spokan they remained Stedfast in this Refusal. Credit is apparently due for this steady attachment and affectionate Conduct to their Husbands in such trying Situations, as the Articles offered were of inestimable Value in their opinions, and such as would have flattered their Vanity; not that their Beauty or Appearance created any violent Desire for the possession of their

Persons. Such Questions were put merely to try, howfar they conceived Good Conduct was binding in the Matrimonial State, and I may say from these Circumstances that a Contract of that high Importance to Civil Society is among these poor and uncivilized Indians preserved in its greatest Purity.

By Saturday afternoon the explorers had completed their investigation of the inlets. Beautiful as was the inland sea, it was a dead end, offering no waterway to the interior. Had the apocryphal Greek, Juan de Fuca, actually entered the strait now named for him and sailed, as alleged, for twenty days he would have ended not in the North Sea, as myth would have it, but at Mud Bay.

The Puget party dined at Johnson Point. "A favorable breeze sprung up from the Southward which we made use of to return to the ship." The wind strengthened to a gale; though rain began to fall heavily Puget risked sailing by night. The boats swept north through the tide race of the Narrows, crossed the lumpy waters between Point Defiance and Vashon, and rode the gale and current up Colvos Passage. At two in the morning they were back on the *Discovery,* having completed their assignment in two hours less than seven days.

When Puget returned, Vancouver was off on a survey of his own. Saturday morning he had taken the *Discovery*'s yawl and the *Chatham*'s cutter and started down the passage on the east side of Vashon Island, following the shore opposite that assigned to Puget.

It was another brilliant day; the Mountain was out but clouds of smoke hung over the eastern shore where the Indians had fired the underbrush to drive out deer. The cutter and yawl made good time down East Passage. From the southeastern shore of Vashon-Maury, Vancouver noticed "a very abrupt division in the snowy range of mountains immediately to the south of mount Rainier," and "flattered ourselves we should find the inlet [around Brown's Point] take an extensive easterly course." But it was almost noon, so before looking into Commencement Bay they landed between Brown's Point and Dash Point to determine latitude from the position of the noonday sun—41 degrees, 21 minutes—and have dinner.

A clamming party of about a dozen Indians met them at the beach. After distributing presents to "these friendly people," Vancouver drew the customary line on the beach and indicated that the visitors did not wish to have the home-folks standing over them while they ate. Two Indians asked if they could share the meal and were given permission. The English watched with amusement as the Puyallup attempted to master the use of spoons for the soup, and knife and fork for the fish. One tried to secrete a knife under his breachclout but when detected returned it, laughing.

While at Restoration Point, Vancouver had purchased for a bit of copper a deer the Indians had caught in a net on Blake Island. The *Discovery*'s cook had prepared a venision pie for the exploring party's main dish. "The Indians ate of the bread & fish we gave them without hesitation," Vancouver reported, "but on being offered venison pie, though they saw us eat it with great relish, they could not be induced to taste it. They received it from us with great disgust and presented it round to the rest of their party, by whom it underwent a very strict examination. Their conduct left no doubt in our minds that they believed it to be human flesh."

The red men lectured the whites on the theme that people should not eat people. Vancouver felt this misapprehension to be one "which it was highly expedient should be done away" lest it lead the tribesmen to noncooperation or hostility. He pointed to a deerskin one man was wearing. The Indian shook his head and pretended to chew on his arm, then "threw the pye on the dirt with gestures of great aversion and displeasure." Eventually Vancouver remembered a haunch of uncooked venison in the cutter. This was displayed to the Puyallup "by which means they were undeceived, & some of them ate of the remainder of the pye with a good appetite."

During the picnic, the natives offered travel tips to the tourists. They pointed north and spread their arms wide to indicate an extensive waterway. When asked about the opening around Browns Point, they pointed to the curve between thumb and forefinger to indicate a compact bay. By bending an arm and pointing to the crook of the elbow, they indicated that the inlet to the south was larger but that it led nowhere.

Vancouver had his doubts: "The little respect which most Indians bear to truth, and their readiness to assert what they think is most agreeable for the moment, or to answer their own particular wishes and inclinations, induced me to place little dependence on this information."

So, lunch over, the English rowed around the point. The Indians had been right: "We found the inlet to terminate here in an extensive, circular, compact bay." This was not what Vancouver had hoped for: it offered no path through the mountains. But like Puget and Menzies, the captain admired the view:

The waters washed the base of mount Rainier. . . . The forest trees, and the several shades of verdure that covered the hills, gradually decreased in point of beauty until they became invisible, when the perpetual clothing of snow commenced, which seemed to form a horizontal line from north to south along this range of rugged mountains, . . . and seemed as much elevated above them as they were above the level of the sea; the whole producing a most grand, picturesque effect. The lower mountains as they descended . . . became gradually relieved of their frigid garment; and as they approached the fertile woodland region that binds the shores of this inlet in every direction, produced a pleasing variety.

Vancouver failed to notice the Puyallup River, which seeped through the tideflats at the head of the bay. (He and his party were not good on rivers. In a period of four weeks they failed to recognize the Columbia, the Puyallup, the Nisqually, and the Fraser.) Accompanied by a small flotilla of canoes, they crossed the bay and ran along the southern shore to the entrance of the Narrows.

Though Vancouver had little doubt that Puget had preceded him, he decided that since the other party had been assigned the righthand shore, he would follow the left, so that "in the event of Mr. Puget having been unable to accomplish the task assigned him, our survey might be completed without another expedition into this region." He spent three days repeating part of Puget's work south of Point Defiance.

On Tuesday evening, May 29, Vancouver returned to the *Discovery* and compared notes with Puget: "By our joint efforts, we had completely explored every turning of this extensive inlet, & to commemorate Mr. Puget's exertions, the south extremity of it I named Puget's Sound."

The whole body of water south of the Strait of Juan de Fuca, Vancouver designated as Admiralty Inlet. Usage has reversed the meanings. Today Admiralty Inlet refers to the stretch between Point Wilson and Elliott Bay, whereas Puget Sound embraces the entire inland sea.

What did these eighteenth-century visitors think of the waterway whose existence they revealed to the western world? The age of steam was then dawning in England, but Vancouver and his officers were as yet untouched by the Industrial Revolution. They thought of Puget Sound in terms of masts and spars—"enough for all the navies of the world"—and of farms and cottage industry.

"To describe the beauties of this region will on some future occasion be a very grateful task to the pen of a skillful panegyrist," Vancouver declared. "The serenity of the climate, the unnumerable pleasing landscapes, and the abundant fertility that unassisted nature puts forth, require only to be enriched by the industry of men with villages, mansions, cottages and other buildings, to render it the most lovely country that can be imagined; whilst the labour of its inhabitants would be amply rewarded in the bounties which nature seems ready to bestow on cultivation."

Menzies agreed; one can almost hear violins in the background: "A traveller wandering over these unfrequented Plains is regaled with a salubrious & vivifying air impregnated with the balsamic fragrance of the surrounding Pinery, while his mind is eagerly occupied every moment on new objects and his senses rivetted on the enchanting variety of the surrounding scenery where the softer beauties of Landscape are harmoniously blended in majestic grandeur with the wild & romantic to form an interesting & picturesque prospect on every side."

In spite of the fact that one of its great mountains was named for him, Third Lieutenant Joseph Baker had doubts of the utility of the region. Conceding that "this large branch of the sea" had excellent harbors, secure anchorages, and abundant material for masts and spars, he was "of opinion that their remote situation from the Sea Coast renders it improbable that they will ever be of much use to Navigators."

James Whidbey, who with Puget had taken the closest look at the sea in the forest, wrote home to suggest that the area would make a suitable half-way house for graduates of the new prison colony at Botany Bay in Australia. "Instead of returning to England to become a fresh prey on the Public, the [transportees could after serving their time] be sent to this country and settled at the head of Fuca Straights—where there is country equal to any in the world."

As for Puget, he was enthusiastic about the area that bears his name:

The Land in the Southern Inlets of these strates is most greatfull to the Eye. . . . rising in Small Hillocks and Mounts till the more inland parts. It is overlooked by Lofty Snow Mountains and indeed Nature as if she studied the Convenience of Mankind, has so disposed of the Trees as to form on the Rising Grounds the most beautiful Lawns on which I have seen Grass Man Height. Little would the Labour be in its Cultivation, yet the Natives either from Ignorance or Indolence prefer the Stony Beach to the more healthfull and delightfull plains which distinguish this favored Land from the Rest of the Coast of America. . . . An Island distinguished in the General Chart by the name of Whidbey's Island is absolutely as fine a tract of Land as I ever saw, at least apparently so.

The Eyes
of Exploitation . . .

L OVELY as was the land, glowing as were Vancouver's descriptions in *A Voyage of Discovery to the North Pacific Ocean and round the World,* Puget Sound attracted no visitors (at least, none who left records) until 1824, and no settlers until 1833. Distance, as Lieutenant Baker had predicted, was the problem. The farmlands were half the world away from markets, the spar-trees three thousand miles from the nearest shipyard. The Sound itself was several days' sail from the open ocean. Furs were few. What the inland sea had to offer was more readily available elsewhere.

It was a time of war and the threat of war. The French Revolution and the rise of Napoleon tied up British ships, merchant as well as naval. New England ships dominated the trade in sea otter skins between the Northwest Coast and China until the War of 1812, when British sea power drove American vessels from the eastern Pacific and the British-owned North West Company bought, at gunpoint, John Jacob Astor's post at the mouth of the Columbia.

The period was a time of trade wars that included armed battle. The Hudson's Bay Company, which in 1660 had been given a three-hundred-year monopoly on trade in the area draining into Hudson's Bay, and the North West Company, which operated out of Montreal, were struggling for control in the Canadian Midwest. Men died in the Pemmican War; worse, profits disappeared. Not until the Hudson's Bay Company absorbed its rival in 1821 and expanded its operations to the Pacific did fur traders become interested in Puget Sound.

It was a time of stalemated diplomacy. Unable to agree on a dividing line between their claims in the Pacific Northwest, the United States and Britain agreed in 1818 to a ten-year period of joint occupancy. The Oregon Country—by which was meant all the land between Russian America in the north, Spanish America in the south, the crest of the Rockies, and the Pacific Ocean—was open to citizens of either country. The arrangement, leaving the eventual nationality of the Puget Sound country uncertain, was no incentive to settlement.

And it was a time of trouble with the Indians. They had learned to look on the whites not as visitors bearing luxury goods but as invaders. The tribes were still numerous enough and powerful enough to make dangerous the approaches to Puget Sound whether by sea or by land.

In 1818, while the North West Company still controlled Fort George at the mouth of the Columbia, a Scot named James Keith was chief factor. Keith was celebrated for the good luck that got him out of scrapes his bad judgment created. (Not forever; on a trip home to Scotland he slipped on garbage in the cobbled street of Glasgow and died of a fractured skull.) Among Keith's employees was an Indian named Oskonton, one of numerous Iroquois imported from the East as hunters. Assigned to a beaver brigade on the Cowlitz River, Oskonton became diverted in pursuit of a Cowlitz girl left unattended by the men of her village who were away on a deer hunt. He wouldn't take no for an answer, but she so strenuously resisted his advances that Oskonton wound up dead. His hunting companions paddled back to Fort George to report murder most foul.

Factor Keith sent a newly arrived clerk, Peter Skene Ogden, with an escort of Iroquois warriors to investigate the homicide. The guardian Iroquois complicated the inquest by opening fire as soon as they reached the village where Oskonton had perished. Before Ogden could restore order they had killed a dozen Cowlitz.

Better at diplomacy than at managing his Iroquois minions, Ogden placated the Cowlitz by arranging a marriage between Chief How-how's daughter and one of the young gentlemen at Fort George. The record does not say how the bridegroom was selected, but in due course the bridal party was escorted downriver from How-how's village to the fort. An armed guard was necessary because the Chinook at the mouth of the Columbia opposed visits by other tribesmen to the trading post. Fur trade nuptials (valid only for the duration of the man's stay in Indian country) were celebrated, and the new relationship between Nor'westers and Cowlitz was strengthened by three days of drinking, feasting, and present giving. How-how started home in high spirits, happy with the alliance, but Chinook waited in ambush, attacked his party, and drove them back to the fort. Guards, hearing shooting and seeing Indians running toward the walls, locked the gates and opened fire. One of How-how's companions was wounded before the whites realized their mistake and opened the gates.

How-how had had it. He was not to be placated by more presents.

The Cowlitz declared their river off-limits to whites and eastern Indians. The river route north toward Puget Sound was still closed when George Simpson visited Fort George six years later.

Simpson was the illegitimate son of a well-to-do Scot, and the protégé of a major stockholder in the Hudson's Bay Company, Lord Colville. After HBC swallowed the North West Company, Simpson became governor of the Northern Department of Rupert Land, which included the Oregon Country. Though the Pacific Northwest was vast, the profits it brought the HBC were meager. On November 8, 1824, Governor Simpson arrived at Fort George by canoe to find out what was wrong.

Small, rotund, fastidious, observant, and intelligent, as well as brusque, determined, and ungenerous, Simpson examined everything and liked almost nothing: "The Establishment of Fort George is a large pile of buildings covering about an acre of ground well-stockaded and protected by Bastions or Blockhouses, having two Eighteen Pounders mounted in front and altogether an air or appearance of Grandeur & consequence which does not become and is not at all suitable to an Indian Trading Post. Everything appears to me on the Columbia on too extended a scale *except the Trade.*"

Simpson was appalled to learn that little attempt had been made to carry the trade north. Since "the disgusting and inhuman scene of Carnage" at How-how's village, he complained, "we have never ventured beyond the banks of the Cowlutch. The Dangers of a visit to the Northward were Magnified to such a degree as to the treacherous and blood thirsty character of the Natives that it would have been considered the height of insanity to think of opening any intercourse or communication with them; but after repeated enquiries I could not obtain distinct information to justify all this alarm and seeing the importance of gaining a knowledge of Frazers River & the adjacent country . . . I resolved on fitting out an Expedition."

The assignment to find a passage for small boats between the Columbia River and the Fraser River fell to James McMillan, a middle-aged Scot, twenty years in the fur trade, one of the most experienced wilderness men in Hudson's Bay Company employment. He decided to try to reach Puget Sound by way of Willapa Bay, Grays Harbor, and the Chehalis River, thus by-passing the Cowlitz and How-how's hostile tribesmen. To make the trip he chose a party of forty. There were three clerks (that is, men holding the rank of officer), a French-Canadian translator, and a motley of boatmen drawn from the remarkably international collection of laborers at Fort George: seven Iroquois, six Hawaiians, twenty-one French Canadians, an Englishman, and William Cannon, an American.

On Thursday, November 28, McMillan's brigade embarked in three open boats in the rainiest time of the year to pass through the rainiest part of the country. A journal kept by a thoughtful Irishman named John Work, one of the clerks, describes what was surely the soggiest trek in the annals of Northwest exploration. They sailed in light rain across the wide bay at the mouth of the Columbia and camped in a drizzle near today's Ilwaco. For two days, "under a weighty rain," they portaged boats and supplies for six weeks—kegs of peas, oatmeal, pork, grease, butter and rum, bags of flour, biscuit, and pemmican—across the spit to Willapa Bay, their trail half-swamp, half-creek, but bordered by "many good cranberries."

In a day and a half they sailed the twenty-mile length of the oyster-bordered mud puddle that lies between Willapa hills and North Peninsula, and landed on the fist of land separating Willapa Bay from Grays Harbor. No waterway penetrated the barrier, so they portaged, dragging the boats across Toke Point to the Pacific shore. One of the French Canadians went lame and had to be carried.

Tuesday dawned fair; the wind was light, but the ocean beat heavily on the slaty beach. Afraid to risk the rowboats in the open sea, McMillan had them carried out beyond the first line of breakers. Then six men embarked with poles to keep them from drifting onto the beach while the rest of the party waded ahead, waist deep in the icy waves, towing the craft north. In eight hours they made 4,620 yards.

Wednesday they splashed north another two miles, then cut a path eastward and portaged to Grays Harbor through "one continuation of swamps, where the men with their loads were often on their knees in water and mud." Seven days' labor had brought them forty miles.

Their second week began with "drizzly rain broken by weighty showers." Through murk so thick they sometimes could not tell where gray sea ended and gray shore began, they rowed eastward. About ten o'clock Friday morning they reached "the river at the bottom of the bay" and stopped for breakfast before starting upstream. "It was with difficulty a fire was made."

The Chehalis is a beautiful river—but not a river convenient to ascend in rowboats, in late November, with a storm front hanging over Grays Harbor, the stream rising, the current at its strongest, the shores wet and marshy, and even the Indians in bad spirit: "We were surprised to find them all under arms on our approach, and at some of the villages assuming threatening attitudes, shouting from behind the trees and presenting their arms, particularly their bows and arrows, as if in the act of discharging them."

McMillan learned that the son of a Chinook chief, hoping to prevent direct contact by the whites with Indians to whom his people had been selling English goods, had spread the rumor that this was a war party: "They were soon undeceived and a present of a little tobacco to some of the chief men dismissed all appearances of hostility."

For a week the exploring party labored upstream. The Chehalis, noble in its lower reaches, narrowed and became choked with willow. Rain and terrain strengthened the current. Often the men had to pole. On Sunday they turned into a small tributary, the Black, which led north. "Navigation got very troublesome." The stream was choked with driftwood; the banks were covered with rotting salmon, dead after their spawning effort. Day after sodden day the men rowed and poled and pushed and portaged up the diminishing stream, aware now that only in the rainy season could boats use this route.

It was not all misery. One night the rain stopped long enough for them to steam their clothes back to mere dampness before the campfire. They bagged two deer and an elk. They saw signs of beaver. They encountered a friendly party of Chehalis who, for a price, agreed to carry the lame Canadian back to Fort George. He was tied on a horse, given a week's provisions, and wished well. (He survived.)

At the end of their second week they reached Black Lake. They rowed its length and set to work widening the five-mile Indian trail to the Sound so the boats could be portaged: "This labour is attended with a great deal of difficulty. As we advance the road gets worse. It is in many places wet and miry, the trees are of a very large size, many of them fallen, and the ground among them so thickly covered with underwoods, particularly an evergreen shrub called by the Chenooks Lallal [salal] that cutting a road through for the boats is a tedious and laborious task. The portage is 8090 yards long, and except a little plain at its commencement, thickly wooded with different kinds of trees, pine, maple, cedar, ash and wild cherry. Some of the pine trees are very large. I measured some of them, one of the largest was upwards of five fathoms [thirty feet] in circumference, another twenty-eight feet around."

Monday morning, December 4, 1824, they emerged from the woods and took to the Sound on Eld Inlet, the first whites to visit it since Peter Puget. The day was chill but, after morning fog, clear. They paused at Johnson Point to dine on mussels and wonder at the sun-ray starfish: ("Another kind of fish in a curious shape was also in plenty. This is a shapeless animal with long toes jointed together in the middle").

After camping north of Nisqually they put in at Chambers Creek where Work reported "a village of the Nisqually Nation consisting of six houses. These are miserable habitations constructed of poles covered with mats." It was called "Chilacum" (Steilacoom). There they recruited three Snohomish Indians—a woman and two men—to act as interpreters and guides. Thus reinforced, they pushed on through the Narrows, past Commencement Bay (being the first to note that "it receives the Qualax [Puyallup] River"), and spent the night on Vashon Island, "where we see the marks of some horses the Indians have on it. The appearance of the shores is much the same as yesterday, still bold and high, composed of clay and generally wooded to the water's edge. We found abundance of mussels at low water." The next day they passed out of the area Vancouver had designated "Puget's Sound."

In the following two weeks McMillan's brigade reached the Fraser, ascended the river to the first rapids, and having completed their assigned survey started back. On December 23 they passed Restoration Point and a few hours later were driven ashore at Three Tree Point, "it being too rough to proceed." The next day, again in weighty rain, they returned one of their guides to Steilacoom. Arising early on the twenty-fifth they were on the water by 4:00 A.M. and "reached the portage at 10, where the people immediately commenced carrying and had the boats and baggage more than half across the portage at night. On account of the heavy rain the road is much more wet and miry than when we passed last, yet we got on more expeditiously as the road is cleared." Work's journal does not mention that it was Christmas Day.

Convinced that the Black River would not make a suitable route for the fur trade, McMillan decided to risk the Cowlitz. He rented some horses from the Chehalis Indians and, leaving the bulk of the party to return by the route they had come, McMillan, Work, and seven companions went cross-country to the Cowlitz. How-how's people apparently had decided they would not hold against the Hudson's Bay Company their misadventures with the North West Company. McMillan was able to obtain two canoes, one large, one small, in which the party ran the turbulent river to its juncture with the Columbia in a day, paddled downstream through the night, and arrived at Fort George at ten in the morning.

The expedition had taken exactly six weeks. It established the Cowlitz as the best way to reach Puget Sound and the Fraser River. And it delighted Governor Simpson: "I must say that since my acquaintance with the Indian Country I have seen nothing of the kind gone through so satisfactorily; in the space of 42 short rainy Winter Days when the people would otherwise have been laying idle at Fort George it has been accomplished without incurring an Expence of ten pounds."

Simpson had worked out a grand strategy for reorganization of the fur trade in the Oregon Country. That the four established posts west of the Rockies returned fewer than twenty thousand beaver and otter skins a year "cast a very Severe reflection on those who have had management of the Business, as on looking at the prodigious expences that have been incurred & the means at their command I cannot help thinking that no economy has been observed."

Galled at the cost of shipping food from the British Isles to the fur posts—North West Company officers had even imported salmon from Scotland to the Columbia—Simpson decreed that the area be self-sufficient. Fur traders must henceforth farm as well: "It has been said that Farming is no branch of the Fur Trade, but I consider that every pursuit tending to lighten the Expence of the Trade is a branch thereof."

Since Fort George lay on the south side of the Columbia in an area likely to go to the Americans when the boundary was drawn, Simpson ordered it replaced by a post on the north bank. South of the Columbia, and especially along the Snake River, HBC fur brigades were to scour the land, trap out all beaver, and "create a fur desert" across which the Americans might hesitate to move; to the north, in areas safely British, conservation would be the rule. A fort was to be built on the lower Fraser, which Simpson wishfully believed "to be formed by nature as the grand communication with all our Establishments on this side of the mountains." Along the Northwest Coast, where the Yankee sea captains had been trading for fur with the Indians and freighting supplies to Russian America, HBC was to enter aggressive competition. Ships were to be built on the Columbia for the coastal trade and a large vessel would be sent from England to carry furs, spars, and pickled salmon to China.

When Simpson started back to Hudson's Bay in March of 1825, he left Dr. John McLoughlin, the chief factor, "to put the Machinery in full play." For the next twenty years, McLoughlin was the most important man in Northwest America. He looked the part: six feet four, heavily boned, his prematurely gray hair shoulder-length (the Indians called him White Eagle), gray-blue eyes beneath ferocious eyebrows, complexion pink, temper notoriously short—a man not casually to be disobeyed.

Simpson had a few doubts about his huge subordinate. In his private notebook he described McLoughlin as

. . . very zealous in the discharge of his public duties and a man of strict honor and integrity but a great stickler for rights & privileges and sets himself up for a righter of wrongs. Very anxious to obtain a lead among his colleagues with whom he has not much influence owing to his ungovernable violent temper and turbulent disposition, and would be a troublesome man to the Comp'y if he had sufficient influence to form and tact to manage a party; in short, would be a Radical in any Country under any Government and under any circumstances; and if he had not pacific people to deal with, would be eternally embroiled in "affairs of honor" on the merest trifles arising I conceive from the irritability of his temper more than a quarrelsome disposition.—Altogether a disagreeable man to do business with as it is impossible to go with him in all things and a difference of opinion almost amounts to a declaration of hostilities, yet a good hearted man and a pleasant companion.

The quarrels were to come later. At the start McLoughlin carried out Simpson's plans with energy and effectiveness. It was McLoughlin who selected Jolie Prairie, across the Columbia from the mouth of the Willamette, as site for the new headquarters (though Simpson was the one who named it Fort Vancouver "to identify our claim to the Soil and Trade with the discovery of the River and Coast on behalf of Gt Britain"). It was McLoughlin who dispatched Peter Skene Ogden as head of the Snake River expedition to scour the Idaho area of furs, McLoughlin who sent a party under Chief Trader James McMillan back to the Fraser, by way of the Cowlitz and Puget Sound, to start building Fort Langley, McLoughlin who supervised the planting of grain, the start of sheep and cattle ranching, the cutting of lumber, and the pickling of salmon at Fort Vancouver, all facets of Simpson's grand design.

Competing with the American ships trading along the coast was McLoughlin's toughest job. The Yankee skippers were experienced free-lancers; they did not scruple to use liquor and firearms as trading goods, and if they failed to obtain enough furs from the Indians they usually could make expenses by hauling freight for the Russian-American Company at Sitka.

McLoughlin was handicapped by the fact that HBC vessels sent from London were few, small, often crank, sometimes under charter that restricted the way they could be used. They had to cross the fearsome Columbia River bar coming and going; that usually led to delay, sometimes to damage or destruction. The five-month trip to Northwest America was not a popular run and did not draw England's best sailors. The captains who came to the coast for the HBC were often alcoholic, sometimes timid, occasionally both.

Governor Simpson knew the problem. Of an officer he and McLoughlin encountered at Fort George, Simpson said, "His talent as a Navigator I know nothing about, but his talent as a Grog Drinker I understand is without parallel and I shall be agreeably surprised if he and his Ship ever reach the Port of Destination." Of that worthy's successor, Simpson observed that "his Prudence amounted to pusillanimity." McLoughlin reported to Simpson that the next captain to arrive was "so much addicted to Liquor I conceive it would be hazarding the safety of the Vessel to give him charge of her. I have several times perceived he made free with Liquor before Breakfast, often have I seen him intoxicated before dinner, very seldom have I seen him perfectly sober after dinner." One brigantine left the Columbia with lumber for Chile and made port in Tasmania, the captain claiming compass error.

Nor was it easy to build ships at far remove from British yards. Shipwrights were as scarce on the Columbia as marine hardware. Of the two vessels put together at Fort Vancouver, the thirty-ton *Broughton* proved too small for the fur trade and was used as a tender; the sixty-ton *Vancouver* was a floating disaster that soon found her shattered destiny in the Queen Charlotte Islands.

Not until Aemilius Simpson, a lieutenant in the Royal Navy as well as a relative of the governor, came across the continent by canoe to take command of the trading vessel *Cadboro* did McLoughlin have a captain he could trust. And even he had peculiarities: Simpson was thought to be "excessively the gentleman." In dankest North America he refused to go on deck without kid gloves and "if the occasion was perilous or peculiar, his gloves must be of white kid. Form was nine tenths of the law with him, and the other tenth was conformity."

As for the *Cadboro,* she was a two-masted schooner of about seventy tons, none too nimble in bad weather. (She was eventually wrecked in a gale near Port Angeles.) Her greatest liability was her size. Though she carried thirty-five men and six cannon, Governor Simpson, often casual about other men's safety, conceded she was too small to intimidate Indians: "There are hundreds of War Canoes on the Coast longer and higher out of the water than she is, carrying from 40 to 50 men each." McLoughlin concurred. He described the *Cadboro* as "very lame in way of defense to be on such a coast as this." Nonetheless she was soon at war.

In January 1828 four men under Clerk Alexander McKenzie, having taken Christmas mail to Fort Langley on the Fraser were on their way back to the Columbia by way of Puget Sound. While camped on Lummi Island, they were attacked by Clallam Indians. All the men were killed and the Indian wife of one of them was taken as a slave. The Indian side of the story was never recorded, but McLoughlin reported to London that "they committed this crime without having the least difference with our people & murdered them merely for the sake of their apparel and Arms, & the murderers had Dances among themselves to celebrate the deed, & sent us word to come & revenge it, that they were ready."

Some Indians living near Fort Vancouver volunteered to go north and punish the Clallam. McLoughlin declined their services. He feared that "accepting their offer would be kindling war among them, cause a great deal of innocent blood to be shed, give them a claim on us & lower us in their opinion." Revenge belonged to the Company.

The supply ship *Eagle,* a 193-ton brigantine, happened to be on the Columbia. McLoughlin asked to borrow her since "a Vessel of her size would have a very imposing appearance in the eyes of the natives & add much in their estimation to our respectability." Captain J. C. Graves countered that using his brig as a battleship "might vitiate his Insurance."

The little *Cadboro* was pressed into service. Since she was too small to carry all the men needed, McLoughlin ordered Lieutenant Simpson to take her around the Olympic Peninsula and rendezvous off Dungeness Spit with a strike force of fifty-nine "workers and gentlemen" under Chief Trader Alexander Roderick McLeod, who would come by canoe up the Cowlitz and Puget Sound. This logistical arrangement yielded an unexpected dividend. En route north, McLeod's party chanced upon eight Clallam in a canoe and killed them all.

The combined HBC fleet—the *Cadboro* plus the war canoes—assembled in front of the defiant Clallam village. For the first time on the Sound, ship cannon were loaded with deadly intent. But before war, negotiation. McLeod sought the return of the Indian widow captured on Lummi Island; the Clallam sought to inveigle a small party of whites into visiting them ashore.

After five days of unsuccessful parlay, McLeod attacked. Flame and smoke spurted from the ships guns. Cannonballs splintered the beachwrack where the Clallam warriors lay concealed. Under cover of the cannon fire, landing parties rowed ashore, charged into the village with torches, set it afire, smashed forty-six dugouts, and returned unharmed to their floating fortress.

The Clallam who survived the assault sent out a canoe with the captured woman. The whites were not satisfied. They proceeded to Port Townsend and put to the torch the largest of the Clallam villages, a line of long-houses stretching two hundred yards along the beach. In all, McLoughlin estimated, twenty-nine Indians were killed. No whites were wounded. "Though the loss the murderers have suffered may appear great & ought to deter them & their countrymen from committing any acts of violence towards us," McLoughlin reported to London, "still I doubt if it is sufficient for that object."

Officials were still worried about the Indians four months later when Governor Simpson passed the Clallam villages on his way to Fort Vancouver. He had come to the coast by way of the Fraser River rather than the Columbia, hoping to prove the northern stream a better route for the fur trade. It wasn't. Simpson, after surviving its rapids, declared the Fraser "extremely dangerous even to perfectly light Craft under the most skillful management, & in the most favorable state of the water, & not under any circumstances to be attempted by loaded Craft." After five days rest at Fort Langley while the canoes were repaired, Simpson, Chief Trader McLoed, and thirty men set out in three canoes for the run south up Puget Sound.

"Immediately after our leaving the River," Simpson reported, "a telegraphic communication was made all along the coast that an Enemy was abroad, by Smoke during the Day and Large Fires at night on the different projecting heads." The Company canoes stayed close together and the men had rifles and pistols primed and shotted as they swept past the destroyed villages. "The Natives did not think it proper to interfere with us and by pushing on late and early, the weather being favorable, we got [in three days] to a Neck of Land between Puget's Sound and a Stream falling into the Columbia. We Burnt our Boats to prevent their falling into the hands of the Indians, crossed the Cowliz Portage, got Canoes from the Natives at the head of the Cowliz River, and reached Fort Vancouver on the Night of the 25th October, having between that Date and the first of May performed the longest Voyage ever attempted in North America in one Season, about 7000 miles."

"It is eating gold," Simpson had snarled as he checked on the imported foodstuffs that fed the fur posts when first he visited the Columbia. But this time Fort Vancouver delighted him by its economy.

The piggery produced 10,000 pounds of cured pork in 1828. The herd of two dozen or so faintly domesticated longhorns that had grazed on salty grass at Fort George had, since their transfer to Jolie

Prairie, multiplied tenfold; in spite of demands from employees, especially sailors who arrived ravenous for fresh meat, there was an absolute ban on slaughtering any other than an occasional scrub bull when rennet was needed to curdle milk for cheese making. Tons of salmon purchased from the Indians for a pittance (seventy-five hundred were bought for sixty dollars in one month) were brined in 250-pound barrels. Young apple trees were in blossom, the vineyard in leaf. Fourteen acres were planted to peas, eight to oats, five to barley. There were fields of corn and wheat. The post had a two-year supply of grain in storage.

Such self-sufficiency satisfied Simpson's Scottish soul and set him to scheming about increased sales and the politics of plenty. If the Oregon Country could produce a surplus of food for the posts, that surplus might be sold to the Russians up north. If the Russians had a sure source of supply, they would not need to use American ships to bring in food. If the Yankee traders lost their Russian business they would be severely handicapped in competing with the Hudson's Bay Company in the maritime fur trade.

While Simpson was inspecting the Oregon Country, British and American diplomats were again failing to agree on how the area should be divided. When the ten-year agreement for joint occupation, negotiated in 1818, ran out, the best the State Department and Foreign Office could do was agree to extend it indefinitely. Simpson, on his return to London, persuaded the directors at Beaver House that it was in the Company's interest to establish more posts, some south of the Columbia that could serve as pawns to be sacrificed in the next negotiation, others north of the river to solidify the British claim. Puget Sound, lying between the 49th parallel that the United States proposed as boundary and the Columbia suggested by Britain, was a logical place for a new post. The area might not be rich in fur but, as Vancouver and Puget had reported and Simpson had seen for himself, it had agricultural possibilities.

In the early spring of 1833, the veteran Archibald McDonald was sent north from Fort Vancouver with a party of eight to trade on Puget Sound. That was usual. But he was also instructed to pick out a possible site for an establishment in the southern Sound. After finishing his trading he returned to the mouth of the Nisqually and on the hill rising above the north shore his party knocked together a rude storehouse, twenty feet by fifteen, with dirt floor, log walls, and cedar boards for the roofing. There he left William Ouvrie and two hands to guard a small store of potatoes, garden seeds, and trade blankets while he reported back to Fort Vancouver.

On May 8, McDonald was invited to have high tea at the fort with Chief Factor McLoughlin and to meet a fellow Scot just arrived aboard the Company barque *Ganymede*. The newcomer, Dr. William Fraser Tolmie, was twenty-one years old, a recent graduate in medicine from the University of Glasgow. He was a slight, sandy-haired, serious young man who smelled strongly of skunk.

Young Tolmie confessed that while walking along the Columbia admiring "a range of undulating hills perhaps 500 feet high with the colossal Mount Hood in the background, the finest combination of beauty and grandeur I have ever beheld" he chanced to see "a busy animal with a large cocked tail, striped white and brown, about the size of a large cat about 100 yards ahead. He made off, but seeing him tardy in his movements, I gave chase and soon gained on him and admired his beauty as he ran with cocked tail spread out like a fan, or the tail of a turkey cock. He stopped under the shade of a huge pine, grinned and stood at bay. I let fly and soon settled his hash. Immediately thereafter a most diabolical smell declared him a pole cat."

Not even the whiff of civet spoiled the pleasure the two Celts took in each other's company. McDonald and Tolmie hit it off. The young doctor was scheduled to sail on the company ship *Vancouver* to Fort Simpson up by the Russian-American border, but it was arranged that instead of going all the way by ship, he would accompany McDonald to Nisqually by canoe and horse, and board the *Vancouver* when she visited the Sound. This would give him a chance to botanize and learn more about the Northwest flora, to say nothing of its fauna.

So, a few days later, Tolmie packed, checked his firearms, said au revoir to a bed of dahlias he had planted on arrival ("they were nearly an inch high and numerous"), and joined McDonald in a canoe manned by four husky Hawaiian paddlers. "Majestic Columbia rolling smoothly along and its wooded and winding banks rejoicing in the noonday sun." After only two hours downstream from Fort Vancouver they put ashore to dine on pickled pork, cold duck, biscuit, and a bottle of porter.

As the canoe swept past the Indian villages, the veteran Scot told the tenderfoot about the history of the region:

Mr McD pointed out to me one of the men who five weeks ago having quarreled with a person living in the same lodge stole on him as he lay in front of his dwelling & shot him dead—the surrounding tribes assembled to the number of 3 or 400 & the murderer according to their custom satisfied all who claimed kindred with the deceased with presents & thus expended all his substance which was considerable. When spoken to by McD soon after the deed, he expressed no contrition but said "The sun was high when I killed him. It was not in the dark. I have paid the price of his blood & what more can I do?" He now seems as cheerful & devoid of care as his fellows.

Progress downstream was slow. Four men were driving the oxen and horses overland and the canoe party occasionally landed to help them. The canoe caught up with the *Vancouver* and Dr. Tolmie treated a seaman for malaria ("Quinine and Emetic doses of Ipecacuan"). It took them three days to reach the Cowlitz and another three for the Hawaiians to fight the current up to the portage, Tolmie noticing everything with the enthusiasm of a newcomer, the trained eye of a scientist, and leaving the first detailed account of the route now followed by Interstate Five between Longview and Tacoma.

His journal tells of turkey vultures hunched in the trees, of a partridge ("very tender"), of trouble in the Indian lodges ("found my trousers swarming with fleas, who were travelling rapidly upwards and required active measures to subdue their ambitious propensities"). They found outcroppings of coal, but of poor quality, and met Indians who shared their meagre supplies with the visitors.

With greenhorn enthusiasm, Tolmie jumped into the river to help push the canoe past an obstruction and was almost swept under a log jam. He survived and "assisted in poling and paddling to keep up the animal heat and comforted the inward man with a tass of aquavita."

Tolmie wrote a detailed description of an Indian fish trap, "a barrier formed across river here about 40 yards wide—7 tripods constructed of strong poles were placed across & supported by these poles stretched horizontally gave attachment to a perpendicular row of small wands sufficiently close to prevent the passage of salmon or large trout upwards & fastened in bed of stream also supported by the tripods were frames to which net bags might be fixed & into which the fish would fall in attempt to leap barrier."

At Cowlitz Landing they met the cattle party and set out on horseback along the Indian trail, "execrable—knee deep in water & mud" into which he was several times nearly spilled by low-hanging branches. He was not too miserable to admire the blue-flowered camas and the yellow buttercups. On the second day they camped with several Indian chiefs: "The most important was dressed in a blanket, capot, blue vest and trowsers, a foot too long, english hat and Blucher boots. He was a little old man, very forward & intrusive, wishing to invade the precincts of our tent, hitherto kept sacred. He succeeded however in favoring Mac with a Colony of fleas who kept him in purgatory all night. The old fellow was going to a meeting for the purpose of deliberating on the propriety of accepting two slaves as a peace offering from the northern tribes for the murder of two of his kinfolk."

On the third day Tolmie puzzled over the mounded prairie north of Centralia, a phenomenon now believed to be caused by the retreat of the last ice age glaciers, and on the fourth day they rode ahead of the rest of the party, through "pretty green hills, sprinkled with young oaks, and descending a steep bank arrived at the proposed site of Nusqually Fort on a low flat about 50 paces broad on the shores of Puget's Sound."

The travel-worn Scots stashed their gear in the storehouse, hurried past a group of men roasting mussels around a beach fire— Canadians in blue capots with red military belts, their black hair hanging below their shoulders; Hawaiians in work-pants but with buttercups woven in their hair; Nisqually naked to the breachclout but boldly painted—and plunged uncomplaining into the chill waters of the Sound, "smooth as crystal & bordered by a sloping beach of shingle." Refreshed, they climbed the north hill and inspected the site McDonald had picked for the post buildings. It lay along a small stream the Indians called Sequalitchew "which in its devious course through the plain presents points well adapted for Millsetts."

The next day, Sunday, Tolmie strolled by himself northward into what is now the lake district suburb of Tacoma, admiring "the long range of snow speckled mountains on the peninsula opposite, to the highest summit of which the classical name of Mount Olympus has been given, the foreground filled with a densely wooded island [Anderson] indented with one or two bays about a mile in length." Reaching a beautiful, nearly circular lake about ¼ mile round [Old Fort Lake]," he noted that waterlilies "floated on its unruffled bosom while Flora adorned its margin with a profusion of yellow ranunculia & others unknown." On a grassy bank shaded with oak, the young man stretched out and thought appropriate Sabbath thoughts for more than an hour. Resuming his hike, he lost his way but eventually sighted the Sound and followed the cliff back to base camp.

"A beautiful walk of more than a mile could be formed along the face of this hill, until it should terminate in the vale of Nusqually," he thought. "With slight aid from the axe, splendid prospects might be obtained. When tired of the shady wood you could emerge into the boundless prairie, to which any nobleman's park which I have seen cannot once be compared either in size, beauty, or magnificence." That night he promenaded the beach with McDonald. "What a pity," he mused, "that a country which so easily could afford subsistence to man is yet uninhabited."

The Nisqually people, of course, did not count. The process was under way which would transform the land of the Indians into the possession of a British monopoly; then into homesteads for settlers and an Army post; a satrapy of du Pont de Nemours; and, in 1979, a potential marshaling area for the Weyerhaeuser Company.

McDonald laconically noted the first step: "The ploughman with his Oxen fairly at work on the potatoes at an early hour this morning. They are simply ploughed in under the green sod in a chosen piece of ground."

Pierre Charles, a broad-chested mixed-blood from Montreal, was in charge of construction. He knocked together near the beach a lean-to of posts and canvas for himself, a pen for the oxen, and a house of "red pine" logs to serve as store and lodging, the whole surrounded by a picket fence so haphazard it blew over in a gale. "The space occupied by this infant establishment is perhaps 100 square yards, & is enclosed on all sides by tall pines except toward the NE where it is open to the boundless and picturesque prairie," said Tolmie. "It is gratifying to witness this first step toward colonization."

They began to worry about the *Vancouver,* which was to take Tolmie to Fort Simpson. The sloop had left the Columbia when they did; when she had not arrived by June 6, Tolmie and McDonald on impulse started north by canoe to look for her, relying on Indians along the way for sustenance. They bought salmon and elk roasted over coals on a split stick, and "for 5 loads of powder and ball" a large woolly dog, still alive, which one of the Hawaiian paddlers "soon dispatched with a blow of his ponderous axe & on our stopping to breakfast on the bank of Hood Canal cut up and potted him in a trice."

The *Vancouver* had been delayed by nothing more serious than calms. They met her coming out of the Strait of Juan de Fuca, first "a white speck in relief against the tall trees," then "a most agreeable sight, with swelling sails, stemming the powerful tide as she rounded a sandy point." They boarded her, but on their way south an express canoe interrupted the idyll with an emergency call for the doctor. Tolmie was paddled post haste to Nisqually to treat Pierre Charles, who in shaping a log with an axe had missed the wood and split his foot.

The young doctor saved his patient's life and foot but, when the *Vancouver* sailed for Fort Simpson, Charles still needed attention. Tolmie missed the boat. It was six months before there was another. In the interval he played pediatrician to the infant settlement.

By June 14, things were going so well that McDonald could boast in the Journal of Occurrences at Nisqually House: "Canoes arriving by sea—dozens of horses & riders by land—two ploughs at work on an endless plain & a ship riding at anchor before the campus, a scene

I venture to say not very common in the Indian country, far less at a new settlement. Trade upwards of 80 skins."

A few days later, McDonald was transferred back to Fort Vancouver. The twenty-one-year-old Tolmie found himself "commander of a trading post in a remote corner of the New World with only a force of six effective men in the midst of treacherous, bloodthirsty savages, with whom murder is familiar." He had no trouble surviving until C. F. Heron arrived the following week to take over.

Chief Trader Heron was large, Irish, noisily religious, given to quiet nips at the bottle and loud denunciations of others' folly. Little about Nisqually pleased him, including its location. Within a week he announced that everything was to be moved to the mouth of the Deschutes (where Olympia later grew). Then he decided that the soil at "The Shutes" was inferior so that it would be better to move to a plateau on Johnson Point, then that this would be too far between water and plain. Nisqually would have to do after all unless perhaps some land that William Ouvrie liked farther north would suffice. He dispatched Tolmie to inspect the area between Three Tree Point and the mouth of the Duwamish, but Tolmie was not impressed by the location that later arrivals chose for Seattle's first settlement.

What did impress Tolmie, whenever it was out—and the summer was largely clear—was the Mountain. His journal glows with poetic references to "stupendous Rainier enbosomed in cloud," "its gelid vesture," "its pyramidal form," "its trifid crest," but most of all to its seeming nearness. "It looks only fifteen miles away," he decided, as he studied it from a canoe in Commencement Bay.

Mountain climbing for sport was not an avocation among fur traders. They had hardship enough. But the Mountain was there, Tolmie wanted to go, and he found an excuse. There might be herbs on the Mountain that would help those suffering from "the intermittants," a fever pandemic among the coastal Indians. On August 27, "Obtained Mr. Heron's consent to making a botanizing excursion to Mt. Rainier for which he has allowed 10 days."

For the price of a blanket, Lachalet, a powerful young Nisqually who was exchanging language lessons with Tolmie, agreed to be overall guide and to supply horses. Nuckalkat, a Puyallup whom Tolmie mistakenly took to be a native of the Mountain, agreed to lead the way beyond the horse trail; he was to be paid in ammunition. Three other Indians, including a muscular Puyallup named Quilniash, went along because the Mountain was there.

The party left on the afternoon of August 29, Tolmie astride an iron-gray stallion. They made only eight miles before camping at the lodge of Nuckalkat's father near the north end of Lake Steilacoom. They "supped on Sallal," no hardship for Tolmie, who thought the purplish berries "intended by Providence as a staple article of food, neither cloying the appetite by its lusciousness nor dissatisfying by insipidity." During the night a branch fell from a tree and so bruised Tolmie's thigh that he was afraid he would have to cancel the trip, but the pain lessened with movement.

At sunrise, they headed for the Puyallup with Tolmie this time on a gentle brown mare. They paused to breakfast on dried clams, dried goatsmeat, bread, and more salal. Noon found them at a bark lean-to belonging to a Klickitat family, with whom they shared a "savage repast" of dried elk boiled in a bark kettle. Tolmie liked it well enough to buy a supply of jerky for four rifle balls and three rings. In mid-afternoon they struck the Puyallup, forded it near the present site of McMillan with one of the Indians carrying their duffle on his head, and crossed the plain, the ferns sometimes higher than the horses' heads. When they reached the forest they left their mounts and followed Nuckalkat through the woods, twice crossing the river on logs Tolmie deemed "unsteadfast." Their second night they spent on a sandbar, the milky gray Puyallup pouring past, the crowns of fir and cedar dark against the sky. When Tolmie awoke, the Indians had two salmon roasting on spits over the campfire. They left the gills and air bladder on a stick over the embers of the fire to let the next camper know that fishing was good. It was their last moment of comfort.

All through the third day they struggled with the terrain, fighting through forest to avoid the Puyallup canyon upstream from today's Electron, then lurching along the boulder-strewn border of the river-bed, their packs a menace to balance. The Indians moved at "a sure trot" to which Tolmie confessed himself "very inferior." Trees and clouds hid all but the next hills when they made camp. During the night the rain began, the steady, pounding rain that marks the end of summer on the Sound.

They breakfasted on the last of the dried elk, which they cooked in water brought to a boil by dropping hot rocks into a shell of bark, then set out in pouring rain, Tolmie dressed Indian fashion, bare-legged in a green blanket. He found it awkward and traded for Lachalet's hooded capot, which "has been on almost every Indian at Nusqually. However I found it more convenient than blanket." They came out of the woods on the Mowich River, about two miles west of the present Mount Rainier National Park boundary, and found shelter from the rain in a semi-cave the river had cut in the bank: "The floor is very rugged." Tolmie missed two shots at a sawbill duck, so they dined on boiled salal berries, which reminded him of sowens, a Scottish porridge made from the husks and siftings of oatmeal. They were near the limit of supplies and endurance. "Propose to ascend one of the snowy peaks above," Tolmie wrote before turning in.

In the morning they followed the Mowich upstream three miles to its forks. From a natural amphitheater they could see a torrent of rain and snow melt pouring off North Mowich glacier in a three-hundred-foot waterfall. Several peaks were within striking distance. Tolmie chose the one that seemed to have the most snow and, after a nice cup of tea, started up with Lachelet and Nuckalkat. Only the last quarter mile was snow covered, "ancle deep." Dense mist covered Rainier, puffs of wind occasionally giving glimpses of the peak.

Back at camp that night Lachalet asked if he could bundle up with Tolmie to share warmth, which was not great. "Lay shivering all night—roused my swarthy companion twice to rekindle the fire." But the sky cleared. At sunrise Tolmie went back up the peak and "found the tempr. of the air 33°—the snow was spangled and sparkled brightly. It was crisp & only yielded a couple of inches to the pressure of the foot when walking. Mt. Rainier appeared surpassingly splendid & magnificent." That was the climax.

From there it was all downhill. They were back at Nisqually in two days. Heron noted in the Journal of Occurrences that "Dr. Tolmie returned safe after collecting a variety of plants." Tolmie was so tired that his only notes for the next day were "Nothing particular." Later he realized he had ruptured himself and sent to Vancouver for a truss.

So ended the first tourist approach to the Mountain that has attracted millions. Tolmie was the first to visit what is now Mount Rainier National Park, the first to reach the snowline, the first to report the existence of its great glaciers. And on October 15 he had another first. After preparing the skins of a pileated woodpecker and a guillemot he took his customary walk in the gloaming. "Had a fine view of Tuchoma or Mt. Rainier, appearing in relief against the cloudless firmament," he wrote on returning.

This is the first report of the Puyallup-Nisqually word for the mountain. It preceded by thirty years the publication of Theodore Winthrop's *Canoe and Saddle* in which the word was spelled *Tacoma*.

Indians were coming great distances to exchange beaverskins for blankets and tools: Makah from Neah Bay, Clallam from the Strait of Juan de Fuca, Skagit and Snohomish from the northern Sound, Muckleshoot from the hills and Klickitat from the mountain passes, Duwamish and Suquamish from the central Sound, Chehalis from Grays Harbor.

One day in August when an unusually diverse group had gathered, the men to gamble and trade, the women to dig camas on the Nisqually plain, Heron drew the leaders of the various bands into assembly. The one who most impressed Tolmie was Silah (Seattle), "a brawny Soquamish with a Roman countenance & black curly hair, the handsomest Indian I have seen." Heron turned the gathering into a sort of confessional. Each leader was asked to recount his misdeeds, starting with murder and ending with theft. After hesitation came bragging: one-upsmanship in what was being put behind:

Chilialucum [Steilacoom] began and confessed having murdered four men, but pleaded guiltless of any other crime. Watskalatchet none. Lachalet killed the murderer of his uncle and a slave of the former chief's. Scaldh [another spelling of Seattle] in his youth slew a great chief and stole a fathom of very fine payaquas [shells] from the Klalum. Babyar, after coughing, blowing & humming frequently, declared himself guiltless of any evil action but recollecting himself shortly after said that he had killed 5 men & stolen their property, also stole two slaves. Chiatzaan being called in said he had for a long time been a physician & conductor of the religious ceremonies, that he had never done any harm, but afterwards acknowledged himself the murderer of five (besides those killed by his medicines).

Heron then made a speech informing the chiefs that murder was contrary to the Almighty's express command. They all promised not to kill anybody again unless they had to, and made a mark with a pen on a sheet of paper on which their names were written. After the treaty was signed and everyone was feeling the relief of confession and the fellowship of redemption, the whites hinted to the chiefs how helpful it would be if the log storehouse on the beach were moved up by the little lake where the permanent post was being built. The chiefs thought that was a fine idea: they told their people to do it. By evening the logs were on the new site.

The post now consisted of the store, which was divided into a trading room and a room for cleaning and storing skins; a house fifty feet by thirty for the chief trader; a second house thirty feet by twenty for "the people," and sheds for the Hawaiians. The buildings were of logs, but a sawpit had been dug and men who had been chosen for their skill with paddles were trying to master the art of slicing boards of standard dimension for flooring and paneling. "Owing to the badness of our saw, and sawyers, we make but slow progress at cutting boards," Heron complained, adding, "as indeed we have done all along at every kind of work, owing to the incapacity of our people."

Nevertheless, when Tolmie left for Fort Simpson on the *Cadboro* in mid-December, Nisqually had the look of a real fur post, the buildings solid and protected by a wall of upright logs with blockhouse bastions at each corner, another link in the chain of forts that extended from Hudson's Bay to the Columbia River. But its role soon changed. By the time Tolmie returned to Nisqually ten years later as chief factor, it was more a ranch than a trading post, and it belonged to an organization known as the Puget's Sound Agricultural Company. The transformation was brought about, as so often happened in the history of Puget Sound, by events and decisions in distant places.

Governor Simpson and John McLoughlin no longer saw eye to eye. Cattle had come between them. The herd at Fort Vancouver was prospering and its success gave McLoughlin a new perspective on the economy of the Pacific Northwest.

Although the HBC cattle had been brought to the Columbia as a source of food, McLoughlin was aware of another possibility. Ship captains calling at Fort Vancouver reported that Alta California, long a drain on the Spanish and Mexican economies, had at last found something to export: hides. The Industrial Revolution was drawing farm folk to the industrial cities, and they were giving up wooden clogs, rope espadrilles, and cloth slippers in favor of leather shoes. Leather was in increasing demand. Suddenly the great herds of semi-wild cattle that roamed the brown hills of Alta California had value; during the 1820s the Mexicans began to slaughter the herds for their hides. There was no market for the meat—much of it was left to rot—but the fat was rendered into tallow for candles. A thousand-pound beast yielded about a hundred pounds of raw material, worth on the average four dollars. The hide bonanza drew ships from half-way around the world. Richard Henry Dana's two years before the mast of the *Pilgrim* were on a voyage from New England for California hides. Eighty thousand cattle were slaughtered in Alta California in a three-month period of 1831.

To John McLoughlin ranching seemed the wave of the future. "The fur business must soon be knocked up," he told young Tolmie shortly after the doctor's arrival, but "the rearing of cattle for the sake of hides and tallow could be carried on to a greater profit than that from all the furs collected west of the Rockies." The Oregon Country should be not a fur farm but cattle country. McLoughlin wanted to go into the hide business on his own. In 1832 he wrote Governor Simpson that he and other Hudson's Bay officers would like to form an independent company to raise cattle; they would supply meat to the fur brigades and sell hides on the world market. Simpson agreed that "cattle raising on a large scale on the banks of the Wilhamet, or the Cowlitz Portage or elsewhere . . . appears to hold out prospect of becoming an extended & highly profitable branch of trade," but he recommended to the HBC directors that the business be carried on "by the Honble. Company, not by individuals." The directors concurred. They informed McLoughlin that the HBC had "a right to the best & undivided time and attention of every Chief Factor & Chief Trader." McLoughlin must not moonlight as a rancher; instead he was to buy more cattle—five thousand more—in California on behalf of the Company.

McLoughlin's Irish temper and Celtic parsimony were aroused. He replied that "nothing in the Deed Poll [contract of employment] deprives me of the Right of investing my means in any business I think proper, except in trading directly or indirectly with the Indians; and forming a hide & tallow Company is certainly distinct from the fur trade." For the HBC to demand that its factors organize and operate a new line of business on the Company's behalf, one for which the Company was not chartered, would mean that the factors would do all the work while the stockholders reaped all the benefits.

Correspondence took from eight months to a year for each exchange of letters. The dispute dragged on until 1837 when McLoughlin was summoned to London for a conference with the governor and the executive committee. Americans were beginning to settle in the Oregon Country, though south of the Columbia. The British government had indicated it wanted the HBC to encourage activities which, unlike trapping, would lead to British settlement. Farming and ranching were to be pushed for both political and economic reasons. The Russian-American Company had agreed to lease the HBC 350 miles of Alaskan coastline for ten years, the payment to be in agricultural supplies from Oregon.

Simpson found a way to compromise with McLoughlin. A new company, the Puget's Sound Agricultural Company, was created to handle the ranching and farming enterprise, with an authorized capital of two hundred thousand pounds. Ownership of stock in PSAC was limited to those who already held HBC stock, a device that left the agricultural enterprise technically independent while assuring its cooperation with the fur company. McLoughlin was paid an additional five hundred pounds a year, plus a share of the profits, to manage the PSAC. The HBC made to its subsidiary a gift of joint ownership in the land, buildings, and livestock at Nisqually and at a new establishment on the Cowlitz that was to concentrate on wheat, barley, oats, peas, and potatoes, while Nisqually raised livestock.

By 1840, Nisqually was a great ranch. Some barter for beaver continued in the store; the skins were paid for with PSAC goods, then sold to the HBC, but the real function of the station was raising livestock. A head shepherd—Mr. McLean—was imported from Scotland. The sheep were divided into flocks that grazed from present-day South Tacoma to Yelm and Muck Creek. The shepherds—some French Canadian, some mixed-bloods, a few Nisqually—lived with their flocks in huts scattered across the plain, or in wanigans, shacks built on two-wheel carts hauled by oxen. The sheep were moved daily to prevent overgrazing, and were folded nightly to concentrate manuring and protect them from wolves and coyotes, which were numerous and bold. At certain seasons the rams, which had been imported from England for improving the breed, were herded separately to distant pastures, thus regulating the period of lambing. The sheep were washed and shorn in summer and the wool pressed into bales and sent to Vancouver for reshipment to England.

Like the sheep, the cattle were of stock originating in California but improved by the importation of British bulls, about one for each twenty-five cows and heifers. During the summer, about 120 cows were tamed and milked at the dairy, which stood five miles north of the fort. As soon as a third of the young cattle were habituated to being handled, they were released with their calves and replaced by others, so in the course of the season the whole herd became domesticated. The milk was made into cheese, most of which was shipped to the Russians at Sitka.

All the cattle, except the milch cows, were penned at night, partly to get them accustomed to being herded and driven, and to protect them from predators, but chiefly to improve the soil for agricultural purposes.

It is a scene to conjure: the mountain, pastel in the sunset, looming over the plain with its scattered oaks and border of fir, the lean, long-horned cattle moving restlessly ahead of bareback cowboys who shouted at them in Nisqually. For all of the cowboys were Indians.

The Eyes of Empire . . .

N O American ship had been on Puget Sound, at least none the government knew about. Only an occasional fur trader in British employment had visited the inland sea and they did not report back to Washington. American ignorance of the Puget Sound area was so great that Albert Gallatin, who represented the United States in negotiations with Britain over the Oregon boundary, in 1826 asked the former Astorian, Ramsay Crooks, who had at least been as far as the Columbia, to estimate its value.

"The country north and west of the Columbia, extending north to the 49th degree of latitude and west to the sea," wrote Crooks, "is extremely worthless; along the sea shore rocky & poor, with little other timber than pine and hemlock, farther inland sandy and destitute of timber, a very small portion of the whole fit for cultivation, and in the meanwhile affording hardly any furs."

Ten years later the government had few facts on which to base policy. President Andrew Jackson asked Secretary of State John Forsyte to find someone who might "obtain some specific and authentic information in regard to the inhabitants in the country in the neighborhood of the Oregon or Columbia River." Forsyte found William A. Slacum.

Slacum was a thirty-four-year-old Virginian, on leave of absence from the Navy while recovering from tic douloureux (a painful neurological disorder of the face) and bad investments. While on naval duty as a purser in the Pacific he had as a private venture sent a ship and cargo from Valparaiso to Gueymas, receiving payment in drafts on the Sonora state government, which Mexico subsequently refused to honor. Slacum planned to return to Gueymas to get his money. The secretary of state asked him to visit the Oregon Country and, without revealing that he was a government agent, take a census of the population—British and American, red and white—determine the

41

national sympathies of the settlers, learn the salient facts about the geography, geology, marine facilities, and climate, and report back.

The assignment appealed to Slacum's patriotism, his curiosity, his self-importance, and his naval officer's suspicions about British intentions in the Pacific. Besides, there was an expense account. May of 1836 found him on the west coast of Mexico, suffering the misadventures common to Mexican travelers. He bought mules and provisions for an overland trip to California but gave it up when warned about the heat and Indians. He bought a twenty-ton vessel, *Joven Teresa,* but she proved unseaworthy. He chartered the twelve-ton *Lorentano,* but she couldn't make it around the tip of Baja in a storm and he went back to Mazatlan. He crossed over to La Paz and finally found passage to Honolulu by way of San Blas, arriving in November.

At Oahu, Slacum chartered the brig *Loriot* and Captain Bancroft at $700 a month, bought a small supply of trading goods, and set sail for the Columbia. They arrived December 22 in a storm. "The bar presented a terrific appearance, breaking entirely across the channel from the north to the south shouls," but Captain Bancroft found the channel, causing Slacum to report the passage less fearful than reputed.

Slacum spent Christmas with the Hudson's Bay Company detachment at Fort George, and on New Years Day, 1837, presented himself to Chief Factor John McLoughlin under the guise of an American businessman awaiting the arrival of partners coming west overland and desirous of learning all he could about the Oregon Country. McLoughlin was not deceived; his men told him that the *Loriot* had arrived almost without cargo, an inconceivable waste of opportunity for a businessman. "This," he wrote in his private journal, "must be an agent of the American Government come to see what we are doing."

McLoughlin decided the best tactic was to tell the truth, to help Slacum see how strongly entrenched the Hudson's Bay Company was. He not only answered all questions accurately and fully but provided Slacum with a canoe and six Hawaiian paddlers to carry him on an inspection trip to the Willamette, where the Americans were concentrated, there being not a single Yankee settler north of the Columbia.

Agents assigned to the clandestine gathering of information are often tempted to exceed their assignment and attempt to influence developments they were supposed only to observe. Slacum succumbed. He assured the French Canadian HBC men who had retired to farms on the Willamette that "their pre-emption rights [to the land they were developing] would doubtless be secured to them when our government should take possession of the country." He encouraged American settlers to petition Congress to redress their grievances against the Monster, as they called the Hudson's Bay Company.

In league with the Methodist missionaries and the Oregon Temperance Society he pledged money to buy out a still with which two former fur trappers, Ewing Young and Lawrence Carmichael, proposed to turn the surplus wheat and corn of the Willamette into whiskey. When the two entrepreneurs agreed for the general good to abandon the enterprise without recompense, Slacum helped organize the Wallamette (sic) Cattle Company, with Ewing Young as its leader, to go to California, buy cattle from the Mexicans, and drive them north through the Sacramento and Willamette valleys. Slacum not only put up money for the project; he furnished the cattle party transportation to California on the *Loriot*, not an unmixed blessing since the brig went aground inside the Columbia bar and was considerably delayed. Nevertheless the project was Slacum's most significant contribution to the American cause. It furnished the American settlers their first cattle and broadened the base of their farming activities in the Oregon Country.

During his three weeks on the Columbia, Slacum was too busy on activist projects to get up to Puget Sound. That did not prevent him reporting on it:

I beg leave to call your attention to the topography of *Pugitt's sound*, and urge, in the most earnest manner, that this point should never be abandoned. If the United States claim, as I hope they ever will, at least as far as 49 degrees of north latitude, running due west from the Lake of the Woods on the above parallel we shall take in Pugitt's sound. In a military point of view, it is of the highest importance to the United States. If it were in the hands of any foreign power, especially Great Britain, with the influence she could command (through the Hudson Bay Company) over the Indians at the north, on those magnificent straights of Juan de Fuca, a force of 20,000 men could be brought by water in large canoes to the sound, *Pugitt's*, in a few days, from thence to the Columbia; the distance is but two days' march via the Cowility. I hope our claim to 54° of north latitude will never be abandoned; at all events, we should never give up *Pugitt's sound*, nor permit the free navigation of the Columbia, unless, a fair equivalent was offered, such as the free navigation of the St. Lawrence. . . .

A new president was in office when Slacum reported back to Washington in September 1837. Martin Van Buren received the report on the Oregon situation with interest perhaps tempered by shock over Slacum's expense account, a work of exuberance and ingenuity, part of which the president declined to recommend for payment. Slacum was still trying to collect when he died three years later, aged thirty-nine.

There was nothing clandestine but much that was controversial about the next American naval officer sent by the government to study the Oregon Country.

Lieutenant Charles Wilkes arrived in uniform, with government ships, and he made no attempt to hide his purpose. Wilkes made a good first impression. He was forty when he took command of the United States Exploring Expedition in 1838, a tall, loose-jointed officer whose lank frame and air of dishabille were the despair of a generation of Washington tailors. An able astronomer and competent mathematician, he was one of the Navy's few scientists; though erratic in spelling, he commanded a grandiloquent prose style, occasionally effective; as a commander of men he was a disciplinarian in the beat-'em bloody tradition of the wooden-ship navy but as demanding of himself as of his people. Wilkes's personality was his problem. He was proud, touchy, secretive; he looked on unavoidable accidents as personal affronts and on disagreement as conspiracy. Like Bligh of the *Bounty,* he should always have sailed alone. Had he been God, many a saint would have fled Heaven.

His appointment to command the first major American scientific expedition stemmed from attrition among other candidates rather than his own merits. Feuding and jealousy within the Navy eliminated so many of those proposed for leadership that the influential Washington *Globe* snarled, "It is impossible to make heroes of men who adopt the maxims and principles of cobblers and tinkers. A service constituted of such materials and disorganized by such unworthy principles of discord can neither merit nor receive the affection and respect of a great generous nation." Wilkes had the advantage of being obscure enough to have few enemies, an insufficiency he did not permit to endure.

Whatever his deficiencies, Wilkes was decisive. He immediately settled a long dispute as to whether the United States government should send the best available scientists or simply Navy men who needed the training. Wilkes went Navy. Except in the fields of botany, philology, horticulture, conchology, and mineralogy, his experts were officers. Nathaniel Hawthorne volunteered as historian, but Wilkes preferred to tell his own story.

Only four months after Wilkes was assigned command, the six vessels of the expedition—the 780-ton sloop-of-war *Vincennes,* the 650-ton sloop-of-war *Peacock,* and the 224-ton *Porpoise;* two former New York harbor pilot boats, the 110-ton *Sea Gull* and the 96-ton *Flying Fish;* and the store-ship *Relief*—sailed from Norfolk, their assignment to encircle the globe, en route exploring the Antarctic, charting the islands of the South and Central Pacific for harbors useful to American whalers and ships in the China trade, and charting and making studies of the Oregon Country and San Francisco Bay to determine their possible value to the United States.

That Wilkes was able to put to sea so soon was considered proof of his "go-aheadness," though a high price was paid for the haste: the ships were in poor repair and indifferent sailers; the scientific gear might be new and exquisite but the food was inferior and the clothing shoddy. Still the first months at sea were pleasant. Most of the 433 men seemed to admire Wilkes. James Dwight Dana, the twenty-three-year-old mineralogist from Yale, had been upset by the downgrading of civilian scientists but found Wilkes personally "a far more agreeable man than was expected." Midshipman William Reynolds, at twenty-two a seven-year veteran of naval service, thought him "of great talent, perhaps a genius." But by the time the expedition approached the Oregon Country three years later, morale had curdled. Reynolds, looking over an early description of the commander in his secret journal, interlined revisions:

"In my humble opinion (*woefully changed since*) Captain Wilkes is the most proper man who could have been found in the Navy to conduct this Expedition and I have every confidence (*soon lost it*) that he will accomplish all that is expected, if accidents do not interfere, of a kind that cannot be avoided. Well who knows (*who did know how things would change?*) what will be the termination of this cruise?"

Wilkes's aloofness—he dined alone, shared authority as little as possible, kept plans and destinations secret until the last moment—soon alienated fellow officers, especially those who were his senior in experience and equal in rank. The civilian scientists detected scant interest in their work and began to mutter about "damned quarterdeck insufferability." The enlisted men suffered most. Wilkes freely applied the dozen stripes of the cat-of-nine-tails which was the maximum punishment allowed by the Navy; when that failed to achieve ungrumbling acceptance of orders, he ignored regulations and ordered twenty-four, then thirty-six, and in one instance forty-one lashes.

Disaster struck early. The little *Sea Gull* disappeared with all hands during their first summer in the Antarctic. Distrust of the commander's judgment increased. Wilkes accused two officers of cowardice; they were cleared by fellow officers at a hearing but asked for, and received, transfer home on the next supply ship. Others were sent back without asking.

During their second summer in the Antarctic, they made the first charts of the continental shore along today's Wilkesland, but the feat lost luster when Wilkes's officers accused him of reinterpreting the log to deprive a rival French expedition of the first sighting of the southern continent.

While they were charting the archipelagoes of the South Pacific, two midshipmen, one of them Wilkes's nephew, were killed by natives of the Fiji Islands. Wilkes sent parties ashore to destroy the two nearest villages and kill all men of fighting age. Some officers accused the commander of exceeding and disobeying his Letter of Instructions from the secretary of the Navy. He responded that his instructions were to do what he thought best when in the Pacific, and such orders could not be exceeded.

Wilkes kidnaped a Fiji chief, Vendovi, who was rumored to have presided some years earlier at a feast at which eight sailors from the Boston whaler *Charles Daggett* were the main dish. The islanders had even complained, it was said, that one of the Americans tasted too strongly of tobacco. Vendovi was to be taken to the United States for trial, or at least diet modification. He was a big, friendly man, scrupulously neat and clean, who learned to play the jews' harp and soon became a favorite of the crew. Anybody Wilkes didn't like was all right, including man-eaters.

Not even the chaplain, bowlegged little Jared Elliott, was exempt from the general disharmony. Elliott took his ministry seriously. He worried about the seamen's morals and sought to keep them from reading French novels. When the expedition reached Hawaii, he urged the missionaries to safeguard the sailors' virtue by sequestering their female parishioners. The sailors responded by making a formal complaint that the chaplain was too friendly with the lovely wife of one of the ministers, a dereliction they feared would lower their own morale. Wilkes suspended Elliott from conducting divine services.

When the *Vincennes* and *Porpoise* departed for the Oregon Coast, leaving the *Peacock* and *Flying Fish* to complete the charting in the Central Pacific before joining them, disharmony rode with the ships on the westerly winds. The weather was so pleasant that Wilkes felt obliged to remind his men they were not on vacation. "He would have quarters beat," a sailor complained, "take charge of the quarterdeck and sing out through the speaking trumpet, 'Silence fore and aft, wet and sand the decks, knock out your ports, take off your muzzle bags, withdraw your tampions and cast loose your guns.' " Then the temperature fell thirty degrees in twenty-four hours, they caught a series of gales, the ships lunged through heavy waves, taking water through the hawser holes, the decks awash. No need for scrubbing now.

Only twenty-two days out of Hawaii, after the fastest passage recorded till then, they raised Cape Disappointment. Their first glimpse of the guardian headlands of the Columbia was ominous. Driven by the unchecked winds of the Pacific, the dull green waves rolled slowly shoreward, gathered speed as the bottom shoaled, smashed white against the sandbars, and merged with the outpour of the mighty river which carried the rain and spring snowmelt of a quarter million square miles. The breakers, beautiful but deadly, stretched in unbroken line from Cape Disappointment to Cape Adams.

The Hawaiian pilot Wilkes had brought from the islands because he claimed to know the Columbia could not suggest where the channel might be. Wilkes ordered quarterboats lowered but the weather worsened and they were forced to return. The sloops stood off shore. The next morning, the weather no better, Wilkes decided to chart Puget Sound before doing the river. He laid a course for Cape Flattery.

On the morning of April 29, a day of haze and high wind, the *Vincennes* and *Porpoise* were racing north through the murk under heavy sail. Suddenly, about 10 A.M., "Breakers under the lee! Breakers under the lee!" The white water was less than a pistol shot distant. The helmsmen fought to hold the ships clear.

R. B. Robinson, a purser's clerk on the *Vincennes*, stood transfixed,

waiting with breathless interest, expecting every moment to feel the strike, our ship driving bows completely under. A man aloft reported land on the lee bow, over breakers. The Captain would not believe it, at first, as his reckoning places us at some distance from land. We were going at a tremendous rate through the water and in less than a minute I saw land myself from the weather passway about one point on the lee bow. It looked very high, shaped like a sugar loaf, and real dismal through the mist and spray. The sea was breaking tremendous heavy against it, and over some smaller ones just showing their heads out of the water alongside it. We lay well up and weathered it by about a third of a mile. As we passed abreast of it we saw an aperture through the center of it of considerable size, and leeward was a still higher and larger rock or island. As we weathered it we passed clear of the breakers and left as we thought all danger astern but just as we were congratulating ourselves on our narrow escape the cry of Breakers Ahead and to Leeward brought all hands to stations. We had but faint hope of saving the old barkey. We got a cast of lead in five fathoms, the breakers making a clean breach over the bows and almost drowning the armorers who were shackling the chains. As we were just passing out of this dangerous situation a large rock was discovered about a pistol shot to leeward but it was passed almost as soon as discovered and we were out of the labyrinth of dangers triumphant and grateful for our miraculous deliverance. We now stood off again to get an offing. Had this occurred at night instead of daylight, not a soul of our whole crew would have lived to reach land.

Wilkes praised all hands for their seamanship, a compliment not returned. George Sinclair, sailing master of the *Porpoise,* felt they had escaped disaster by good luck, not good management. The commander, he wrote, "insisted on running by his own reckoning and as a matter of course, and thereby he came within an ace of losing both vessels."

Two days beyond their brush with disaster on the Point Grenville rocks, the ships anchored in Discovery Bay, forty-nine years to the day after Vancouver.

Wilkes was unsure how the presence of United States naval vessels, obviously sent to strengthen their country's claim in the disputed land north of the Columbia, would be received by the Hudson's Bay Company garrison at Fort Nisqually. To test the British attitude, Wilkes dispatched a message by longboat asking the help of a pilot and interpreter. After waiting a week he decided that no answer was answer enough and started south on his own. The next day, off Whidbey Island, a day so gusty that the *Vincennes'* lee guns sometimes went muzzle under, a dugout came alongside with William Heath, a dark-haired Englishman off the HBC supply ship *Cowlitz.*

Heath piloted them to Port Orchard, where they spent the night. The next morning the *Vincennes'* crew put on a display of bad seamanship. They set out a light warping anchor while raising their heavy bower anchor and began to set sail; the kedge failed to hold and the ship drifted ashore. They worked her clear before she was hard aground but then the starboard anchor was let go by mistake. "We were humbugging around for two hours," the purser lamented, concerned that all this took place under British eyes. But the cruise south under clearing skies calmed even Wilkes.

The Americans took the west channel past Vashon Island and anchored about 7:30 P.M. across from Point Defiance, a mile north of the Narrows and only a cable's length (720 feet) from shore, Wilkes remarking the extraordinary deepness of the water, seventeen fathoms (102 feet).

"We have a splendid view of Mt. Ranier, which is conical & covered about ⅔ of its height with snow," said the first American to describe it. "Last evening the weather cleared sufficiently to see it and also Mt. Baker at the Entrance of Admiralty Inlet. If the weather should prove calm in the morning I shall make a survey of this part of the Sound. I deem it highly important because vessels are likely to be detained here in consequence of the difficulty in getting through the Narrows, which I trust we shall pass tomorrow and reach the Fort."

The morning brought favorable wind and tide so no surveying was done. Again they had trouble keeping the ships off shore when they raised anchor, but once underway, clear sailing.

"This is one of the most Majestic sheets of Warter I ever saw in all my life," observed the usually dour John W. W. Dyes, one of the scientists' helpers, who specialized in taxidermy and temperance lectures to his mates. "The forrist trees of the largist size grow to the Very Warter's Edge where you may cut a mast or stick for a Line of Battle Ship. I never saw Sutch large forrist trees in any part of the world before. This is principally Pine tho there is considerable oak maple and other branch wood common in the U States."

Wilkes too admired the waterway: "Nothing can be more striking than the beauty of these waters without a shoal or rock or any danger whatever for the whole length of this Internal Navigation, the finest in the world."

At eight that morning, Tuesday, May 11, 1841, the *Vincennes* and *Porpoise* dropped anchor below the bluff just south of Sequalitchew Creek, a little seaward of the black-hulled, paddle-wheeled *Beaver,* the first steamship on the Northwest Coast. "Appears to be a fine vessel," commented purser's steward Robinson. From the water they could see no sign of the fort, but soon a boat bearing two officers rowed out to the flagship.

For the first time, British and American officials faced each other on the water their countries coveted. Alexander Canfield Anderson, the slight, thoughtful chief trader at Nisqually, and Henry McNeill, the burly, short-tempered captain of the *Beaver,* introduced themselves to Wilkes. They promised the Americans "all assistance in their power" or, Wilkes added skeptically in his journal, "at least that was their offer. A few days will show the extent of it."

Anderson meant it. The Hudson's Bay Company gave Wilkes some supplies, loaned or sold equipment, helped line up Indian guides and interpreters, showed the Americans around the post. The fort begun by Heron was complete now. As described by the *Vincennes'* armorer, William Brisco, the stockade was an oblong, 200 by 250 feet, of "upright posts eight or ten feet high, at each corner a Sentry Box or house large enough to hold fifteen or twenty persons, perforated with holes of sufficient size to admit the muzzle of a musket." Lieutenant Sinclair noted that "the site was never chosen by an Engineer or wasn't calculated to stand a seige, as its inmates are compelled to go nearly a mile to get their water." Besides, "the Stockade is falling to decay and they are about to build another in a better site."

The new establishment was to be farther north, closer to the farm and dairy. Wilkes inspected the farm and was surprised to find peas about eight inches high, strawberries and gooseberries in full blossom, and lettuce already gone to seed, some plants three feet high. Out on the plain wheat was growing but not doing well: "They do not average even two Bushels to the acre. I think Rye would have answered better."

Robinson, the purser's steward, hiked up the Nisqually valley about fifteen miles to an Indian fishing station:

We descended a bluff covered with Pine about 200 feet deep & almost immediately came to the river which ran very Swift. It is about 30 yards wide and close to the banks were several huts, just erected, and a basket work dam, just finished. The stakes for the dam were about 3 inches apart, and there was a double line of them, about four feet apart, and cross pieces to support them both, & on which the Indians stand and spear the Salmon as they leap the barrier. Between the two rows of stakes are nets spread to catch those who fall between the lines. They catch a great quantity of salmon, which they dispose of to the company agents.

When the fish were brought to the Station, Nisqually women cut out the backbones and chopped off the heads. The salter placed them in a large hogshead with a quantity of coarse salt. There they remained for several days until they became quite firm. The pickle this process produced was boiled in a large copper kettle; the blood which was floated by the boiling was skimmed, leaving the pickle clear. The salmon were then taken out and packed in forty-two-gallon casks, more salt was added, and the casks were sealed and laid on their sides with the bunghole left open. The pickle recovered from the boiling process was poured in until the cask was full. A circle of clay about four inches high was made around the bunghole, into which the oil from the salmon rose. The oil was skimmed, and as the salmon absorbed the pickle more was poured in. When the oil ceased to rise, the clay circle was removed and the cask sealed. Salmon cured in this manner would keep at least three years. The preserved salmon was sent to Vancouver and relayed to the interior posts as emergency food. Any surplus was sold in the Hawaiian Islands.

But livestock remained the principal source of income at Nisqually. Robinson noted "horned cattle in great abundance" and about a thousand sheep. "I am astonished that our Country should let them get such a secure footing as they already have got on this land."

Wilkes was busy organizing parties to chart the shore and survey the interior. Anderson gave him permission to build two log work-shops on the hill above the Sequalitchew. One housed the telescopes and the pendulum clock which was used ashore to check the accuracy of the ships' chronometers; the other served as a storehouse and as drafting room for the chart makers. Under one corner of the observatory, Carpenter Amos Chick buried two pennies, one minted in 1817, the other in 1838, both borrowed from John Dyes, and a bit of doggerel written by Robinson about the British-American rivalry for land still occupied by the Nisqually.

Though far from our homes, yet still in our land
True Yankee enterprise will ever expand
And publish to all, each side of the main
We triumphed once and can do it again.

A problem, a problem, oh! hear great and small
The true owners of the country are still on their soil
Whilst Jonathan and John Bull are growling together
For land which by rights belongs not to either.

Philosopher, listen & solve me this doubt
Which has troubled so many wiseacres about.
By what right does the Bull claim pasturage here
Whilst he has plenty of pasturage elsewhere?

The *Porpoise* was first to start surveying. She was the best sailer of the expedition ships, 224 tons, 88 feet long, two-masted, rigged as a brigantine, carrying sixty-five men and under the command of Cadwallader Ringgold. Lieutenant Ringgold had spent twenty-five of his thirty-nine years in the Navy; he was scion of a distinguished Maryland family and bore the name of his maternal grandfather, the Revolutionary War general John Cadwallader; his commission as lieutenant had been issued before that of Wilkes. Unfortunately he knew nothing of surveying; Midshipman William Reynolds groused that "the mysterious properties of a right angled triangle are utterly beyond his comprehension." Fortunately, Lieutenant Sinclair, the sailing master of the *Porpoise,* though he longed to be home, could still lay down the latitude and longitude of strange places and fix them on a chart. Sinclair surveyed for Ringgold.

Wilkes assigned the *Porpoise* to go above the Narrows and work northward along the east side of the Sound. Coming out of the Narrows on Saturday, May 15, Midshipman Joseph Sanford noticed on the west bank "a pretty little bay that is concealed from the Sound." Investigating by long boat, he found that "the passage is about 10 or 15 yards wide and it gradually widens until it forms a circular basin." Sinclair, after a visit in the ship's gig, pronounced it "an excellent little Bay about 2½ miles to the north of our anchorage on the 11th." He named it Gig Harbor.

The *Porpoise* anchored along the west shore on Sunday. The officers went hunting. Sinclair bagged a pheasant and a few squirrels, admired the forest, and, as he usually did, found something to complain about in the natives: "They cook their salmon by sticking sticks into it and letting it hang over the fire, and by way of seasoning they take up their blankets and scratch their backsides over it." The Puyallup had a bawdy sense of humor.

On Monday morning, May 17, the *Porpoise* anchored below the bluff of present-day Tacoma. "Called this anchorage Commencement Bay," Sinclair noted. "Sent the boats out Surveying. . . . Boats returned at Sunset, having discovered a fine harbor entering Vashon Island on the SE Side [Quartermaster Harbor] and two small rivers Emptying into Commencement Bay." The rivers were probably the two channels of the Puyallup, though one might have been the Hylebos.

Midshipman Sanford was among those who visited the head of the bay. "A fine sheet of water. . . . A flat off from its head for ½ mile. Plenty of [word undecipherable] surrounded by a range of low hills covered with splended trees. A snow covered range in the distance to the East, of which Mount Rainier is the loftiest peak."

The next day, with fine weather and variable winds, two boats visited the tideflats. Sanford's boat could not get into the south channel of the Puyallup. Working northward on a rising tide, Sanford entered a twisting, reed-shrouded stream, possibly the north channel of the Puyallup but more probably the Hylebos, which he followed about three miles, until "it branched into numerous little streams which completely bisect the bottom land for some distance, as could be seen, beyond the point reached. The face of the country on either side of the bottom is very much broken by hills."

The other boat seems to have entered the main channel of the Puyallup, which then pointed west up today's Fifteenth Street. It met the smaller north channel (today's main stream) near the present Interstate Five bridge: "These rivers form a small flat off their mouths which is [word undecipherable] at low water but at high water boats may go up and fill with water. Followed them about two or three miles up. Low meadowlands on their Banks covered with fine grass on which vast numbers of Duck and geese were feeding. There was an opening in the hills to the Southward as though another small stream came in [Delin Creek] but there was no water for the boats to go up."

Wednesday they moved north and anchored in Quartermaster Harbor, which proved more extensive than they had supposed. One of the boats located "a portage communicating with an anchorage. It is a mere strip of Sand, so that Vashon is nearly two islands." Wilkes, in completing his charts, named the eastern portion Maury Island honoring William L. Maury, nephew of the Navy hydrographer who had turned down command of the expedition. The designation of Vashon and Maury as separate islands was one of the few changes Sinclair's survey made in the chart prepared by Puget and Vancouver which, the Virginian acknowledged, "is of the greatest assistance to us in cutting out our work."

A few days later Sinclair's people took the measurement of the future site of Seattle. Studying their findings, Wilkes was unimpressed: "The anchorage is of comparatively small extent, owing to the great depth of water as well as the extensive mud flats; these are exposed at low water. Three small streams enter the head of the bay, where good water may be obtained. I do not consider the bay a desirable anchorage: from the west it is exposed to the prevailing winds, and during their strength there is heavy sea."

He named it Elliott Bay. There were three men named Elliott on the expedition: the unpopular chaplain, Jared Elliott; a ship's boy, George Elliott, who about the time of the charting was receiving eight lashes for insubordination at Nisqually; and Midshipman Samuel Elliott, a member of the *Porpoise* survey crew that charted the bay. Although he sometimes named places for men he had disciplined, Wilkes almost certainly meant to honor Midshipman Samuel Elliott.

While the *Porpoise* was working north along the east shore, longboat crews based on the *Vincennes* at Nisqually charted the twistings and turnings of the Sound south of the Narrows. Puget had charted the general outline; the Americans now filled in the details and the depths. They did discover an inlet the British had overlooked, the long, narrow, crooked arm extending to the present site of Shelton. Wilkes named it Hammersley Inlet for Midshipman George Hammersly, though with characteristic abandon he spelled it with one more *e* than did its namesake.

Anxious to emphasize an American connection with an area discovered and occupied by the British, Wilkes made lavish use of the names of people on his ships in his charts of Puget Sound. His principal cartographers—Lieutenant George M. Totten and Thomas A. Budd—and passed Midshipman Henry Eld had the three southernmost inlets named for them.

The civilian artists and draftsmen, Titian Ramsey Peale (son of Charles Willson Peale, noted for his portraits of George Washington), John Drayton, and Alfred T. Agate gave their names to passages, Agate's causing lasting confusion to rock gatherers.

Hale Passage between Fox Island and the mainland bears the name of the expedition's expert on languages, Horatio Hale, who compiled a definitive dictionary of Chinook Jargon (and whose mother wrote "Mary Had a Little Lamb"). Charles Pickering, the naturalist (whose book, *The Races of Man,* was to receive a memorably unkind review from Dr. Oliver Wendell Holmes: "The oddest collection of fragments that was ever seen . . . amorphous as a fog, unstratified as a dumpling and heterogeneous as a low priced sausage"), gave his name to the passage separating Hartstene Island from the mainland. James Dwight Dana, who shipped as geologist but who produced a major study of coral zoophytes, is remembered by Puget Sound pilots not as a Yale professor but for a passage.

Whatever his limitations as a commander, Wilkes was generous in his name giving. Foe as well as friend received such immortality as comes from having one's name in use after death. Lieutenant Augustus Case, whom Wilkes detested with reciprocity, drew equal billing on the charts with Lieutenant Overton Carr, who rather liked his commander: both had inlets called after them. Lieutenant Henry Hartstene, who demanded to be sent home after being abused by Wilkes for what he and others believed to be an act of heroism in the Antarctic, has his name on the largest island in the southern Sound, though not in the manner he spelled it. James Sinclair, who could not make up his mind whether Wilkes's greatest defect was his incompetence or his arrogance, is remembered by the inlet he most admired, the southwestern arm of Port Orchard. Even the cannibal chief, Vendovi, had an island between Lummi and Guemes named for him, and the nearby Viti Rocks for the area in the Fijis he called home.

Nor were crewmen overlooked. S. L. Fox, an assistant surgeon; Stephen W. Days, hospital steward; and Lewis Herron, barrel maker, had islands named for them. Sailmaker Henry Wilson and Gunner's Mate Daniel Green had points on Hartstene Island and Hale Passage named for them. Quartermaster Harbor, lying between Vashon and Maury islands, honors Wilkes's petty officers as a group, while individual points were given the names of Quartermasters Dalco, Henderson, Heyer, Neil, Piner, Pully (now Three Tree Point), Robinson, Sanford, Southworth, and Williams.

The British were not totally left out. Anderson Island honors Alexander Canfield Anderson, the chief trader at Fort Nisqually, whose generosity surprised Wilkes. Ketron Island was so called in an attempt to recognize the helpfulness of William Kittson, the HBC carpenter. McNeil Island recalls William Henry McNeill, (two *L*'s), the Yankee captain of the steamer *Beaver* who became a Hudson's Bay Company chief factor.

Wilkes seems to have recognized his problems with spelling. When it came to naming something for George Musalas Colvocoresses, a Greek refugee from Turkish massacre in 1822, the captain gave up. He simply called the waterway west of Vashon Island, Colvos Passage. (Colvocoresses, in his best-selling *Four Years in a Government Exploration Expedition,* published in 1852, managed to spell Wilkes's name correctly every time.)

Washington, D.C., was anxious to have the Oregon Country explored by land as well as sea. In one of his more wayward moments, Wilkes assigned the inland expedition to Lieutenant Robert Johnson, a handsome young Virginian with a fondness for liquor and a distaste for camping out. Others in the eight-man party included Charles Pickering, the naturalist, a quiet little man who could outwalk a camel, and William Dunlop Brackenridge, thirty-one, former head gardener at the Edinburgh Botanical Gardens, not unaccustomed to hiking. These "proven pedestrians," as they styled themselves, were miffed to find themselves getting marching orders from a tenderfoot.

For that matter, Wilkes wasn't happy with his choice. "Johnson not off yet," he noted on May 18, "fussing, fidgeting and delaying our time. No cruppers, then no packsaddles, then no girths, all his time being wasted bargaining for horses. Still waiting for a guide. No end to delay."

When a guide was found it was Pierre Charles, whose foot Dr. Tolmie had saved. He led them through Naches Pass, the first recorded crossing by whites. The trail was bad, the horses reluctant; in desperation they hired a dozen Indians to carry the beasts' burdens. The day the party crossed the divide, Lieutenant Johnson fell in a stream, rendering their chronometer useless; next, the marine sergeant broke their barometer; finally Johnson's horse ran off with their artificial horizon. Surveying became a matter of guesswork.

They survived a crossing of the flooded Yakima on rafts made from their inflatable, India-rubber groundcloths, but they were cold, hungry and weak. They traded their worst horse for dried salmon and patties of sun-dried camas root and plodded hopefully toward the juncture of the Columbia and the Okanogan, where they expected supplies. Their only fresh meat was whistling marmot, which Indians traded at the rate of one rifle ball, one marmot.

Arriving at Fort Okanogan, they were outraged to learn that their baggage included twenty-five pounds of pork, three whole cheeses, and three cases of sardines. When Johnson made presents of the sardines and two cheeses to the British, Brackenridge was outraged: "Had I then had the least idea that such conduct would have been approved of by the Commander—or that he had direct orders to act as he did—I would certainly have taken the shortest way for the U. States, viz—across the Rocky Mountains."

From the Okanogan the surveyors moved through the great rut of the Grand Coulee to Fort Colville, over to the Lapwai Mission on the Clearwater (where Henry Spalding generously gave them new horses for old), on to Fort Walla Walla, then back through Naches Pass, now clear of snow, and down to Nisqually. Brackenridge, the gardener, summed up their impressions: "Not two acres out of a hundred in the interior would repay a farmer's efforts" and "a Sailor on shore, is as a fish out of Water."

Wilkes had been on an inland trip of his own. With the draftsman, Joseph Drayton of Philadelphia, R. R. Waldron, the pompous purser, and a French Canadian guide he crossed The Portage to the Cowlitz, rented a canoe, and ran down the river, then up the Columbia to Fort Vancouver. He was charmed by Dr. McLoughlin ("a tall fine-looking person, of a very robust frame, with a frank manly open countenance and a florid complexion"), who entertained him in the great hall while the bagpipes skirled, and supplied him with equipment from the company store and a bateau complete with oarsmen for a visit to the Willamette.

Wilkes was dismayed by most of his countrymen south of the Columbia, "an uncombed, unshaven and dirty-clothed set," though he found some of the missionaries tolerable. He was a disappointment to the Americans as well, they having anticipated another Salcum who would sympathize with their complaints against the HBC Monster but getting instead advice to be patient "until the government of the United States should throw its mantle over them." Premature attempts to end joint occupation, Wilkes warned, might leave the American minority governed by the Catholic, French Canadian majority.

When Wilkes returned, a fur brigade under Peter Skene Ogden had arrived at Fort Vancouver from up the Columbia. He found them an impressive assemblage, "decked in gay feathers, ribans, etc., full of conceit, and with the flaunting air of those who consider themselves the beau-ideal of grace and beauty; full of frolic and fun, and seeming to have nothing to do but attend the decorations of their persons and seek for pleasure; looking down with contempt upon those who are employed about the fort, whose sombre cast of countenance and business employments form a strong contrast to these jovial fellows."

Ogden volunteered to take Wilkes back as far as Cowlitz Landing. The Columbia was in flood and, with fourteen paddlers fresh and anxious to show off, their canoe swept down the Columbia to the Cowlitz, thirty-five miles, in two and a half hours. Upstream was slower but Wilkes marveled at the *élan* and endurance of the French Canadians as, stimulated by songs and pauses every half hour, for smokes, they swung their paddles at sixty beats to the minute, dawn to dusk. They beached at Cowlitz Farms on the third day, and Wilkes rode into Nisqually two days after that. "All well," he wrote in his journal.

The men of the *Vincennes* were not overjoyed to have him back. "At 4:30 he came on board," Dyes noted sourly, "and all hands was called to witness the punishment of Owen Roberts, who received 18 lashes of the cat of nine tales for Refusing to do Double Duty by the order of Mr. Carr." On July 3, three men from Lieutenant Case's longboat party tasted the whip. "The skipper has kicked up a terrible breeze all around the board," says another journal, "keeping everybody on the 'qui vive' and making everybody uncomfortable, as he always does."

Wilkes decided to throw an Independence Day party. Since the Fourth fell on a Sunday, they would celebrate a day late. The Glorious Fifth dawned clear. The sun, rising from behind the dark line of the Cascades into the salmon-tinted sky, was greeted with twenty-six consecutive shots from a cannon, one boom for each state of the union. The cannonade set the crows to complaining and raised a cloud of gulls. Indians gathered at the landing. Clambake today! White man's potlatch!

Shortly before ten o'clock, everyone except the officer of the day and the poor pariah of a chaplain, who was not invited, left the *Vincennes* and climbed the bank to the log-cabin observatory above the mouth of the Sequalitchew. They formed a line of march, the fife and drum in the lead, followed by the men of the starboard watch in crisp whites, the marines in blue, the larboard watch in white, the civilians wearing whatever, and Vendovi in a Fiji wrap-around and second-hand boots. Officers not assigned to watches brought up the rear.

In single file they started along a narrow path bordered by rhododendrons in bloom, poison oak, salal, oregon grape, and Solomon's-seal. The air was sharp with the scent of evergreens; Douglas squirrels scolded and crows commented as they made their way to the Old Fort palisade. The Americans gave three cheers for the British, independence from whom they were celebrating. The Hudson's Bay people cheered back. The Americans cheered again, the prisoner Vendovi joining in the hurrah for freedom, then to the tune of "Yankee Doodle" they moved out, two abreast now, through thinning woods, across a shallow dale bright with buttercups, and onto the plain where stood the Puget Sound Mission Station.

The only Americans living north of the Columbia were at the station, which was supported by the Methodist Episcopal Board of Missions. The site had been selected in 1838 by Jason Lee, the head of the Oregon mission. The following spring there arrived William Holden Willson, a cantankerous young eccentric with a passion for cats, folk medicine (Lee feared Willson would "send some of us to an untimely grave"), and "the habitual use of tobacco, even immoderately." But Willson had his good points. Before finding life on a New Bedford whaler immoral he had been ship carpenter; so by the time the missionaries arrived in 1840 everything was shipshape at Nisqually Station; it looked more solid than the Old Fort. The main house—thirty-two feet by eighteen—was of logs, with floors and doors of boards cut in the HBC sawpit. The outbuildings, too, were of log, and the whole, including garden plot, was enclosed by a palisade of sharpened posts.

The mission party consisted of twenty-nine-year-old Dr. John P. Richmond, a short-sighted, lantern-jawed Marylander who held degrees in medicine and theology; his wife, America, a handsome, dark-haired woman who had been widowed when very young, and their three children, a fourth soon to be the first white child born on Puget Sound. Also with the party was Chloe A. Clark, a school teacher, sent to lift the Nisqually children from the pit of ignorance. Inevitably Chloe married Willson, the Reverend Dr. Richmond officiating at the first Puget Sound wedding.

Nisqually Station was less firm spiritually than structurally. Like most of his fellow missionaries in the Pacific Northwest, Dr. Richmond was beset by doubt. "Instead of thousands of Indians I have found but a few hundreds," he complained, "and these are fast sinking into the grave. Extinction seems to be their inevitable doom, and their habits are such that I am fearful that they will never be reached by the gospel." He had already told Lee he intended to return east, a decision which drew from the bearded Jason a sputter of indignation: "To know, that there is, in the M. E. Church, a conference Preacher, who could enter the Missionary field, with the express stipulation, that he should remain *ten* years, at least, and before he had labored *one*, determine to abandon it, fills my heart with *grief;* and I am ready to cry out, where is justice? Where is conscience? Where is Methodism? How are the mighty fallen?"

The Mission Station was to be abandoned in 1842, but when the

Vincennes crew saw it that July 5, 1841, it looked flourishing and the presence of an American family with "fine fat children, rosy cheeks, was quite a novel sight to us." The crewmen cheered the Richmonds and the Willsons and marched on to the picnic grounds. The site had been suggested by the Indians, a stretch of clear land between the little lake the Nisqually called Sequalitchew and a larger one, Spootsylth—now American Lake.

Everything was ready. Preparations had begun the day before. The commissary had obtained a bullock from the Company herd, driven it to the picnic grounds, and slaughtered it by the roasting pit. John Sac, a tattooed Maori who had joined the expedition in New Zealand, was chef. He had the carcass spitted, the ends of the pole slung in the forks of two conveniently spaced trees, and a windlass attached to keep the beef turning over a trenchful of alder coal, while bread baked alongside. Tables stood under oaks bordering the little lake; poles were tied to posts driven into the ground, fir boughs laid across the poles, canvas spread over the boughs as tablecloth.

Reaching the picnic grounds the sailors planted five stands of colors, the marines stacked rifles, the officers ordered the men to "Fall out," and the first official American Fourth west of the Rockies was under way.

Sailors raced wildly over the six miles of prairie on horses rented from the Indians; others played football or cornerball, an early variant of baseball; still others danced on a portable door, brought from the ship, to a fiddler's lively tunes. The Nisqually, who watched the whole show with appreciative amusement, delighted at the trouble the Americans were taking to entertain them, were puzzled by the violin: "They tried to determine how it was possible for the Little Box as they called it to make so manney strange sounds," said Dyes. "They thought that we'd passed with a devel and he must be in the little Box. They examined the fiddle but when they found it was hallow, they were even more surprised and said the devel was invisable to Indians."

At noon Wilkes ordered ten rounds of musketry and another twenty-six-gun salute. The first shots from the brass Howitzer went well, but when Quarter Gunner Daniel Whitehorn rammed home a new cartridge it was ignited by debris from the previous shot. The blast so mangled Whitehorn's left hand that both the *Vincennes'* surgeon and the missionary doctor recommended immediate amputation to prevent tetanus. Whitehorn refused the operation. He was taken back to the ship on a litter. (He survived but never recovered the use of his hand and was discharged on pension when the *Vincennes* reached the United States.) "The incident put a momentary stop to the hilarity," Wilkes reported, "but men-of-war's men are somewhat familiar with such scenes and although the accident threw a gloom over the party, the impression did not last long."

Speechmaking began in the early afternoon under a blazing sun. Wilkes' thermometer read 120 degrees, which tells us more about the instrument than about the real temperature. The missionary led a prayer, the sergeant of marines read the Declaration of Independence. Wilkes read scripture. The sergeant led in the singing of "My Country 'Tis of Thee" and "The Star Spangled Banner." The Reverend Dr. Richmond put on his spectacles, set aside his pessimism, and read a speech of confident patriotism:

We entertain the belief that the whole of this magnificent country, so rich in the bounties of nature, is destined to become a part of the American Republic. . . . The time will come when these hills and valleys will be peopled by our enterprising countrymen, and when they will contain cities and farms and manufacturing establishments, and when the benefits of home and civil life will be enjoyed by the people. . . . The future years will witness wonderful things in the settlement, the growth and the development of the United States and especially of this coast. This growth may embrace the advance of our dominion to the frozen regions of the North, and south to the narrow strip of land that separates us from the lower half of the American continent. In this new world there is sure to arise one of the greatest nations of the earth. Your names and mine may not appear in the records but those of our descendants will. . . .

There is no record of how the Hudson's Bay people who heard the speech, or the Indians, reacted to Richmond's redistribution of property, but the sailors, having been given verbal deed to the continent, went back to cornerball and dancing. Wilkes and Lieutenant Case took time out to calculate the height of Mount Rainier, missing it by more than two thousand feet. Uncharacteristically, they were low.

Dinner was piped at four. "The Main Brace was spliced," wrote Purser Robinson, "and all hands had an extra allowance of old Rye, and the Bullock was eaten with great relish by all hands. Considering it was roasted by Sack, it was done well. I made a hearty meal off it." It was after midnight when they returned to the ship.

The celebration marked a comma, not a period, in the expedition's feuding. Controversy flowed on. When the Johnson-Pickering-Brackenridge party returned from the far side of the Cascades, the *Vincennes* was about to leave for the San Juan Islands, then for the mouth of the Columbia, to rendezvous with the *Peacock* and *Flying Fish* after they completed surveying in the Hawaiian Islands.

Wilkes decided to send Johnson overland to Grays Harbor, along the route pioneered by the Work-McMillan party in 1824–25. While composing instructions for the survey, he learned that Johnson had made the factor at Fort Colville a present of a bowie-knife pistol issued to Pickering.

Wilkes was outraged. He amended Johnson's orders to say that "no government property is to be disposed of except through absolute necessity, in which decision the officer who accompanies you must decide." Johnson protested that the order made him, a lieutenant, subject to veto by an inferior officer, passed Midshipman Henry Eld. Wilkes brooked no back-talk. He ordered Johnson below to think things over. When the young Virginian reappeared, he was wearing an Indian rain hat he thought might be useful on his trip. Wilkes refused to talk to him "as he was dressed very unofficerlike and showed marked disrespect in his manner and dress to the rules of the Ship and Navy." Again he sent Johnson below. Johnson reappeared "in some temper and in the same dress." Wilkes had him arrested, charged with "wasting government property," and disrespect to orders. He was acquitted. Eld was put in command on the westward survey with Colvocoresses as second in command.

Thus organized the explorers set out for Grays Harbor. Brackenridge and Pickering, those proven pedestrians, thought even less of Eld and Colvocoresses as forest scouts than they had of Bob Johnson. "About the poorest hands to conduct an expedition of this sort that I have ever fallen in with," was Brackenridge's estimate. Still, the trip west from Puget Sound had its moments.

On Eld Inlet they negotiated with a female chief for horses to use on the portage to Black Lake. "The squaw chief seemed to exercise more authority than any chief that had been met with," said Eld. "Indeed her whole character and conduct placed her much above those around her. Her horses were remarkably fine animals; her dress was neat, and her whole establishment bore the indications of Indian opulence. Although her husband was present, he seemed under such good discipline as to warrant the belief that the wife wore the breeches." This would seem to be Princess Charlotte, the handsome, alcoholic daughter of the famous Chinook chief, Concomley, and wife of a Cowlitz chief. Tolmie had thought her "the best looking native I have seen, about the middle size, a dark brunette, with a large dark languishing eye, pearly teeth & finely formed limbs & there is a grace in all her actions."

The canoe trip down the Black and Chehalis proved difficult. Eld complained that "the turns sometimes were so short that the larger canoe would be in contact with thickets on the banks at both ends." The stream was narrow and the trees were huge, even by Puget Sound standards. Eld paced off 260 feet along the length of one fallen cedar. On the Chehalis they were astonished to find on the south bank a stand of upright planks, rudely carved with stylized representations of human figures which had been painted with bright red pigment. Eld sketched them.

When they reached Grays Harbor on the last day of July, the wind was strong from the southwest, the tide at flood. They had great difficulty getting their dugouts out into the bay. Unexpectedly the woman chief appeared in a high-prowed, ocean-going canoe. She had them towed to the safety of a sheltered cove, and disappeared.

For two weeks Eld's little party waited for the *Vincennes* to pick them up. They exhausted their supplies and lived off berries, clams, and a few dead fish washed up on the shore. In mid-August a supply party reached them from the Columbia with provisions—and bad news. The *Peacock,* arriving from Hawaii, had gone aground on the Columbia River bar. All hands were saved but the ship was a total loss.

Wilkes was in the San Juans when a canoe from Fort Nisqually relayed word of the disaster. He broke off charting the archipelago and sailed to the Columbia. For the next two months he was at his best. He arranged shelter for the shipwrecked crew. He bought for seven thousand dollars the brig *Thomas Perkins,* a New England merchantman, renamed her *Oregon,* and pressed her into charting work. They surveyed the river from the upper range of tidewater at the Cascade Rapids to the crazy-quilt pattern of shoals that made up the bar.

Wilkes's charts of the Columbia bar were beautiful, but he feared they might be useless. The sands at the river mouth shifted so swiftly that by the time he finished the survey the chart of the first part was outdated.

His report to Congress on his return to Washington in 1842 stressed the hazards of the Columbia. He urged that the United States not be stuck with the river as its only outlet to the Pacific. Puget Sound and San Francisco Bay were the areas he coveted for the nation: "Mariners, without exception, clothe the entrance to the river with dangers; and none have had the hardihood to attempt its entrance except under the most favorable circumstances, and almost every vessel that has attempted a passage, in or out, has met with some disaster more or less serious; even those who have been deemed the most expert navigators, and we have reason to believe had the best information respecting it, have not escaped uninjured."

About the Oregon Country and its worth, he was enthusiastic: "It is very probable that Upper California will become united with Oregon, with which it will perhaps form a state that is destined to control the destinies of the Pacific. This future state is admirably situated to become a powerful maritime nation, with two of the finest ports in the world—that within the Straits of Juan de Fuca, and San Francisco."

On June 29, 1842, the aging Alexander Baring Ashburton sat at his desk in the sweltering heat of a Washington summer writing a dispatch to Lord Aberdeen, the British Foreign Secretary, about his efforts to negotiate with Secretary of State Daniel Webster a settlement of the many disputes that plagued American-British relations.

For the most part things were going well. But they were as far apart as ever on the proper dividing line in the Oregon Country. The United States was as unwilling to yield anything below the 49th parallel as the British were to concede the area north and west of the Columbia River. And now, the tired old diplomat reported to his master, a new factor made early agreement unlikely:

"With reference to the subject of Boundaries, I am sorry to have to express my apprehension that I shall not be able to do anything with that on the Pacific. The exploring expedition just returned from a cruize of nearly four years brings a large stock of information about the Columbia River. The public is at present busy with this subject and little in a temper for any reasonable settlement. It must, therefore, I fear, sleep for the present."

It was to be a short and uneasy sleep, disturbed by the rattle and creak of covered wagons rolling west, by the clamor of American politicians for possession of all the Pacific Coast as far north as the Russian-American border, by the proposal of the governor general of Canada that he lead an army of 150,000 men south through the United States, making treaties with each separate state as it was conquered.

The Oregon Country became an issue in the American presidential election of 1844. James K. Polk, the Democratic candidate, favored the admission of Texas to the Union as slave territory and, to balance things, all Oregon as free territory—that is, all the area between the 42nd parallel and the Russian boundary at 54 degrees 40 minutes. The British ambassador wrote from Washington that "leading interests" in the United States would see that the Oregon question did not lead to war, that "mischievous declarations in Congress" could be discounted, and that much of Polk's talk was "nothing more than Electioneering manoeuvre."

When Polk won the election, the British waited to see if as president he talked as tough as he did as candidate. He did. In his inaugural address on March 2, 1845, President Polk threw down the gauntlet: "Our title to the country of the Oregon is clear and unquestionable. . . . Already our people are preparing to perfect that title by occupying it with their wives and children. . . . The jurisdiction of our laws and the benefits of our republican institutions should be extended over them in the distant regions which they have selected for their homes."

A sailing packet rushed the news of the speech from New York to London, arriving March 27. On April 3 Governor George Simpson of the Hudson's Bay Company was called to Number 10 Downing Street to discuss the Oregon situation with Prime Minister Robert Peel and Foreign Secretary Lord Aberdeen.

Simpson distrusted the Americans, especially the type seen in Oregon. "Desperate characters," he styled them. "People among whom the Bowie Knife, Revolving Pistol and Rifle take the place of the Constable's baton." In 1843, fearing the Americans might seize Fort Vancouver, he had ordered construction of a new fort on Vancouver Island, which would be better protected from "those troublesome people." Simpson urged that a naval squadron be sent to the Oregon Country, that marines occupy Cape Disappointment and install cannon commanding the entrance to the Columbia, that two thousand troops be sent overland to Oregon from Canada, and that Indians be armed and trained for guerilla warfare.

Peel wanted peace. England faced other problems—trouble in India, famine in Ireland—of more concern than the boundary in Oregon, but if war with the United States did come, the British Navy had 90 steam vessels to the Americans' three, 636 sailing vessels to the Americans' 77, and 17,681 cannon afloat to the Americans' 2,345. Peel could afford to speak softly but make gestures reminding Polk of British seapower. Already HMS *America* was on her way to the Columbia. Not only was the fifty-gun frigate the most powerful warship ever sent to the Pacific, but her commander was the brother of the Foreign Secretary, and one of her junior officers was the prime minister's son. Surely this would impress the Americans. But in case it did not, Peel dispatched two secret agents "to gain a general knowledge of the capabilities of the Oregon territory in a military point of view."

Chosen for the undercover assignment were Lieutenant Henry J. Warre, aide-de-camp to the governor general of Canada, and Lieutenant Merwin Vavasour of the Royal Engineers. They were to pass themselves off as "young gentlemen of leisure travelling for the pleasure of field sports and scientific pursuits." It was a cover that offered an unlimited expense account and the opportunity to spy in some luxury.

Warre and Vavasour went west from Montreal to Fort Garry

(Winnipeg) by express canoe in the company of George Simpson and the omnipresent Peter Skene Ogden. Traveling with Simpson meant traveling in style: paddlers piggybacked the gentlemen ashore from the canoe lest they dampen their boots in Her Majesty's service; their tents were pitched for them; bagpipers marched around the campfire as they dined. But beyond Lake Winnipeg they were on horseback in a party commanded by Ogden, who had no fondness for frills. Or for Warre and Vavasour.

Warre complained of the hardships of the trail: "Our daily journeys commenced with the early morn and ended where a sufficient supply of wood and water could be obtained to prepare our frugal meal—a tent our only covering." Such talk irritated Ogden, who had spent more than half of his fifty-one years in the wilderness. He had no more consciousness of hardship than a mountain goat. Any tent was a luxury; any junior officer who would find it remarkable to sleep in one was beneath contempt. "Two more disagreeable companions I never travelled with," he reported to Simpson, adding that rather than cross the Rockies again with the likes of this pair he would forego seeing his companions ever again.

Working westward in the Okanogan country the British agents encountered the Jesuit missionary, Pierre Jean De Smet. A good listener, the priest had little difficulty penetrating the lieutenants' disguise and getting an exaggerated idea of their mission.

"It was neither curiosity nor pleasure that induced these two officers to cross so many desolate regions and hasten their course toward the mouth of the Columbia," he wrote to his bishop in St. Louis. "They are invested with orders from their Government to take possession of Cape Disappointment, to hoist the English standard, and erect a fortress for the purpose of securing the entrance of the river in case of war. John Bull, without much talk, attains his ends and secures the most important part of the country, whereas Uncle Sam loses himself in words, inveighs and storms."

The agents were impressed deeply and unfavorably by the Big Bend of the Columbia in eastern Washington: "The barrenness of the soil, the total absence of wood and water, completely excludes all hope of its ever being adopted to the wants of men." Nor, on reaching Fort Vancouver some seventy-three days after leaving Winnipeg and losing more than half of their sixty horses en route, did they think much of Governor Simpson's notion of sending an army across continent by canoe and cayuse. "Quite impractical," they reported. "Facilities for conveying troops to the Oregon Territory by the route we have lately passed do not exist to the extent Sir George represents."

Fort Vancouver was more to the young officers' taste. At

McLoughlin's table the civil amenities were observed. Men were seated by rank, the correct toasts were pledged, the wine was excellent, there was talk of empire and trade. The company commissary was well stocked, and as "gentlemen of leisure" they dare not be parsimonious. Their expense account lists purchases of the best in beaver hats at $8.88 each, frock coats at $26, cloth vests, figured vests, tweed trousers, nail brushes, hairbrushes, handkerchiefs, shirts, tobacco, pipes, wines, whiskies, and enough extract of roses to make fragrant the available female population. Nor was that the end of their indulgences. Ogden lamented to Simpson, "Master V remains a disagreeable puppy, and at times most disquieting, particularly when under the influence of brandy and opium."

While Warre and Vavasour were luxuriating at Fort Vancouver, another British observer arrived, the prime minister's son, William Peel. HMS *America* had reached the Northwest Coast two months behind schedule. Drawing too much water to enter the Columbia, she anchored at Discovery Bay. Captain the Honorable John Gordon detailed Lieutenant Peel of the Marines to carry a dispatch to Dr. McLoughlin announcing the presence of the frigate, and to determine "the actual state of the Country on the Banks of the River Columbia and the district called Oregon."

Peel took the *America*'s launch to Fort Nisqually, where he obtained horses from the Indians and a supply of potatoes from the company store, then crossed the portage to the Cowlitz and reached Vancouver by canoe. He and Warre and Vavasour hit it off splendidly. When Peel returned to the *America,* the secret agents accompanied him. The three lieutenants took time out to join some Hudson's Bay Company cowboys in a round-up of cattle on the rainswept Cowlitz plains, a pursuit Warre described as "not unattended with personal danger as these animals are extremely fierce and often become the attacking party, in which case we were obliged to trust to the speed and activity of our horses."

They cast a military eye on the settlement at Cowlitz Farms, noting that "in the vicinity is a R. Catholic church built of squared timber, musket proof, situated on a rising ground having command over the surrounding plain. The position is good but the buildings are unprotected and incapable of offering any defenses. The church might be loop-holed and made very defensible."

The relocated Fort Nisqually they found to be "incapable of making any defense. The buildings are not even surrounded by pickets." The Old Fort, abandoned since Wilkes's visit, had fallen into decay and was without water. Their field notes summarized the state of the only settlement on the Sound: "20 men, 5795 sheep, 1857 cattle, 100 acres cultivated. Excellent stream of water near the Fort at all seasons. No wells. 1 large warehouse. 1 large and 1 small dwelling house. Accommodation for about 50 men. The ground is dry & the situation fine for camping."

If Britain fought the United States for possession of the Oregon Country, the young officers declared in their final report, Nisqually would be the best place to land troops, "the Straits of Juan de Fuca and Puget's Sound being accessible to vessels of any tonnage and at all seasons." The troops could provision themselves off the herds of sheep and cattle before marching south.

The Columbia, on the other hand, could not be entered much of the time. Even getting out was difficult. They told of two vessels that needed almost a month to work downstream from Fort Vancouver to Astoria against the prevailing southwest winds, then spent another forty-seven days waiting for the weather to permit an exit across the bar.

Warre and Vavasour recommended seizure of Cape Disappointment and Cape Adams to control the entrance to the Columbia, occupation of Oregon City on the Willamette "to over awe the present American garrisoning of either the Cascade Rapids area or The Dalles against an American approach overland.

We entertain no doubt as to the practibility of cutting off, or otherwise obstructing, the passage of any body of troops from the United States in their descent from the south branch of the Columbia [Snake River] because of the ruggedness of the present route; and the obligations they are under of keeping to the beaten track to obtain water and wood, and from the fact that troops brought 2 or 3000 miles across any country would be harrassed from their long march and rendered unfit for active service on their first arrival.

The reports and contingency plans of the secret agents did not reach England in time to influence Robert Peel's decision to accept the 49th parallel to the Strait of Georgia as the boundary. Warre and Vavasour's trip is remembered not for its impact on events but for their description of conditions in the Oregon Country; especially for the paintings and sketches Warre made in his guise of Victorian tourist.

William Peel, the prime minister's son, did get back to England while the issue of the Oregon boundary remained unsettled. He brought with him a report from the captain of the *America* and his own observations.

Captain John Gordon would have fit comfortably on the bridge of HMS *Pinafore*. Elderly, eccentric, of explosive temper, he had not been in command of a craft larger than a punt for thirty years when assigned the *America*. He owed his appointment to competence—the competence of his brothers, one, Foreign Secretary, another, First Lord of the Admiralty. A creature of quick and abiding prejudice, Sir John cultivated an early dislike to the Northwest Coast into hatred. He couldn't get his ship into the Columbia. He couldn't find the entrance to Victoria harbor. The wind died when he was two hours from Port Discovery and he was becalmed for days. This was a place where things went wrong. The crowning insult bestowed upon him by this land of difficult anchorages, endless rain, and fir-dark shores of unbearable sameness came when he finally found Fort Victoria. Chief Factor Roger Findlayson took his fellow Scot fishing. Salmon abounded. The spawning run was on and Indians were harvesting its bounty with net, spear, and club. They were even throwing them ashore with their hands. But Gordon was skunked. He insisted on whipping the streams with his fly-rod, and spawning salmon do not bite. "What a country, where the salmon will not take the fly," he protested. According to Findlayson, he "would not give one of the barren hills of Scotland for all he saw around him."

So hostile did Gordon find the Oregon Country that he attributed the westward movement of American settlers to a conspiracy on the part of the United States government against its people. Why, sir, they trick those poor chaps into selling their farms and crossing the desert and the mountains in the certainty that when they arrive they will be so dismayed that they will go south, south sir, and occupy California, which is worth having. A plot, sir, a devious Yankee plot.

Then the rains began, the real rains of fall, and Gordon too fled south to Hawaii, then to Mazatlan. British merchants in Mexico, fearful of rising lawlessness in that troubled land, asked him to carry their money back to England, which a naval captain was permitted to do, and for a percentage. The honorable captain saw things their way. He took on board something like a million dollars and sailed for home, "without orders, with gold," as the Admiralty put it when he faced court martial. Gordon was found guilty of leaving station without permission, suffered reprimand, but was allowed to take the legal cut from the money he had rescued.

The captain's notions about Oregon almost certainly carried little weight with Peel. But his son's report may have carried more. Lieutenant Peel had been sent home by way of Mazatlan and Vera Cruz and arrived February 10. What had impressed him in Oregon was the population explosion among the Americans. It began with the wagon train of 1843 that brought "about 1000 persons with a large number of wagons, horses and cattle, traversing the vast desert section of the country." That first great train tipped the population balance toward the Americans.

And still they came:

Some are induced to come over from not finding a market for their produce in that country [Missouri]; others come mostly from speculation and a habit of restlessness; some either to get rid of their debts or to escape justice. . . . The American Settlements on the Wallamette, running south, and those on the Sacramento, running north, will, I am afraid be very soon united. Their junction will render possession of Port San Francisco to the Americans inevitable, and that harbor has so many advantages, is so safe from attack, and the land round its enormous girth is so rich and accessible, that when once in their possession it will, I fear, give the Americans a decided superiority in the Pacific.

Nor were the newcomers all heading south. "The cultivable part of it, however, cannot be said to extend more than 60 or 80 miles in length, and 15 or 20 miles in breadth. Nearly all of the Prairie land is now taken up, and the Immigrants are too indolent to clear the woods. They are consequently forming new settlements on the banks of the Columbia, at the mouth of the same river, and on the beautiful but not very rich plains to the north, in the neighborhood of Nisqually and Puget's Sound."

Americans had reached the Sound, not like the Methodist missionary guests of the Hudson's Bay Company in 1840, but as settlers.

The canoe system of the British fur trade, pioneered by the explorers of the North West Company and perfected by the Hudson's Bay Company under Simpson, was an elegant construction. It delicately balanced the lightness of birchbark canoes, the endurance of the French Canadian paddlers, the portability of the ninety-six pieces into which all canoe cargo was divided, the length and slope of innumerable portage trails, the strength of currents in the river systems, the prevailing winds on the open water traverses, the depth of snow in a thousand defiles; all these came together into a pattern lovely and serviceable as a spider's web, capable of moving men and supplies across a continent, capable of supporting a fur empire.

There was precious little elegance to the Oregon Trail, which started on the Missouri and ended on the lower Columbia. Its merit was brute practicality. The Americans had found they could roll wheels over the Rockies at South Pass in Wyoming. Where Americans could go on wheels, they went as families: the missionaries first, then the land-hungry farmers.

To the north, the swift birchbark of the British, driven by hardy paddlers, moving trade goods. To the south, the awkward wagons of the Americans, pulled by oxen, carrying families. The race was to the slow.

There was an exquisite appropriateness in that first party of Americans to reach the Sound in the fall of 1845. They symbolized, as Lieutenant Peel indicated, the filling up of the Willamette Valley by the covered wagon pioneers and the overflow of American settlement across the Columbia. The dam of HBC opposition had broken. And they symbolized, too, the diverse motivations at play in the great migration that began in 1843—patriotism, curiosity, land-lust, health, poverty, prejudice. All played a part in bringing the Bush-Simmons party not only across the plains and over the mountains to the Oregon Country but across the river and through the trees to the inland sea the British had monopolized.

An odd pair, these family men: Michael Troutman Simmons, thirty, born in Bullock County, Kentucky, one of ten children; George Washington Bush, at least fifty-four, maybe sixty-six, born in Pennsylvania or New York, if not Louisiana, an only child, a man of color, his mother Irish, his father possibly East Indian, probably black. Simmons, big-framed, bearded, blue-eyed; Bush, big-framed, bearded, brown-eyed. Simmons, by his sworn testimony all but illiterate; Bush, by others' testimony, well-educated. Simmons, a self-taught millwright; Bush, a mountain man turned rancher.

They met in western Missouri where Bush raised cattle and wheat, and Simmons ran a gristmill he had put together from an illustrated book on mechanics by the cut-and-see-if-it-fits method. It is not known how much the Bush and Simmons families influenced each other in the decision to join the covered wagon train to Oregon in 1844, the year after the first mass crossing of the plains by Americans, but they formed the nucleus of a group of Clay County residents, which included Simmons' mother- and father-in-law and his wife's brother and sister-in-law and their neighbors, the James McAllisters.

Big Mike westered for all the standard reasons: he was, to begin with, a mover-on. His mother left Kentucky with her brood of ten when he was still a boy. They settled in Pike County, Illinois. From there Michael went to Iowa, where at the age of twenty-one he married fifteen-year-old Elizabeth Kindred, small enough to stand under his outstretched arm. After five years they moved to Missouri and now, another four years later, it was time to think of moving on. Times were tough in the Midwest, drought-stricken tough; Missouri was full of talk about the Willamette, a land of deep soil and blessedly frequent rains, where crops never dried up a land that might be lost to the British who wanted it, the politicians said, not to cultivate but as a preserve for beavers and the wild Indians who hunted beaver—and to encircle the United States and block Uncle Sam's way to the Pacific. It was patriotic to go west, and patriotism might turn a man a profit. Congress was considering a bill to guarantee each settler in the Oregon Country 640 acres—a square mile—with another 120 acres for every child. To Simmons, father of three, that meant 1,000 acres. Why not Oregon?

To Bush, at fifty-four going on sixty-six, wealth and land were not the problem. Color was the problem. Historians and genealogists may debate Bush's ancestry but to the man himself what mattered was that he, and his children, could fall within the reach of laws restricting nonwhites from possession of land, from citizenship, even from the right to testify in court against white men. The chance to be himself had drawn Bush to the frontier, that cutting edge of American independence, but others who also sought freedom brought with them the virus of discrimination. One recourse open to white men who found it difficult to compete with slave labor was to move on. Opposing slavery, they saw in the exclusion of blacks the surest way to prevent slavery. Institutionalized exclusion moved with the American frontier, ahead even of apple pie.

"The prejudice of race appears to be stronger in the states which have abolished slavery than in those where it still exists," reported Alexis de Tocqueville, "and nowhere is it so important as in those states where servitude has never been known." Ohio in 1807 excluded blacks from residence unless they posted bond of five hundred dollars for good behavior. Illinois in 1813 ordered every free Negro to leave the territory under penalty of thirty-nine lashes every fifteen days until he did so. Michigan, Iowa, and Wisconsin denied blacks the franchise. Indiana and Illinois in 1840 wrote Negro exclusion laws into their constitutions. Congressman David Wilmot, author of the Wilmot Proviso which excluded slavery from free territories, explained his object as "to preserve for free labor of my own race and color those new lands." Horace Greeley in urging young men to go west, meant young white men. "The unoccupied west," said Greeley's *Tribune,* "shall be reserved for the white Caucasian race." Though the Missouri census of 1830 listed Bush as a "free white person," there was clearly a question about his ancestry. Perhaps it would be different in Oregon.

Bush bought six broad-wheeled Conestoga wagons, apparently furnishing four to the Kindreds and the McAllisters. In the family wagon he nailed at least $2000 in coin and bullion in a false bottom. The little party ferried the Missouri at the crossing where Joe Robidoux, a retired fur trader for whom Bush had worked in the west, had a log-cabin warehouse. There was enough traffic going by to cause Robidoux to lay out a town, which, as a government official put it, "with proper self-regard he named after himself, St. Joseph."

On the prairie west of Robidoux Crossing the pioneers gathered to organize the wagon train. Simmons was elected "Colonel," second-in-command, an honor somewhat diminished by the election of the blustering Cornelius Gillium as "General," but one which gave him a title he carried to his grave.

So they set off along the Oregon Trail, a trail not yet rutted deep. They were beleaguered not by Indians but by unseasonal rain, then drought, then the shortages and disasters and dissensions inevitable to such a caravan. A man died of cholera; his wife gave birth to a daughter then fell under the wagon wheel, which shattered her leg. There could be no waiting. The train moved on and the injured woman gasped out her life in the jolting wagon. The Bushes helped look after the orphans. Farther west, an Indian rode off with Bart and Rachel Kindred's baby boy, then brought him back with a new buckskin shirt, beaded moccasins, and his wife's compliments.

The journals give glimpses of other moments beyond the routines of the trail: Simmons in flaming argument with Gillium; the Simmonses abandoning Elizabeth's heirloom oak chest at a crossing of the Platte, Bart Kindred and Bush hunting antelope for the party, Bush warning men sent on ahead that they'd be crossing hungry land and should shoot and eat anything big enough to hold a bullet.

One day Bush and a young Englishman, John Minto, who kept a journal, were ahead of the party, "he riding a mule and I on foot. He led the conversation to this subject [of prejudice]. He told me he should watch, when we got to Oregon, what usage was awarded to people of color and if he could not have a free man's rights he would seek the protection of the Mexican Government in California or New Mexico. He said that there were few in that train he would say as much to as he had just said to me."

Minto later was detailed to ride ahead to Fort Vancouver, get supplies, and meet the party at The Dalles with a barge. When the Bush-Simmons wagons got there December 7, Minto informed Bush that the Provisional Government of Oregon, an ad hoc settlers' organization which had no legal power but did reflect the mood of the populace, had just voted to exclude blacks. The method was to be periodic whippings for any black, slave or free, man or woman, who sought to stay in Oregon. This barbarous penalty was never exacted, but its presence on the books greeted the man of color and his party on arrival.

There is no hint in any known journal of the influence the black exclusion law had on the decision of the Bush-Simmons group to settle not on the "American" side of the river but on the north, where the Hudson's Bay Company dominated, and soon afterwards to migrate to Puget Sound. The journals and later volumes of reminiscence speak only of love of country, of the desire to penetrate an area from which the HBC sought to exclude Americans.

Most of the Clay County contingent wintered at Washougal on the north side of the Columbia, upstream from Fort Vancouver. Bush, the experienced cattle man, stayed on the south side at The Dalles, looking after their herd as well as some cattle of other members of the train. Simmons rented a three-walled sheep pen at Washougal, paying a Hawaiian a yellow, homespun shirt (wellworn), and moved his family in. In the spring, Elizabeth Simmons gave birth to a son conceived on the trail. His name reflects their venture and the river of their destination, Christopher Columbus Simmons. The Indians called him Kickapus, the White Seagull.

Already Big Mike was ready to move on. In the spring he and five other men set out by canoe to look at the land around Cowlitz Prairie and the Sound. The Cowlitz was high with rain and snowmelt. They struggled up as far as the forks, pulling themselves along by the branches that showered them with water at the touch, avoiding trees that swept down on the flood, but Simmons recalled a bad dream he had had in Missouri of disaster on a river, and they went back to Washougal.

In July Simmons tried again, this time with a party of eight and a French Canadian guide. They spent several weeks on the Sound, getting as far as Whidbey Island and Hood Canal, but selected for settlement the area at the extreme southern reach, where the Deschutes River falls into Budd Inlet. Simmons saw in the plunge of the river from the prairie to sea level at Tumwater the power needed for grinding grain and cutting lumber.

Bush was at Washougal when Simmons and the scouting party returned in September. The younger Kindreds, Bart and Rachel, chose to settle near Astoria, where Bart became a bar pilot, but the rest of the Bush-Simmons group, thirty-one in all, stuck together. In the last week of September, with the fall cloud cover low over the hills and the rain incessant, they set out for the Sound, a party of men driving the cattle overland, the others, including all the women and children, moving by flatboat down the Columbia to the Cowlitz, then transshipping to canoes for the upstream struggle. They paddled and poled and pushed to the Cowlitz Landing, just upstream from today's Toledo, and set out along the Indian trail. Although it had been improved by traffic between Fort Nisqually and Cowlitz Farms, they needed fifteen days to move fifty-eight miles. Elizabeth Simmons, suckling her six-month-old son, remembered the crossing as the worst time of her life.

A year and a half after leaving the Missouri the party was on Puget Sound. Simmons claimed the area at the falls, where the Olympia Brewery now stands. Bush chose higher, open land to the south, more suited to farming and ranching. The Kindreds were in-between. The McAllisters eventually decided on a claim close to the Nisqually.

That fall they worked together to build a house, forty feet by twenty, walled by split logs set upright, roofed with cedar boards, the floor of dirt, with a huge clay fireplace in which they cooked. The whole party shared it while the individual cabins were being built. They slept four or five to a bed, the beds made on slats laid across stout pegs set in the log walls, one family shielded from the next by a screen of blankets.

The weather was awful. Big Mike had told them he was leading them to Eden, but Eden froze over. The HBC people at Nisqually said it was the worst winter they had experienced, heavy rains followed by heavy snow and prolonged cold. There was not time to both hunt and build. For the first few days the party lived on the dried peas and oats they had carried across the prairie, but Dr. McLoughlin had given "Col. Symonds" a letter of introduction to Dr. Tolmie, who had returned to Fort Nisqually in 1843 as chief factor. It authorized the Americans to buy on credit such food as they required for personal use. The Nisqually House blotter records the first sale on November 11, 1845: "2 bu. salt" and "1¼ gal molasses." Before winter was over, the Americans ran up a bill at the company store for two hundred bushels of wheat, one hundred bushels of peas and ten head of cattle.

The Indians helped, too. They showed these inland people where to gather oysters and mussels, where to dig clams, how to catch crabs. They sold them venison and bear meat; ducks, geese, and swans netted in the swamps; camas root, skunk cabbage root, salal cakes, dried geoducks, and dried salmon. The Bush and Simmons children never lost the taste they developed that winter for the food of the land.

On June 15, 1846, Robert Peel in his study at Number 10 Downing Street read over a treaty already agreed to by the Americans. It divided the Oregon Country between the United States and Britain along the 49th parallel from the crest of the Rockies to the middle of the Strait of Georgia, then by the main channels separating the continental shore from Vancouver Island. That same day George Washington Bush was planting spring wheat on the prairie and Michael Troutman Simmons was working on the foundation for a gristmill below the Tumwater falls on the Deschutes.

There is not the slightest evidence in the official records that the presence on Puget Sound of the Bush-Simmons party had any direct influence on the British decision to give up the north bank of the Columbia. The American settlers had no power other than the power of suggestion. But they did symbolize the facts that Americans on wheels were flowing westward through the funnel of South Pass, that they came as families, that the longer Britain waited to divide the Oregon Country, the stronger would be the American presence in the disputed land. A congressman had told his colleagues that war with England was unnecessary: "We will win the battle for Oregon in our bedchambers. We will outbreed them."

Prime Minister Peel was not inclined to dispute the imperatives of geography and sex. A boundary at 49 degrees north latitude was as favorable a settlement as Britain was likely to get. Sir Robert signed the treaty that afternoon, listed it as one of his major accomplishments in a speech to Parliament that evening, and resigned from office, satisfied that he had established a basis for lasting peace between Britain and the United States.

On Christmas Day 1847 the first child was born to the Bush-Simmons group after their arrival. Lewis Nesqually Bush was born on American soil.

The Engineer and
the Indians

O N April Fool's Day 1852 a long-nosed, spade-bearded Swede
was grubbing in the golden skunk cabbage at the southeastern edge of Commencement Bay. It was hog-work, leveling the
soggy silt washed back by the tides from the outfall of the Puyallup
River, not the type of labor a master carpenter preferred. But Nick
Delin was preparing the ground for industry. In this patch of bog,
where the no-see-ums hovered and the blackbirds flashed their un-
derwing rubies, he would build a dam to impound the waters of two
rivulets flowing from the gulch to the south and use the water from
the millpond to drive a saw in a mill of his own devising. The spade-
bearded Swede in the swamp at the far edge of nowhere, crushing insects against his forehead as he rubbed back the sweat, was the cutting edge of technology on the Northwest frontier.

We know little about Delin's early life. He was born Nicholas
Dahlin somewhere in Sweden sometime in 1817. He was apprenticed
as a carpenter and after learning his trade crossed the Gulf of Finland
to St. Petersburg in Russia, where he worked as a cabinetmaker.
After five years he left for New York, then left New York for Massachusetts, left Massachusetts in 1849 with some 150 other adven-
turers bound around the Horn for the California gold fields, left San
Francisco for Portland the next year, and in 1851 moved on to Puget
Sound.

The scattered farms of the Bush-Simmons party had given rise to a
village. There Delin found work and learned the brief history of
Olympia. Big Mike Simmons had completed his grist mill below the
falls of the Deschutes in 1847, furnishing it with grindstones chiseled
from granite found on Eld Inlet. Now the settlers could eat their own
wheat, though the first years were unusually dry, the crops were
small, and most grain was needed for seed.

The gristmill in operation, Simmons started building a sawmill.

Seven other settlers teamed up with him and on August 20, 1847, they entered a "Corporate commercial venture" to be called the Puget Sound Milling Company. The mill was built half a mile below the falls, far enough down the river that logs could be floated in from the inlet. It was another by-guess-and-by-god contraption, its most spectacular feature a flumehouse that looked like a skyscraper privy. No matter, the flume channeled enough water to the wooden paddles of a flutter wheel turbine to drive a stiff old upright saw that the Hudson's Bay Company had retired from service on the Columbia. A separate gig water wheel was rigged to propel the carriage back after each slice was cut from the log.

Simmons was manager, but twenty-three-year-old Antonio B. Rabbeson, a garrulous jack-of-all-jobs who had crossed the plains from New York "to kill buffalo, deer, elk, etc., and have a good time," passed himself off as an experienced operator. He agreed to run the mill "for three bits every hundred board feet sawed." Rabbeson claimed the honor of hoisting the gate to let the first water down the flume to start the wheels of industry creaking on Puget Sound. The contraption cut lumber, but not rapidly. At its seldom best it produced three thousand board feet a day.

When they had twenty-five thousand board feet on hand, the mill-owners rafted it to Nisqually. Dr. Tolmie bought the lot at sixteen dollars a thousand, paying one hundred dollars in cash and writing off the three hundred for the mill irons. The Simmons party paused on their way back to the Deschutes to celebrate their triumph with a clambake. The Hudson's Bay Company transshipped the Sound's first milled lumber to Hawaii.

Among those drawn to the area by the prospect of the mill was Edmund Sylvester, a native of Deer Island, Maine, who had come west looking for a place on salt water. He was in Portland when he heard a mill was being constructed. Sylvester joined a tragic young Presbyterian divinity student, Levi Lathrop Smith, in claiming the land next to Simmons at the mouth of the Deschutes. (Smith had left Wisconsin after falling in love with a girl considered unsuitable because she was half Indian and all Catholic. He later drowned when he suffered an epileptic seizure in a canoe, leaving Sylvester in possession of the land that became Olympia.) Sylvester and Smith felled a medium-sized cedar, bucked it into sixteen-foot lengths, split out boards, and built a cabin sixteen feet square, roofed, walled, and puncheon floored from the single tree. They fenced two acres and planted a garden, but events in California changed everybody's ideas about the future of Puget Sound.

The same week in January that Simmons' mill started cutting, a carpenter named James Wilson Marshall, a dour chap who had crossed the plains in the same train as Bush and Simmons, was constructing a flue for a small sawmill on the American River in California. He picked up from the millrace a flake of yellow metal "about the size and shape of a small mellon seed."

Although rumors of a gold strike spread through northern California, there had been other such tales and the new ones were widely discounted. The editor of the California *Star* thought they were designed to draw customers to the sawmill and warned editorially of "as superb a take-in as was ever got up to guzzle the gullible." He went to investigate the fraud but returned in May to run through the streets of San Francisco waving a quinine bottle filled with yellow particles and shouting, "Gold, Gold! Gold from the American River!" His paper suspended publication: the printers had become prospectors. "The blacksmith has dropped the hammer," wrote a man on the scene, "the carpenter his plane, the mason his trowel, the farmer his sickle, the baker his loaf, the tapster his bottle. All are off to the mines, some on horses, some on carts, and some on crutches."

Those who left for the gold fields were replaced by others who came to mine the miners. Prices for lumber soared as San Francisco grew and burned and rebuilt and burned again. The impact was first felt on Puget Sound when a load of lumber Tolmie bought from Simmons at the standard $16 a thousand was purchased by the supercargo of a visiting merchantman for $60 a thousand. "A tolerable good speculation," one HBC official gloated. But within a few weeks lumber was going at $150 a thousand.

The Puget Sound lumber industry had found a ready market. Now its problem was labor. Nearly half of the men in the area took off for the golden hills of California. Among those who locked up their cabins and left their gardens unhoed and unharvested was Edmund Sylvester. With three men from Missouri and a yoke of oxen he muscled a covered wagon south to the Sacramento Valley. The trek took five months. By the time he reached the gold fields, Sylvester was homesick for his stump-ranch. But he didn't want to go home by land.

San Francisco was crowded with idle ships that, having hauled the Forty-niners around the Horn, could find neither cargoes nor passengers bound elsewhere. Sylvester picked out a likely brig, the *Orbit*, built in his home state of Maine. With three other quickly cured Californians—Colonel Isaac Ebey, Benjamin Franklin Shaw, and S. Jackson—he bought her for seven thousand dollars. They retained Captain William Dunham to take her north, and Dunham invited a friend, Charles Hart Smith, from his hometown, Eastport, Maine. The other passengers were John M. Swan, who had found prospecting injurious to his health, and Henry Murray, a New York ship carpenter.

It seems to have been a happy voyage. Captain Dunham was so pleased with the company he decided to stay. (And stay he did, forever. His horse pitched him head-first against a rock while he was inspecting the Nisqually plain.) Ebey and Smith persuaded Sylvester to abandon farming in favor of city planning. They even suggested the name for his townsite, Olympia, deriving from Mount Olympus and the Olympic Mountains. "The Indian name here was not suitable," Sylvester thought. "It was one that could be converted into a blackguard meaning. It was Schictwood, signifying Bear; this happened to be a good place for hunting bear. Tumwater was called Schictass by the Indians. These were not proper names."

The arrival of the *Orbit* and the surveying of Sylvester's claim for a town led Big Mike Simmons into a series of financial misadventures from which he was never fully to recover. He had already sold his claim on the falls and his share in the mill to Clanrick Crosby, a ship captain (and brother of the great-grandfather of singer Bing Crosby). Now Simmons bought controlling interest in the *Orbit* and accepted from Sylvester a gift of two town-lots on which he promised to operate a general store.

Simmons sent the *Orbit* to San Francisco with lumber. Charles Hart Smith went along as supercargo to sell the shipment and buy mercantile goods for the store; he did so well that Simmons made him manager. On the *Orbit*'s next voyage her captain tried to enter the Columbia, grounded on the bar, and went over the side with all the crew. The brig floated free on the rising tide and some local people claimed her as salvage. Although Simmons came down from Olympia, retrieved the brig, and brought her back to Puget Sound, a court held she belonged to those who had found her. The *Orbit* was sold at auction by the United States marshal. A party of Olympians bought and dispatched her to Hawaii with piling, but she was caught in a storm and limped into Esquimalt on Vancouver Island, her "rigging and sails very much demoralized." Her captain sold her to the HBC for a thousand dollars. She was quickly repaired, sailed for the Hudson's Bay Company for a decade, and then went into the trans-Pacific trade.

Simmons meanwhile had sent young Smith south with another consignment of lumber and money to purchase more trading goods. Smith sold the lumber, pocketed the proceeds, and was not seen again. Simmons was broke. Like many another self-reliant pioneer he looked around for a government job and caught on as Olympia's first postmaster. Tony Rabbeson, who had sold his share in the Puget

Sound mill to Bush, had a government contract to bring the mail weekly from Cowlitz Landing to Olympia on horseback. There were so few letters he carried them in his pocket and distributed them house to house on arrival. Tony thought the selection of Big Mike as postmaster peculiar, noting, "He can't read."

It was amid this change and turmoil that Nick Delin, the quiet Swede, reached Olympia and quickly attracted attention by his competence. The demand for lumber was growing; new mills were being built up and down the Sound. Delin found financial backers for a mill on Commencement Bay.

After he smoothed out the ground around what is now Twenty-fifth and Dock streets in Tacoma, Delin hired Sam McCaw, a young Irishman who lived near Steilacoom and had a team of oxen, to drag the foundation timbers into place. He paid $150 for three days' work, an extraordinary price at the time. Most of the other work, Delin did himself. The mill stood on tall pilings, a gaunt shed facing the bay with a broad trough extending down into the stream (Delin Creek) up which sawlogs could be moved.

A little to the south, Delin built his house, twenty-four by thirty feet, one and a half stories tall, its exterior of upright planks, the inner walls of hand-planed cedar weatherboard twelve inches wide. It was simply but handsomely furnished, for Delin was not only cabinetmaker but Scandinavian.

Nearby was a typical pioneer garden, a bit larger than most since it supplied food for the mill hands: corn, beans, pumpkins, squashes, potatoes, peas, turnips, cabbages, melons, cucumbers, beets, parsnips, carrots, onions, tomatoes, radishes, lettuce, parsley, sweet fennel, peppergrass, summer savory, and sunflowers. Delin had a few chickens, a dog and a cat, but he had yet to find a wife.

He needed only three or four helpers in the mill. Jacob Burnhardt, a twenty-nine-year-old German who had come out from Illinois, built a log cabin at the edge of the bluff near today's Seventh and Pacific, but Delin built small houses near the mill for his other workers. Into one of them a young English couple moved: William Sales to work in the mill, his twenty-four-year-old wife, Eliza, to cook. On October 23, 1853, she gave birth to their son, James, the first white child born in what is now Tacoma.

The mill started cutting lumber sometime late in 1852. The Puyallup Indians thought it a wonderful show, watching solemnly as one of the mill hands rolled a two-foot fir log onto the crude carriage, fastened it with iron dogs, and Delin shoved the lever that released water down the flume. The mill wheels slowly turned and the muley saw rose and fell against the face of the log. Yellow sawdust cascaded to the floor and the air grew heavy with the scent of fresh-cut wood.

Delin's mill could do two thousand feet a day on the days when the saw didn't hang up too often. It took him nearly six months to make enough lumber to form a shipload. Then, since it all had to be rafted down the creek and out to the *George W. Emery* and hand-loaded over the side, several more weeks passed before the brig sailed for San Francisco. But Commencement Bay was now a port of call.

Most of Delin's logs were brought in by settlers who were clearing their land. He paid not in cash but in lumber. He ran an ad in the Washington *Pioneer* of Olympia:

SAW LOGS! SAW LOGS!

The undersigned will let a contract for furnishing his mill with saw logs on the following terms: he will allow $6 per log to be paid for in lumber at $20 per thousand. Application to be made immediately at his mill on the Puyallup Bay

N. De Lin

In the fall of 1853 the local population was increased by the arrival of the first party of settlers to struggle over the Cascades. A wagon train, led by James Longmire, had come up the Yakima Valley and through the Naches Pass—the route taken in 1841 by Lieutenant Bob Johnson of the Wilkes Expedition—rather than following the Columbia to the Cowlitz, then dog-legging north.

The Longmire party expected a wagon road but found only the Indian trail that had been imperceptibly widened in places that summer by a party of west-side settlers hoping to encourage immigration. The trail was a torment. The wagons crossed the Naches River sixty-eight times. At one point on the west side the party had to slaughter some oxen to provide rawhide ropes to lower wagons down a cliff. But thirty-four of the thirty-six wagons and all 171 pioneers made it to the Sound. Nick Delin had not only a fresh labor supply but a local market for lumber as they scattered to homesteads around Pierce County.

One wagon brought Peter Judson, forty; his wife Anna, thirty-six; their sons Steven, fifteen, and Paul, thirteen; and their niece, Gertrude Meller, thirteen, who had lost the rest of her family to cholera on the trail. Originally from Cologne, Judson had lived in Illinois before starting for California; along the way he changed his mind and joined the Longmire train. His fellow German, Jacob Burnhardt, was ready to give up on Puget Sound. Judson bought Burnhardt's cabin at the foot of today's Stadium Way for thirty dollars and filed claim on 321 acres stretching from Seventh to Twentieth streets.

Such land as was naturally clear, about six acres in all, they immediately sowed with grain and in the summer of 1854 harvested oats where the post office now stands and wheat near the Union Depot site. The Judson boys threshed out thirty-five bushels of wheat with flails and rowed it to the Simmons gristmill on the Deschutes for grinding.

Young Steve yoked the family's six oxen and snaked logs down the gully the Indians called Shu-bahl-up, "the sheltered place"—today's Old Town. The logs were stored in a lagoon, then towed one at a time by rowboat to the Delin mill. With the aid of one faller, a Swede named Peter Anderson, Steven could keep ahead of Delin's saw.

Besides supplying Delin with sawlogs, his new neighbors provided the thirty-seven-year-old bachelor with a wife. On November 25, 1854, Gertrude Meller, then fourteen, married the mill owner in a ceremony performed at the Judson's new house on the present site of the Union Depot. Portly little Sherwood Bonney, another member of the Longmire party, who had just been elected Pierce County justice of the peace, performed the ceremony.

There was now a community of whites on the south shore of the bay. The Sales had staked a claim on the bank of the Puyallup, where they had as neighbors three German-American veterans of the Mexican War—Jacob Kershner, Peter Runquist, and Carl Gorisch—as well as Adam Benston, a Scot who had arrived as a servant of the Hudson's Bay Company. On the waterfront west of the Stadium gulch, a cooper named Chauncey Baird had built a small cabin alongside a big shed in which he assembled fir barrels. These he sold to John Swan and Peter Reilly, the first commercial fishermen on the bay. When the salmon were running, Swan came up from Olympia and with Reilly dragged in enormous catches with seines set between Shubahlup and Cho-cho-chluth—"the maple wood"—where the Smelter now stands. There are no recorded figures, but pioneer memoirs spoke of hauls of two thousand salmon. The fish were brined and shipped to San Francisco.

With logging, sawmilling, farming, barrel making, seining, and fish-packing under way the little community seemed ready to coalesce into a town. Instead there was war, and all was lost.

1852 was an election year. While Nick Delin was grubbing about his swamp on Commencement Bay, the Democrats were mucking about in the heat of a Baltimore summer, trying to pick a presidential candidate. After thirty-four ballots, the early front runners had faded and the dark horses had proved the merit of their long-shot status. No one was close to the two-thirds vote needed for nomination. Then somebody from Virginia placed in nomination Franklin Pierce.

Franklin who? You remember Pierce. From New Hampshire. Lawyer. Served in the House, then the Senate. Youngest member. Didn't much care for Washington. Resigned—they say his wife made him—and went home to make money. Volunteered for the war with Mexico. Enlisted as a private, made colonel before he saw combat and general within a year. Thrown from his horse in his first battle, and invalided home. Not a hero exactly but a reasonable facsimile. Charming fellow. Not fanatic. Few admirers but no enemies. Just what we're looking for.

"My God, gentlemen, you could not have told a more astonished man," Pierce said when a delegation from the convention waited on him in his rose garden with word that on the forty-ninth ballot he had been nominated for president.

The Whigs also looked to the military for a candidate. They usually did. They had won in 1840 with General William Henry Harrison and in 1848 with General Zachary Taylor, only to have each die in office. Millard Fillmore, who inherited the presidency from Taylor, looked like a loser. The Whig convention stampeded to General Winfield Scott, known to admirers of his deeds in the Mexican War as the Hero of Molina del Rey, and the Captor of Chapultepec; to others as Old Fuss and Feathers.

One of the most effective workers for Pierce was a thirty-four-year-old brevet major in the Army Corps of Engineers, Isaac Ingalls Stevens. He was a diminutive man with a large head, dark, curly hair and beard, and wide-set brown eyes. A phrenologist felt his skull and mistook him for a poet. He not only was graduated at the head of his class at West Point but was first in every class he took. Wounded and decorated for gallantry in Mexico, Stevens now served as assistant in charge of the Coast Survey Office. He lived at Mrs. Kelley's, one of the most politically powerful of the rooming houses that served as unofficial clubs for men of like interest in Washington. But what made Stevens uniquely useful in the Pierce campaign was that although he had been on Scott's staff and had written admiringly about the general in his book *Campaigns of the Rio Grande and of Mexico,* he preferred Pierce for president.

Pierce won and Stevens, who in his son's words was "feeling the powers and ambition of a leader and not content to remain longer a subordinate," asked a favor. He wanted to be governor of the Territory of Washington, which had just been split off from Oregon. The new territory was enormous, embodying all of Idaho and much of Montana as well as present-day Washington. It was a wilderness larger than New York and all New England combined, but with no town larger than 250, a white population of fewer than 4,000, and only one road.

Stevens' energy was as overwhelming as his ambition. As soon as Pierce nominated and the Senate confirmed him as territorial governor, he asked the secretary of state to make him superintendent of Indian Affairs for the territory (which was done), and to make him Indian treaty commissioner to negotiate agreements with the tribes he was serving as superintendent (he was promised favorable consideration later). He asked the secretary of war to put him in charge of the most northern of four transcontinental surveys Congress had authorized to locate a possible route for a railroad to the Pacific. When Secretary of War Jefferson Davis hesitated, Stevens went over the Mississippian's head and assured President Pierce that he was "the fittest man for the place." He got it.

Confirmed as governor in mid-March, Stevens wrangled $90,000 of the $150,000 appropriated for all four railroad surveys, organized 250 men, and was ready to depart from base camp (which he thoughtfully called Camp Pierce) just west of St. Paul by June 3. All this in eleven weeks. In the next six months he proposed, in the admiring words of his son and biographer,

. . . to traverse and explore a domain two thousand miles in length by two hundred and fifty in breadth, stretching from the Mississippi River to the Pacific Ocean, across a thousand miles of arid plains and two great mountain ranges, a region almost unexplored and infested by powerful tribes of predatory and warlike savages; to determine the navigability of the two great rivers, the Missouri and the Columbia, which intersect the region; to locate by reconnaissance and to survey a practicable railroad route; to examine the mountain passes and determine the depth of winter snow in them; to collect all possible information on the geology, climate, flora and fauna, as well as the topography of the region traversed; and finally to treat with the Indians on the route, cultivate their friendship, and collect information about them.

Even Stevens could not do all that in the time allowed. He delegated the Cascades to Captain George B. McClellan, who was to proceed directly to the West Coast and look for a route connecting eastern Washington with Puget Sound.

McClellan and Stevens were old friends, fellow West Pointers, comrades-in-arms in Mexico, much alike physically—short, handsome, notable horsemen; but in temperament, except for vanity, they were opposites. Stevens was impetuous, quick to decide and act, slow to concede error: facing the Grand Canyon he might give the order to charge. Little Mac was brave but implacably cautious, determined that everything should be in perfect readiness before he moved: facing a molehill he might make camp and think about the problem.

The east and west survey parties met in mid-October at Fort Colville, and shared a night of conviviality with Angus McDonald, the factor, who treated them to steaks cooked in buffalo fat, and Scotch, and whose last memory of the evening was of Stevens subsiding off his chair in the midst of a speech by McClellan about a Highland ancestor's bravery at Culloden Moor. Estrangement began the morning after.

Stevens, certain before he started that the northern route would be feasible, had swept westward on a wave of self-confidence, sweet-talking the Indians with assurances of the Great White Father's concern for their welfare, touting the fertility of the Great Plains as "far surpassing the Empire of Russia for the cultivation of the great staples," and minimizing the difficulties of crossing the Rockies ("I was a good deal surprised to find how small an obstacle this divide was to the movement of a wagon train"). Nothing he had seen between the Missouri and the Columbia made him think it would be difficult to connect his territory with the United States.

Lethargy mixed with apprehension had marked McClellan's search for a pass through the Cascades. After reaching Fort Vancouver he spent three weeks getting ready; when he took the field his party averaged only three miles a day through open country. On seeing the higher Cascades from eastern Washington he lamented, "There is nothing but mountain piled on mountain, rugged and impassable." He failed to locate some passes, failed to recognize the utility of others, and accepted as gospel Indian hearsay about danger and difficulty. As a survey it was a fine trout fishing trip. The picnickers panned for gold, too.

McClellan's informal report to Stevens that the river route was the way for rails to go touched off an argument that has never been fully resolved: whether the best route through the mountains was that taken by running water—the gravity route through the Wallula Gap and the Columbia Gorge; or the more direct way up through a pass. Neither man had any doubts, but Stevens was in command. He told his subordinate to try again. Stevens had begun to suspect McClellan of pusillanimity, McClellan to look on his old comrade as "a civilian and a politician."

The parties separated to go to Walla Walla by different routes. Stevens, of course, got there first, and learned that only six weeks earlier the Longmire party had made it through McClellan's impassable range with wagons, livestock, women, and children. When McClellan arrived with more excuses than accomplishments, Stevens assigned Chief Engineer Lander to try the Naches Pass and ordered McClellan to proceed to Puget Sound and attempt to cross from the western side.

Lander picked up a false rumor that a party attempting to follow the Longmires had been trapped by blizzards. He gave up without approaching the pass. McClellan lolled around Steilacoom looking for supplies, then tried to cross Snoqualmie Pass, as he put it, "without tent, blanket or overcoat." He soon turned back, having decided "if the attempt to reach the pass was not wholly impracticable, it was at least inexpedient."

Stevens meanwhile had started for Olympia to organize the government. He descended the Columbia by boat, inspected Vancouver, and started for the Cowlitz under a weighty rain from a putty sky. His men were soaked before they got to the canoes. The great river, high, heavy, slate-colored, flowed sullenly toward the sea. The rain fell harder as the canoes turned up the Cowlitz; sky, air, river, and bank merged into the gray murk. Water sloshed in waves in the bottoms of the dugouts. Water seeped through the governor's buckskin undershirt and he made a note not to wear it again in such a climate. They ate wet, slept wet, and sat wet on the four days to Cowlitz Landing, where they bedded under a welcome roof, eight to a room in the farmhouse, their clothes steaming in front of the fireplace.

Before dawn they set out by horse, dragging their small wet circle of horizon north across the prairies, the mountains hidden, the road a bog, sheets of rain gusting after them on the sou'west wind. The forest patches were dim as grottoes, the sword fern flattened, salal and Oregon grape glistening, the musk of deer heavy in the saturated air. The path flowed like a stream and they rode alongside it, past the ice-age deposits they thought to be Indian burial mounds (Wilkes's people had dug fruitlessly in them, and for the next half century treasure-hunters would turn tons of glacial silt in hopeless quest), off the prairie, and back into the woods, the horses' hooves sucking mud, the streams a danger, and then out at last onto another prairie, this one under cultivation, the lamps of early evening gleaming in the windows. The owner of one farm, alerted by the bark of his dogs, came to invite the party to dinner. It was always so with George Bush. He was happy to share not only his food but his seed grain. "Pay me back in kind when you can," he would say, "or pass it on to someone who needs it."

Stevens had grown up on a farm, had ruptured himself pitching hay. He could appreciate what Bush had done with his land. The soil of Bush Prairie, like that in all the Puget Sound basin except for a few river bottoms, is the residue of the last ice age, the sterile scrapings the glaciers carried from the mountains of British Columbia and dropped when the ice melted. The topsoil was thin, but the land could be worked and made to yield harvest to those who loved it and treated it with intelligent concern.

The Bush farm was, except for the spread held by Simon Plamondon down by the Cowlitz, the most valuable privately held land in the territory. The cultivated portion of his 640 acres was mostly in wheat and oats. The garden produced enough cabbage to keep a sauerkraut barrel brimming. The root house held a bounty of beets, turnips, carrots, and potatoes. Sheep, cattle, and hogs grazed and rooted the uncultivated acres; hens and turkeys fussed in the chicken yard. Beef was drying in the smokehouses; salmon, too, and clams. There was a stand of fruit trees, too young to bear, but thriving.

There were also problems. Congress in September of 1850 had passed the Donation Land Law, which provided land for the early settlers. It allowed every male settler, including "American half-breeds," who had occupied and cultivated land for four consecutive years before December 1, 1850, to claim a half section, 320 acres; if married—and settlers were given until December 1, 1851, to get married—his wife could claim a like amount to hold in her own right, with the government surveyor designating which half belonged to which partner. Settlers coming later, up to December 1, 1855, could claim 160 acres, their wives likewise. Titles to the land would not be given until treaties were made with the Indians relinquishing to the United States their ownership of the territory.

For Bush there was a catch: the phrase "white citizens and half-breeds." Joe Meek, the former mountain man who as United States marshal took the 1850 census in Oregon, listed Bush as Negro. The patriarch of the prairie could not claim the land he had developed. He was at risk of having his farm claimed by some late arrival. How much of this background the governor learned while having supper with the settler neither his reports nor Bush family tradition tells.

Leaving the Bush farm, Stevens rode on across the Kindred claim, along the Deschutes past the gristmill and the sawmill, and into the rain-drenched mudhole that was Olympia. It consisted of twenty or thirty frame houses and about as many log cabins set among stumps on unpaved streets, the town enclosed on three sides by a horseshoe of hills opening onto the inlet; handsome at high tide, a mudflat at low. The population of 250 whites and mixed-bloods made Olympia the metropolis of the territory, and though Steilacoom, Port Townsend, Seattle, Bellingham Bay, and other places with "a claim and a name" could dream their dreams of glory, Olympia was the probable capital of Washington. After all, it boasted a thin newspaper and a rudimentary hotel.

Stevens hurried to the Washington Hotel and commenced governing. Most other appointed officials had already arrived, among them Charles Mason, the twenty-three-year-old territorial secretary recently graduated from Brown, a gentle-looking youth with soft brown hair and beard, rimless glasses, and a deferential manner that masked a capacity for decision; Edward Lander, the chief justice of the territorial supreme court, a lantern-jawed Harvard graduate whose gaze could snuff candles; Collector of Customs Sampson Moses; and U.S. Marshal J. Patten Anderson.

The marshal had completed a census of the new territory. He found 3,965 citizens, exclusive of Indians. There were 1,682 white and mixed-blood males over eighteen, eligible to vote. Stevens proclaimed the existence of organized government, established election districts (somewhat favoring Puget Sound over the Columbia district in representation), and set January 30 as the date for an election to choose a nonvoting delegate to congress and twenty-five territorial legislators. Stevens also appointed Mike Simmons to be Indian agent for the tribes on Puget Sound, and Benjamin Franklin (Frank) Shaw and Orrington Cushman, the region's most exuberant teller of tall tales, to help Simmons.

Politicking began at once and in a pattern still recognizable. The Whigs reached quick agreement at their convention and nominated William Wallace as delegate. The Democrats split left and right, as well as north and south, rivalry between the Sound and the river being the main issue. Simmons wanted to be delegate but after some ingenious manipulation of proxy votes (one delegate controlled nine proxies) the Columbia River candidate, Columbus Lancaster, was chosen. Simmons stalked out and ran as an Independent, only to suffer the usual humiliation of the party bolter, receiving 18 votes compared to 690 for Lancaster and 500 for Wallace. The Democrats won control of both the house of representatives and the council (senate). The first legislators were a young lot, averaging twenty-eight years in age. There were ten farmers, seven lawyers, four mechanics, two merchants, two lumbermen, a civil engineer, and a surveyor.

Stevens called the legislature into session in Olympia, February 27, 1854. In the atmosphere of a small town Odd Fellows Club, with red-white-and-blue bunting above the platform and a fire in the pot-bellied stove in a second floor hall of an unpainted frame building on the slough called Main Street, the frock-coated governor addressed the first joint session of the first legislature.

He predicted prosperity. He deplored "the extreme inefficiency and defectiveness of mail arrangements," as well as the lack of funds for federal roads. He called on the United States to buy out the Hudson's Bay Company holdings in the territory. He cited the need for a school system in which "every youth, however limited his opportunities may find his place in the school, the college, the university, if God has given him the gifts." He asked for military training classes in high schools and the creation of a militia subject to federal call. But most of all he talked about railroads and Indians.

The railroad—"the magnificent and gigantic enterprise of connecting the Mississippi and the Pacific with iron roads"—would become the shortcut to the Orient, the Northwest Passage that nature had neglected to provide for ships. World trade beckoned: "The Eagle of our country's majesty has winged his course to the distant east, and Japan, China, Australia and Hindoostan will be brought into fraternal and mutually beneficial communion with us."

As for the Indians, whom he estimated to number ten thousand, two and a half times the white population of the territory, "for the most part a docile and harmless race, disposed to obey the laws and be good members of the State," they would have to give up most of their land. He recommended that the legislature ask Congress to authorize treaty negotiations and "make appropriation to actually extinguish their title throughout the Territory, reserving to them such portions as are indispensable to their comfort and subsistence."

It was a speech in the great tradition of the pioneer West, looking to Washington for the fulfillment of public needs—a railroad, highways, mail service, land development. The legislators responded enthusiastically, turning Stevens down only on things that must be done by the local citizenry, such as the formation of a militia. The rest of his shopping list they endorsed. They gave the governor permission to leave the territory and lobby Congress for beneficial legislation, and added an item. They asked Congress to make George Washington Bush eligible to receive land under the Donation Land Act, a request that was granted.

The legislature's memorial assured Congress that Bush, "a mulatto," with his family "has resided upon and cultivated said tract of land continuously from said year 1845 to the present time, and that his habits of life during said time have been exemplary and industrious: and that by a constant and laborious cultivation of his said claim, and by an accommodating and charitable disposal of his produce to emigrants, he has contributed much towards the settlement of this Territory, the suffering and needy never having applied to him in vain for succor and assistance; and that at the present time the said George Bush has a large portion of his said claim under a high state of cultivation. . . ." The same legislature, however, rejected a bill asking that Bush be granted full citizenship and the right to vote. That right, Bush never achieved.

Back in the East, Stevens defended his report on the northern route against Secretary of War Davis' contention that he had seriously underestimated the cost of construction. He fought off Davis' attempt to hold him personally responsible for cost overruns on his survey. But the mood in the Capitol convinced him that Congress would not soon appropriate the enormous amounts needed for construction of a transcontinental line. With three routes suggested—north, central, or south—there was an automatic two-to-one opposition in Congress to any proposal favoring one of them.

So Stevens turned his attention to the second priority, the Indian problem. He secured appointment from the State Department as Indian treaty commissioner to negotiate formal treaties between the United States and the Indian nations residing in his territory. "Conflict of interest" was not a phrase then current in Washington. No one saw anything improper in the fact that Stevens represented the white citizenry as governor, the tribes as Indian superintendent, and the U.S. State Department in negotiating with those same tribes. Nor that he would be determining reservation boundaries for tribes whose continued presence along the right-of-way he advocated for the railroad might prove an impediment to its construction.

Stevens returned to Olympia in December 1854 and immediately focused his enormous energy and the powers of his various offices on the task of extinguishing, as quickly as possible, the Indians' claim to their traditional lands so that settlers could be given legal title.

The Nisqually rushes fullborn, strong enough to roll rocks, from its nourishing ice high on the side of the mountain. The river slants steeply through the forest of wiry, short-branched conifers shaped by thin soil and deep snow, curves across tilted plateaus where volcanic-blown minerals and decayed vegetation nurture trees old when Columbus sailed, then knifes through canyons of dark basalt to emerge on the blanket of sterile soil laid down twelve thousand years ago when the mile-thick ice covering the Puget Sound area melted. Time has enriched the glacial till, grass grows on the prairie, camas too, and the wild buttercup; but few trees.

Almost at salt water, on a slight rise beside a small stream the Indians called She-nah-nam—Medicine Creek—a few scraggly firs stood out above the flatland in 1854, offering not shade but a landmark. To these trees for so long the memory of men knew not the contrary, the Indians of the southern Sound came to party and sometimes to parlay. And it was to Medicine Creek that Isaac Stevens as treaty commissioner summoned "the chiefs, head-men and delegates of the Nisqually, Puyallup, Steilacoom, Squawkskin, S'Homamish, Stechass, T'Peeksin, Squi-aitl and Sa-heh-wamish tribes and bands occupying the lands lying round the head of Puget's Sound and the adjacent inlets" to make a treaty with the United States of America which would hold good "as long as the grass shall grow and the sun shall rise." Treaty making would start the day before Christmas.

The wind flowed in from the ocean, heavy with moisture. The Mountain was not out, nor its supporting cast. A curtain of leaden clouds, stretched between the tops of the foothills, rolled to the northeast dragging strands of rainfall through the tree tops. The showers began as the first Indians, up-river Nisqually, rode up to the conference site, their horses steaming; it rained or drizzled for the three days of the treaty council. No sunshine warmed Medicine Creek.

The advance party of whites had arrived earlier. Mike Simmons, Ben Shaw, and red-bearded Orrington Cushman, "Old Cush," supervised preparations. The council tent was raised under the grove of firs. In front, partially covered by the tent awning, was the table of officials. A mound of roasting potatoes and several barrels of molasses and ship biscuits, a combination the Indians considered a delicacy, was kept under armed guard.

Through the day the tribesmen arrived, more than seven hundred all told, the Nisqually men riding while their women walked, most of the others coming by water, dark dugouts materializing out of the rain-shrouded Sound. They pitched tepees or threw together shelters of woven mats and poles, their camp an arc on the waterside of the trees. They talked, uneasily, in flat Indian voices of what was to come.

The Stevens party arrived in the afternoon, its appearance an anticlimax. The Indians were accustomed to the high ceremony of a Hudson's Bay Company welcome for visiting officials: men resplendent in uniform, cannon fire, drums, pipers. To honor the new white chief of the Bostons, tyee of a people so strong the rival King George men had surrendered authority without battle, the Salish tribes expected a celebration splendid beyond the memory of grandfathers. Stevens sloshed ashore from a canoe, his flannel shirt open at the throat, twill pants bloused and tucked into his boots forty-niner style, the ensemble topped by a black felt hat with a pipe rather than a feather in its band. Practical garb to be sure, acceptable to Jacksonian democracy, but to the Indians, with their sense of occasion and concern for dignity, an affront.

Nor was the rest of the party impressive in person or apparel. Among those accompanying Stevens was his twelve-year-old son Hazard, a sturdy, handsome lad but hardly an official to be taken seriously by the Indians. Charles Mason, the boyish, fuzz-bearded territorial secretary, peered at the encampment through rain-blurred glasses; he was not imposing. The might of the military was represented, in toto, by First Lieutenant William A. Slaughter of the Fourth Infantry, stationed at Fort Steilacoom, a solemn young man; his dark, muttonchop whiskers reached the corners of his down-turned mouth and gave him the expression of someone perpetually confronting the unacceptable. The canoe trip may have upset him. Ulysses Grant, who came west on the same ship, recalled Slaughter as the sea-sickest soldier he'd ever seen: "It almost made him sick to see the wave of a tablecloth when servants were spreading it."

Others had been brought to Medicine Creek because they were familiar with Indians. Simmons, Cushman, and Shaw were there as old settlers. James Doty, who had once taken a census of the Blackfeet, served as secretary to the treaty council. George Gibbs had come west as a geologist for the McClellan part of the railroad survey; he had read *Hiawatha* and was trying to fit Longfellow's concepts into the realities of Indian existence, and he was assigned as surveyor for the proposed reservation boundaries.

In gathering darkness the last band of Nisqually swam a herd of ponies across the river and staked them out near the campgrounds. A flotilla of Puyallup, accompanied by subagent John Swan, paddled up Medicine Creek. The commissary distributed biscuits and molasses to all camps. While the people feasted, dipping biscuits in molasses in the manner they dipped salal cake in fish oil, Stevens and Simmons visited some of the leaders, after which Indians and whites retired to their shelters to listen to the drumming rain and review plans for the morrow.

In theory the Medicine Creek Council was a negotiation between independent nations, on par with the meetings of British and American diplomats to decide the boundaries of the Oregon Country. Stevens represented the State Department. The president of the United States would review the terms agreed to and send the treaty to the Senate for advice and consent. When satisfied and signed its terms would be law.

But the parties did not meet on equal terms. The most reliable estimate of Indian population, that made by Warre and Vavasour ten years earlier, credited the Puyallup with 484 people, the Nisqually with 258, and all other tribes represented at the conference with about as many more. The Indians were scattered in some twenty permanent villages. There were more whites than Indians in the immediate region. Though the total Indian population in the territory considerably outnumbered the whites and the Indians if united, might have wiped out the white settlements, the fact was they were not united.

The Puyallup and Nisqually were not accustomed to European-style diplomacy. They permitted Stevens to choose the place and set the time for the meeting, to determine the language in which negotiations would be conducted, to decide which peoples would be lumped as a nation for treaty purposes, even to decide which Indians would be spokesmen for their people. Stevens was dominant.

Stevens regarded himself as a friend of the Indians, their protector and benefactor. He admired individual Indians, especially for their endurance and bravery. He sorrowed for them as a people whose time had passed. He wanted to be fair and believed he was fair. But that the westward march of the Anglo-Saxons was Progress, that Progress was good—a manifestation of divine purpose—that the Indians must step aside for the whites, make way for a people more technologically advanced, Stevens did not doubt. What was best for this tragic race, he believed wholeheartedly, was that they be removed from the path of progress and left to peter out their sad destiny in isolation. His problem was how to get them quickly and peacefully to accept their fate.

Stevens first thought of moving all the Puget Sound Indians across the Cascades, but the old settlers warned that the Indians would fight. He then suggested one big reservation at the head of Hood Canal where the tribes would have little intercourse with whites, but again the experienced hands warned this would lead to war among traditional enemies. So he compromised. The Indians would be given two reservations on the east side of the Sound, one south of the Nisqually, the other on the bluff between Old Town and Point Defiance in Tacoma—a total of 2,560 acres, plus Squaxin Island, a heavily forested, little-coveted lump of land in the southern Sound. For ceding to the United States all of today's Thurston and Pierce counties plus parts of King, Mason, and Kitsap counties, they would not only get to keep the reservations but would be paid $32,500 over a period of twenty years, plus $3,200 moving expenses. And they would be promised "the right of taking fish, at all usual and accustomed grounds and stations, in common with all citizens of the Territory, and of erecting temporary houses for the purpose of curing, together with the privilege of hunting, gathering roots and berries, and pasturing their horses on open and unclaimed lands" provided that the Indians not take shellfish from beds staked by citizens, and that they castrate all stallions not intended for breeding, and confine the studs.

There was an escape clause, Article Six. It provided that the president might, when in his opinion the interests of the territory required it, move the Indians from the reservations to other suitable places within the territory, or consolidate them with other friendly tribes or bands.

"Do you think you can get the Indians to sign?" Stevens asked Frank Shaw.

"I can get them to sign their death warrant," Shaw replied.

For the Indians there was no leader like Stevens. Their pattern of life denied such concentrated authority. Persuasion was all: the experienced were listened to in council, but persuasion rested on continuity, on agreement about the nature of the world. In a cosmos adrift, uprooted by strangers, authority of past performance was lessened. The rains of the moon of darkness were falling as they should fall in December but did they mean now what they meant in the time of their fathers? The Indian world was no longer the world they had known.

On Christmas morning, the skies still wept. Red men and white men gathered under the Medicine Creek grove. Stevens gave to the Indians his aides had decided were responsible certificates proclaiming their authority to negotiate with him.

Among those honored was Leschi, a prominent Nisqually. He was in his thirties, about Stevens' age but half a head taller and more powerfully made. His skin was light. His features had a strong Indian cast, with a thin, straight mouth, short chin, heavy brow; his mother, a Klickitat (some say Yakima), had not flattened his forehead in infancy. His black hair was parted slightly on the left and cut straight below the ears. He was dressed in plain work clothes purchased at Nisqually House and he wore neither paint nor ornament.

Leschi was a favorite of Dr. Tolmie, who considered him intelligent, honest, friendly, and adaptable. Such white ways as seemed useful, Leschi had adopted. He had learned to farm; he planted wheat and corn on land near Muck Creek, lived with two wives in a substantial house of cedar. He had the largest herd of horses on the prairie, and had lent a dozen packhorses to settlers who sought to improve the trail through Naches Pass. Leschi represented what many whites felt the Indians should become: a farmer in overalls, attached to his land.

Nevertheless, the whites worried Leschi. Their ways were not always understandable to him. They were untroubled when they changed the mother earth in ways from which she would not recover in the time of their children's children. Whites cut down trees not just for fire and shelter but to load on ships and send away; they did not even talk to a tree before using it. Nor did they share willingly with each other. They closed off the land on which they built houses. They barred their doors. They were strange and they were powerful. They were dangerous.

Indians from the east warned of the whites' lust for land; told of tribes dispossessed; warned that the Americans would get the Nisqually to sign a paper, then would send them off to a land far away, where it was always dark, where fierce little men attacked any stranger, where the mosquitoes were big as herons. Leschi had asked white friends, Dr. Tolmie and James McAllister, about this; they had said that while it was true a land of ice lay far toward the fixed star, the Americans would not send the Indians there. But Tolmie and McAllister were white men, and if part of the story was true, might not it all be. Leschi listened carefully when the speeches began.

Stevens spoke in the name of the Great Father who lived far off but knew of his Indian children and their needs. "The Great Father feels for his children. He pities them, and he has sent me here today to express these feelings and to make a treaty for your benefit. The Great Father has many white children who come here, some to build mills, some to make farms, and some to fish; and the Great Father wishes you to learn to farm, and your children to go to a good school; and he now wants me to make a bargain with you, in which you will sell your lands, and in return be provided with all these things. . . ."

As Stevens spoke, Frank Shaw translated into Chinook Jargon, and men from each band translated the Jargon into Nisqually-Puyallup. The Jargon was a bastard tongue, consisting of a few hundred words from the languages of the salt-water tribes with a flavoring of English and French. It had developed early in the fur-trade era for communication between whites and Indians along the Coast. Serviceable for barter, travel, kitchen talk, and rude courtship—"what do tonight?"—it was ill suited for expressing philosophic concepts or legal abstractions. Shaw could speak Nisqually-Puyallup; he had offered to translate directly, but Stevens told him to use the Jargon. Shaw thought sign language would have done as well.

After Stevens' speech, Secretary Doty read the proposed treaty, article by article. Shaw did what he could to turn into the simplicities of Jargon the complexities of English legalese. "The said tribes and bands of Indians hereby cede, relinquish, and convey to the United States, all their right, title and interest in and to the lands and country occupied by them, bounded and described as follows, to wit: Commencing at the point on the eastern side of Admiralty Inlet, known as Point Pully, about midway between Commencement and Elliot Bays. . . ." And so forth. The Indian translators did what they could to turn the Jargon into Nisqually-Puyallup, and the men squatting in the rain did their best to understand.

The readings lasted well into the afternoon. When they were over Stevens recessed the council until morning, leaving the Indians to discuss the proposal. Any questions?—come to him or to his assistants.

The Stevens party felt this first of treaty councils was going well. There was cause for celebration. Old settlers later told of a party of such proportions that Shaw or Old Cush found it prudent to hide the remaining whiskey. The Indians, too, had tales to tell of Christmas night at Medicine Creek. They say the Nisqually puzzled over what they had heard and at last realized they were to give up all their land except the hillside rising south of the Nisqually flats, which they called The Rock, not because it was rock but because little would grow on it. Indian tales tell of a delegation that went to the council tent to talk to Stevens. As they approached they heard someone ask, "What if the Indians won't give up the land?" and Stevens reply, "My soldiers will drive them off and wipe them from the face of the earth. Shoot them as we did that skunk this morning." There is no way of knowing.

The rain turned to drizzle on December 26 when the council gathered for the last time, but the day was chill. Breath showed as fog as the Indians listened to a second reading of the treaty, and another speech by Stevens:

"The paper has been read to you. Is it good? If it is good, we will sign it; but if you dislike it in any point, say so now. After signing we have some goods to give you, and next summer will give you some more; and after that you must wait until the paper comes back from the Great Father. The goods now given are not in payment for your lands; they are merely a friendly present."

There was, the formal record says, "some discussion." Indian accounts say that Leschi denounced the proposed reservation as no good. It embraced too little land and that land was poor; if the Great Father expected his red children to become farmers he should not assign them farms that would not support even their dogs.

When it came time for the signing, say the Indians, and some old settlers as well, Leschi and his half-brother Quiemuth refused. Mike Simmons is said to have exclaimed, "Damn them, if they don't sign, I'll do it for them." The Indians claim Leschi tore up the certificate of chieftainship he had been given, stomped on it, ground it into the mud with his heel, left the treaty grounds, and rode away. None of this appears in the formal record.

Sixty-two Indians had certificates of leadership. Their names were written phonetically by Secretary Doty at the bottom of the treaty. Beside each name is a mark, supposedly put there by the Indian as a signature. The first is Qui-ee-metl, the third is Lesh-high. Nineteen whites signed as witnesses, Simmons first, the governor's twelve-year-old son last.

Presents of food, blankets, and trinkets were distributed. By nightfall most of the Indians were back at the winter villages their representatives had just agreed to relinquish. Stevens, Mason, Doty, and Shaw returned to Olympia. Simmons and Cushmen went north to make preliminary arrangements for treaty councils with other salt-water tribes. George Gibbs stayed at Nisqually to survey the proposed reservation.

A few days after the treaty council, Frank Shaw rode over to the Nisqually. There he encountered Leschi and Stahi, another Nisqually leader. "They were very much dissatisfied and they complained very much," Shaw said later. They accused him of deceiving them in his translation. He denied it and said he had repeated exactly what the governor had said. "They wanted to get a new treaty. They asked me to report their dissatisfaction to the Governor. I told the Governor, but the treaty was sent to Washington."

The Treaty of "The United States of America with the Nisqualli, Puyallup, Etc." was ratified by the Senate on March 3, 1855, and signed by President Franklin Pierce. Forty years later the pioneer jurist James Wickersham, in an address to the Washington State Historical Society, summed up the proceedings at Medicine Creek. The treaty was, he said, "a contract obtained through over-persuasion and deceit; through promises not in the record; by imposition upon minds unaccustomed to written contracts; a contract obtained from the weak by the strong; from the ward by the guardian; from the child by the parent, and wholly without consideration—unfair, unjust, ungenerous and illegal."

By then much water and blood had flowed down the rivers of Puget's Sound.

The Territory of Washington extended across eleven degrees of longitude and six of latitude; it covered nearly two hundred thousand square miles. Governor Stevens wanted treaty title to all of it, right now. After his success at Medicine Creek he quickly persuaded the other tribes of the Sound and Strait to accept reservation status. In the spring of 1855 he crossed the Cascades to continue his work of liberating the land from the aboriginal occupants.

The great horse tribes of the lower interior—the Nez Perce, Yakima, Cayuse, Walla Walla, and Umatilla—were numerous, independent, well armed, and well informed. After Medicine Creek, Leschi had visited the Yakima and told them of the tactics employed by Stevens. The tribes devised a treaty strategy of their own. They would demand as reservations all of the land on which they customarily hunted. Since their hunting grounds overlapped, this in effect would constitute all the land of the interior. Nothing would be left for white immigrants.

The test of wills commenced on council grounds near Walla Walla late in May of 1855. For more than two weeks the allied chieftains held firm. But Stevens, a single power negotiating with an alliance, used his advantage brilliantly to separate the Nez Perce from the other tribes, play chief against chief, band against band, until in the end the Indians signed. They ceded to the United States forty-seven thousand square miles.

"Thus ended in the most satisfactory manner this great council," Stevens wrote in his journal. To the State Department he claimed that the council demonstrated that policies of firmness and pressure would prevail. To the Oregon *Weekly Times* he and the Indian treaty commissioner for Oregon sent a dispatch outlining the boundaries of the lands the Indians were giving up and stating that "the country embraced in these cessions and not included in the reservation is open to settlement. . . . This notice is published for the benefit of the public. . . . Oregon and Washington papers please copy."

Copy they did. Would-be homesteaders headed for the Yakima, Walla Walla, and Umatilla valleys to pick out claims. They were not welcomed by the Indians, who looked on their presence as a breach of their understanding with Stevens that the tribes would remain undisturbed until after the treaty was ratified.

At this inopportune time, gold was reported around Fort Colville. It was not a major strike, but a man with a pan could make from five to fifteen dollars a day—this at a time when common labor paid forty dollars a month. The shortest route lay through Yakima land. Gold-hungry prospectors joined the land-hungry farmers moving into the Yakima Valley. The Indians were angry and resistent, the whites tough and adamant. Violence was inevitable.

The first casualty was Henry Mattice of Olympia, who crossed Naches Pass on his way to the gold fields. The Yakima said he had raped the young daughter of a chief. Later two more men from Olympia were found dead on the trail.

The Indian agent assigned by Stevens to the Yakima was A. J. Bolon, a member of the territorial legislature from Clark County. He was a young Irishman with flaming red hair, quick temper, and a reputation for fearlessness that some equated with foolishness. Hearing of trouble he started alone to the village of Kamiakin, a powerful Yakima chief. On September 21 Bolon paused at the Ahtanum Mission of the Oblate Fathers on a creek flowing into the Yakima, conferred with the priests for two hours, then rode on. He was never seen again by whites. Rumor soon had it that Bolon denounced the Yakima around the council fire in Kamiakin's village, threatened reprisals by the United States Army, and started back to The Dalles, only to be shot in the back, stabbed, and cremated. His horse, too, was killed and burned.

Governor Stevens was in Montana, negotiating with the Blackfeet and out of touch with territorial affairs. In his absence, Charles Mason was acting governor. On September 24, after learning of the deaths of the prospectors but before he heard that Agent Bolon had disappeared, young Mason wrote to Major Gabriel J. Rains, the ranking Army officer in the Pacific Northwest, "to request that a detachment of the troops under your command may be dispatched at the earliest moment to the Yakima country to administer punishment to that tribe, and to furnish protection to such citizens as may be remaining there."

Major Rains ordered Major Granville Haller of the Fourth Infantry, stationed at The Dalles, to the Yakima country with 102 men and a howitzer. At the same time William Slaughter, the sea-sick lieutenant stationed at Steilacoom, was to take fifty men through Naches Pass and rendezvous with Haller at Ahtanum Mission. Neither party got there.

Haller's force crossed the Columbia on October 2, and marched over the rolling bald hills called the Klickitat Mountains and into the Klickitat Valley. At three o'clock on the afternoon of October 5, while working through the underbrush down a long hill toward the river, the soldiers found themselves facing more than a thousand war-painted Yakimas who were not willing to be punished. In a three-day battle the Indians chased Haller's men twenty-five miles, killed five, wounded seven, forced the soldiers to abandon their howitzer, and captured a herd of cattle that had been sent with the troops as provisions.

Slaughter's party from Fort Steilacoom were working their way up Naches Pass when a dispatch rider brought word that Haller had been driven from the field. They retreated to the White River Valley to await further orders.

The Indian War had begun. In their first encounter with United States soldiers, the Yakima had routed troops sent to intimidate them and had scared away a supporting force without battle. The Americans were impressed. Haller, after getting back across the Columbia to the safety of The Dalles, wrote to Major Rains to say it would take a thousand regular Army troops to subdue the Yakima. At the time the entire United States Army numbered about 10,000 troops, only 2,000 of whom were west of the Rockies. Of that number only 350 were in the Northwest.

The situation was awkward. The white population of the territory was almost entirely west of the mountains, as were the troops. The Yakima were east of the mountains. To punish them—and Major Rains, a veteran of the Seminole War, had no doubt they must be chastised—would require stripping the West of defenses, thus risking attacks by the salt-water tribes on the scattered towns and farms. It was a chance Rains felt must be taken.

Rains sent an urgent dispatch to Olympia on October 9 asking Mason to raise, equip, and loan him two companies of civilian volunteers, "to take the field at once." He specified each company should consist of "one captain, one first lieutenant, one second lieutenant, two musicians, four sergeants, four corporals and 74 privates." The same day the acting governor received a dispatch warning that the Palouse Indians had joined the Yakima, and that the Walla Walla and Cayuse were likely to do so.

Mason on October 14 requested volunteers. The calls were oversubscribed but, although Mason asked each man to furnish his own arms and equipment, few did so. The settlers were lightly armed, and most chose to leave their weapons with their families. Mason requisitioned some muskets, carbines, pistols, and swords from the sloop-of-war *Decatur* at Seattle, and the revenue cutter *Jefferson Davis* at Steilacoom.

Volunteers reporting to Fort Vancouver were attached to the regulars there and assigned to move up the Columbia and enter the Yakima valley from the southwest. Volunteers reporting to Steilacoom were sent to the White River where they joined the force waiting under Slaughter. Captain Maurice Maloney was sent from Vancouver to lead the Steilacoom force through Naches Pass.

Mason immediately issued a second call for volunteers, this time seeking four companies. Men proved willing to join only on condition they would not be sent across the mountains. The citizens of the Grand Mound area held a mass meeting at which they proclaimed their willingness to build a blockhouse, garrison it, and protect their area, but not to leave their farms and families unprotected.

On October 16 James McAllister, whose claim was on Medicine Creek, wrote to Mason from "Nisqually Bottoms" to say, "We have information and are satisfied that Leschi, a sub-chief and half Clickitat is and has been doing all that he could possibly do to unite the Indians of this country to raise against the whites in a hostile manner and has had some join in with him already. Sir, I am of the opinion that he sould be attended to as soon as convenient for fear that he might do something bad. Let his arrangements be stopped at once."

Six days later a volunteer cavalry company, which chose the name Puget Sound Rangers, mustered at Olympia. Charles H. Eaton, who had crossed the plains with the Bush-Simmons party, was elected captain; McAllister, lieutenant. The Rangers, forty-five in number, were given an assignment that might have frustrated an army—to patrol the mountain passes from Snoqualmie to the Lewis River in southwest Washington "intercepting any Indians that may be found travelling the mountains from the seat of war" but not committing "any act which will have a tendency to cause tribes that are now friendly to become hostile"; however, "should you meet any unusual or suspicious assemblage, you will disarm them and should they resist, disperse them, and put any who resist or use violence to death, or send them to Fort Steilacoom in irons. Any Yakima Indians or other savages of the tribes now at war whom you may discover west of the Cascades, acting as an emissary to incite the tribes now at peace to join the war party, you will hang."

The Rangers felt they knew the Indian most likely to incite the local tribes. James McAllister and Leschi had been friends. Leschi had come to the red-headed Scot to tell him, "I will never raise a hand against you or yours, but if you join the army, I cannot be responsible for whatever others may do, for the Indians are going to fight." Charles Eaton's relations with Leschi were even closer: he was married to Leschi's sister. But the two officers felt their duty clear. On October 24, they rendezvoused with seventeen of the Rangers on the Yelm Prairie and set off for Leschi's farm.

Leschi was plowing when someone on a sweaty horse galloped up to warn him the Rangers were coming. He left the plow in the furrow, ran to his best horse, and took to the forest. The Rangers set out after him.

The war had come to Puget Sound.

The week that began Saturday, October 27, left wounds not yet healed.

The Rangers, after three dismal, dangerous days beating the bushes for Leschi, were camped on the Charles Bittings claim on the west bank of the Puyallup, south of today's Sumner. Exhausted, out of supplies, and perilously short of men, Captain Eaton sent five Rangers to Olympia for fresh animals and provisions, and two others to Grand Mound to try to drum up recruits.

Jim McAllister and Mike Connell, a civilian with a claim near the White River, volunteered to scout for hostiles on the prairie near today's Buckley. "Be back this evening," Eaton said. "I will return if alive," said McAllister.

That afternoon Eaton and Private J. W. Wiley, editor of the Olympia *Pioneer and Democrat,* rode out to inspect a slough that was said to be almost impassable for horses. They found it boggy, but Eaton estimated that it would take a small party only an hour or so to firm it up with cutting from the heavy underbrush alongside. As Eaton and Wiley were returning to Bittings' cabin they heard a rifle shot, then another, and after a pause a fusillade of four or five, then silence.

"My God," Eaton exclaimed, 'My God! Our boys are gone." They galloped ahead, found McAllister and Connell dead, then fled as a party of mounted Indians approached. The Rangers holed up in Bittings' cabin through the night, one man suffering a minor gunshot wound. In the morning the Indians were gone, but so were all but one of the Rangers' horses. The Volunteers trudged back to Fort Steilacoom, their pursuit of Leschi a costly failure.

A neutral Nisqually had already carried word to the McAllister cabin on Medicine Creek that James was dead.

The George King and Harvey Jones families had been farming marginal land in Wisconsin, trying to raise crops in a ravine so deep that the dew was dry on their neighbors' fields before their own caught sunlight. Coming west in search of a place with its full share of daylight, King and James in the fall of 1854 took claims near the farm of William Brannon on the bank of the White River between today's Auburn and Kent. They put up log cabins, dug wells, broke ground, set out seeds for an orchard, planted grain and vegetables. They saw their last sunrise October 28.

It was Sunday and Harvey Jones, who was feeling poorly, stayed in bed. His wife, her seven-year-old son by a former marriage, the two Jones children, and a hired man, Enos Cooper, were having breakfast when they heard the distinctive half-cough, half-grunt that Indians made instead of knocking. Mrs. Jones opened the door. When the Indian edged away, and she opened it wider to see who he was, she caught sight of a second Indian crouched at the corner of the house, his rifle pointing at her over the butt of a log. She screamed, shoved back the children, slammed the door, and dropped the crossbar into its slot. From outside came the crack of guns and the thud of one-ounce balls striking the walls and splintering the door.

Mrs. Jones found her husband's five-shooter. Poking it through the window, she fired blindly until it was empty. The firing outside stopped. She took the children to the bedroom, told them to lie on the floor, and covered them with a feather bed. John, the seven-year-old, crawled out to watch and told later what happened.

Harvey Jones got out of bed and was tottering toward his wife when he lurched and cried, "Oh, God, I am shot." She caught him. "Oh, Harvey, don't say so," but when she opened his shirt, there was a wound near the nipple. She helped him back to bed. He died as bullets continued to crash through the windows.

Enos Cooper at Mrs. Jones's urging tried to escape. He pried off a window stop with an axe, removed the lower sash, lunged through, scrambled to his feet, and ran for cover. He did not make it. Mrs. Jones went out the window. She was felled only a few feet from the house with a shot through the lungs.

The attackers battered open the door with a fence rail and found the three children. They were taken to Nelson, a White River Indian who had frequently visited the Joneses. He was seated on a stump directing his followers as they prepared to burn the house. Nelson told the children they would not be harmed. He assigned an Indian to take them to a cabin which sometimes served as a school but the guide led them in the wrong direction, then disappeared. The seven-year-old took charge. He led the four-year-old girl and two-year-old boy to a cabin where they hid for a time. Then they went cautiously back to their house. It was burning.

"I came on my mother, prostrated upon the ground, some hundred feet or so southwest from the remains of our dwelling. She was yet alive. She told me I must take the children and go to Mr. Thomas's. I did not want to leave her but she told me it was best, that she could not live and that I might save the children."

They reached the Thomas place, two miles distant, but found it deserted. John met an Indian named Tom, whom he trusted. Tom hid the children until dark and smuggled them by canoe to the mouth of the Duwamish. Another Indian brought them to the *Decatur,* anchored at Yesler's wharf.

Meanwhile the raiding party had gone from the Jones farm to that of their neighbor Brannan. He had heard shooting and had barricaded the house. According to a pioneer recollection of an Indian account, one Indian was killed as they rushed the house, and Brannan crushed the skull of another with the butt of his rifle when they broke in, but then he was killed. Mrs. Brannan fled with her ten-month-old baby in her arms. She was overtaken, stabbed in the back, and dragged to the well. The attackers threw the baby down the well, then dropped her in after it, head down.

The Kings' house was attacked next. One of the King children was killed with an axe. King was shot. Mrs. King fought with an axe, wounding one Indian before she was shot, then beaten to death with the axe handle. George King, the surviving child, was carried off into captivity. (He was released unharmed the following spring.) Two other farmhouses were burned before the raiders withdrew.

That same Sunday morning, Captain Maloney's troops from Steila-coom completed their ascent of the disorder that is Naches Pass. There was a dusting of dry snow on the ground when they crossed the summit. That evening they camped on the eastern side at the headwaters of the Naches, the pallisades of its narrow canyon loom-ing over them.

A civilian scout had crossed ahead of the troops. He was John Edgar, a husky, hard-drinking Englishman who had come to the Sound as a shepherd for the Puget's Sound Agricultural Company. After the boundary settlement he took American citizenship and made the first claim on the Yelm Prairie. There he lived with a hand-some Nisqually-Yakima wife and several youngsters. Edgar was a good man and a useful citizen. He had helped survey the route for the immigrant road through the pass. He was a leader in the cam-paign to have Washington made a separate territory. In August 1852, on impulse, he and R. S. Bailey, Sidney Ford, Jr., and perhaps Frank Shaw, had made the first approach to the summit of Mount Rainier. They got to the fourteen-thousand-foot level—ten thousand feet above Tolmie's pioneering effort—and reported the view "most enchanting."

Now Edgar moved cautiously down the east slope of the pass. Not cautiously enough: the Yakima captured him. He was able to con-vince his captors that he was on his way to warn his wife's relatives of the approach of an avenging army. They let him go and he raced back to warn Captain Maloney that an abundance of Yakima eagerly awaited the Americans' descent into the valley.

Almost simultaneously a rider reached Maloney's camp from Stei-lacoom. He was William Tidd, a small, soft-spoken English carpenter who had one of the fastest horses in the territory. Tidd had been dispatched to warn Maloney that Major Rains's force had been de-layed at Fort Vancouver but hoped to get going in a week.

Maloney thought it over. Ahead lay possible glory but probable di-saster. Edgar told him that perhaps two thousand Yakima were wait-ing for his small force. There was only one path down the Naches, no way to outflank the hostiles. The season was late. Rain could raise the Naches to difficult heights, snow could close the pass. Even if he

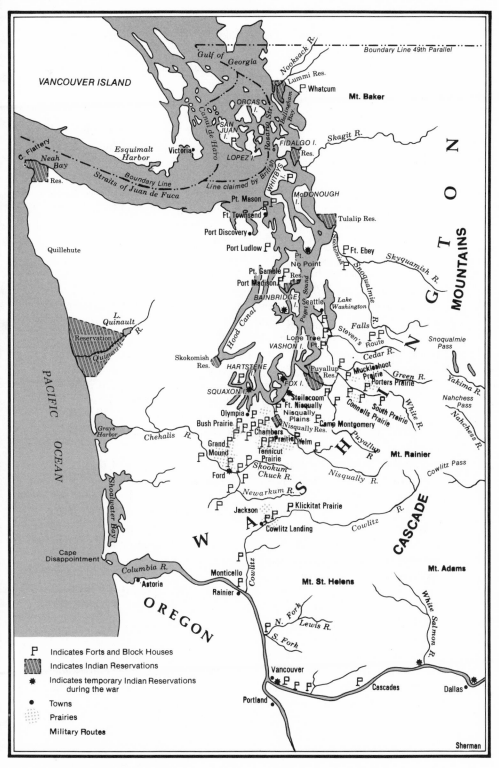

Military map from the Indian War period (based on a map in the records of the Washington Territorial Volunteers)

fought through the ambush to the Yakima Valley he would be out of supplies before Major Rains could join him. Maloney wrote a dispatch to Fort Vancouver: "I have concluded that it is my duty to return to Steilacoom."

Tidd agreed to carry the message back to Fort Steilacoom for relay to Rains. Six Volunteers were detailed as escort. Colonel A. Benton Moses, a twenty-eight-year-old veteran of the Mexican War who had come to Puget Sound with his brother, Sampson Moses, the collector of customs, was in charge. The other five were Sheriff John Bradley of Pierce County, Dr. M. P. Burns, an eccentric surgeon from Steilacoom, Joseph Miles, George Bright, and the ubiquitous Tony Rabbeson, who had been head sawyer at Simmons' mill, mailman, deckhand, and carpenter.

By Wednesday, Tidd and his guardians were off the mountainside and racing across the prairie near Buckley. Coming out of a patch of woods they found themselves in a camp of Indians from several tribes. Whites and Indians were edgy. Moses asked what the Indians knew about a burned cabin along the trail. Nothing. What were their feelings toward the whites? *Tum-tums kayas cloe cop Boston*—their hearts were right toward the Americans. Oh, sure: Dr. Burns muttered something about shooting a few varmints. Moses, who could count, shushed the surgeon and pretended to be interested in purchasing moccasins from a woman. Seeing some Indian men moving into the woods, Moses signaled for his party to ride on.

After a few miles they came to the slough Eaton and Wiley had inspected on the day McAllister and Connell were killed. It was still unimproved. As the horses plodded through, single file, hooves sucking mud at each step, a burst of musket fire poured out of the tangle of willow and salal. Moses was struck on the left side of his back; the shot passed immediately under his heart and came out through the right breast, piercing a letter in the pocket of his overcoat. He managed to stay in the saddle. Miles was shot through the neck, he fell in deep mud, blood pumping from the wound. His companions called for him to grab his stirrup leather; they took his horse's bridle and, spurring their own mounts, managed to drag him out of the slough before he lost his grip. Miles, too weak to move, gasped that he was dying, and said they should escape. They left him. Tidd caught three slugs of buckshot in the head as they rode away but the pellets did not penetrate the skull.

About a mile and a half from the slough Moses fell from his horse. He was too weak to get back on. His companions carried him some two hundred yards off the trail, wrapped him in their coats, and hid him in the brush, then rode on looking for help. At Fennell's Creek, spotting signs of another ambush, they dismounted, and charged into the brush, three on one side, two on the other. The Indians fled, but after the skirmish the Volunteers could not find their horses. They walked back to where they had left Moses, told him what had happened, and promised to return as soon as possible. The dying man raised himself on one elbow as they left and whispered, "Boys, if you escape, remember me."

Nearing Fennell's Creek they saw a party of Indians on the far side and ducked into the underbrush. All except the excitable Dr. Burns. He muttered the hell with it, waded into the creek, sloshed across, and disappeared into the stand of alder on the far side. There was a wild yell, three shots, and silence.

The four remaining whites stayed hidden until dark, debating whether to try to reach Maloney's force or strike out for Steilacoom. Deciding on Steilacoom, they floundered toward it in the dark, sometimes waist deep in water, sometimes entangled in thickets of underbrush and fallen timber. When they rested two would lie on the ground with the others on top to provide warmth. About daylight they reached the immigrant road from Naches Pass but were afraid to follow it for fear of being seen. Instead they went cross-country to the Puyallup, reaching it about noon and working along the bank looking for a place to cross. At the edge of Lemon's Prairie, east of present-day Alderton, they hid until long after dark, "all the while shaking with cold so much our cartidge-boxes rattled like cow-bells." Two Indians took cover in the willow thicket overlooking the ford they had just crossed. Although the whites might easily have shot the hostiles, they were afraid gunfire would attract more Indians and crept away "scraping sticks and leaves from under our feet as we stepped, until out of hearing."

Again reaching the immigrant road, and with no more rivers to cross, too tired now to worry about concealment, they plodded through the darkness toward Fort Steilacoom. George Bright collapsed; he staggered off into the bracken, lay down, and was instantly asleep. His companions could not arouse him, so they trudged on. About three o'clock Friday morning they reached the Tallantire claim on Clover Creek. Tallentire and a friendly Nisqually hunted until dawn before locating Bright.

About ten that morning the survivors reached Fort Steilacoom. A party of Volunteers was sent to bring in the bodies of Miles, Moses, and Burns. Pausing at the Lemon claim on the Puyallup to look in the barn for horsefeed, they found Burns hiding in a barley sack. He was indignant at having been given up for dead and wrote a boastful complaint to the adjutant general of the Volunteer Forces:

Sir—Please contradict the report that I was killed by the Indians on Wednesday last. I killed seven with my own hands. They hunted me through the brush for one mile with dogs and lighted sticks, and every one who carried a light I shot. The only wound I got was a skin wound in the forehead from a buckshot. I lived in the brush on leaves and shot an Indian this morning for his dried salmon and wheat at Mr. Lemon's. Give my respects to Bright and Rabbeson, and let them know I am safe—only I had to throw away my boots and my feet are badly hurt. I lost my horse, instruments and medicine case. My horse was shot in the kidneys in the swamp where we received that murderous discharge of balls and buckshot. I remain respectfully

M P Burns
Surgeon Captain
Hays' Command

Burns's horse was found unharmed a few days later. Those who knew the doctor best discounted most of the other details of his tale, but there was no disputing that he had somehow survived.

On the day of the White River massacre, Stephen Judson was walking westward from Delin's mill at the head of Commencement Bay. In the draw where Fifteenth Street now runs down to the water, he saw some Indian men dancing around the lodge of Shil-wahl-ton, a minor chief among the Puyallup.

Steve went to join the fun. He was surprised to find that many of the dancers were strangers to him. Even his Puyallup friends and hunting companions, his tillucums, ignored him. All except Shot-face Charlie who, as he danced past, whispered "Klat-aw-a, Klat-aw-a"— Get away, get away.

This was the first hint the settlers on the bay received that they might be in real danger. That evening a friendly Puyallup brought them word of the deaths of the Kings, Joneses, and Brannans. The Delins and Judsons at once loaded everything portable onto the scow used to move lumber out to visiting ships and set off for Steilacoom. Sail, oars, poles, and the current carried them as far as Cho-cho-chluth, before change of tide. They waited offshore until dawn, when the current carried them into the Narrows and helped them to the safety of the town of Steilacoom. Steve and his father returned overland to Tacoma, rounded up their oxen, and returned to what became a camp of refugees.

Distance was the curse of pioneer life. The mountains and the plains, the perils of the trail, the twelve-thousand mile voyage to round Cape Horn, the diseases of the Panama crossing—all cut settlers off from the life they had known, while the lack of roads in the wilderness left each homestead an island. Neighbor, meant an hour's walk; the town, a day's journey.

On the lonely farms of the Puget Sound country, families reacted with horror and panic to word of the killings on White River, the ambushes on the prairie. Every sound became an alarm. The familiar was cause for concern. Was that really a towhee rustling the leaves? a blue jay scolding? Why were the crows alarmed? the frogs silent?

As word spread about the massacre, nearly all the homesteaders started for the nearest settlement. Daybreak of October 29 found them streaming down the emigrant road toward the military base at Steilacoom. "As we approached the Fort," one recalled, "each converging road was lined with loaded wagons carrying all sorts of plunder hastily gathered together. Some had come with but little, not even waiting to bring bedding, while others had been less heedless and brought a great share of their goods. Others it would seem had left nothing behind, even bringing the chicken coop, cats, dogs, pigs and all, and many were driving their cattle before them. 'But what shall we do?' was the question. There was no room at the fort."

Indeed, there was hardly a fort. No stockade had been erected, no blockhouse. Instead there were some frame buildings set beside a parade ground. The property (now the site of Western State Hospital) had been rented from the Puget's Sound Agricultural Company by Joseph Heath, who came from England to recoup a fortune dissipated in drink and gambling. Heath learned carpentry, built a handsome wainscoated house, but died a lonely death of pneumonia in February 1849. The Hudson's Bay Company reclaimed his land and rented his house to the United States Army the following July when an artillery company was transferred up from Fort Vancouver. Captain Bennett Hill took over the big house as headquarters and put his troops in the barns. Barracks were later erected, but Fort Steilacoom's defensive posture against Indian attack was approximately that of an English country house.

Still, the very name was comforting. Women and children were put in the barracks. The men were assigned tents. The livestock were herded together and a watch posted over them. Some families found shelter in the town of Steilacoom two miles away. A strange euphoria washed over the displaced persons. They would soon be back on their farms. No doubt of it. "Twenty men and a howitzer could chase them siwash into the hills. Ten white men and a canoe could clear the Sound. Yes siree."

Such civilian confidence was not shared by the military. Second Lieutenant John Nugen had been left at Steilacoom with a handful of sick soldiers and a scant supply of arms when Captain Maloney started for Naches Pass. "I have nearly all the women and children in the county at the post and will of course protect them," he wrote Olympia on November 1. "I would respectfully request that all the men in this section of the country be called out, as I am firmly of the belief that we are to have a general Indian war in this vicinity. Send me down cartridges at the earliest moment, as it is reported the Indians are to make an attempt at taking our fort tonight."

The attack on Steilacoom never came, but the difficulties of warfare against a hunting people in their own forests soon became clear even to the civilians.

Captain Maloney's troops, emerging onto the prairie near Buckley after retreating from Naches Pass, found burned cabins, the bodies of Moses and Miles, and signs that a considerable party of hostiles had broken camp only hours earlier. Scouts traced the Indians to the White River canyon. Maloney assigned fifty regulars under Lieutenant Slaughter and fifty Volunteers under Captain Gilmore Hays, a transplanted Kentuckian from Budd Inlet, to an attack.

The Indians of Puget Sound first fought United States army regulars, supported by civilian Volunteers, on November 3. The Indians were concealed behind brush and rock on the six-hundred-foot-high east bank of the canyon. The troops, approaching from the west, found the river was too high to be forded without great difficulty. A soldier began chopping down a tree to serve as bridge, but he was picked off by a sniper. All the fighting was at long range. As darkness closed in, both sides withdrew.

The Battle of White River had been noisy, indecisive, and almost bloodless. Slaughter and Hays estimated thirty Indians killed, but they reached that total by counting as dead any Indian who did not remain in sight after being shot at. The Nisqually later claimed they suffered only one casualty and were greatly encouraged by the standoff.

The next day Maloney and Hays led 150 troops back to the canyon. They found the ford undefended, crossed it, climbed the far bank, and worked north in two columns to the Green River. Hays's company encountered Indians holed up in tangled woods with the Green protecting one flank, a slough the other. Hays ordered an attack, but thought it over, and countermanded his order, "knowing full well we would lose more men than the enemy, who were prepared to fire and run." The whites were learning the problems of guerrilla warfare, if not the solutions.

Three days later, Slaughter was reconnoitering along the Puyallup. The gallant, mountain-climbing John Edgar went ahead with a small scouting party. He felled a tree to bridge the river and started across with two men. An Indian concealed on the far side waited until the whites were in perfect line, then killed Edgar and wounded the other two with a single bullet. On learning of the loss, Maloney decided he was just furnishing the Indians with target practice. He marched all his troops back to Steilacoom.

For the next three weeks, the Americans planned, drilled, and gathered arms. The HBC sent fifty stands of rifles, ten barrels of powder and a supply of ball from Fort Victoria, a contribution doubly important since it ended the Indians' hopes that the British might side with them against the Americans.

Most Puget Sound Indians remained, if not friendly, outwardly neutral. The Americans decided to concentrate the nonhostile natives in camps on islands where it would be easier to keep them from contact with the disaffected. Indians who refused to go to restricted areas would be considered enemies. Hays's company of Volunteers was stationed at Muck Creek to cut off Indians approaching from the Cascades toward Nisqually Valley. The sloop-of-war *Decatur* was to guard the northern Sound and keep the much feared Haida and Kwakiutl from raiding southward in their great war canoes. Army regulars from Fort Steilacoom, under a new commander, Captain Erasmus Keyes, just arrived from San Francisco, and a company of Volunteers from Seattle under Captain C. C. Hewitt were to converge on the forest between the White and the Green to encircle the main band of Puget Sound Indians believed to have followed Leschi, Quiemuth, Nelson, and Kitsap on the warpath.

The great round-up began on November 24 with comedy: the Indians stole forty of the unfortunate Lieutenant Slaughter's horses the first night. It ended two days later with tragedy. Slaughter and Volunteer Captain Hewitt were conferring in an abandoned cabin two miles above the juncture of the Green and White Rivers. As they sat silhouetted against a bonfire, Indians opened fire at close range from the surrounding forest. The twenty-seven-year-old Slaughter died instantly, a bullet through his heart. Two soldiers were killed and five wounded, one of whom died later. The survivors solemnly returned Slaughter's body to Fort Steilacoom and Lieutenant Nugen was sent to Olympia to break the news to his young widow, who was visiting at Governor Stevens' home.

"It is impossible to operate against the Indians with any effect in the country on the White, Green and Puyallup Rivers at this season of the year," Captain Keyes reported to Acting Governor Mason. "I know it to be so from personal observation. To continue such a course will break down all our men and effect no harm to the Indians. Our pack animals are broken down, and we must establish our forces on our own ground in places where they will not suffer at night and where they can best protect the settlers."

The regulars gave up the chase for the winter and withdrew to garrisons. The Navy, too, was discouraged. "I trust I shall be pardoned for stating it as my opinion that the war in this territory is assuming a most serious aspect," Isaac L. Sterett, commander of the *Decatur*, wrote the secretary of the Navy from Seattle on December 5. "The valor and prowess of the Indians has been greatly underrated. The forces now in the field and indeed the whole military resources of the Territory are totally inadequate to conduct the war with success, even to afford protection to the settlers. It is the opinion of well informed men that it will require regiments instead of companies, and years instead of months to conquer these tribes."

A few days later Commander Sterett had more bad news for the secretary. On a cruise to show the flag to the Indians, the *Decatur* had located, the hard way, an uncharted reef extending three hundred yards east of Restoration Point on Bainbridge Island. She made it back to Seattle but was badly hulled and would be out of action indefinitely.

The war west of the mountains settled into a siege within a siege. The Indians kept the farmers away from their fields and the townsfolk coralled behind the log stockades they hurriedly raised to protect the larger communities. The whites kept the Indians away from accustomed places for fishing, hunting, and gathering.

As the wet fall gave way to one of the coldest winters on local record, Indian quarreled with Indian in their dismal camps in the deep forest. It was the same with the settlers, clustered in towns and blockhouses away from the homes they had been creating, the fields they had been cultivating, the stock they had been raising, the dreams of a new life in a fruitful land shattered.

Some could not bear the waiting and brooding in refugee idleness. Neighbors joined to build small blockhouses central to several claims. The men could go out by day to do some work on the farms and return to the blockhouse at night. Twenty-two of these wooden fortresses stood west of the Cascades by the end of winter, but life in them was at best miserable. With dozens of men, women, and children cooped up in the muddy, stinking compounds through the short days and long rains of a Puget Sound winter, subsisting on food both poor and scanty, prospects dim and misery contagious, they bickered and quarreled about the causes and purposes of the war, about anything from manners to mattresses to morals.

Andrew Jackson Chambers was one of four brothers who with their father came west in 1847. He had a claim between the Nisqually plains and Yelm Prairie, and a blockhouse was built on the property within sight of his house. His wife and daughter, after a few nights impounded with "forty children and thirty dogs and a lot of screaming women," told him they would take their chances sleeping at home. And they did.

Chambers was elected lieutenant in Gilmore Hays's company, but had a flaming quarrel with his captain when ordered to go out and requisition horses. He considered that to be horse stealing and refused to do more than scout for Indians. One day his patrol reached his father's place at the mouth of Chambers Creek. After running some stray horses into the corral, his men began selecting mounts for themselves, some taking two.

"What do you think you're doing?"

"Well, we might as well have them as leave them for the Indians."

"We're here to protect the property of people, not take it."

Chambers made them turn the horses loose. The men complained to Hays. The next time Chambers was scouting, Hays called a meeting of the company and elected somebody else lieutenant. Thirty years later, Chambers was still angry. "In consequence of my having incurred the displeasure of Captain Hays," he complained in his memoirs, "my name was never mentioned in any of the reports."

Anguish, though, was the predominant mood of the blockhouse period.

"Can you sympathize with us on this side of the Great Columbia," the Rev. John H. Devore asked in a letter to a Methodist colleague in Oregon. "Have you one consoling word to utter in our behalf? Our country is laid waste. We hear nothing but the clangor of arms and the war-whoop. We lie down at night after bidding each other farewell and resign ourselves into the hands of the God of battles, not knowing that we shall ever behold the light of another day. When we find that we have lived to see the light of another day, oh! how thankful. . . . How intolerable this state of suspense!"

Most of the Puyallup and the nonhostile Nisqually, totaling between four hundred and five hundred persons of all ages, had been removed to Fox Island, north of Steilacoom. John Swan, the Commencement Bay commercial fisherman, was assigned to distribute government food and supervise the camp.

On the afternoon of January 5, 1856, a flotilla of canoes pulled up on the rocky beach in front of Swan's cabin. He came out to greet them and was startled to recognize Leschi and several other hostile leaders. Leschi spread his arms to indicate he had come in friendship. He promised that the Indians would not harm Swan—they wanted to talk.

Leschi had a lot to say and said it in the soft, unstressed voice of Indian argument. He had not gone to war, he had been driven to war. He denied any responsibility for the White River slayings; they were the work of *cultus* (bad) Indians; the Nisqually were not fighting women, children, or unarmed men. He said that George King, the boy taken captive during the massacre, was across the mountains and was being educated to be a chief, not a slave. Leschi said that the Indians wanted peace, that if the whites wanted peace there could be peace talks but the Indians would not negotiate with Simmons. They had thought Simmons a friend but had been deceived. Get a new agent for the Puget Sound tribes and the Indians would talk peace.

One of the nonhostile Puyallup slipped away and paddled to Steilacoom with word that the Nisqually were on Fox Island and Swan was their prisoner. Captain Keyes detailed thirty men to Captain Maloney for a rescue attempt. They sent a dispatch rider to Fort Nisqually and asked to borrow the steamship *Beaver* to transport the troops. Dr. Tolmie agreed, but it was morning before Maloney put to sea in the borrowed paddlewheeler. Leschi's party was still on the island, their six canoes drawn up on the beach before Swan's cabin with armed warriors guarding them. Only after reaching the island did the soldiers realize they had forgotten landing craft. The *Beaver* carried only one small lifeboat. Maloney hesitated to send five men ashore in it, a bunched target, to confront six times as many Indians. While the captain was trying to figure out a way to rescue Swan, Swan came to the beach, got unmolested into a dugout, and paddled out to the *Beaver*. Swan said there had been no violence. Leschi promised there would be no trouble unless Maloney started it. Everybody urged Swan to stay aboard. He refused. He had given his word to the Indians he would return, and he did.

Maloney, in disgust, took the *Beaver* back to Steilacoom. Just another damn wild Indian chase. But when he got to the dock he was delighted to find another steamer, the USS *Active,* tied up. She was a coastal survey ship, not a warship, sent from San Francisco to serve as transport and courier.

Her commander, James Alden, and the Army officers decided not to try a landing on Fox. The *Active*'s boats were too small to carry a howitzer, which Maloney felt would be needed. Anyway they didn't have a howitzer. So Keyes, Maloney, and Alden took the *Active* up to Seattle to borrow a heavy boat and a howitzer from the *Decatur*.

Guert Gansevoort, a tough, competent, short-tempered Dutchman, had taken command of the *Decatur* a few weeks earlier. He did not like Commander Alden, whom he considered his subordinate. Alden interpreted his instructions from the Coast Survey as leaving him free to decide when to take orders from Gansevoort. Now he wanted

Gansevoort's cooperation. Patiently he explained that he and the Army men planned to use the launch and howitzer to blockade the mouth of the Puyallup, while the steamers tried to catch Leschi's canoes in open water. Impatiently Gansevoort said that the plan was cumbersome and time-consuming. Two steamers ought to be sufficient to chase canoes.

Captain Keyes butted into the argument. His contribution was not likely to convert Gansevoort. The soldier said the capture of Leschi would be worth more than the *Decatur* and all the property aboard her: "Why if I could secure Leschi's capture I would if necessary march out the people from Fort Steilacoom and burn every building and everything at the post to secure such an object."

Gansevoort thought that not so much silly as insane. He would not loan them anything. The *Active* left Seattle without the launch or howitzer. Not that it mattered. Leschi was already well up the Puyallup on his return trip. But the Army, Navy, and Coastal Survey officers were thundering and volleying at each other in official reports long after the crisis was past.

During his thirty unmolested hours on the island, Leschi recruited fifteen Indians to his cause, most of them women. Before leaving he invited Swan to visit the Indian camp on the Green to negotiate peace. The hostile canoes paddled boldly north through the Narrows. Near Point Defiance they encountered a canoe paddled by Peter Runquist, Jacob Kershner, and an unidentified black man, who had been in the Puyallup Valley digging potatoes on abandoned farms. Leschi forced the Americans to accompany his flotilla for about a mile, then levied tribute of enough potatoes to feed his party before letting them go.

"I tell you, sir, that nigger's wool turned white as the top of Mount Rainier," Runquist said when they got back to Steilacoom, in words reflecting the unselfconscious racism of the day. "It did for a fact, sir, and no mistake. Well, yes, I guess we were all skeered a little; well, a good deal. We fellers couldn't tell what them buggers might take a notion to do, for a fact, sir, and no mistake. They just turned our canoe around and took us along with them; that they did for a fact sir, and no mistake." But after the Indians told them to go, "Golly, didn't we paddle. Feared the buggers might change their minds, for a fact, sir, and no mistake."

Leschi's bold visit and plea for peace drew an admiring editorial from the weekly Puget Sound *Courier* in Steilacoom: "It is in vain that we look for a parallel case of bravery in the annals of Indian warfare," said editors E. D. Gunn and William Affleck. As for Swan, "His conduct is deserving of the highest praise, as by remaining on the reserve his influence tended greatly to counteract the evil influence of Leschi's visit by keeping the friendly Indians from being led away. Well would it be for us if those who had dealings with the Indians did as did Mr. Swan, who would not, after being taken prisoner, break his parole with them. Had we a few such men in the Indian Department we would not now have cause to lament the existing state of things."

The editors of the *Courier* were Whigs. In praising John Swan they were shooting at Governor Stevens. The treaties and the war were becoming political issues.

Governor Stevens returned to the capital of his territory on January 19, 1856. He had made an extraordinary trip through hostile country to reach Olympia and arrived to a hero's welcome—a thirty-eight-cannon salute, the cheers of the citizenry, a torchlight parade down the frozen mud of Main Street, a banquet. He was in a fighting mood, angry over what he considered the Indians' betrayal of his paternal trust. He promised those toasting him "war until the last hostile Indian is exterminated."

Two days later Stevens stood before the legislature to report on the war, its cause, its progress, its goal. He demanded war not just to the death of all nonsubmissive Indians, but war waged by the citizens of the territory independent of the United States Army. For in Major General John E. Wool, commanding the Department of the Pacific, Stevens saw a threat to the territory nearly as great as that posed by Leschi of the Nisqually or Kamiakin of the Yakima.

General Wool had come from the Presidio in San Francisco to Fort Vancouver in November to direct the campaign against the Indians. He was not impressed by its importance. He was seventy-one years old, a veteran not only of the Mexican War but of the War of 1812. He was not West Point: he was before West Point. He had soldiered forty-four years. The general knew war, war's abuses, and the abuses of peace. He knew Indians (he had supervised the tragic exodus of the Cherokee to Oklahoma) and he felt he knew the settler mentality. Of war, Indians, and settlers, he was most suspicious of settlers, especially those who volunteered to fight Indians and then asked to be paid for fighting Indians.

Wool wanted all Indian fighting left to the professionals. He looked on settler volunteers not as keepers of peace but as lynchers for profit, better at rape than battle, and at their best when concocting expense accounts for services unrendered. In a statement to Congress, Wool argued that "as long as Governors of the Territories exercise powers, as I believe, unknown to the President, and individuals raise volunteers and make wars on the Indians whenever they please, and Congress pay the expense, so long will we have war in Washington and Oregon Territories."

Stevens had forwarded Wool a plan calling for a massive sweep through eastern Washington in late winter. Wool replied that the campaign seemed "very extended" and observed, "I have neither the resources of a Territory nor the Treasury of the United States at my command." In Wool's opinion the trouble in Washington Territory was just a brush fire, to be contained, then damped down with as little fuss as possible. After all, most of the Indians were sitting it out. Wool proposed to protect the settlements, isolate the hostiles, and let their mutiny burn down to discontent. Fewer than two hundred Indians were under arms west of the Cascades. Surely four hundred army men and several ships of war "constitute a force which if rightly directed ought to be sufficient to bring to terms two hundred warriors."

To Stevens this was imbecilic if not timid. If the Army wouldn't carry the war to Indians, he would:

"Fellow citizens! War has existed for three months, and still exists. A war entered into by these Indians, without a cause; a war having not its origin in these treaties, nor in the bad conduct of our people. It originated in the native intelligence of restless Indians, who, fore-seeing destiny against them, that the white man was moving upon them, determined that it must be met and resisted by arms. We may sympathize with such a manly feeling, but in view of it, we have high duties."

Stevens recalled his pleasure in making treaties "to civilize and render the condition of the Indian happier." His hopes had been be-trayed: "Nothing but death is a mete punishment for their perfidy—their lives should pay the forfeit. The tribes at war must submit un-conditionally to the justice, mercy and leniency of our government."

The young governor paid two-edged tribute to General Wool as a "gallant and war-worn veteran," but insisted that the Army's use of territorial Volunteers had amounted to a breach of faith: "I do not think the volunteers of this Territory should be mustered into the United States Service. I am ready to take responsibility of raising them, independent of that service. The spirit of prosecuting this war should be to accomplish a lasting peace—not to make treaties but to punish their violation."

It was an emotional speech, a powerful speech, made in wartime by a leader just returned from danger. The legislature gave Stevens his head. Through the winter and spring of 1856, the general and the governor waged their separate campaigns against the Indians, and each other.

For the Indians, too, discontent and divided counsel. Holed up in the hills, away from families and the comforts of their winter villages, short of food, without weapons effective against fortifications, the men from the different tribes could not agree on how the war should be fought.

The older men counseled waiting. Through the grapevine that started with the Indian wives of white settlers, they heard that the war was unpopular with many Bostons. Wait: perhaps better treaties would be offered. But there were younger men who would not wait; they did not want new writings on paper; they wanted no whites on their land telling them what to do and where to live. They had gone to war, not into hiding.

Five days after Governor Stevens' declaration of a war of extermination, the Indians attacked Seattle. Coming down from their hideouts in the foothills, they crossed Lake Washington in canoes on the afternoon of January 25 and disappeared into the forest. During the night they crossed over the dividing hill and took positions at the edge of the clearing and swampy areas facing the east side of the village. Their presence was no secret. Friendly Duwamish told the Americans of the approach of hostile tribesmen, though the reports seem to have multiplied by ten the actual numbers. There could not have been more than one hundred and fifty.

Seattle had about a hundred able-bodied civilians, but most of them had volunteered for the abortive campaign in which Lieutenant Slaughter was killed. Only thirty re-enlisted. Most settlers were content to leave the defense of the village to the *Decatur,* which had a hundred sailors and a small detachment of marines. Commander Gansevoort sent ashore the marines, and sixty sailors, in four groups of fifteen each, to guard the town on the night of January 25. Nothing happened.

At 7:30 the next morning, the sailors rowed back out to the sloop for breakfast; half an hour later, Henry Yesler, who owned the wharf and sawmill off which the *Decatur* was anchored, came on board. He had word from "a trustworthy private source," presumably a friendly Indian, that the hostiles were in three parties spread in an arc behind the village, with their greatest force concentrated opposite the southern part of town, which stood on a knoll with the bay in front and a swamp in back. The dominant building was a hotel of

Puget Sound basin, satellite photograph
Courtesy of Earth Rotating Orbital Satellite

Captain George Vancouver Courtesy of Provincial Archives, Victoria

Port Townsend (from a plate in Vancouver's Voyage of Discovery) Courtesy of Photo. Coll., UW Library

Above: *Mount Rainier, from the southern part of Admiralty Inlet (from a plate in Vancouver's* Voyage of Discovery); below: *Mount Rainier (from a 1911 painting by A. H. Barnes)* Courtesy of Photo. Coll., UW Library

Left: *Lieutenant Charles Wilkes;* right: *Vendovi (from Wilkes,* U.S. Exploring Expedition) Courtesy of Photo. Coll., UW Library

Wreck of the sloop-of-war Peacock *at the mouth of the Columbia, July 18, 1841 (from Wilkes,* U.S. Exploring Expedition) Courtesy of Photo. Coll., UW Library

The Reverend John P. Richmond and his wife, America

"Pine forest, Oregon" (from Wilkes, U.S. Exploring Expedition) Courtesy of Photo. Coll., UW Library

Lieutenant William A. Slaughter and Mary Wells Slaughter

Edward Lander Courtesy of Washington State Library, Olympia

Isaac I. Stevens Courtesy of Photo. Coll., UW Library

Leschi of the Nisqually Courtesy of Photo. Coll., UW Library

Puget Sound and Mount Rainier from Whidbey Island (from Stevens, Reports of Explorations and Surveys . . . 1853)

The sloop-of-war Decatur Courtesy of Photo. Coll., UW Library

Gertrude and Nicholas Delin

The old Delin mill (from a sketch made in 1878 by J. D. S. Conger) Courtesy of Washington State Historical Society

Job Carr

Marietta Carr

Anthony Carr

Howard Carr

Above: *Job Carr's house, Tacoma's first post office (photograph by Anthony Carr)*; below: *Tony Carr's house, ca. 1868–70, with Marietta Carr, Josie Bird, and Tony* Courtesy of Rick and Francie Carr

Morton Matthew and Mary Ann McCarver

Jay Cooke

Janet Elder Steele

The Steele Hotel Courtesy of Tacoma Public Library

Salmon fishing in Puget Sound Courtesy of Tacoma Public Library

Picnic, ca. 1873

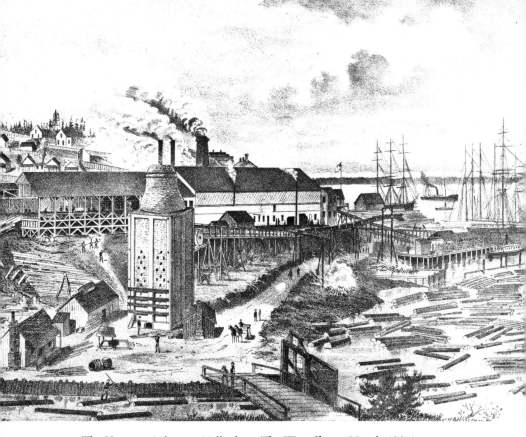

The Hanson, Ackerson Mill (from The West Shore, *March 1884)*

Saloon, 1890s Courtesy of Tacoma Public Library

Charles B. Wright in the 1880s;
Annie Wright, 1884 (from T. P.
Harney, Charles Barstow Wright)
Courtesy of Photo. Coll., UW Library

Tacoma, 1871 Courtesy of Photo Coll., UW Library

Pacific Avenue, Tacoma, 1877 (from Stanley Wood, Over the Range to the Golden Gate)

The Blackwell Hotel Courtesy of Tacoma Public Library

William B. Blackwell

Alice Blackwell

"Constructing the big tunnel" (*from* The West Shore, *1887*)

"Across the switchback" (*from* The West Shore, 1887)

Nelson Bennett

Henry Villard Courtesy of Photo. Coll., UW Library

Jacob Weisbach

Governor Watson Squire

J. W. Sprague Courtesy of Tacoma
Public Library

Ezra Meeker Courtesy of Photo.
Coll., UW Library

"Tacoma's Twenty-seven" Courtesy of Photo. Coll., UW Library

"The Committee of Fifteen" Courtesy of Photo. Coll., UW Library

The Annie Wright Seminary (from The West Shore, *1884)*

Ezra Meeker's home, Puyallup (original drawing by Carl Darmer, 1889)
Courtesy of Architectural History Collection, UW Library

General Office building, Northern Pacific Railroad (*from* The West Shore, *1888*)

The Tacoma (*from C. Clark,* Tacoma, the Western Terminus) Courtesy of Photo. Coll., UW Library

Allen Mason
(*from* The West Shore, *1888*)

Whitworth College, 1907, formerly the home of Allen Mason (*photograph by A. Curtis*) Courtesy of Photo. Coll., UW Library

The forest of masts at dockside (photograph by E. A. Lynn); the Republic *discharging tea at Tacoma (photograph by T. Rutter)* Courtesy of Dennis Andersen

"Mount Tacoma from City Hall Tower" (*photograph by A. H. Waite, 1894*)
Courtesy of Photo. Coll., UW Library

The Foss Launch Company Courtesy of Tacoma Public Library

The Foss family: Thea, Henry, Lillian, Weddell, Arthur, and Andrew
Courtesy of Henry Foss

"There are millions more at Tacoma just like this monster"; Colonel Chauncey Griggs to left of sign Courtesy of Tacoma Public Library

Graduating class of Washington College, 1892 (photograph donated to UW Library by Zoe Semple) Courtesy of Photo. Coll., UW Library

Coal bunkers at Tacoma (from C. Clark, Tacoma, the Western Terminus)
Courtesy of Photo. Coll., UW Library

Rummage-collecting carriage on Tacoma waterfront (photograph by Wilhelm Hester) Courtesy of Photo. Coll., UW Library

The Ryan Smelter (from Tacoma Illustrated) Courtesy of Photo. Coll., UW Library

Logging Wright's Park, 1885 (photograph by C. E. and Hattie King) Courtesy of Photo. Coll., UW Library

"Morgan's Hellhole": the Theatre Comique (photograph by A. H. Waite)
Courtesy of Photo. Coll., UW Library

Govnor Teats addressing the Tacoma and Seattle contingents of Coxey's Army, April 29, 1894, from the balcony of the Park Hotel, Puyallup

Deputy United States marshals who handled Coxey's Army, at the old passenger station in Puyallup

sorts operated by a lady known as Mother Damnable, well versed in the entertainment of sea-faring men.

The sailors rowed back ashore. Most of the women and children of Seattle were brought out to the ship. The howitzer, manned by nine seamen and guarded by marines, was placed near Mother Damnable's and pointed at the forest where most of the Indians were supposed to be. Civilians who had arms took positions in or near the central blockhouse; its cannon were manned by marines. The four divisions of sailors were positioned on the perimeter, partly protected by low barricades.

At 8:45 A.M., with all forces in place, Gansevoort gave the signal. The howitzer lobbed an exploding shell into the forest across from the knoll, and a moment later, from out in Elliott Bay, the ship's guns fired into the same spot. From the woods came the protests of crows, the war cries of Indians, and scattered rifle fire. The sailors raked the trees with disciplined volleys from rifle and carbine, while the howitzer and cannons harrumped whenever fire from the forest indicated a concentration of the enemy. When the whites centered their attention on the trees behind the southern swamp, the Indians drifted north to a point where they could shoot down on Yesler's wharf. When the heavy guns turned to that area, the Indians spread out more widely. By noon the battle had become a desultory duel at long range. An Indian would lean out from behind a tree or rise from behind a log, fire quickly, and duck back. Moments later shells would explode where he had been.

By mid-afternoon things were so quiet that Commander Gansevoort ordered all four divisions of sailors brought back to the *Decatur* for "rest and refreshment." They took the precious howitzer with them, but left the marines to guard the central blockhouse with its two nine-pounders. Bullets dimpled the gray-green water as the launches pulled from the wharf but no one was hit, and the Indians made no attempt to rush the town.

Through the fading hours of winter daylight there were occasional shots from the woods and replies from the ship or the blockhouse. Then, with evening, silence. In the morning the *Decatur* fired into the woods where the Indians had last been seen. There was no reply.

The Battle of Seattle was over. Two whites had been killed. One was a fourteen-year-old boy who, a week earlier, had shot and killed a deserter from the *Decatur* who was trying to break into his sister's house; the other was a thirty-year-old man who apparently walked in front of a Volunteer's gun. No one was wounded. Two houses, at opposite ends of the village, were burned: one set on fire by the Indians, the other by a shot from the howitzer. There were no known Indian casualties.

Both sides were dismayed, the whites by the realization that the enemy really would attack a town, the Indians by their first experience with exploding shells rather than cannonballs.

Nine days after the skirmish at Seattle, seventeen hostile Indians led by Leschi and Kitsap appeared at Muck Creek, north of the Nisqually, where a number of former Hudson's Bay Company men married to Indian women had claims. The hostiles had let it be known that the "squaw men" would not be molested if they did not take up arms, so most stayed on their farms.

The delegation went to the home of John McLeod, a thirty-four-year-old Scot whose wife was Nisqually. Leschi told McLeod that neither he nor any of his band had taken part in the raid on Seattle, which he felt was foolish. The Indians wanted peace, but a just peace, one that left them land that could support their people. He spoke with what the Scot described as "savage earnestness" of the wrongs his people had suffered. He wished to have two pieces of paper taken, on one to be written the wrongs done by the Indians to the whites, on the other the wrongs inflicted on the Indians. Send both to Washington and let the Great Chief decide who was most to blame: the Indian whose lands were taken or the white man who deceived the Indian and took the land. The Indians asked that John Swan, whom they trusted, be sent to their camp on the Green River for a conference.

With the permission of Lieutenant Colonel Silas Casey, who had assumed command of the regular troops at Fort Steilacoom, Swan went to visit Leschi in his hideout in the forest between the White and Green rivers. An Indian guide led him to the camp "in a large swamp near the Green, where they have their women and children. This swamp is near the base of the mountains, difficult to reach and almost impenetrable. All approaches are watched by spies. Another trail leads from the swamp into the mountains, on which they would doubtless try to retreat in case of an attack."

For two nights and a day Swan lived with the hostiles in their secret camp. He counted about 150 men of fighting age and estimated that between 10 and 20 more were on lookout duty. Nearly all were from the salt-water tribes; he saw fewer than 20 Indians from east of the Cascades and the chiefs denied that many Yakima and Klickitat had come through the pass. It seemed to Swan that ammunition was short, food scanty and poor, morale low. Leschi complained that some Duwamish who had visited the hideout, stole his horses. He asked Swan to tell the Americans that his people would lay down their arms if guaranteed no reprisals against those who had gone to war—and if assigned a better reservation.

The Indians might be despondent but they were not yet defeated.

In early March they twice attacked troops who were building roads, ferries, and blockhouses on the plains leading to the Cascades. On March 1, young Lieutenant Augustus V. Kautz, who a year earlier had welcomed assignment to Fort Steilacoom because "there is plenty to eat, and little to do, and pleasant surroundings," was leading fifty regulars from the Connell claim to the Muckleshoot. Descending the south bank of the White at the point where Slaughter and Hays had encountered Indians the previous November, they found themselves surrounded. Kautz got his men to cover, a messenger broke through and brought reinforcements, and the attackers were driven off. One soldier was killed and nine wounded, including Kautz, who received a bullet through the leg and earned a citation for gallantry. Indian losses could not be determined.

The following week Leschi's full force, including some women warriors, caught 110 Volunteers by surprise as they moved out from Camp Connell on the morning of March 10 to build a blockhouse overlooking a ferry site on the White. The Indians were in ambush behind logs and brush on high ground, but the Volunteers were able to outflank them, drive them from the redoubt, and chase them more than a mile before losing contact. Two Indian dead were found, and discarded clothing which indicated that others had been wounded. The Volunteers suffered four casualties, none fatal.

"I regard the victory of this day as complete—a grand triumph," Volunteer Major Gilmore Hays declared in an official report to His Excellency I. I. Stevens, Governor and Commander in Chief. "The Indians had together their whole force. They picked their ground. They brought on the attack without being seen by our troops. They exceeded us in numbers nearly, if not, two to one, and we whipped and drove them before us."

A few days after the third fight on the White, Leschi led the retreat of seventy of his dispirited people through the snow-clogged pass into Yakima country. Others quietly returned to their villages. Fifty women and children surrendered and asked for food. The fighting in the west was over, but not the squabbling.

Winter was ending. The growing tips of the sullen firs turned chartreuse. Willows reddened. The bowed heads of trilliums broke the moss of the forest floor. On the reservation islands the friendly Indians longed for the deer runs of spring, the fields of camas. In the blockhouses the settlers thought of the warming earth, the seed unplanted, the birthing stock. And some thought with envy and hatred of their neighbors with Indian wives, who had been spared the war, who lived untroubled on their claims, who—it was rumored—furnished the hostiles with supplies, gave them advice, even perhaps directed the war.

Governor Stevens shared these suspicions. He announced that in his humble judgment there was no such thing as neutrality in an Indian war: "Whoever can remain on his claim unmolested is an ally of the enemy and must be dealt with as such." He told Isaac Smith, the acting territorial secretary, to "march to the settlements occupied by the French and other foreign-born settlers and remove them to Fort Nisqually," but Smith returned, mission unaccomplished.

The Washington Mounted Rifles were now brought from the Columbia to Puget Sound. The Mounted Rifles were a cavalry unit recruited in the Vancouver area and led by Captain Hamilton J. C. Maxon, a flamboyant horseman with a mustache big as a snowplow and a voice that would stampede buffalo. Maxon had earned a reputation as an Indian hater during the pursuit of the Cayuse after the Whitman Massacre. "A jovial man with more belly than brains," said a colleague, but his men loved him.

Stevens ordered Maxon to sweep the upper Nisqually and Puyallup clear of hostile Indians. He was to consider hostile any Indians he encountered except fourteen Chehalis mercenaries who could be identified by their uniforms, blue flannel shirts and blue caps with red bands which had been sewed for them by the governor's wife and other Olympia women. Swinging through the Eatonville area, the Mounted Rifles surprised a party of Indians harvesting salmon on the Mashel. The Volunteers killed them all, some by gunfire, some with the butts of their rifles. Among the seventeen Indian dead were fifteen women and children. Maxon's men suffered no casualties in the "battle."

On his next patrol, Maxon encountered the former Hudson's Bay Company employees settled at Muck Creek. He was aware that Governor Stevens wanted them sequestered, and he considered the farmers' presence on their farms treasonable. He sent five men— Charles Wren, John McLeod, Sandy Smith, Henry Smith, and John McPhail—under armed guard to the governor.

There was no jail in Olympia; indeed, there was no civilian jail in the territory. Civilization had not advanced that far. Stevens forwarded the prisoners to Fort Steilacoom and requested Colonel Casey to hold them in the Army guardhouse until evidence was found on which they could be tried for giving aid and comfort to the enemy.

Casey was regular Army. His commander was General Wool, not Governor Stevens. He doubted that locking up civilians was legal.

On the other hand there was a war on. So he incarcerated the settlers but wrote the governor to say, "I trust the charges against them will be investigated as soon as possible in order that justice may be done. It will be impractical for me to retain them long." Stevens was no man to fret over legal niceties. "Even if the evidence should fail to convict one of them," he replied, "the peace of the country requires that those not convicted be kept in close confinement till the end of the war."

Wartime shortages in the territory did not include a shortage of lawyers. Steilacoom, as a county seat and site of the Third Territorial District Court, was oversupplied. There were barristers of all political persuasions, including adherents of the new Republican creed. Stevens' detention of citizens without formal charge was an issue that cut across party lines and united lawyers in defense of the law. On the evening of April 1, twenty-four-year-old Frank Clark, chairman of the Pierce County Democratic Committee, and William H. Wallace, forty-two, a former Whig candidate for congressional delegate, set out by canoe for Whidbey Island, where the district judge lived when court was not in session, to obtain a writ of habeas corpus for the release of the Muck Creek five.

John Chapman, clerk of the Third District Court, was a Democrat, a territorial legislator, and an ally of Stevens. He sent a message to the governor saying the writ would almost certainly be issued and added darkly, "There is something mysterious in this matter."

No one ever accused Stevens of being indecisive. He reacted swiftly, firmly, and illegally. He put Pierce County under martial law and suspended the operation of the civil courts, citing "grave cause of suspicion that certain evil-disposed persons of Pierce County had given aid and comfort to the enemy" and that "efforts are now being made to withdraw by civil process these persons from perview of the [military] commission."

Colonel Casey sent a dispatch to Olympia informing the governor that martial law or no martial law, "I doubt whether your proclamation can relieve me from the obligation to obey the requisition of the civil authority." He would have to release the prisoners if presented with the writ. "I request therefore that you relieve me from their charge."

Stevens sent Benjamin Franklin Shaw, now a staff colonel in the Volunteers, to transfer the prisoners from Steilacoom to Fort Montgomery, a blockhouse on Clover Creek in the Spanaway area. It was manned by Volunteers responsible to the governor. So when Wallace and Clark paddled in with the writ of habeas corpus, signed by Judge Francis A. Cheneweth, ordering Casey to produce the prisoners, they were in the custody of a different officer in a different organization. A new writ would be needed. The 160-mile round-trip to Chenoweth's home on Penn Cove by canoe was not only time-consuming but dangerous. Clark and Wallace decided to wait until the first Monday in May when a session of the district court was scheduled for Steilacoom.

Judge Chenoweth fell ill. Chief Justice Edward Lander of Olympia, whose younger brother had served under Stevens on the Railroad Survey, agreed to substitute on the bench. Lander knew the question of the legality of martial law would arise and he foresaw a conflict of interest. Holding a commission in the Volunteers from Acting Governor Mason, he might be ordered to enforce martial law, including the suppression of the courts. He wrote Stevens resigning "any and all commissions." Stevens rejected the resignation and ordered Lander to help Colonel Shaw enforce the rule of the military in Pierce County.

Lander decided his responsibility was to the Constitution, not to the governor. On Monday, May 5, he arrived by boat in Steilacoom. As he approached the courthouse he was met by Colonel Shaw, who said the governor requested that the court session be delayed a month. Lander replied that was beyond his power. Shaw pointed out that the governor, in his capacity as commander in chief, had detached a company of Volunteers from Indian chasing and assigned them to make sure court was not held; they were present and armed. Lander thought of a compromise; he would declare the court in session, then adjourn for two days without transacting any business.

"So," Shaw wrote Stevens, "I permitted him to go to the courthouse."

Lander also wrote to Stevens. He suggested that the governor had overreacted. Perhaps he would now abrogate the proclamation "as the present conditions of the county seem not to require it as strongly as before." Stevens reply was to send a message to Colonel Shaw with its main point underlined: *"Martial law must be enforced."*

Judge Lander went to Colonel Casey. Would Army regulars protect the court from Stevens' Volunteers? Casey said he had no authority to use soldiers for that purpose. Lander had one more card to play. He commissioned four deputy United States marshals and furnished them with writs ordering every male citizen of Pierce County over sixteen years of age to appear at the courthouse Wednesday morning, with arms, to serve as a *posse comitatus* to protect the court.

Some of those summoned could find no arms. Some found excuses. But thirty citizens with guns in their hands answered Lander's summons. The territory teetered on the brink of civil war.

A cloudless May day. Squirrels chattering in the firs. The year-old courthouse gleaming white in the mid-morning sun. Twenty blue-clad Volunteers under Captain W. W. DeLacy, an Oregon engineer, and Colonel Shaw lined up on the dirt street, their long-barreled, government-issue rifles in stands nearby. Inside the courtroom the panel of citizens called for jury duty, but also thirty men, the *posse comitatus,* most carrying hand guns but some with rifles or fowling pieces, ready to defend the rule of law. They have agreed that if an attempt is made to arrest the judge they will shoot first at Frank Shaw.

The door opens. It is the judge, a man of impressive bulk and massive dignity. He comes to the bench, instructs the bailiff that anyone carrying a gun past the bar that separates the working court from the spectators' section is to be arrested, then takes his seat. The bailiff declares the honorable court in session. The judge begins to call the names of jurors summoned to duty.

The door opens again. Colonel Shaw and Captain DeLacy stride in, uniformed, stiff, somber, the Volunteers behind them looking uncertain. They line up outside the bar, facing the bench, their long-barreled rifles enormous in the small room. The judge continues to empanel the jurors.

Colonel Shaw speaks. His voice is loud, formal, as military as he can make it. He declares that Pierce County is under martial law. The functions of all civil officers have been suspended. He has orders from the commander in chief to prevent court being held. Arrest the judge.

Volunteers start toward the bench. The bailiff tries to block their path but is pushed aside. The citizens of the posse are on their feet, shouting, pistols pointed at Colonel Shaw.

Lander pounds his gavel, stands. Rather than be the cause of bloodshed, he will submit to arrest. Shaw takes the judge, his clerk, and the court records to Olympia. The courthouse is closed. To preserve law and order, the instrument of law has been removed.

Even while the chief justice of the territorial supreme court was being transported back to Olympia, a prisoner of the governor, indignation meetings began in Steilacoom. Six lawyers were members of the *posse comitatus.* They assembled outside the court as the Pierce County bar, and declared the morning's proceedings a violation of law "which if tamely submitted to would be entirely subversive to our liberties." The same lawyers took part in a torchlight meeting that night and passed resolutions condemning Stevens. The petitions were forwarded to the Congress, the secretary of state, and the president.

When Judge Lander reached Olympia, he raised an interesting legal point. Thurston County was not under martial law. He was released and he waited in cold fury for the start of the regular session of his own court, May 14.

The controversy over martial law and the arrest of the judge spread. The pro-Stevens *Pioneer and Democrat* of Olympia found martial law necessary; the Whig Puget Sound *Courier* of Steilacoom found it outrageous and unconstitutional. Governor Stevens published, anonymously, a manifesto under the title *Vindication of Governor Stevens.* George Gibbs, the Harvard lawyer who had served Stevens on the Railroad Survey and at Medicine Creek, wrote to the secretary of state in Washington replying to the *Vindication* point by point. He concluded that the heart of the matter was the question "whether a public servant shall be allowed to override all law, even the highest; to usurp at his sole and absolute discretion absolute power over life and liberty, or whether the law of the land is to control him." To Stevens the question was "whether the Executive has the power in carrying on the war, to take a summary course with a dangerous band of emissaries, who have been the confederates of Indians throughout, and by their exertions and sympathy can render to a great extent, the military operations abortive."

Stevens charged ahead with his plan to try the Muck Creek settlers in military court. He appointed five Volunteer officers, including Captain Maxon, to constitute the court. The court martial was set for May 20.

On Sunday evening, May 11, attorneys for the Muck Creek men went to Judge Lander's home in Olympia and obtained new writs of habeas corpus, which they served on Governor Stevens. He immediately declared Thurston County under martial law, posted an armed guard around his office, and stationed a cannon in front of the courthouse.

Wednesday morning, Judge Lander convened the federal court as scheduled. He dispatched U.S. Marshal George Corliss to inform the governor that the chief justice awaited his response to the writs of habeas corpus. Stevens shrugged off the request. Judge Lander sent Corliss back with a summons demanding Stevens' immediate appearance in court to show why he should not be held in contempt. Stevens laughed and refused to go. Lander issued a summons ordering the governor to appear on contempt charges. Adjutant General

James Tilton and Volunteer Captain A. J. Cain tossed the marshal out in the street when he attempted to serve it.

Stevens moved to the offensive. He sent Volunteers to arrest Lander. They brushed aside Marshal Corliss who tried to keep them out of the courthouse, found the judge barricaded in the clerk's office, kicked open the door, and for the second time that month placed the chief justice of the territory under arrest. Stevens offered to let Lander go if he would promise to be a good boy and not play judge until the war was over. Lander refused. He and his clerk, Elwood Evans, were locked up at Fort Montgomery along with the Muck Creek settlers.

Lyon "Sandy" Smith was the first of the prisoners to have his day in military court. His attorneys immediately raised two points. First: the Volunteers were not militia, they were an ad hoc organization created by Stevens and the legislature; they had no basis for existence under the Organic Act creating the territory and therefore had no authority to set up courts to try anyone. Second: the accused was charged with giving aid and comfort to the enemy in wartime; that amounted to a charge of treason; treason was a civil offense, beyond the reach of any military court.

The five laymen who comprised the court martial pondered the arguments and decided the court was "legally and constitutionally created" but that the offense described "constitutes the crime of treason and this court as a military court has no jurisdiction." The judge advocate sent word to Stevens that the case had collapsed. Governor Stevens received the news along with word of another legal setback.

Judge Chenoweth had regained his health if not his good temper. He had returned to Steilacoom on May 20, the day the court martial opened at Fort Montgomery. Chenoweth, in chambers, wrote writs of habeas corpus for the Muck Creek contingent, the chief justice, and his clerk. The writs were served on Shaw and demanded that he produce the prisoners at the courthouse the next afternoon at 1:00 P.M.

Chenoweth directed the Pierce County sheriff to deputize fifty men to protect the court. Colonel Shaw and Captain Maxon assigned thirty members of the Washington Mounted Rifles to proceed from Fort Montgomery to Steilacoom to prevent Chenoweth from holding court.

The Volunteers were led by Lieutenant Silas Curtis, a slim, blond, blue-eyed schoolteacher from Vancouver. He had enlisted to protect the territory from Indians and seems to have had doubts from the start about this tangential assignment. Arriving in Steilacoom he found the place alive with deputy sheriffs who seemed to feel that the protection of the court was worth a shoot-out with the strangers from down on the Columbia.

"They are here in force," the young lieutenant wrote Stevens from the scene. "I see fifty or sixty about the town. The Judge is at the military station [Fort Steilacoom] and I suppose the commander of the post is called on to protect the court. I shall make no forcible attempt to arrest the Judge until I receive further orders from Captain Maxon or some higher authority. I will try to prevent a collision until I hear from you."

This moment of caution, a thoughtful temporizing by a young schoolteacher in uniform, may have averted tragedy. There was no clash between Volunteers and deputies at the courthouse that Saturday, May 24. But what if it had been Captain Maxon who led the Mounted Rifles to Steilacoom?

At noon on Saturday, Chenoweth's bailiff told the judge that Colonel Shaw refused to honor the writs, saying he took orders from his commander in chief, not the judiciary. Chenoweth quickly wrote an opinion declaring Stevens' proclamation of martial law "a monstrous assumption of arbitrary power without the shadow of legal authority," and cautioning the territorial Volunteers to weigh the orders given by their superiors; those directed at subduing Indians should be obeyed, but anyone following orders to seize citizens, invade temples of justice, and arrest judges not only risked the penalties of the law but put in jeopardy their hope of getting Congress to pay the Volunteers for their military services. He ordered that copies of his opinion be posted in public places. At 1:00 P.M. Judge Chenoweth donned his robes and took the bench to hear a case in Admiralty, "Dun and others vs. Steamer *Water Lily*," but first he wrote out a warrant for the arrest of Colonel Shaw on the charge of contempt of court.

Governor Stevens received, almost simultaneously, the news that the military court he had created would not try the settlers on the charges he presented, and that a federal judge had ruled his proclamation of martial law "without shadow of authority." His choice was to submit to the court's authority or shoot some civilians. Governor Stevens lifted martial law.

What followed was anticlimax, more interesting as political farce than as political force. Stevens ordered that Judge Lander be let out of the lock-up. Colonel Shaw appeared before Judge Chenoweth on contempt charges but, after receiving the governor's statement that Shaw's services were needed in the field in eastern Washington, the colonel was released on his personal recognizance. Eventually he was fined twenty-five dollars.

Stevens ordered the Volunteer judge advocate to file new charges against the Muck Creek people but, apparently by pre-arrangement, the officers of the court martial decided they would be more usefully employed in the field. They canceled the trial and turned the prisoners over to civil authorities. Three were brought to trial in Steilacoom before a visiting judge. After presenting Stevens' evidence, which proved to be a mishmash of rumor and strained interpretation, the district attorney conceded he had not made a case. The prosecution asked that charges be dismissed. The settlers went back to their farms.

Chief Justice Lander waited until July before again summoning Stevens to answer charges of contempt. Stevens' attorneys asked that the governor be tried by a judge whom he had not put in jail. Lander refused to disqualify himself. He declared Stevens guilty of contempt and fined him fifty dollars. Governor Stevens granted Citizen Stevens a stay of execution of the sentence pending a review of his conduct by the man who had appointed him, President Pierce.

That did not work either. Attorney General Caleb Cushing advised the president that "under the Constitution of the United States, the power to suspend the writ of habeas corpus belongs exclusively to Congress. The power to suspend the laws and substitute military in the place of civil authority is not within the legal attributes of a governor of one of the Territories."

Secretary of State Marcy, on the president's request, wrote Stevens to say that "martial law never can be excusable when the object in resorting to martial law is to act against the existing Government of the country or to supersede the functionaries in the discharge of their proper duties. The latter seems to have been the principal grounds you had for proclaiming martial law. Your conduct, in that respect, does not therefore meet with the favorable regard of the President."

The next session of the territorial legislature passed a joint resolution of censure, declaring that Stevens "acted in direct violation of the Constitution and Laws and of the United States, and that any such attempt to exercise unconstitutional power tends to the subversion of our institutions and calls at our hands for the strongest condemnation."

Friends paid Stevens' fifty-dollar fine.

By August 1856 it was clear that fighting west of the Cascades was over. Roads connected the settlements. Blockhouses impervious to Indian attack guarded river portages and key farming areas. Neutral

Indians were shielded on island reservations from contact with those who had taken up arms. The whites had demonstrated they could not be driven into the sea; what was not known was how long they could afford a garrison existence. The war was being fought on credit and there was no assurance the federal government would pay the bills being run up by the territorial Volunteers.

With no fanfare, Governor Stevens went in late summer to the camp of the sequestered Nisqually and Puyallup on Fox Island. This time no oratory. This time Stevens listened, listened to the Indians, listened to subagent John Swan, listened if not to the voice of conscience at least to the need for a lasting peace. He agreed to new, different, and larger reservations for both tribes.

The Nisqually would not have to leave the valley and move onto the 1,280-acre patch on the slope south of their river, land they called The Rock. Instead they were left 4,700 acres straddling the Nisqually from near its mouth to the juncture with Muck Creek.

The Puyallup gained even more. Instead of the original 1,280 acres of high bluff fronting Commencement Bay between today's Old Town and the Smelter, they were conceded 23,000 acres east and north of the bay.

(Old settlers like to yarn about how Stevens outfoxed the Indians. The tale, as told in Hunt's *History of Tacoma,* would have it that Squatahan of the Puyallup asked for a reservation embracing the northern part of the Nisqually plains, a large part of the Puyallup Valley extending almost to Alderton then northward to the Sound, and from there westward by such lines that it would cover all of the Point Defiance peninsula. Stevens agreed but stipulated that Squatahan would have to furnish a guide to show the surveyors the boundary lines. Tobasket, the guide, started from Fern Hill but the surveyors got him off course so he struck the Puyallup downstream from the point intended. Then they asked him to swim the stream with the surveying line and the current carried him downstream, accounting for a jog. From there they steered him south so that he came out around Brown's Point rather than at Redondo. Finally he made a mistake of his own, landing toward the head of the bay rather than at Point Defiance.) This tale reveals more about the old settler mentality than about the actual survey.

Governor Stevens recommended to Washington that the new reservations be created under terms of Article Six of the Medicine Creek Treaty, which gave the president authority to assign tribes to different areas. Commissioner of Indian Affairs George Manypenny approved. In January 1857, President Pierce signed the executive order creating the new reservations.

Leschi's band had not fought in vain.

Governor Stevens might tacitly admit the original reservations had been inadequate but he could not forgive the Indians who forced him to admit it. "Nothing but death is mete punishment for their perfidy," he had told the legislature. "Their lives only should pay the forfeit." He meant it. Stevens wanted blood.

When Indians who had fled across the mountains began surrendering to the regular Army in eastern Washington, Stevens wrote Colonel George Wright to "put you on your guard in reference to Leschi, Kitsap, Nelson and Quiemuth, and suggest that no arrangement be made which shall save their necks from the executioner."

Colonel Wright, following General Wool's policy of conciliation, accepted the surrender of the war leaders and on their promise to fight no more if there were no reprisals, he released them to find their own way back to their reservations.

Learning of the Army's leniency, Stevens refused to accept custody of Indians returning to the reservations "until the murderers among them are arrested for trial." The returnees asked the Army for help; Colonel Casey agreed to feed them until they were accepted at the reservation, and he warned Stevens that "the Indians on the Sound, there is no doubt, can, by neglect and ill-usage, be driven to desperation." Stevens replied indignantly that "I do not believe any country or any age has afforded an example of the kindness and justice which has been shown toward the Indians by the suffering inhabitants of the Sound." he renewed his demand that the Army help arrest men he described as having "committed the murders in a time of profound peace, under circumstances of unsurpassed treachery and barbarity." Casey responded that the treatment of the surrendered Indians seemed "a case in which the rights and usages of war are involved, and in consequence I consider myself and military superiors the proper persons to judge." He had the temerity to remind the governor that "if in dealing with the Indians, a spirit of justice is exercised and those who have charge of them are actuated by an eye single to their duties and the peace of the country, there need be no further difficulty."

Leschi had made his way back to his native land. At a meeting arranged with his old Hudson's Bay Company friends, Dr. Tolmie and Edward Huggins, he asked them to tell Colonel Casey that if assurance were needed that he would fight no more, he would cut off his right hand. Tolmie carried the message to Fort Steilacoom, but Casey "considered it most prudent that Leschi should for a time remain in the woods, as prejudice ran against him."

Although Leschi stayed in hiding, word leaked out that he was in the area. Volunteer Adjutant General Tilton offered a reward of fifty blankets for his capture. On November 13, Leschi's nephew Sluggia and a second Indian, Elikukal, met the fugitive on the pretext of delivering a message, overpowered him, and delivered him to Sidney Ford, an officer in the Volunteers, who the next day delivered him to Stevens. It was the first time the two men had met since Leschi tore up his certificate at Medicine Creek almost two years earlier.

Stevens ordered that Leschi be tried immediately for murder. The governor, who had sought to try the settlers in military court, insisted on trying the Indian in civilian court. It was his contention that the uprising had not been a war between nations signatory to the Medicine Creek Treaty but a series of terrorist attacks by vicious individuals. It was decided to charge Leschi with the murder of Volunteer Colonel A. Benton Moses in the slough on Connell's Prairie as Moses escorted William Tidd back to Steilacoom from Naches Pass.

Judge Chenoweth had completed a session at Steilacoom and was on his way home to Whidbey Island by boat when an express canoe overtook him and brought him back to reconvene court. Attorneys Clark and Wallace, allies in the defense of the Muck Creek settlers, were appointed to opposite sides in this case, Clark and Joseph Smith representing the United States, Wallace and Henry Crosbie defending the Indian.

Captured on November 13, Leschi went on trial for his life November 16. The government's case was based largely on the testimony of Tony Rabbeson, a member of the escort party. He swore he had seen Leschi at the Indian camp where they had paused and again at the scene of the ambush where Moses was killed. The defense argued that as a warrior of the Nisqually nation, Leschi could not be accused of murder for killing a man in uniform in wartime; and that he hadn't been there anyway.

Judge Chenoweth left to the jury the issue of whether a state of war existed. If there were war, Leschi was to be found innocent. The judge said a declaration of war could consist of acts as well as words; that in Indian warfare a formal declaration was never expected, that with civilized nations it was often omitted; that the fact of war between nations often preceded the formal declaration and in such cases shielded combatants from individual responsibility. If no state of war was found to exist, Leschi was guilty if he were found to have killed, or been an accessory to the killing of, Colonel Moses.

On the first ballot, the jury stood eight for conviction, four for acquittal. Ezra Meeker was one of the minority. "The balloting went on and on," he recalled, "eight to four, eight to four, eight to four, with pallor on the cheeks of more than one juror for it was well known that the feeling on the outside was for vengeance. From ballots the jurors passed to words and hot words at that—almost to the point of intimidation."

The jury returned to the courtroom, reported themselves unable to agree, and asked to be discharged. Chenoweth sent them back to try again. Two more voted guilty, but Meeker and William Kincaid held out, the tiny, spunky Meeker arguing, always arguing, Kincaid—who was called "Father" Kincaid because, a widower, he had crossed the plains with seven children—sitting with his head bowed in prayer, refusing to speak except in response to the poll of jurors: Not Guilty, Not Guilty, Not Guilty, until at last he said, "I never will vote to condemn that man," and they believed him. The jury was dismissed and a new trial was scheduled for the following March.

The day after the jury was discharged, Leschi's half-brother Quiemuth turned himself in to James Longmire and asked to be taken to Governor Stevens. They arrived in Olympia well after midnight. Stevens accepted Quiemuth's surrender. Longmire agreed to spend the night with the prisoner in Stevens' office, there being no jail: "Blankets were brought for me and Quiemuth, and we lay down, one on each side of the fireplace, I being next to the door. The Governor left lights burning in the office, bade us good night and again retired, and I was soon in a deep sleep, from which I was aroused by a great noise, I hardly realizing what it was or what caused it. I sprang to my feet, and as I did so I heard the sound of persons running out of the house, and the lights were out. I saw by the dim firelight a man fall and heard a groan, and rushing to the man, I found it was Quiemuth, speechless and dying."

Governor Stevens burst in, saw Quiemuth dead, and asked, "Who in hell has done this?"

"I don't know," said Longmire.

"In my office, too! This is a club for General Wool."

Quiemuth had been shot in the arm and stabbed through the heart. No one was ever charged with the murder.

The second trial of Leschi began in Olympia on March 18, 1857, with Judge Lander on the bench. This time attorneys Clark and Wallace were united on the defense team. The testimony paralleled that in the first case, but the judge did not leave the question of whether war existed to the jury. He instructed them that the only question before them was whether Leschi was involved in Moses' death. The verdict was "guilty charged, and that he suffer death." The judge set June 10 as the date of execution, but the case was appealed to the territorial supreme court. In December the court sustained the jury's verdict.

Leschi during the long delay was kept in the guardhouse at Fort Steilacoom. He greatly impressed the officers, including Lieutenant Kautz who had been wounded in battle with Leschi's band at White River. Before sentence was passed on Leschi the second time, Kautz and Dr. Tolmie visited Connell's Prairie, and measured the routes described by Rabbeson in his testimony in which he claimed to have seen Leschi both at the Indian camp and at the ambush. Their conclusion was that it would have been impossible for Leschi to have made the trip as described. Kautz drew a map illustrating the routes, and attorney Clark petitioned for a new trial on the ground of new evidence. The petition was denied.

On December 18, 1857, Leschi was brought before Judge Lander and was asked if he had anything to say before sentence was passed. Frank Shaw translated as Leschi spoke in Nisqually.

> I do not see that there is any use of saying anything. My attorney has said all he could for me. I do not know anything about your laws. I have supposed that the killing of armed men in war time was not murder. If it was, the soldiers who killed Indians were guilty of murder, too. The Indians did not keep in order like the soldiers and could not fight in bodies like them, but had to resort to ambush and seek the cover of trees, logs, and everything that would hide them from the bullets. This was their mode of fighting and they knew no other way.
>
> Dr. Tolmie and the red-headed chief [Cushman] warned me against allowing my anger to get the best of my good sense as I could not gain anything by going to war with the United States but would be beaten and humbled, and would have to hide like a wild beast in the end. I did not take this good advice but nursed my anger until it became a furious passion, which led me like a false god.
>
> I went to war because I believed the Indians had been wronged by the white men and I did everything in my power to beat the Boston soldiers but for lack of numbers, supplies and ammunition I have failed. I deny that I had any part in killing Miles and Moses. I heard that a company of soldiers was coming out of Steilacoom and determined to lay in ambush for it but did not expect to catch anyone coming the other way. I did not see Miles or Moses before or after they were dead, but was told by other Indians that they had been killed. As God sees me, this is the truth.

Leschi, who had been converted to Christianity during his captivity, made the sign of the cross. "Ta-te mono, Ta-te lem-mas, Ta-ta hal-le-hach, tu-ul-li-as-sist-ah. [There is the Father, this is the Son, this is the Holy Ghost, these are all one and the same.] Amen."

Judge Lander set the date of execution as January 22.

The day before Leschi was to hang, an Indian appeared before United States Commissioner J. M. Bachelder in Steilacoom and complained that Sheriff George Williams and his deputy were selling liquor to the Indians. Bachelder issued a warrant for the arrest of the sheriff and his deputy. An acting United States marshal locked them up. Williams refused to turn Leschi's death warrant over to anyone else. His deputy had been scheduled to do duty as the hangman. The date of execution passed without the warrant being acted upon. A new date would have to be set.

The tactic of delay was credited to Frank Clark. It raised no sympathy for his client. Mass meetings passed resolutions protesting the trickery. Even Ezra Meeker, the hold-out against conviction, signed one of the protests.

A new date was set for Leschi's execution: February 19, 1858. On February 3 the territorial legislature rushed through a bill calling the supreme court into special session. The next day the court met and rejected the last motions from the defense. The governor refused clemency.

Leschi's execution took place in a gentle valley on the prairie a mile east of Fort Steilacoom. Charles Grainger of Olympia was chosen to be hangman. With a dozen deputies he escorted Leschi from the Fort Guardhouse across the open land to the gallows where about three hundred spectators were assembled. Leschi studied the gallows calmly.

The noose hung from a beam set across two six-by-six timbers twenty feet high. Steps led to a platform six feet from the ground. A trap had been cut in the stand. Some observers said Leschi seemed to sag slightly as he first looked at the noose but quickly composed himself. His step was firm as he mounted the platform and stepped into place on the trap, under the noose. He turned to Grainger and thanked him for his kindness. He said quietly that he was not guilty of killing Moses, that Rabbeson lied, and that he would meet Rabbeson before his God and tell him so. He bowed to the spectators, prayed silently for several minutes, and spoke for the last time. He said he had made his peace with God and desired to live no longer. He bore malice to no man save one, upon whom he invoked the vengeance of heaven.

When Leschi finished speaking, Grainger drew the hood down over his eyes and adjusted the rope. "He did not seem to be the least bit excited at all," said the hangman. "No trembling on him at all, nothing of the kind. That is more than I could say for myself. Leschi seemed to be the coolest of any on the scaffold."

At 11:35 the trap was sprung.

"I felt I was hanging an innocent man," said Grainger.

The few Indians who attended the execution removed the body from the scaffold, placed it in a plain box on an ox cart, and buried Leschi in a secluded spot under some trees. The Indian War on Puget Sound was over. The last symbol of resistance was gone.

A generation later the Nisqually reburied Leschi near the mouth of Muck Creek on the reservation he had won for them.

For Isaac Stevens there were four more years of politics, controversy, and war. In the summer of 1857, while the Leschi case was still before the courts and the governor's Indian policies were under attack from regular Army officers, old Whigs, new Republicans, and a few Democrats, Stevens decided to carry his case to the people. He was governor by appointment. He chose to seek the highest office the voters of the territory could bestow: territorial delegate.

The Democratic convention nominated Stevens, fifty to ten. He ran against Alexander S. Abernethy, a newcomer to the territory and the first man to campaign under the banner of the new Republican party. Although slavery dominated national politics, the territorial election centered on local issues and personalities. Stevens turned the campaign into a referendum on the legitimacy of the Indian War and the territory's claim for payment from the federal government for the services of the Volunteers. A vote against Stevens seemed to be a vote for General Wool and against the $1,300,000 sought by the Volunteers. Stevens won handsomely. With the aid of Joe Lane, the representative from Oregon, he maneuvered through Congress a bill appropriating money to pay the Volunteers.

On the great issue of slavery, Stevens took an equivocal position. He called himself an Abolitionist Democrat, by which he meant he was an antislavery man who put preservation of the Union ahead of abolition. The right of self-determination for each state outranked the rights of all men to freedom. As territorial delegate to the Democratic convention in 1860, Stevens put forward Joe Lane of Oregon, a southern sympathizer, for president. When Stephen A. Douglas was nominated, Stevens joined the delegates who bolted and staged a rump convention and created another party, the National Democrats. Stevens again nominated Lane, who got on the ticket as John Brackenridge's running mate.

The National Democrats were not without impact. They ran third but drew enough votes away from Douglas to elect Abraham Lincoln. South Carolina seceded, fighting started, and Stevens, a Union man above all, offered his services to the North. He was suspect because of his political background and months passed before he was entrusted with command of the Seventy-ninth Regiment of the New York Volunteers.

On September 1, 1862, General Stevens led his regiment in an uphill charge against Confederate troops behind a stone fence near Chantilly in northeast Virginia. Four times men carrying the regimental colors fell under the concentrated fire from the hilltop. As the fifth man stumbled and the troops wavered, Stevens himself caught the falling standard and carried it up the slope. A summer storm broke. Thunder joined the crash of artillery, lightning flashed brighter than the guns and in this melodramatic setting, at the moment when his men swept over the Confederate barricade, Isaac Ingalls Stevens fell dead, the flagstaff in his hand, a bullet in his brain, the regimental colors covering his head and shoulders. He was forty-four.

At the time of Stevens' death in 1862 the lovely curve of Commencement Bay lay almost as it was when Puget and Vancouver came by in their longboats in 1791 and the men off the *Porpoise* surveyed it for Wilkes in 1841.

Delin's mill stood now on the creek at the head of the bay, spared destruction by the Indians who had no quarrel with the gentle Swede and enjoyed the rhythmic rise and fall of the saw and the revolution of the paddle-wheel turbines. But the fun was out of sawmilling for Nick after the war; the profit too. Steam mills to the north were driving down the price of lumber. So he sold out for thirty-five hundred dollars to James L. Perkins, who had a government job on the Puyallup Reservation. With his brother Andrus, another cabinetmaker, Delin moved on to Olympia, then to Seattle—where he helped construct the columned building that housed a common school that styled itself a university. Delin ended his days in Portland. Young Perkins, who bought him out, found the mill difficult to operate and impossible to profit from, and anyway he would rather play the fiddle. So he sold to Milas Galliher, twin of Silas who ran a hotel in Steilacoom. Milas, whose interest was more in land than in logs, let it lie idle. The mill now stood up to its floorboards in skunk cabbage and cattail, and silt clogged the lower reaches of Delin Creek.

The frame house the Judsons had built out of Delin lumber on the open ground where the Union Depot was later built had not survived the war. It burned: cause unknown but suspected. Peter looked on the charred frame and gave up on what became the heart of Tacoma.

He took a claim on land south of Steilacoom, a bad guess, but understandable. Judson's boy Steve lived out his ninety years in the Steilacoom area, a useful man. He served seven years as sheriff, two terms as county treasurer, and several terms in the territorial and state legislatures. His brother, John Paul Judson, qualified as a lawyer and won election as territorial superintendent of schools.

Reilly and Swan, the bay's first commercial fishermen, stopped fishing. Reilly faded from the scene. Swan took a claim on McNeil Island, which he eventually sold to the government as a prison site. Chauncey Baird, the cooper, abandoned barrel making when the fishing stopped. The German-Americans on the Puyallup shifted their claims to areas outside the reservation. The Sales took land on the prairie.

Save for the silent mill, the stumps of firs logged for the saws but already shrouded with sworn-fern and bracken, some gardens gone to seed, the bay lay as the Indians had always known it, ready for rediscovery.

The Quaker, the Boomer, and the Railroad

O N July 2, 1864, President Abraham Lincoln signed a bill chartering the Northern Pacific Railroad Company and providing a grant of 40 million acres of the public domain—the greatest real estate give-away in American history—as incentive for the company to lay rails from Lake Superior to Puget Sound. The signing of the act incorporating the Northern Pacific fell on the fifty-first birthday of an about-to-be-discharged Union soldier, Job Carr, Jr., whose service entitled him to a 320-acre homestead claim. Within weeks he was on his way to Puget Sound to try to deduce where the rails would probably reach salt water, there to stake his claim.

Job Carr was a modest little man. It was said you would hardly notice him in the kitchen on horseback. Before going into the Army he had worked as machinist, millwright, painter, paper-hanger, and nurseryman. His 130 pounds were spread over a five-foot eight-inch frame. His eyes were brown, his hair brown and lank, his beard brown and vigorous. A fourth generation Quaker who employed *thee* and *thou* all his life, he disliked controversy ("If thee so wishes it, have it thy way"), but detested slavery and revered the Union: his Quaker grandfather, Caleb Carr, had been on General Washington's staff. Three months after the firing on Fort Sumter, Carr, though forty-eight years old and the father of four, enlisted as a private in the Twenty-sixth Indiana Infantry Regiment. He was wounded in the arm at Shiloh and again, critically, at Stone River on New Year's Day 1863. His estranged wife, Rebecca, the matron of the regimental field hospital, helped nurse him back to health, but when Job was invalided out of service they amicably went separate ways, she to marry again, become a spiritualist medium, and a champion of woman suffrage, Job to start west in quest of the terminus site and a life without violence or controversy.

By December, he was on the Sound looking at waterfront property and talking to old-timers. He went first to Olympia to examine the government land office maps and listen to men like Edmund Sylvester, the town founder, who had no doubts that the Northern Pacific would make Budd Inlet the Boston of the West. At Steilacoom, Lafayette Balch, the founding father, talked in terms of a greater Portland, Maine. And Seattle, recovered now from the shock of Indian attack, was chockablock with boosters ready to recite passages in the Railroad Survey in which Isaac Stevens said Snoqualmie was the best pass and Elliott Bay the most promising port. Carr listened to them all and went back south to Commencement Bay.

Except for Milas Galliher, who occasionally visited his idle mill, no one lived on the shore between the Puyallup River and Steilacoom. Carr stayed at the home of A. Williamson Stewart, the government carpenter and wagon maker for the Puyallup Reservation. Two other reservation employees, William Billings, who taught farming, and Dr. Charles Spinning, physician and agent to the tribe, invited him on a fishing trip to Gig Harbor on Christmas. Although after leaving the Army Job had scruples against hunting and fishing, he went along for the ride, wanting to have a look at the waterfront.

Christmas morning, a Sunday, dawned clear, the Mountain glorious with new snow, a slight frost on the tips of the evergreens. They paddled the northern route to stay out of the whitecaps kicked up by a stiff north wind. That took them along the south shore of Browns Point—reservation land, out-of-bounds for homesteaders—and Vashon Island, but coming back in the afternoon the canoe followed the shore along the northern side of the Point Defiance peninsula. For the rest of his life Job Carr cherished the moment they came to the place where the high banks folded into a gentle draw leading to the crest of the hill. A creek trickled through the trees into a pond that lay behind a natural bar at waterfront. "I raised on my feet and exclaimed, 'Eureka! Eureka!' and told my companions there was my claim." Somebody must have told him to sit down, he was rocking the boat.

Carr had no doubts: this was the place. His companions pointed out other sites worth considering, especially the old Judson claim, now abandoned. Job did not argue but he would not consider it. He would choose no land that anyone else had ever claimed. That only led to arguments. There was a Carr family tradition that an ancestor had been beaten out of vast holdings in New Jersey in a disagreement over title.

By early January, Job was on the claim at Shubahlup, "the sheltered place," falling trees to enlarge a small clearing facing the water, bucking logs to cabin length and rolling them into place between today's Carr and McCarver streets. He lived with the Stewarts on the reservation until the cabin was habitable, commuting by canoe in dawn and twilight. When the weather was very good or unexpectedly bad he spent the night at Shubahlup, which he called Eureka, sheltering Indian-style beneath big slabs of fir bark leaned against a cedar log, his companion a yellow cat called Tom, a present from Mrs. Stewart.

Once the cabin was roofed, Carr took a job part of the time tending the burrs in Andrew Byrd's gristmill on Chambers Creek. In his spare time he put up the interior boards, covered them with cloth, then paper. The cabin was divided into two sections, a bedroom on the west side, a kitchen–living room, facing a clay fireplace in which a bark fire burned most of the winter, built against the east wall. A low-ceilinged loft furnished sleeping space for visitors. Job added a front porch after his two sons, both veterans of the war, joined him in 1866.

Howard, the younger, arrived first, still recuperating from his experiences as a prisoner of war. Too young for military service, he had contrived to enlist in New York under an assumed name and while still seventeen was thrown into the bloody battle at Cold Harbor ("After working half the night we had fair breastworks, which we embraced as tight as we ever did our girl but at 6 o'clock A.M. we have a charge, which was simply *butchery* to us, and no good. In afternoon charged again with same results, and the ground *covered* with dead and wounded. Sam Patch and I was cooking coffee when he got terribly wounded from back of his neck to his Seat and I was knocked into the sink, darn em. Close call"). He saw Grant plain ("He had a Cigar, but stood fire like a sojir—no fear"). The next day Howard was captured with two thousand others and sent to the hellhole of Andersonville Prison ("Nov 25: Escape tunnels not found, no grub. Dam em we are starving and my birthday today. 18 years old, but I can't eat anything. We drink water all the time. Hundreds are dead"). His weight dropped from 138 pounds to 92. His prison mates were assuring him he was a goner. Then an exchange of prisoners ("*Nov. 30.* Went on board the Beauregard and down the river to our boats. A *million* Cheers for the *dear old flag.* We all cried with joy and oh! think. *Clothes. Hard tack. Coffee, Sugar. Salt. Soap. Washed clean.* Hair *cut* with *Shears*, not with a *Knife*, and real old style *northern Sow Belly.* This is *too much,* and *doctors,* and real northern *Potatoes* and *onions,* and *pepper,* genuine too. A new quart-cup *full* of old Govt Java—and a *new* <u>Blanket</u>. Think of all this. After *starving* and *freezing naked dam* the *conflageracy.* I'm too full of Joy and Coffee. *Reese* and I *hugged* each other & cried like two babies. 'Cause we're glad.' Poor Berry got left.") Three years later he was still complaining of hunger.

After visiting his mother and sisters in Richmond, Indiana, Howard worked his way west, pawned his clothes for twenty dollars in San Francisco, bought a steamer ticket to the Columbia River, and walked from the mouth of the Cowlitz to the Sound, arriving on July 28, 1866, a dime in his pocket.

Anthony, the older brother, joined him a few months later. He was twenty-five years old, a lean young man slightly taller and heavier than his father, with light brown hair and eyes, a sweeping long-horn mustache, and a clean chin. A photographer by trade, he had enlisted in Company B of the Ninth Indiana Infantry—the Iron Brigade. The Army enrolled him as an "artist" and sent him, bulky camera, wet-plates, chemicals, and all, into Confederate territory to photograph topography. He once carried a message to Lincoln, which he insisted on hand-delivering to the president. Lincoln arranged for him to have a bath before he left the White House.

The Army taught Anthony telegraphy, but he fought as an infantryman too and was invalided out of service in 1863 with a letter of commendation from his commanding officer (". . . at Bull Run you stood by the old flag and done your whole duty until you were stricken down by the enemies of our Country. You have been a good soldier and a brave man"). Anthony rode west to Idaho with a party of prospectors, found no gold, lost his pack animals to the Indians, and on his return to the States, broke, re-enlisted. He was captured in Texas in the last land battle of the war, weeks after Lee's surrender, but after twenty-eight days simply walked away from prison camp.

Anthony took a steamer to Atchison, Kansas, hired on as a mule-driver for a wagon train going to Salt Lake City ("Wrote several letters and went to the Theater. Brigham and five of his wives were there"), caught on with another party headed for California, took a steamer to the Cowlitz, and walked to Steilacoom in four days "over the muddiest road I ever saw." The road went past the Byrd gristmill on Chambers Creek "where father was. Found him. Glad and all that. Had a big pow-pow and a big supper, you bet." Howard joined them and the three vets refought the war: "Pow-wow continued. Weighty subjects considered. Andy Johnson a rascal in general. My throat sore in particular."

The Carr brothers took claims adjoining their father's. The set formed a rough triangle with its base on the beach and the point running up the draw. John Meeker, a deputy United States surveyor, was hired to survey the claims. Charley Ross, who with his brother cut paths and carried chains, long remembered that they camped in the Carr cabin: "Mr. Carr and Uncle John Meeker occupied the only beds, while we slept on the bare floor. We complained a little and Uncle John was full of pity. 'Come on, boys,' he told us, 'Get out your pocket knives and hunt for a soft board.'"

There were no soft spots. It was a hard and lonely life for a young man. The land was promising, the weather mild compared to the Midwest, but the nights were long and filled with thoughts of girls who were half a continent away. The good moments are laconically noted in the diaries—"Caught 50 pounds rock cod"; "Shot a buck"; "Letter from mother. Nice"; "Went to Narrows. Caught 300 salmon";—but the refrain was loneliness—Ah, Liz; Ah, Em; Ah, Carrie; Ah, Ah, Ah—and the slow leakage of days, the lack of money and of the opportunity to make money.

Howard, who had arrived in July with a dime in his pocket, greeted 1867 by writing bitterly, "Happy New Year to all. How fortunate for a young man to have a fresh start in a new country on the first of the year—with *ten cents.*" In February he took off for California. He prospected vainly in the Sierra, hurt his ankle badly when thrown down a steep hill by a runaway mule he had retrieved. In July he gave up ("I'm getting older, uglier, poorer and meaner by the day"), sold his claim, and bought passage to the East Coast via Nicaragua. He had decided to get married.

Almost broke when he arrived in New York, Howard wired his mother for money, walked to Philadelphia spending thirty-five cents in ten days—all for food. He found one hundred dollars awaiting him: "bought me a 50 dol suit of clothes and things and a ring for the Girl I want." But she turned him down ("hadn't the moral courage") and he went back to Puget Sound.

Instead of a bride, Howard took with him his sister, Marietta. Mattie was a dark-haired, dark-eyed girl, slightly built—five feet two and a half inches, 105 pounds—and in delicate health, but she was venturesome and wanted to see the world. Mrs. Carr paid their passage by ship. They left New York September 20 and entered the Strait of Juan de Fuca November 10, but the winds failed and after a week Howard "hired two Injuns to take us in canoe to home. Lots of fog. Got to upper end Vashon Island at 8 P.M. Camped and it rained on us some in the night. Off at 7 and arrived at 8 at home, Shubollop. Father was home. And this is the round trip. And quite a one too. But what will be the end?"

It wasn't so lonely with Mattie there. She was a notable cook, could play the dulcimer and the accordion, had a sweet singing voice, and was good-looking. There was much company, mostly unmarried. There were picnics, boatings ("Mattie caught four bullheads, I caught cold"), and dances. There were evenings of just the family in front of the big fireplace, singing, reminiscing, playing the dulcimer, flute, and accordion, reading Shakespeare—*Merry Wives of Windsor* was the favorite—while the rain thrummed on the shake roof and winter waves pounded the beach. Howard and Anthony improved their claims. Mattie learned telegraphy. Anthony opened a photo studio in Steilacoom, and split shakes for cash. Howard and his father worked in the Byrd mill. The boys cut a trail from Steilacoom to Shubahlup, visited the reservation, flirted with what girls there were ("Ah, Jane. Sweet ain't the word for it"). But the days became weeks, weeks flowed into months, and there was no word from the East that work had begun on the Northern Pacific. Waiting for the railroad was worse than waiting for a sailboat.

In April 1868 their fortunes changed.

NEW PHOTOGRAPHIC ESTABLISHMENT,

TACOMA, PIERCE COUNTY, W. T.

A. P. CARR, PROPRIETOR.

Every kind of Picture pertaining to the Photographic Art.

Carte de Visite in vignette or full length, plain or enamelled.

Also, the wonderful Porcelain picture, the finest and most elegant of all photographs.

The neat and convenient article known as " Gems" made to order.

Or, if you wish a picture life size, or any size less, of any kind or description, they can be had at the above Gallery.

The Latest Improvement!

PHOTO-CRAYONS OF ANY SIZE.

Remarkable for elegance of finish and truthfulness of representation.

Views of points on the Sound and in the country on hand, or to order.

Advertisement in Washington Territory West of the Cascade Mountains *by Ezra Meeker* Courtesy of Photo. Coll., UW Library

On the afternoon of April 1, 1868, a tall, blue-eyed man with sandy-gray hair and a face elongated by partial baldness sat astride his worn horse and looked out at Commencement Bay from the bluff above the southern shore, the old Judson claim. He had ridden north from Portland to study the Puget Sound country and he liked what he saw: an Indian canoe moving across a bay streaked by silt from the river which flowed across tideflats green with seagrasses; the Mountain high and white against the eastern sky; a small sawmill in a swale of skunk cabbage to his right; to his left a shallow cove; the forest all but unbroken, the land undeveloped, the magnificent sheet of water awaiting ships.

Looking out from the bluff, Morton Matthew McCarver saw not the all-but-empty bay, nor did he smell the clean, thin scent of fir. He envisioned a city: wharves and streets and steamships and locomotives; a county courthouse, perhaps a state capitol; he breathed the heady incense of coal smoke and new-sawn lumber, heard the clang of trolleys and the wail of factory whistles.

But McCarver saw cities wherever he looked. He was a boomer, one of the nineteenth-century Americans irresistibly drawn to undeveloped land, no more capable of resisting the impulse to look at a field and proclaim a metropolis than other frontier types were of foregoing a drink or a look at the hole card. Booming was his vice. He shunned alcohol and helped circulate the Northwest's first manifesto extolling prohibition; his language was mild, his family life exemplary though intermittent; he was upright, god-fearing, and a sucker for a stretch of empty waterfront or a hint of industrial development. Though he deplored all games of chance, his optimism about property futures was steady and unearthly. As he lay dying, seven years after his first look at Commencement Bay, his last requests were for someone to read him from the local paper any stories about road building or coal mining.

McCarver was born on a farm near Lexington, Kentucky, in 1807. His father died when he was a child; his mother, a stern woman, brought him up within a religious philosophy that advocated celibacy and deplored dissipation. (He was a lifelong teetotaller but the father of ten.) The boy ran away to the Southwest at fourteen. Poor, with little schooling and no friends, he found himself competing for work done by slaves. The experience left him with a lifelong prejudice against blacks. He went home, broke, only to have his mother turn him away, saying they were "dead to each other on earth."

The young man drifted west. In Illinois he found a wife but not prosperity. He fought in the Black Hawk war and, when the treaty was signed opening Indian land in Wisconsin to settlement, claimed the site that became Burlington. When Wisconsin was divided into two territories in 1838, the southern portion became Iowa and Burlington its capital. McCarver was appointed commissary general of the territorial militia. The pay was trivial but the honorific "General" served him the rest of his life.

At the age of thirty-five, after a decade in Burlington, McCarver was the father of the town and of five children, but he was ten thousand dollars in debt, his prospects poor. The price of corn and hogs, the measure by which the farming West judged prosperity, was at a twenty-year low. Iowa echoed with talk of greener pastures. The great migration of 1843 was aborning. McCarver was ready again to move on. There were greater towns to be created beyond the Rockies.

In the spring of 1843, McCarver took leave of Mary Ann, their children, and their town, and joined the pioneers gathering at Independence, Missouri. A man of imposing appearance, the general was elected to the Council of Nine, which governed the wagon train. The office was no easy honor. Disputes among the nine hundred travelers were frequent. Some were insoluble, some ludicrous. A bachelor had a wagon so large it was called Noah's Ark, so cumbersome it required the muscle of a score of men to get it up the worst slopes. Eventually the council demanded to know what was in it. The owner allowed as how he was transporting near a ton of soft soap with which to woo the womenfolk out west. The unromantic councilmen made him leave it beside the trail for the possible benefit of puzzled Indians.

McCarver played Solomon in such cases but chaffed at the slow pace of the cow column. What if someone else spotted the ideal site for the great city of the West while he was listening to debate about cow-pies in the drinking water? He had struck up an alliance with the captain of the wagon train, a young lawyer named Peter Burnett, who also fancied himself a town builder. After the train reached Fort Hall, about ten miles from present Pocatello, the two men agreed that McCarver should ride on ahead and try to outguess destiny.

The site McCarver selected was near the confluence of the Willamette and the Columbia. They called it Linnton in honor of Senator Lewis Linn, the sponsor of much legislation promoting westward immigration. McCarver deluged editors and other opinion makers with letters booming the prospects of his townsite ("There is growing in a field less than a mile from the place where I am writing a turnip measuring four and one-half feet around . . ."), but neighboring Portland became the metropolis of Oregon.

Elected to the provisional legislature in May of 1844, McCarver was chosen Speaker. His influence and prejudices were reflected in two of the measures passed that year. One banned the distillation or sale of ardent spirits "lest they bring withering ruin upon the prosperity and prospects of this interesting and rising community." The other threatened black immigrants with the lash if they stayed in Oregon.

Giving up on Linnton, McCarver bought out a settler who had

land near the falls of the Willamette. He farmed, planted an apple orchard, and sought political appointment. Mary Ann brought the children west but died the following year. McCarver soon married Julia Ann Buckalew, a twenty-two-year-old widow who had lost her husband on the trail. She brought one child to the marriage and bore McCarver five others.

When gold was found in California, McCarver joined the stampede south. A few days of panning on the Feather River convinced him that he would do better at promoting than at prospecting. He persuaded John Sutter, Jr., to put him in charge of laying out a town at the juncture of the Sacramento and American rivers, but the elder Sutter overruled young John and assigned the work to a lawyer who had just arrived from Oregon. Thus McCarver found himself displaced by his former partner, Peter Burnett, who made one hundred thousand dollars from the arrangement and went on to become California's first governor.

McCarver bought land in Sacramento, built a store, invested in a river schooner (though even a river trip made him seasick), brought his family south, and entered politics. He won election to the town council, the territorial legislature, and the California constitutional convention. At Monterey, where the state constitution was drafted, McCarver wasted his influence and oratory on a bigoted attempt to win acceptance of an article barring free blacks from California ("They are idle in their habits, difficult to be governed by the laws, thriftless and uneducated"). While he was thus fruitlessly engaged, floods ruined his Sacramento property.

McCarver gave up on California and went back to Oregon to tend his apple orchard. It did well. "McCarver's Big Red Apples" were noted for beauty and flavor. He bought a bark, *Ocean Bird,* and shipped some apples to Hawaii but sold her after discovering that going to sea was no cure for seasickness. He invested in a river steamer but it blew up. During the Indian War he served as commissary general of the Oregon militia—and as spokesman for civilian opposition to General Wool. When Isaac Stevens resigned as governor of Washington Territory, McCarver sought the appointment but lost to a Virginia lawyer, Fayette McMullin, who wanted the job because the territorial legislature had the power to grant divorces. (McMullin stayed in Washington only long enough to get a bill of divorcement.) McCarver joined in the gold rush to the Fraser River and the silver rush to Idaho, where he ran a general store in Bannock City only to lose it in a fire.

Time was running out on the old boomer in 1868 when he heard that the Northern Pacific planned to end its transcontinental on Puget Sound. He was a grandfather now. He had left scratchmarks on the continent but had not created the city of his vision. Here was one last great chance. Securing the promise of financial backing from Lewis Starr and James Steel, president and cashier of the First National Bank of Portland, he rode north alone to try to anticipate the site of the terminus.

On the map Commencement Bay, accessible to Snoqualmie and Naches passes and offering deep water close to shore with protection against all but north winds, looked promising. He went there first. The reality was even better than the promise, and he did not bother to look at other locations. Instead he rode to the Puyallup Reservation and far into the night studied the land office maps and talked to the government people. They told him the head of the bay, where Milas Galliher had started up the old Delin mill only to find the foundations so uncertain that boards came out as wedges, afforded poor anchorage and was silting up. The old Judson claim was high bluff. But at Shubahlup there was deep water close to a gentle slope. The next day McCarver went over to meet Job Carr.

Morton Matthew McCarver at sixty-one was a promoter, a salesman, an optimist. Job Carr at fifty-five was a man of hope and good will rather than driving ambition. McCarver was dissatisfied with his achievements, sure that destiny had intended him to do more. Carr thought a railroad should come to Shubahlup but had been content to wait for others to recognize the merits of the site, meanwhile working at the mill, or painting and papering the houses of other settlers. McCarver talked of the terminal city that would transform the gentle slope into Manhattan, of capitalists ready to build a steam-powered sawmill on Commencement Bay and run a railroad north from Portland even before the Northern Pacific came across the continent. Carr listened to this heady stuff, and to the role he could play in tying together east and west of the nation that had so nearly blown itself apart north and south. He did not hesitate. He would not stand in the way of progress. If McCarver's company needed the Shubahlup waterfront to bring in the railroad, he would not stand in their way. They could have all but the five acres immediately around his cabin. The other 163¾ acres he agreed to sell for $1,600, of which $600 was to be cash, the rest in land McCarver owned in Oregon City, a 100-acre plot that Carr eventually sold for $724, making the payment actually $1,324, or $8.08 an acre. Job retained a claim farther west which included the Puget Gulch.

"Bully! Shout hosannas to all the listening of the earth!" Anthony wrote in his diary after his brother came up to Steilacoom with news

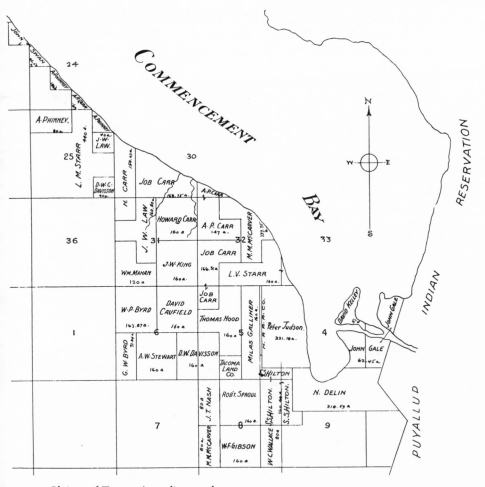

Claims of Tacoma's earliest settlers

of the deal. "Great cause for rejoicing have I. Long will I sing paeans of joy for this day's news. The Spring of Youth has been found. Now will I live, aha!" Later he added, "Bully for Shubollop. It's going to come out after all."

Howard was less euphoric: "M. M. McCarver bought Father out 600 coin and 100 acres land in Oregon. . . . Bully for the company. We may *iscum talla alki* [get rich by-and-by]." He set to work finishing the cabin on his claim.

. McCarver hurried back to Portland to check with his backers before signing any papers. When he returned to Shubahlup he brought with him Lewis Starr, the bank president—himself no tower of financial strength—and two friends from Oregon City, David Caufield and Thomas Hood. They camped for a night below the Stadium Way cliff near the foot of Seventh Street, beside an Indian burial canoe and a boulder marked with hieroglyphs (a treasure casually buried under debris from the grading of Pacific Avenue a few years later). Starr was so impressed he claimed the site, using his brother's name lest he antagonize bank clients in Portland. McCarver filed a pre-emption claim on adjoining land to the west, where Stadium High School and the Stadium Bowl were later built. Hood and Caufield took contiguous claims on the high land behind the Judson claim.

The solitude of Shubahlup ended. The rhythm of axes striking living wood, the screech and thud of falling timber, the clang of sledge on wedge, the beat of hammer on nail echoed across the bay as claimants worked on the cabins they needed for shelter and to prove up. Tom Hood was first to finish and in June moved into a cabin at what is now M and South Ninth. McCarver hired Anthony Carr to build a log cabin for him on the curve below the cliff just east of Stadium High; he called his place Pin Hook and early in August brought his wife and their three youngest daughters, Virginia, Bettie, and Naomi up from Portland, to the delight of bachelors as far away as Olympia and Seattle.

Once back on the scene, McCarver hired a civil engineer from Olympia to survey the former Job Carr property, on which he planned to create a town which he called Commencement City. Howard and Anthony ran the lines. The survey was completed on August 13. It was foggy that morning and to everyone's surprise a steamer began whistling from out in the bay, where no steamer had been before. Anthony, who happened to have his rifle, fired a shot to answer each whistle. Crewmen from the *Eliza Anderson* used the sounds to guide them through the fog to the shore with the first passengers to land from a steamer on Commencement Bay. They were Mr. and Mrs. Clinton P. Ferry, who had come to join the McCarvers, Mrs. Ferry being one of Mrs. McCarver's daughters by her first marriage.

Territorial Governor Marshall Moore, a lawyer from Yale who had risen to the rank of major general during the Civil War, paid a visit soon afterwards. On leaving he asked McCarver to find him some property. McCarver told Anthony Carr that the governor's presence would benefit the entire community. Anthony borrowed McCarver's beloved old gray, galloped to Olympia, and sold Moore forty acres. With some of the proceeds Anthony bought a load of sawed boards from the Galliher mill, rafted them to Shubahlup, and started a big frame house. He was working up nerve to propose to Josie Byrd, the daughter of the owner of the gristmill.

Dreams were coming true and more were aborning. There were

happy rumors everywhere. "Whether construction of the Northern Pacific Railroad is delayed longer or not," said a story in the Seattle *Intelligencer,* "coming next after that in importance is the projected railroad from Portland to Commencement or Puyallup Bay, and the laying out of a new town on that Bay. It is of great significance, as showing the estimation in which our country and the Sound are held by capitalists abroad; it is of further significance in the warrent it gives of increase of business. Backed as the originators of this new town are by immense capital, with the charter of a railroad behind, the hope is reasonable that an impetus will be given to business on the Sound which will never be withdrawn."

Such talk, especially the references to the nonexistent charter and the inflated capitalists, reflected McCarver's talent as a promoter of empty acres. He was booming the new town with every trick of the land-development trade. He showered friends, acquaintances, and especially editors with effusions about the bounties of the bay ("I can frequently with my bare hands throw out enough smelt to supply a camp of fifty men"). He contributed to out-of-town papers a history of railroading in which he started by taking credit for originating the idea of a transcontinental line and ended with the terminus at Commencement Bay. He plugged away even in letters to his backers ("My family say that they have never lived in a new place they liked so well"). And he put every bit of money and energy he possessed behind his words. He bought another 280 acres from the owners of nearby claims. He went prospecting for minerals that would add to the economic base of the terminus.

With Howard Carr and Dan Caufield, McCarver started up the Puyallup Valley in late August to check out reports of iron and coal. The rumored iron proved to be a deposit of inferior bog ore. McCarver returned to town, but the younger men rode on. They camped the night of September 1 on the North Fork of the Puyallup. "Went on up the mountain 6 or 8 miles," says Howard's journal for the next day, "when we struck a 12 foot vein of coal and turned back. Camp on South Prairie Creek." Nothing came of their discovery for several years, and neither Carr nor Caufield benefited from it, but reports of a bituminous bed up the valley boosted interest in the town.

By the end of August all the land on the south side of the bay from the waterfront to the crest of the hill had been claimed. Prices were going up. Job Carr had received eight dollars an acre for land that included waterfront. In August Howard sold two acres back from the water for forty dollars—but lost the money out of his pocket while paddling back to Shubahlup from Steilacoom. "Lost two lots overboard from the canoe," was the way he put it.

In mid-September, to everyone's delight, Philip Ritz of Walla Walla came down on the steamer from Olympia. Ritz was a handsome and cultivated man, a scientific farmer, a contributor of learned letters to assorted editors, a member of a group of Washingtonians who were—vainly, it developed—seeking a franchise from Congress to build a railroad from Portland to Puget Sound. He was also thought to be an agent for the Northern Pacific on an inspection trip. After spending a night with McCarver, Ritz expressed enough enthusiasm that the old boomer tried to sell him one-fourth interest in the entire development project, on condition that Ritz devote his full attention to its promotion. Howard Carr later rode down to Olympia to offer to sell him forty acres. Nothing came of either proposition, but Ritz's visit did put a new name on the map.

Ritz was enthusiastic about *The Canoe and the Saddle,* a humorous account by Theodore Winthrop, scion of the Massachusetts Winthrops, about a visit to Washington Territory in 1853. Winthrop wrote the book in 1859, but it was not published until after he attracted considerable attention by becoming the first Union officer killed in battle in the Civil War. It then became immensely popular. In one of his humorous efforts, Winthrop deplored the "sibilantous gutturality" of the Salish languages but proclaimed *Tacoma* melodious. He admired the Mountain, too. "Of all the peaks from California to Fraser's River," he said of the view from Commencement Bay, "this one before me was royalest. Mount Regnier Christians have dubbed it, in stupid nomenclature, perpetuating the name of somebody or nobody. More melodiously the Siwashes call it Tacoma—a generic name also applied to all snow peaks."

As far as is known, W. H. Cushman brought the first copy of *The Canoe and the Saddle* (and four other books by Winthrop) to Washington Territory shortly after the war. Cushman settled in Olympia, and it is probably no coincidence that a Tacoma Lodge of the Good Templars was organized there on September 2, 1866, and a hotel called the Tacomah House opened for business in the capital eight months later.

During Ritz's visit to Olympia, he read Winthrop's book and was struck by the beauty of the Indian word. While he was visiting McCarver and Job Carr he marveled at the loveliness of the Mountain and spoke glowingly of the aboriginal word. About a month later, after a series of conversations involving McCarver, the Carrs, John W. Ackerson of the Hanson, Ackerson and Co. Mill, and McCarver's Portland partners, Lewis Starr and James Steel, there was general agreement that *Tacoma* would be a better name than *Commencement City* for the city they were planning. (McCarver always credited

Ritz with the suggestion; Ackerson later claimed he was first to suggest the name, having heard it from a Puyallup whom the whites called Chief Spot. Steel's version was that Ackerson favored naming the town after another Puyallup "chief," Sitwell. Job Carr had favored *Eureka* but switched to *Tacoma* after Ritz's visit.)

Late in October, McCarver and his secretary C. P. Ferry were in the offices of the First National Bank in Portland. After discussion with his backers, the old boomer told Ferry, whose handwriting was handsome, to cross out "Commencement City" on the survey map that had been drawn in August, and write in "Tacoma." This was done but McCarver did not immediately have the plat filed with the Pierce County auditor.

Anthony Carr had decided to create a separate town on his claim. On November 30 he appeared in the auditor's office in Steilacoom with a plat for a small community which he called "Tacoma." Three days later General McCarver showed up with his papers, only to find that Pierce County already had a Tacoma. So he called his site "Tacoma City." (Five years later the Northern Pacific platted "New Tacoma." Eventually they coalesced.)

The first newspaper to mention Tacoma was the Portland *Commercial* on November 16, 1868—before either McCarver or Carr had filed their plats. The *Commercial* spoke in terms of the new community's threat to Portland and warned that construction of a Tacoma and Vancouver railroad would sap the life blood of Oregon.

The Seattle *Intelligencer* on November 23 spoke in a more friendly vein about the new community. In a story obviously based on a letter from McCarver, the *Intelligencer* declared: "The name of the new town laid off by General McCarver and known as Commencement City, has been changed to Tacoma after the Indian name for Mount Rainier. It is reported to us that great progress is making in erecting houses on the site, and the building of roads has commenced."

It was almost the last friendly word from Seattle.

On a Sunday in mid-August, Anthony was cleaning and barreling three hundred salmon he had caught the day before. Bill Lane dropped by with two strangers from California in tow. Lane, a freelance logger, had encountered one of the men, clad in blue overalls, on a trail outside Steilacoom and asked if he were looking for work. No, he was looking for a mill site. The stranger introduced himself as Samuel Hadlock, a millwright. His companion, who appeared shortly, was John W. Ackerson, the associate of Charles Hanson. Lane was impressed. Charles Hanson, a Danish sea captain, had entered the logging business in California in the 1850s and was now known as the Redwood Shingle King. If Hanson built a mill, it would be a big one. McCarver talked grandly about a steam sawmill for his new town but everybody now knew that he and his backers did not have the money. Vision, yes; money, no. All of the steam mills on the Sound were built with outside capital for the very good reason that there wasn't any inside capital.

Lane told the Californians that the best site would be around the point at the new town on Anthony Carr's claim, which included the little lagoon where logs were rafted for the Delin mill. So Anthony took them to see his place, then around the bay to look at others, including McCarver's claim at Pin Hook and some locations in Quartermaster Harbor. They chose Tacoma, buying sixty-eight acres from Anthony, seventeen acres from Governor Moore, with McCarver promising to deed Anthony some waterfront property to the west to compensate him for the lagoon. The price was seven hundred dollars. Hadlock wrote Hanson that the property was "the best mill site I ever saw." Not everyone agreed; a Pope and Talbot official told his employer that "if you should blindfold a man and put him in a boat, wherever he landed on the shore would be as well located."

Work on clearing and grading the site started immediately. Anthony helped level his old property. The Lane brothers brought in six hundred pilings from sixty to eighty feet in length for the foundation and wharf, then rafted up five hundred thousand board feet of logs while the mill frame was being raised and the machinery installed.

As the mill took shape in 1869, so did the town. McCarver began selling lots on the townsite to persons he felt would benefit the community. In making sales he sometimes bet on his belief that Tacoma was the place where soon "the iron of rail will meet the salt of sea." When Mr. and Mrs. H. N. Steele bought four lots at Thirtieth and McCarver, they received not a deed but a bond calling for delivery of the deed after five years at a price of one hundred dollars if the railroad had not arrived, three hundred dollars if it had. McCarver lost that bet, but gained in Janet Elder Steele a most useful citizen. Her husband was an occasional prospector given to utter relaxation between fruitless forays for gold, but Mrs. Steele more than made up for his lassitude. She superintended construction of a twenty-four-room hotel and operated it in a manner which (though the competition was less than fierce) earned the Steele Hotel the reputation of having the cleanest sheets and best table of any hostelry between Olympia and Victoria.

On March 25 Tacoma got a post office. It was first located in Job Carr's cabin, with Job as postmaster. Anthony had been bringing the mail from the steamer wharf at Steilacoom, by canoe, horse, or on foot, depending on the weather. After the mill wharf was completed the *Eliza Anderson* stopped there with letters.

The first steamer to call at the mill wharf was the *Gussie Telfair*. She put in on Saint Patrick's Day, bringing McCarver's wife and daughters, who had wintered in Portland where the girls could get adequate schooling. They did not return to the cabin at Pin Hook but to the family's new house, not only weatherboarded but painted, the pride of the community, at Twenty-eighth and McCarver streets. In the clearing in the forest, McCarver planted some seedlings from his Oregon orchard so that later his town could enjoy McCarver's Big Red Apples.

On May 21, the embryo town had its first wedding, when Anthony Carr married his Josie—and on that day gave up keeping his diary.

Also in May, the Pierce County commissioners created the Tacoma Precinct, with H. N. Steele as election inspector, and Job Carr and A. C. Lowell as judges. In the first election, Tacoma went Democratic, giving sixteen votes to Governor Marshall Moore, who was running for delegate to Congress, to thirteen for Selucius Garfielde, the Republican, who was elected anyway and went to Washington where he ended his days running a high-toned brothel and gambling house.

In September a Tacoma school district—Pierce County No. 11—was created. McCarver and associates donated a lot at the southwest corner of Twenty-eighth and Starr streets, and the towns-folk pungled up three hundred dollars to put up a one-room log cabin schoolhouse. James Stewart was hired as the first teacher. One of the McCarver girls, Virginia, was the second. Three families contributed the entire student body, thirteen pupils.

Tacoma could rejoice when on December 8, 1869, the brig *Samoset* cast off from the mill wharf and pointed her Indian chief figure-head toward the Straits and San Francisco, her hold and decks deep with a half million board feet of fresh cut Douglas fir—the first shipment from the Hanson-Ackerson mill. Nineteen more shiploads went out during the next twelve months, most to San Francisco, a few to Central and South America, one to Australia.

By 1870 the new town had its name, its mill, its world market, its industrial payroll, its post office, its school, some politicians and places for them to meet, and a stagecoach line that offered passage to Steilacoom for three dollars, to Olympia for eight. But Tacoma was still looking for its railroad.

A transcontinental railroad was easier to conceive than to achieve.

One summer day in 1830, Peter Cooper ran a tiny steam locomotive he called Tom Thumb along iron rails that had been built for horse-drawn carriages on the Baltimore and Ohio line. From the moment Tom Thumb went into operation it was inevitable that someone would suggest extending the rails from ocean to ocean. Dr. Sam Barlow was perhaps the first: he proposed linking the Hudson River with the Columbia River and estimated the cost at thirty million dollars. Nobody had that much money, including the government. The 363-mile Erie Canal, the largest engineering project undertaken in America up to that time, cost eight million.

Asa Whitney, a New York merchant, proposed in 1845 that the government give thirty miles of public land on each side of the right-of-way to anyone who would build a line from Lake Superior to Puget Sound. This land would rise in value as tracks were laid, and the builder could mortgage the improved land to provide money for further construction. Workers who graded the right-of-way and laid track would be paid in land along the route. Settlement would coincide with construction, and the settlers would provide the line with freight and fares. Whitney offered to build such a line for four thousand dollars a year, plus the land grant, a ribbon of empire twenty-four hundred miles long, sixty miles wide, taking in seventy-six million acres. He could not sell the idea to Congress and he died broke.

Edwin J. Johnson, a professional engineer who had helped build the Erie Canal and the Chicago, St. Paul, and Fond du Lac Railroad, argued that the Corps of Engineers should, to gain experience useful in wartime, build and operate a line from Lake Superior to Puget Sound. Johnson's proposal led Congress to authorize the railway surveys of 1853, of which Isaac Stevens' was one, but sectional and political differences made agreement on a route impossible.

Early in the Civil War it was feared the Pacific states and territories might break away and form a separate republic. In 1862, to preserve the Union and especially to prevent the loss of California, Congress offered charters, land grants, and construction subsidies to the Union Pacific to build west from the Mississippi and to the Central Pacific to build east from San Francisco Bay to a juncture in Utah. Two years later the Union Pacific–Central Pacific land grant was doubled. At the same time a charter was issued for a northern line to the Pacific.

The Northern Pacific was the brainchild of Josiah Perham, the most improbable of railroad promoters. Perham was a Yankee eccentric who, after making and losing a fortune in the wool trade, created the Seven Mile Mirror—an enormous panorama of the Great Lakes and Niagara Falls mounted on rollers. This huge scroll was set on a stage and unrolled before audiences. The moving picture proved so popular that Perham organized railroad excursions to bring customers to Boston. Finding that he made more money from the train tickets than from the theater, he built his own railroad, financing a New England short-line by selling tickets to the end of the track, where he staged a show or held a picnic. With the proceeds he laid more track.

The success of the little short-line gave Perham a great idea. He proposed to lay track from Portland, Maine, to San Francisco, construction to be financed through the sale of one million bonds for one hundred dollars apiece, ten dollars down and a year to pay, with no person allowed more than one bond. The popularly owned railroad was to be called the People's Pacific. The State of Maine gave him a franchise, but his sale of bonds did not pay the cost of printing them. Perham asked Congress for a land grant, but Congress was bestowing its favors on the Union Pacific, which in turn was bestowing favors on congressmen.

Representative Thaddeus Stevens of Pennsylvania persuaded Perham to reorganize, give up his Maine charter, change the point of origin to Lake Superior and the destination to Puget Sound, which would reduce the opposition of the Union Pacific people, and to call the line the Northern Pacific. The bill chartering a railroad under these terms was the one that Abraham Lincoln signed July 2, 1864. It provided for a land grant, but no government subsidy for construction, no government loans, and it prohibited the Northern Pacific from mortgaging the land or the railroad prior to construction.

With such restrictions, Perham could not raise money. Congress extended the July 2, 1866, deadline for starting construction but that was not enough. Broke, bitter, and near death, Perham gave his franchise to a group of New England railroad men and financiers in return for their assuming his debts: $102,000.

John Gregory Smith succeeded as president of the Northern Pacific. A bald, bearded, big-nosed man who looked as if he should have dollar signs on his vest, Smith had no sympathy for Perham's populist notions of raising money. He went straight to Congress and asked for a construction subsidy. Congress turned him down. Smith decided that what the Northern Pacific needed was a board of directors Congress would kowtow to. He called on Thomas H. Canfield, a personable and persuasive Vermont financier, to recruit a cast of imposing personages.

Armed with a copy of the eighteen-page Northern Pacific Charter Act and a sense of mission, Canfield called one evening at the New York residence of William Butler Ogden, president of the Chicago and Northwestern, past president of the Union Pacific, the man who more than any other made Chicago the nexus of midwestern transportation.

"Long after midnight," Canfield reported, "I felt he was won for the cause." Canfield had outlined the difficulties: congressional limitations on financing, one deadline already missed and another approaching, growing uneasiness among voters about land grant giveaways, great distances and scanty population.

"And what is your excuse for asking me to place money at such a risk?" Ogden asked.

"This enterprise is one of the greatest ever undertaken in the world," I answered. "It is equal to that of the East India Company. With the prevailing sentiment of hostility to railroad grants, if this charter is allowed to lapse another year, one never will be granted. The road will open an empire now occupied by savages, and withal, it will be the great highway for the trade of China, Japan, and the East Indies across the continent. It is due to the people of this country and to this nation that you gentlemen whom Providence has placed at the heart of the great transportation interests of this country should step in at this crisis and use your influence and advance money to save this magnificent enterprise from destruction.

"I have suggested the names of twelve men, including ourselves, whom I believe to be honorable men, and whose word once given will serve every purpose. If you go in on that basis, I believe we can secure these men, if they seem to you suitable, and we can pull together until we are in a position to organize."

"It is simply a matter of honor among gentlemen?"

"Exactly," I replied.

"Well, that is certainly a high position on a high and noble purpose. I will take hold with you. The charter must be saved. Meet me at my office tomorrow and we will lay siege to the directors of the Chicago and Northwestern."

The directors capitulated immediately. Ogden and Canfield wrote out on two sheets of notepaper an Original Interests Agreement, which provided that twelve men, most of them associated with major transportation lines, would each put up $8,500 cash. Some of the $102,000 thus raised was used to finance a survey of the proposed route and land grant, the rest to influence Congress. Bills went through extending the start of construction to July 4, 1870, allowing the main line to go down the Columbia River rather than through the mountains (a move which reduced the chance that the Union Pacific might extend a branch from Salt Lake City to Portland) and granting the Northern Pacific permission to mortgage everything in sight: tracks, rolling stock, telegraph line, and land grant.

What the Northern Pacific needed next was someone to sell its authorized $100 million bond issue. The best salesman in the country, and the richest, was Jay Cooke. To be "rich as Jay Cooke" meant to be rich beyond the dreams of avarice—not that Cooke himself was beyond avarice. Starting as an orphan, he had made money even as a grocery boy. By the time he came of age, Cooke was partner in a bank; when thirty, he could boast that in doing business with the secretary of the treasury "we victimized him again;" at forty, he opened what was for a time the largest banking house in America; at fifty, he invented the modern war bond drive to finance the Civil War (complete with instructions that at public sales there must be a soldier fresh from the front, wounded if possible but, if not, bandaged). By the end of the war he was the nation's symbol of financial success.

Asked by the Northern Pacific to market its paper, Cooke slowly thought it over. He sent his own men west to study the land. His engineer predicted construction costs of $85,277,000, which was lower than the NP estimate. His trusted aide, Samuel Wilkeson, described the Far Northwest as "a vast wilderness waiting like a rich heiress to be appropriated and enjoyed." Cooke's own calculation was that he could make $57 million. His partners did not share his vision. They urged, "Let us follow the legitimate banking business." But Cooke said yes. His terms were that he receive a 12 percent commission on every bond sold, plus $200 in stock for every $1,000 in bond sales. He was to receive an equal share in the Original Interest Agreement and in any companies organized to develop townsites. Dazzled by his fame, the board accepted ruinous terms. It proved a hell of a way to finance a railroad.

Cooke began brilliantly. He raised $5,600,000 in thirty days from a pool of Philadelphia financiers to get things going, his fee a mere $1,200,000. He had hoped to dispose of half the bonds to European investors, but the Franco-Prussian War disturbed the market and he turned to the home folks. Sam Wilkeson orchestrated a campaign to make the Northern Pacific sound like a freight from the mint. Newspapers were flooded with stories quoting members of Congress, governors of states, the vice president of the United States on the wonders of the land grant and the security of railroad investment. Wilkeson even put together a circular composed of the arguments made by congressmen who opposed the Northern Pacific land grant because of the fertility of the land and the value of the millions of acres bestowed on the railroad. Selling the Dakotas and Montana as a subtropic paradise was one of the great publicity coups in the history of American merchandising. General William T. Sherman, who had been stationed in the Dakotas and knew the temperature range, issued a statement warning that the grant included land "as bad as God ever made or anybody can scare up this side of Africa. Wilkeson calmly replied that nothing in the record indicated General Sherman had ever been in Africa.

Sophisticates might joke about Jay Cooke's Banana Belt, but the everyday folk who got their information from the papers thought of Cooke as the God-fearing deacon whose genius had helped save the Union and who knew a money-making proposition when he saw one. They dug into the cookie jars and the mattress ticking and bought the Northern Pacific securities—$30 million worth in two years.

On February 15, 1870, a party of undistinguished officials gathered in an unprepossessing open space in the forest twenty-three miles west of Duluth, Minnesota, to break the frozen dirt with pick and spade, then retire to the nearest stove to thaw out. Officially, construction of the Northern Pacific had begun, though no serious work was done until July.

Surveying also started for the spur that was to run from the Columbia River to Puget Sound. There was little doubt the tracks would follow the route of the Indians and the fur traders—up the Cowlitz and across the Chehalis plain—but the point of departure from the Columbia was a problem, and the terminus on Puget Sound remained a mystery for three more years.

John W. Sprague, an engineer and Civil War general, was sent west to select the construction base on the Columbia. He chose a narrow belt of land between the river and the rocky foothills, six miles upstream from the Cowlitz. Ezra Meeker had built a cabin nearby in 1853 but soon moved to Puget Sound, and the land was vacant. It lay downstream from the farthest point of freezing on the Columbia, was less subject to floods than the Monticello plain at the mouth of the Cowlitz, and offered sufficient space for marshaling equipment, supplies, and men for the construction effort. Sprague called it Kalama—"pretty maiden," the Indian name for a lovely stream nearby.

The contract to lay the first twenty-five miles of track, which would carry the line three miles beyond the Toutle River, was won by James Boyce Montgomery of Pennsylvania. He was a thirty-eight-year-old journalist who had abandoned the city desk of a Pittsburgh newspaper in favor of contracting and high finance, and had helped Jay Cooke raise the original $5,600,000 for Northern Pacific construction.

A man of dedicated opinion, Montgomery had a wife, Mary, even more positive. When President Grant offered Montgomery the governorship of Washington Territory, Mary let her husband know that

acceptance meant instant bachelorhood. Her father had been governor of Missouri and she would endure no more politicians. But she
was not against living in the West. When Montgomery won the
railroad contract, she accompanied him and brought considerable
style to the Washington backwoods. The Montgomerys lived beside
the right-of-way in a forty-by-twenty-five-foot tent, with a second
tent of similar size for their three children and their nurse, while a
shake wannigan served as kitchen and quarters for the Chinese cook.

Montgomery imported 750 Chinese laborers, hired from San Francisco contractors who had supplied coolie gangs for the Central Pacific. With 250 whites, they moved a million yards of rock and earth,
built bridges over the Kalama, the Cowemans, the Ostrander, and
the Toutle rivers, and had the twenty-five miles spiked down before
the deadline of July 1871. Montgomery was assigned an additional
ten miles; another contractor, J. L. Hallet, extended the road as far
as Tenino, and in 1872 Montgomery undertook to run it on to salt
water. This contract was announced as covering a hundred miles,
which would have carried the line well beyond Everett, but there was
a secret clause permitting the Northern Pacific to end construction
after forty miles, without penalty. The NP was waging psychological
warfare to keep localities on the Sound bidding against each other
for the terminus, thus holding down the cost of land acquisition.

The Northern Pacific still did not know where it was going to put
its terminus on the Sound. There had been several studies, each of
which started a hundred rumors and raised ten thousand hopes. In
the towns and hamlets fronting the Sound, on lonely farms set
among the high stumps of waterfront land stripped by roving
loggers, even on islands separated from the mainland by channels yet
unbridged, optimistic settlers waited in hope that hardened into belief for the announcement that Jay Cooke was headed for their very
doorstep bearing tidings of increased property value. Pessimists were
those who thought the terminus might be a mile away.

The first report on possible sites for the Puget Sound terminus was
made in 1870 by Thomas Canfield, who had been with the survey
party sent out by Cooke two years earlier. He had been struck by the
fact that everyone assumed the terminus would be on the east side of
the Sound, close to the mountain passes, and that speculators were
gathering land. A site on the west side might be cheaper to acquire.
While on an inspection cruise around the Sound on the steamer
W. G. Hunt, Canfield met the alcoholic but impressive James G.
Swan and hired him at $150 a month to gather information useful to
the Northern Pacific.

Swan was a handsome, white-bearded New Englander who was
not only the Port Townsend town drunk but also a correspondent for

the Smithsonian Institution, judge, journalist, runaway husband and father, secretary of the Puget Sound Pilots' Commission, territorial fisheries commissioner, collector of primitive art, oyster rancher, school teacher, notary public, consul for Hawaii, deputy sheriff, and speculator. He spent four months looking at possible sites and in the end recommended that it be at Port Townsend, where he owned considerable property. His report to Canfield was a masterpiece of balanced denigration of rival ports. To Olympia he conceded "many advantages," especially proximity to Portland, but he pointed out that the waterfront was a mudflat and the shoreline owned by the early settlers. Nisqually was a bog, Steilacoom unprotected against prevailing winds, and Commencement Bay "not a good harbor . . . the great depth of water rendering anchorage inconvenient and almost impractical." Seattle was already too populous and needed a canal connecting the Sound with Lake Washington. Whidbey was an island, Bellingham Bay difficult to enter. That left Port Townsend. Canfield incorporated much of Swan's work in his report, but the directors were not persuaded that west was best.

Olympia in the summer of 1871 was ebullient when surveyors for the Northern Pacific planted a stake at the head of Budd Inlet and began checking grades. Agents thought to be working for the railroad started collecting signatures of Olympians who would agree to covenant certain real estate to the railroad should the route connect the capital with the Columbia. But similar tactics for assembling property to be offered as inducement were being employed by boomers in Seattle and Steilacoom. In Tacoma, General McCarver continued to pick up acreage and options, including the Judson claim and the Delin-Galliher mill property. The rivalry amused the editor of the Kalama *Beacon*. "We take it for granted that the promoters of this great enterprise know as well where they will stop laying their rails as where they began," he editorialized in November of 1871. "Thousands of air castles have been built, and paper cities are multiplying in every direction along the bayous of the Sound Country. Jay Cooke knows, but none of you would lisp it if you were Jay Cooke."

But Cooke did not know, and the myth of Cooke's omniscience was about to be exploded. Cooke did not even know where the next few millions could be found. Costs of construction were far above expectation. Cooke had decided to buy out the Oregon Steam Navigation company to obtain right-of-way down the Columbia, and its cost was high and immediate. A recession was drying up investment capital. Revelation of the Credit Mobilier fraud in connection with the construction of the Union Pacific was eroding enthusiasm for railroad projects. Bond sales fell to a trickle.

With construction costs totaling $5.5 million more than money available, Cooke badgered President Smith to stop acting as if the bond sale money were "the Biblical widow's cruse of oil which would never run dry." Smith replied that to stop spending would further undermine public confidence. Cooke ordered him to "put on the brakes and handle each dollar carefully before laying it out." Smith demurred. Cooke forced him to resign.

George W. Cass, another of the Civil War generals so active in railroading, became the Northern Pacific's third president in October 1872, while on an inspection tour of Puget Sound with Engineer Roberts, Board Secretary Wilkeson, and Directors Ogden, Window, and Wright. They narrowed the contending sites to Mukilteo, Seattle, and Tacoma, with Steilacoom the last to be eliminated and Port Townsend never seriously in the running.

In 1873, as James Montgomery's construction crews pushed track northward past indignant Olympia and across the Nisqually plain, the financial vise tightened on Cooke. He had "loaned" money to influential politicians, including Vice President Colfax and Senator James Blaine, in hopes of getting Congress to double the Northern Pacific land grant, but a congressional committee was studying the Credit Mobilier scandal, the attorney general was threatening legal action, and politicians were panicky and unpliant. Cooke directed his brother to tell the attorney general that the investigations were bad for business: "No man of sense would buy a railroad bond or anything else in this country if such legal proceedings are to be permitted under the sanction of the highest officer of the government." But even the most biddable of cabinet members hesitated to seem helpful to a railroad financier. The Philadelphia *Ledger,* controlled by the rival banking house of Drexel and Morgan, attacked the Northern Pacific as a financial monstrosity and the proposed doubling of the land grant as a looting of the public domain for the sole purpose of saving Cooke's private empire. Bond sales all but stopped.

One possible source of new revenue was the sale of land around the terminus. The Northern Pacific board assigned Judge R. D. Rice, a vice president of the line, and Captain J. C. Ainsworth, its managing director on the West Coast, to make the final recommendation. Late in June, after visits to Tacoma, Seattle, and Mukilteo and conferences with the promoters in each place, Rice and Ainsworth holed up in Steilacoom's clapboard Hotel de Rhinehart to decide, they thought, the future metropolis of the Pacific Northwest.

Mukilteo, up beyond Seattle, might well be the best site, especially since it had much undeveloped land, but it was also the most distant. Miles cost money. Goodbye Mukilteo.

Seattle could make available twenty-five hundred acres and 450 lots within the city, sixty-five hundred acres nearby, forty-eight hundred feet of frontage on navigable water, plus a cash bonus of sixty thousand dollars raised by business interests to offset the higher costs of locating in a developed community.

In Tacoma, McCarver's group had purchased twelve hundred acres it would sell at cost to the railroad, another fifteen hundred acres was available under option, and Hanson would sell the mill and its sixty acres of waterfront for one hundred thousand dollars in gold. That meant a solid body of twenty-seven hundred acres with an unbroken waterfront of more than two miles and riparian rights on another six hundred acres of tideflats. Available to the south toward Nisqually were ten thousand acres of highland including several small lakes and natural parks.

On June 30 the site commissioners wired in code to President Cass reviewing the options and concluding that they "unhesitatingly decide in favor of Tacoma." Cass wired back that the executive board agreed. That left the decision to the full board. While it deliberated in New York, a delegation from Seattle arrived in Steilacoom on a chartered steamer with a last desperate offer. Julius Dickens, the editor of the Steilacoom *Express,* reported mockingly that "the big men from Seattle marched in double file, arm in arm, to the hotel to meet the locating commissioners, their lofty beavers glistening in the noontime sun like an African's phiz in a field of cane. They came, they saw, and—that was all; for the heads of the locating commissioners were too well balanced to lose their equilibrium on meeting this august delegation of great men from the town of sawdust and fleas."

On July 14, Rice and Ainsworth sent identical telegrams from Kalama to Arthur A. Denny of Seattle and Morton Matthew McCarver of Tacoma: WE HAVE LOCATED THE TERMINUS AT COMMENCEMENT BAY. The operator decoding the dots and dashes at Steilacoom was Anthony Carr. He carried the word down the road he and Howard had cleared to the settlement their father had started at the "sheltered place."

The celebration was still escalating when the fine print of the decision arrived by mail. The terminus was not to be west of the Hanson mill on the property McCarver had purchased from Job Carr. It would be three miles to the east on the shelf below the Judson-Delin sites—land McCarver had expected to be in the suburbs. Again the old boomer had been almost right.

Money was running out; time, too. The question was whether the spur could be completed before December 19, the deadline set in the charter. Failure could risk forfeiture of the land grant.

Hazard Stevens, the son of the first governor, was in charge of land acquisition for the right-of-way. Two routes were available for bringing the line into town, one with a gentle grade that would run eastward to the Puyallup and follow the river into town, or a shorter one with a steeper grade that would come through today's South Tacoma and Nalley Valley. They chose the shorter to save time.

Contractor Montgomery speeded the pace of construction. His Chinese crews graded fourteen miles in eighteen days. But the white workers, who did the spiking, grew restive when payroll money failed to arrive. One evening in July, Montgomery told his wife there would be trouble if he did not get sixty thousand dollars in cash from Portland to pay the men on Sunday; she was the only person he could trust to bring it.

Mary Montgomery left Friday morning on horseback, rode ten miles to the railhead, sat beside the engineer in the locomotive on the construction train to Toutle River, where she caught the passenger train to Kalama, then transferred to a steamer bound from Astoria to Portland. Arriving at six in the evening, she went to the home of James Steel, cashier for the First National Bank of Portland, explained her problem, and gave him her husband's check. Saturday morning he met her at the Stark Street landing on the Willamette with the money sacks. The steamer for Astoria had just cast off. The captain shouted down to her to take the Dalles boat and transfer to his ship at the mouth of the Willamette. The steamers were brought alongside and she walked a gangplank between them, followed by two men with the gold. After "a delightful ride in the pilot house" to Kalama, she took the train back to the end of the line, where an escort waited with two horses, one for her, one for the money. She reached camp about nine o'clock that night, a full moon shining overhead. The payroll was met. But there was to be no more money where that came from.

A run started on Cooke's bank, which was most vulnerable. At a quarter past noon on September 18, 1873, Jay Cooke and Company of Philadelphia locked its doors on its depositors. The bubble of railroad expansion had burst. Later that day thirty-seven banks and brokerage houses in New York City shut down. The board of governors halted trading on the New York Stock Exchange. The next day the First National Bank of Washington (D.C.) failed. President Grant called the nation's financial leaders to a conference, but the best advice he got was from Commodore Vanderbilt and it came too late, "Building railroads from nowhere to nowhere is not a legitimate business."

The panic spread. Across the country depositors raced each other to the tellers' cages. It mattered not whether the banks were firm or shaky. The nation's money was ebbing back to the cookie jar, the mattress ticking, and the kettle in the back yard. Mills shut down, lumber camps closed, merchants failed to pay manufacturers, and manufacturers failed to pay suppliers. In the closing months of 1873 five thousand businesses failed. Work stopped on the Northern Pacific main line at Bismarck, North Dakota, not to be resumed for years.

Construction continued on the Kalama to Tacoma spur in the hope of preserving the land grant and of raising money through the sale of city lots in the terminus. No money came from back east. Montgomery advanced $133,000 against his own credit to meet construction costs; creditors attached all his property in Pierce and Thurston counties. Montgomery gave up and was replaced as prime contractor by E. S. "Skookum" Smith, a handyman engineer from New York, who would try his hand at anything: sawmills, coal mining, steamships, politics, even building a railroad without cash.

Smith was a hard-driving man, but when a payday was skipped his crews refused to be driven at all. The construction camp—"Skookumville"—was at Clover Creek. Many of the workers were down-on-their-luck prospectors, working to get a grubstake; they felt they had been cheated by geology and damned if they would be cheated by a corporation. About fifty men put down their sledges and picked up guns. They built a barricade of crossties on the tracks and announced there would be neither work nor traffic until they saw cash on the table.

A construction train came up from the south. The workers captured it and took the engineer as hostage. He was Nickolas Lawson, a Swede, built something like a locomotive himself. Lawson persuaded the strikers to let him carry their demands back down the line. The next day the locomotive chugged back to Skookumville pulling a passenger car loaded with authority: the governor, the chief justice of the territorial supreme court, and J. C. Ainsworth, West Coast manager of the Northern Pacific. Ainsworth was able to talk the strikers into accepting a mixed payment of cash, IOU's, and brass and iron tokens good in trade at the Hanson mill company store. Work resumed.

In November the tracks ran past Gravelly Lake and Steilacoom Lake, down the draw into New Tacoma. The townsfolk gathered to cheer as the first saddle-tank construction "lokey," pushing a kitchen and dormitory car, huffed and clanked through town, sparks from the bolts of fir in the firebox spewing handsomely from the stack, Engineer Ed McCall at the controls and whistle. On the clay cut below the downtown Tacoma bluff, the track gave way and the train rolled over. No one was seriously hurt. A few days later, Nick Lawson brought in a train with real live passengers, William and Alice Blackwell, who had been retained by the Northern Pacific to manage the first hotel in New Tacoma.

A load of rails from England arrived by ship during the second week of December. At three in the afternoon of December 16 the last spike was driven. The citizens of Old Tacoma and New Tacoma gathered to watch the ceremony. The sledge was passed among the dignitaries. General Sprague, who had chosen Kalama, tapped the spike, as did Skookum Smith, Job Carr, and General McCarver. John Bolander, head spiker during the three years of construction, drove it home. We can only guess at the thoughts of Carr and McCarver as they helped fix New Tacoma, not their Tacoma, as terminus. By four o'clock the spike was firm, the speeches were over, and Tacoma was the western end of a transcontinental. But the track led only down to Kalama, after which there was a fifteen-hundred-mile gap in the line to Bismarck.

The Gap Is Closed

A S Jay Cooke's star slipped in the firmament of railroad finance, that of another handsome Philadelphian rose and shone brightly in the west, especially over Tacoma. Charles Barstow Wright was a big-framed, thin-mouthed man of Irish stock who in his early teens had attracted the attention of a Pennsylvania merchant by the persistence with which he huckstered eggs from his mother's henhouse. Put in charge of a trading post out west on the Ohio River when he was fifteen, Charles did well; at twenty-one he moved on to Chicago, then boasting a population of five thousand and growing fast. Within three years Wright cleared ten thousand dollars in land speculation, returned to Pennsylvania, married well, and entered his father-in-law's mercantile business in Erie. The firm prospered. Wright and his father-in-law started a bank, and Charles moved to Philadelphia to manage its office there. He became a member of the Philadelphia stock exchange and a director of the Philadelphia & Erie Railroad. When his wife died of tuberculosis in 1856 he remarried, again advantageously. His second wife's sister was married to Jay Cooke's brother.

During the Civil War, Wright made a million from the Pennsylvania oil fields. He profited not by getting oil from the ground but by getting it to market. There were no pipelines. Oil was transported in wooden barrels or in large tanks cradled on flatbed cars. Wright organized, financed, and managed the Oil Creek and Allegheny, which tapped Pennsylvania's first great field. Just before new areas began to rival Oil Creek, Wright sold his railroad at the top of the market, a feat that attracted appreciative notice from Jay Cooke. The Master invited the Apprentice to join the syndicate that was then raising the first millions to start construction on the Northern Pacific. For the rest of his life, Wright was associated with the railroad, its real estate promotions, and the faction on the board that stood to benefit most from the growth of Tacoma.

Wright was an influential member of the committee sent to Puget Sound in 1873 to choose the terminus. "I looked up at the sloping hills," he said of his first visit to Commencement Bay, "and saw how Nature had done everything except build a city, and I said to myself—Here is the place." When, a few days later, the Executive Committee of the Northern Pacific Board of Directors approved the choice, Wright and a Pottsville financier named Charlemagne Tower (the very name smacks of land development) were delegated "to lay out and own Terminal City."

Laying out cities in the 1870s was child's play. The ideal was a broad rectangle subdivided into squares. All that was required was a map and a ruler. James Tilton, who had been surveyor general of the territory back in the Isaac Stevens era, was still around. They handed him the ruler and told him to start drawing. It has been said that Tilton used as his model a plan for Sacramento that McCarver brought north after his misadventures there, or that Tacoma was patterned after Melbourne, Australia; but chances are that the old engineer needed no pony.

Tilton's sketches do not survive. An account in the *Weekly Pacific Tribune* for October 3, 1873, indicates he made a few modifications to the basic grid plan then in vogue. Three main avenues 100 feet in width paralleled the waterfront. Two others slanted diagonally up the face of the hill, a concession to the difficulties horse-drawn street-cars, not to mention pedestrians, would encounter on a direct climb. The five avenues were flanked by blocks 120 feet deep which ended in 40-foot-wide streets, too broad to degenerate into alleys but not grand enough to detract from the designated thoroughfares. In the middle of town a twenty-seven-acre knuckle of land about 1,000 feet south of the bay was left open for development as a central park or as the campus of a building complex should Tacoma become county seat or territorial capitol. Two smaller parks stood on the north and south flanks of the town.

This first dream of Tacoma failed to get off the drawing board. While Tilton was still making sketches, events and decisions back east aborted his conception. Board members expressed some dissatisfaction with Tilton's proposals for solving drainage problems on the clay-bank hill, but far more important was Jay Cooke's slide toward bankruptcy. As the sale of railroad bonds slowed, sale of land at the terminus offered the best hope of raising working capital. The Northern Pacific in August formed a subsidiary, first called the Lake Superior & Puget Sound Land Company but quickly renamed the Tacoma Land Company, which was capitalized at one million dollars and assigned to develop the terminus and sell the town lots. C. B. Wright was selected by the Northern Pacific directors to head the land company. Almost immediately President Wright began to discuss replacing Tilton with the country's best-known landscape architect, the brilliant, unorthodox, opinionated, highly controversial Frederick Law Olmsted.

A journalist turned planner-administrator, Olmsted had conceived and brought into being New York's Central Park; in 1873 he was embroiled in a widely publicized struggle with Tammany Hall to prevent its commercial exploitation. He had also designed Morningside Park in Manhattan, the Brooklyn Parkway (he coined the term *parkway*), and on commission from the Quincy Railroad he had planned for Chicago commuters the suburban community of Riverside which, as Olmsted put it, emphasized "gracefully-curved lines, generous spaces and the absence of sharp corners, the idea being to suggest and imply leisure, contemplativeness and happy tranquility."

Whether Wright and the board were concerned with prompting happy tranquility at their terminus is doubtful. Probably what attracted them was Olmsted's capacity for getting attention and his reputation for finding novel solutions to difficult problems of terrain. Whatever their reasons, the board summoned Olmsted to the New York headquarters of the Northern Pacific on September 19 (just one day after the closing of Cooke's bank) and commissioned him to make in all possible haste—six weeks—a preliminary study for the townsite.

Olmsted teamed with G. K. Radford, whom he described to Wright as "an experienced sanitary and hydraulic engineer," in creating the plan. He did not visit Tacoma but worked from contour maps and sketches. It is not clear how the two men divided the labor but it is likely that Radford concentrated on drainage problems, Olmsted on creating a town that would blend with sea, forest, and mountain. Sketches in the Olmsted Papers at the Library of Congress show his concept of a lattice-work of diagonals to climb the hill back from the bay.

The plan was delivered to the Northern Pacific on schedule in early December and reached Tacoma the week before Christmas, where it was put on display in the Tacoma Land Office. Residents who had been eagerly awaiting the metamorphosis of the clay cliff into the metropolis of their dreams studied Olmsted's vision with a bemused blend of boosterism and dismay. Thomas Prosch, who had bought the *Pacific Tribune* of Olympia from his father, Charles, and moved it to Tacoma on the strength of its prospects as terminus, reflected the ambivalence of the locals in a long but muted story that appeared on December 23.

The new plan he found "unlike that of any other city in the world," and "so novel in character that those who have seen it hardly know whether or not to admire it, while they are far from prepared to condemn it." He outlined the main features:

The ground laid off is on the southern shore of Commencement Bay 1000 acres in extent, and reaching from the Galliher mill pond two and a half miles down the bay to the Tacoma mill pond. A portion of the mud flat is also laid off, for future use. The most peculiar features are the varying sizes and shapes of the blocks, and the absence of straight lines and right angles. Every block and every street and avenue is curved. The lots have a uniform frontage of 25 feet, but differ in length, averaging, however, 180 feet. The curvature of the blocks does away with corner lots, and their great length with much of the misery of street crossings, where collisions and accidents always happen, and where mud and dust are invariably the deepest. . . .

The three grand avenues are Pacific, Tacoma and Cliff. Pacific leads up the banks, from the rail road dock, and out into the country; Tacoma is about a mile only in length, intersecting up in town with Pacific Avenue and running down to the beach between the old and new towns; Cliff Avenue extends along the brow of the bluff, two miles or more in length. . . . The first is intended for the business of the town, and for country trade and driving; the second takes one past the principal parks; and the third will be magnificent for residences, promenading and driving, as it will be high and sightly, with nothing between it and the water. . . . There are seven parks laid out, consuming about 100 acres of ground, and varying from two to thirty acres each in extent.

Young Prosch felt that time alone would prove the plan's practicality but added, hesitantly, "Certainly, if a large city is ever built here, after that plan, it will be through and through like a park, and have very many important advantages over other cities."

In rival Portland, the *Bulletin* discussed the Olmsted plan with irony. Conceding the originality of the great planner's concept, the paper commented that since "Tacoma is already set upon a hill, or two hills for that matter, it would be ridiculous for such a city to copy after unpretending places like Chicago or San Francisco. Tacoma resolves to have an individuality and to assert it. . . . The curve is the favorite geometrical line at Tacoma. It is supposed to be borrowed from the magnificent movements of the celestial spheres, or other great operations of nature; and with these movements Tacoma is determined to be in harmony. . . . Tacoma, with her new

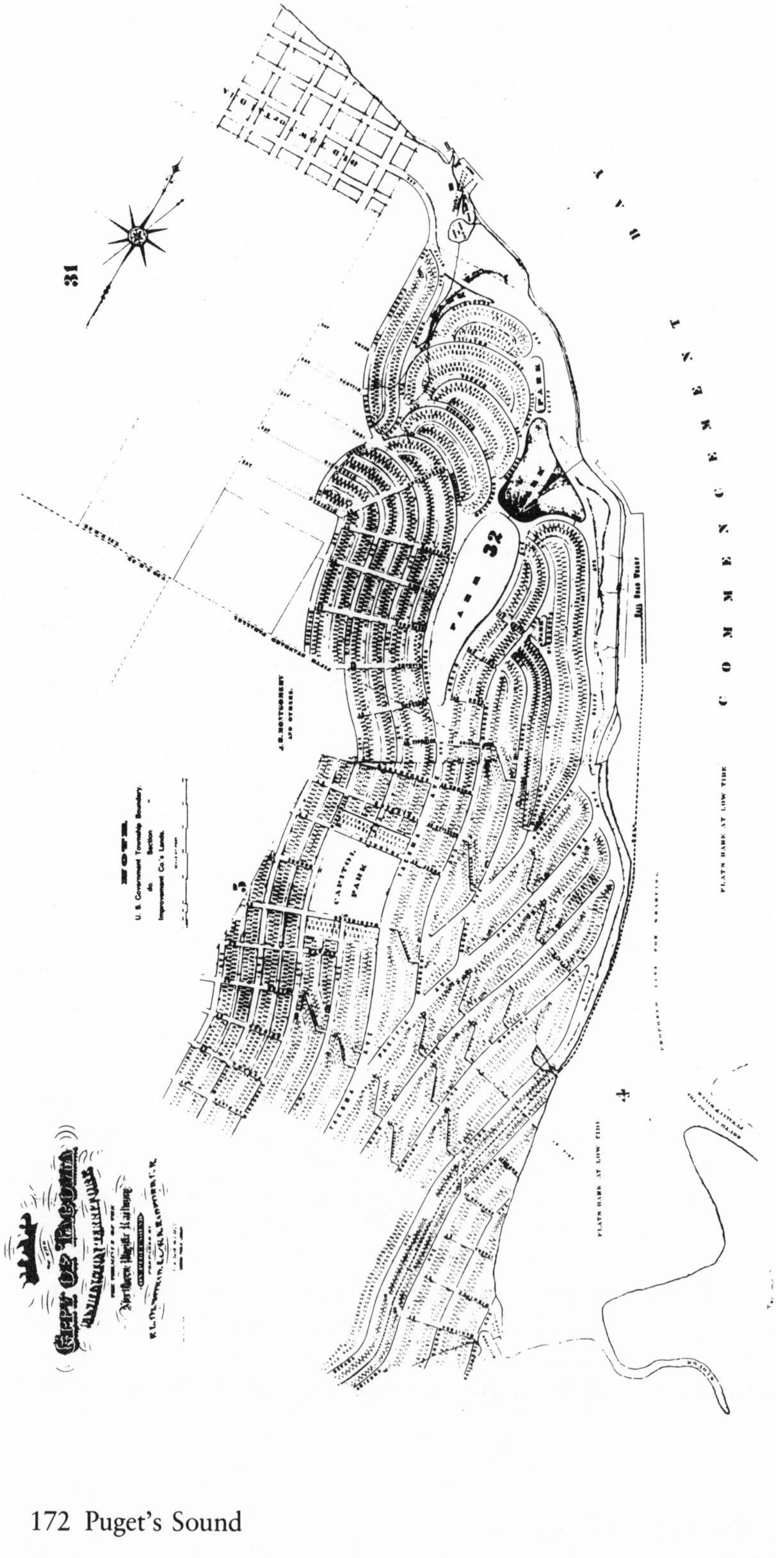

The Olmsted plan Courtesy of Photo. Coll., UW Library

plat, must be almost as perfect as anything can be in this ill-favored world."

Tacomans were not amused. Neither were they enthusiastic. Prosch, in a follow-up story on the plan, concentrated on the assumed wisdom of the managers of the Pacific Division of the Northern Pacific ("Save for unscrupulous, mendacious, hireling editors and their abettors, none have any fault to find with their course") rather than on the plan itself. He allowed that the Olmsted concept was approved by "many men of ripe judgment and unquestioned taste; in their view it will make a beautiful city and is in every respect adapted to the character of the ground." His own opinion he kept to himself.

Even among the scrupulous, the nonmendacious, the unhired, and the nonjournalistic there were to be found sceptics who questioned the incarnate wisdom of the Pacific Division managers, the genius of Olmsted, and the merits of a nonangular street plan. Speculators who wanted to buy corner lots saw no merit in a downtown deliberately left deficient in four-way intersections; Olmsted's dream of a business district without bottlenecks was to them a nightmare. Nor were the engineering crews assigned to run lines amid the downtown stumpage to locate Pacific, Cliff, and Tacoma avenues persuaded by Olmsted's dictum that "speed of traffic is of less importance than comfort and convenience of movement." Early settlers who had seen others profit from the rise of four-square business districts grumbled that the plan for their town resembled "a basket of melons, peas and sweet potatoes." They said that in the street patterns one could find "representations of everything that has ever been exhibited in an agricultural show, from calabashes to iceboxes."

In prosperous times the Olmsted plan might have survived, even benefited from, the controversy and ridicule. Had the Northern Pacific board had the confidence to wait out discontent, the materialized dream might well have answered the doubters. One has only to look at the plan and imagine the parklike city that could have been on the lovely curve of Tacoma's harbor to grieve that the vision was not made manifest. But Jay Cooke's bank had failed, the panic was deepening into depression, the railroad was desperate for capital. With confidence shattered and money short, there was no rush to invest in the western terminus of an ailing and incomplete railroad. The NP bailed out. Late in January, only forty-three days after he had submitted the plan, Olmsted was notified that his ideas would not be used and his services were no longer required. The letter of dismissal, and Olmsted's reply, have never been located. Olmsted never mentioned the rejection publicly.

Theodore Hosmer, Charles Wright's brother-in-law, had been sent west to manage the Tacoma Land Company affairs on site. He was a

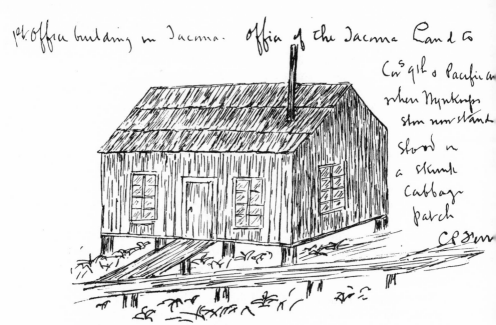

First office of the Tacoma Land Company

man of considerable presence, broad-bodied, thin-haired, with an un-ruly Vandyke. His first office was a shack set on piling over a skunk cabbage patch. To it he called William Isaac Smith, a Virginia Military Institute graduate in engineering whose specialty was light-houses, and assigned him to unscramble the omelette Olmsted and the board had left. And do it fast. They had to start selling lots.

Smith went back to the grid system, eliminating such few frills as Tilton's earlier plan had possessed. His barracks-simple design for Tacoma had the merit of being so conventional that line crews hardly needed specifications. Full speed ahead and damn the topography.

In the rain and slush they graded a road eighty feet wide from the terminal dock to the top of the cliff and on southward. They called it Pacific Avenue. It was an unpaved bog but the citizenry, including the new town's two unmarried girls, turned out to pile brush and slash and help burn out the worst stumps. George Fairhurst, who had been allowed to buy a lot early for a hotel, the California, be-tween Seventh and Eighth added a touch of cosmopolitan refinement to the avenue by laying a board sidewalk in front of his property—a narrow, fifty-foot raft in the sea of mud.

On April 15, 1874, the Tacoma Land Company officially put the downtown section on sale, with fifty-foot lots on Pacific Avenue going for $200, corner lots for $250. The land company headquar-ters, a new frame building at today's Ninth and Broadway, hardly did a land office business. Lots with right angles proved no more salable than Olmsted's curves. Two men bought a lot for a livery stable at Ninth and Pacific, with a public hall on the second floor. Charles Wright bought one of the corner lots and ordered construction of a brick building, real brick—the town's first. Others bought lots on which to build residences. But sales were slow, and in single lots, not city blocks.

Selection as terminus had not proved a shortcut to civic greatness, but the coming of rails meant the end of semi-isolation for the south Sound settlers. Until the line was completed between Tacoma and the Columbia, a trip outside the territory, even to Oregon, meant either the long and sometimes dangerous voyage around the Olympic Peninsula, across the dreaded Columbia bar, and up the river, or a combined steamer, stagecoach, and (sometimes) canoe trip, requiring more than two days at best.

The traveler would run up the Sound in the cranky old *Eliza Anderson* or some lesser steamer. Arriving at Olympia in the evening, he would hope to find lodging at the Washington Hotel, the capital's finest, with an indoor toilet on each floor. If the legislature were not in session he might get a room to himself.

One commuter said that when southbound he always went to sleep in Olympia "in a similar frame of mind as if I were going to be hanged the next morning for horse stealing. Whatever the season, I knew the next day's experience would be disagreeable. In summer the woods might well be on fire. If there was wind, we would be required to help chop up fir trees that had fallen across the road. In winter the ground was covered with mud, and it was a rule of the road that all men had to get out and walk up and down steep hills. As far as the driver was concerned all hills were steep if it was raining, as it usually was."

At four A.M. the driver of a broad-wheeled mud-wagon, known in Olympia as the crazy cart, started through town rounding up the passengers and taking them to the town's stagecoach office. They paid fifteen dollars for the privilege of riding (and walking) the ninety miles to Monticello on the Columbia. In the stage they sat three to a seat. Passengers coveted the center seats in winter for warmth, the window seats in summer for fresh air though it might be mixed with dust or the sweet, sharp scent of burning forest. With the stagecoach driver cracking his whip and blistering the horses with language that drew the pained attention of the town council, the coach lurched off into the pre-dawn gloom. Within a mile it stopped at the first hill.

The men disembarked to trudge up to the plain. In winter several hours passed before there was enough light to reveal the stumps in the roadbed.

Around eight o'clock the stage reached Hogdon's, where there were fresh horses and a hot breakfast of good farmers' fare. Another four hours, broken by a pause at Tilley's to gather and drop mail, brought them to Buchanan's Half-Way House, forty miles from Olympia. The road grew worse. Long after dark, after sixteen to eighteen jolting hours, they came to Pumphrey's in the Olequa Valley for supper and half a night's lodging. It was a memorable experience. Beef was plentiful and cheap, much of it deriving from stock poached from the former Hudson's Bay Company herd at Cowlitz Farms. Squire Pumphrey delighted in carving thick slabs from the roasts, serving each slice onto a guest's plate with a broad-bladed knife which he licked clean and wiped on his shirt between arm and chest after each cut.

In the small hours of the second morning, big Pumphrey pounded on the doors of his lodgers, summoning them to breakfast and the ride to Jackson's or down the river in an Indian canoe. If overland, there was the discomfort of the worst stretch of road on the trip, but the relief of a warm lunch at the Jackson ranch. Taking the canoe meant, as one passenger put it, that "men, women and children were permitted to double themselves up like jack-knives and sit squat in a cedar dugout while two half-naked, smoke-begrimed, salmon-tainted siwashes, one at the bow, the other at the stern, paddled them from Drew's landing down the turbulent Skookum Chuck to the Cowlitz, then through the hundred and one meanderings of that mazy stream to the post town of Monticello."

At the juncture of the Columbia and the Cowlitz a steamer might be waiting. Or it might have taken on a tow of logs or a barge load of wheat and be hours late. In such cases the women and children made the best of it at Huntington's Hotel, while the men adjourned to a saloon. Once aboard the little paddle-wheel steamers they thrashed up the Columbia at a breakneck five knots. By nightfall of the third day after leaving Seattle or Tacoma they were at the Oregon Steam Navigation Company wharf in Portland, where hotel runners and hackmen cried the virtues of such hostelries as Arrigoni's, Dennison House, or the Western, and the streets had lights.

To be able to make the trip in ten hours in a gas-lit parlor car pulled by one of the big Baldwin or Pittsburgh engines seemed nearly as miraculous to the passengers as to the Indians who came to the track, especially at night, to watch the *hiu chick chick* rattle past, hissing steam and trailing sparks. The locomotives burned four to five cords on the run between the Sound and the river; they had to stop twice to stock the tender. The firemen prided themselves on the speed and skill with which they stacked the firebox with two-foot bolts of fir. They boasted of wearing out a pair of leather gloves on each trip.

It was claimed the lokeys could reach speeds of sixty miles an hour, but nobody wanted to be aboard if they tried. The roadbed was uncertain. Since there were no sidings cars had to be left standing on the main line to be picked up on the way back. Locomotives arrived at the ends of the line with cars fore and aft. The engineer needed sharp eyes and a good memory if he was not to encounter a car unexpectedly in the drifting fogs of western Washington.

The first passengers to make the trip to Tacoma from the Columbia were William and Alice Blackwell in the middle of November 1873. They traveled deadhead on a company pass. A Civil War veteran who had been shot through a lung at Antietam, Blackwell was serving as chief clerk at the Sherman House in Chicago when he decided to go west in search of a milder climate. After running a hotel in Portland, he managed the Kazano House at Kalama, one of the most difficult jobs in the hotel business: the Northern Pacific, which controlled the town, prohibited the sale of liquor. Patrons with a thirst had to go by rowboat to scows anchored beyond the city limits in the Columbia. Even so, nobody blamed Blackwell. He was elected mayor of Kalama, unanimously, and when the NP was ready to open a hotel at the terminus the company hired Blackwell to run it.

The hotel was at the end of the wharf at Half Moon Bay, beside the last two hundred feet of track. But the track was not completed when Will and Alice reached town. They were rowed out to the dock by two Chinese. The building wasn't completed either, being only a partially roofed two-story shed containing neither food nor furniture. Four men managed to bring out a bed and mattress in a rowboat, and the operator of a pile driver invited the newcomers to dinner on his scow. But by Thanksgiving Alice Blackwell was able to have the pile-driving crew in for a turkey dinner, and on New Year's Day the hotel was opened to the public.

The Blackwell was soon beloved. Alice supervised the cuisine, which was rich in local fare. There were clams dug by the Indians, salmon caught by commercial seiners and sometimes by guests fishing from the wharf or rowboats, it being not uncommon for the steamer to wait off-shore if a fish was being played near the landing. After all, it might be at the captain's table that night. Everyone joined in raking smelt when the run was on. There was nearly as much venison as beef. Once Blackwell shot a deer from the verandah and it tumbled off the Stadium Way bluff almost to the edge of the wharf.

Alice planted New Tacoma's first garden on the dock, using boxes forty feet long, six feet wide, and one foot deep, filled with rich leaf mold brought her by railroad workers. A partisan correspondent for the Portland *Oregonian* complained, perhaps facetiously, that his trip to Tacoma was "interrupted by our train striking a cow, by a band of Nisquallies beseeching us to buy clams, and by the engineer dismounting to dig dirt for the hotel dining room."

Mrs. Blackwell said she could grow in her boxes "about everything one ordinarily has in a small garden. Added to this, I had long boxes eighteen inches deep on a porch which extended the width of the building. I also had 200 boxes made and painted which held my tender plants that I took in the house during the winter. We had water piped into the building from a spring. My garden thrived and grew finely for when I was tired at night after a long day's work, I rested by working the soil and watering the plants and flowers."

Alice supplied flowers for the first funeral in the new town, that of a sailor who drowned in the bay. His name was not known. The nasturtiums and geraniums supplied the only softening touch at the burial.

Jacob Mann presided at the Blackwell bar. Though he was under orders not to serve more than two drinks a night to any railroad worker and to declare anyone who became the worse for alcoholic wear "an honorary Indian" and thus ineligible to buy more liquor, Mann managed denials with such tact that he was later elected mayor. The decorum in the Blackwell bar was such that when a county commissioner berated the barkeep for refusing him more refreshment, Blackwell ordered him ashore and promised that should he reappear, even sober, he would be shot.

The Blackwell became a great favorite with honeymooners, some of whom had availed themselves of the right of shipmasters to perform marriages at sea. At one wedding celebration, Will was asked to provide champagne. The only bubbly that he had, when uncorked, provided neither pop nor foam. Blackwell was despondent, but his Chinese cook said, "I fix him." Taking another bottle, the cook plunged it in hot water. Thus activated, the bottle produced the traditional sound effects and sent a spurt of lively but warm wine against the ceiling. That evening the waiters brought in the champagne in wicker baskets instead of iced buckets. Anyone who protested was assured that bubbly at the near boil was all the rage in San Francisco. Alice and Will had the town's largest collection of books, and such was their reputation for culture that their word was accepted. For some time hot champagne was the fashion on the southern Sound.

Though she arrived in November, it was March before Alice

Blackwell made it back to the top of the hill where the new town was being laid out. "We were practically three communities at this time," she recalled later. "There were Old Tacoma, Wharf and New Tacoma, or 'on the hill,' as we said, meaning Pacific Avenue from where the city hall was built to about Twelfth Street; A Street from Eighth to the same distance, a few scattered shanty houses a little farther up. There was much feeling between the Tacomas about the name. We would call the old part 'Old,' while we wanted to be called 'Tacoma' (they insisting we were not Tacoma proper and called us 'New'). All business was at the wharf—the railroad and express offices, telegraph, two small stores, and later a printing office."

Old Tacoma's sense of having been betrayed and New Tacoma's sense of being threatened were slow to die. Only a few men like Will Blackwell and Job Carr would remain popular in both. For the old remained rival to the new.

After the Tacoma Land Company put its lots on sale in April, 125 residents of Old Town filed a petition for incorporation as Tacoma City. On May 21, the county commissioners granted their request. Five trustees (councilmen) were elected in June. They in turn chose Job Carr as president. Thus the first settler became, de facto, the first mayor.

The Tacoma City trustees immediately made official protest to Congress and the postmaster general over a proposal to transfer the post office, which had begun service in Job Carr's log cabin, to New Tacoma. They made their point. Tacoma City remained a separate entity with the postal authorities for thirteen more years.

The Tacoma Land Company fought back. When it was proposed that a road be built along the beach to link Hanson's mill with the Northern Pacific wharf and New Tacoma, the company sent its attorney, Frank Clark (the former defender of Leschi), to demand damages. A board of inquiry set the value of company property to be used for the road at forty thousand dollars, and the project was abandoned. For several more years the easiest way to get between the rival towns was by rowboat. John B. Wren inaugurated a water jitney which made four round trips by rowboat daily, carrying passengers one way for two bits, freight for six bits a ton.

Growth was slow but the essentials of a pioneer community were taking shape. In 1874 two of Jay Cooke's nephews opened a bank in New Tacoma. Episcopalians put up Saint Peter's chapel on land donated by Skookum Smith and Lewis Starr in Old Town; Congregationalists raised a tent in New Town. Each community organized a school. Some entrepreneur whose name has not survived opened a dance hall of ill repute toward the head of the Old Town gully; John Pennell, Seattle's pioneer whoremonger, gave New Tacoma the benefit of his experience. There was no shortage of saloons; the saying was that the only way a saloon-keeper could find customers was to host a meeting of saloon-keepers. Each community had rival companies offering drinking water. A bipartisan baseball team, drawn from both Tacomas, played an intersquad game in August. It was called after six innings with the score 29 to 28. After studying the box-score, the team disbanded.

Old Tacoma claimed 177 eligible voters by 1875, while in New Tacoma an informal check on October 1, 1875, showed only 73 inhabitants, not counting those resident on the wharf. Each census was denounced by the community studied. In truth, there was more prejudice than precision in pioneer census taking. Not only did the count reflect the aspirations of the counter, but it was customary to overlook non-Caucasians. New Tacoma, though lusting for population, did not include some 250 Chinese, most of them former construction workers brought to the Northwest by the Northern Pacific, who lived in shacks between the tracks and the bay. Few Indians were counted, not even Indian wives of white men until they became mothers. Blacks were listed if they owned property, which few did. In the Old Tacoma school census for 1877, the superintendent acknowledged that he had failed to include nine pupils—10 percent of the study body—because they were Hawaiian.

But no matter who counted whom, five years after Tacoma was chosen as terminus, it did not boast enough warm bodies to make up a metropolis. There were more Indians on the Puyallup and Nisqually reservations than whites in Tacoma. Then work resumed on the Northern Pacific main line.

After the collapse of Jay Cooke's bank, the financial structure of the Northern Pacific lay wrecked, immobilized. The Panic gave pause to the push of population westward. Settlement between the Missouri and the Red River remained so scant that in winter the NP trains stopped at Fargo, leaving Bismarck, North Dakota, in chill solitude. Puget Sound lay behind the far beyond.

The Northern Pacific owed $33 million with assets between minus and nothing. There was talk in Congress of declaring the charter forfeit and reclaiming the land grant for the nation. Three men took the task of restructuring the company, salvaging something out of the investments, and completing the line. They were General George W. Cass, who had succeeded Smith as NP president and had been called by Cooke "the best railroad man in the country," sweet words that soured as their utterer turned from financial savior of the Union into Judas goat of the investing populace; Frederick Billings, a Vermont attorney who specialized in railroad grant litigation; and Charles Wright.

Billings worked out a scheme in which Cass resigned as president and was appointed receiver. Wright became president. The bondholders foreclosed, took over the railroad's property, and issued new stock—$49 million common, $51 million preferred. Former bondholders received stock in return for bonds, with the catch being that the new paper was worth much less than the old. The corporation was left free of bonded debt and in possession of six hundred miles of completed track, ten million acres of land grant, and a claim to thirty million more acres when the transcontinental was completed. The big losers were the small investors. The old management retained control, and Billings could claim that the company was "rid of all incumbrance and ready to raise money on good security at the dawn of good times."

Good times were years in dawning. Meanwhile company officers made investments east and west to the indirect benefit of the line and the direct benefit of themselves. General Cass and a partner bought a huge tract in the Red River Valley; its wheat production demonstrated the potential of the area, provided the NP with freight, lured settlers, and increased the value of the land grant. Charles Wright concentrated on the far end of the line.

Wright was president of both the railroad and the land company. The subsidiary was originally capitalized at $1 million, with the NP controlling 51 percent of the stock. During the period of the railroad's financial difficulties, this capitalization was increased. Using money borrowed abroad, Wright became the majority stockholder, and stood to profit most if Tacoma blossomed.

Tacomans looked on C. B. Wright as fairy godfather, and he seems to have loved the vision of Tacoma if not the reality. He continued to live back east where he had a marble mansion on Chestnut Street in Philadelphia, a fifteen-acre country estate known as Penn Hill near the Old York Road Station, and a summer cottage at Sea Girt, New Jersey, but he visited Tacoma on ceremonial occasions. His brother-in-law kept him advised on investment opportunities and things the town needed.

Wright gave the Episcopal Church land and cash for a church building in Tacoma, a boys' school, and a girls' school. He authorized the Land Company to donate the site of a courthouse when Tacoma won the county seat from Steilacoom. He approved the donation of twenty-seven acres of company property for a park (now named for him), not neglecting to draw from the town council a pledge of one thousand dollars a year in perpetuity for maintenance. (Wright Park was much appreciated by nearby homeowners who ran cattle on it until the council passed a law forbidding the grazing of anything but milch cows in Tacoma parks.) It was Wright who ordered a track laid on pilings across the mud flats, a move that helped open the area to industry. Wright organized a water and light company (which later he sold to his city at a price the courts found exorbitant) and a streetcar line. When Theodore Hosmer suggested a modest company hotel on the bluff above the city, Wright ordered instead the magnificent Tacoma Hotel, long the town's most cherished building. But Wright's most significant contribution was as advocate for construction of the Cascade Division, the proposed main line through the mountains.

For years after completion of the Kalama to Tacoma spur, no track had been laid. The railroad obviously could not meet the completion date set in the charter. Eastern Washington settlers, restive at their continued isolation, joined Seattle and Portland interests in a campaign to persuade Congress to declare the land grant forfeit—at least the portion through the Cascades. Even in the Tacoma area a considerable number of settlers were sympathetic to the idea of forfeiture, especially since the railroad was keeping off the market the lands it intended to claim under the grant when the line was completed. The possibility of forfeiture was serious.

There was more than land and timber at stake. The coal deposits that McCarver and the Carr brothers had reported in 1868 had been confirmed by professional geologists. One of the most promising fields lay at Wilkeson, almost directly east of Tacoma. Wright bought coal lands for himself and for the Northern Pacific and proposed building a line to the fields. The NP could not raise enough money to finance even that modest venture. Wright put his personal credit behind an order for a shipload of rails, plates, and spikes from England. The fact that work was underway on a line leading into the mountains was cited by NP defenders in the fight over forfeiture of the land grant. They wangled an extension of the deadline for completing the railroad.

Coal from the Wilkeson fields, where the very seams were named for NP officials—Wright, Sprague, and Atkinson—later led to the construction of enormous bunkers along the Tacoma waterfront and enabled the port to become, briefly, the leading coaling station on the Pacific Coast. Wright ordered a new survey in the Cascades for a pass that would bring rails from eastern Washington past the coal fields to Tacoma.

As economic conditions improved, it again became possible to sell railroad bonds. Wright organized the Western Railroad Company of

Minnesota, which built a line connecting with the Northern Pacific, providing an outlet to St. Paul at the head of Mississippi River navigation. Work resumed in 1878 on two sections of the main line, one running from the west bank of the Missouri to the Yellowstone, the other from Spokane Falls to the Columbia at Wallula.

After five years in office, Wright, who needed eye surgery, resigned as president of the Northern Pacific, though he remained influential on the board of directors, and retained control of the Tacoma Land Company. Frederick Billings became president of the NP—just in time to face the new threat posed by Henry Villard.

As Charles Wright was fairy godfather in the mythology of early Tacoma, Henry Villard was the villain. He symbolized the theory that rail traffic from the interior should follow the gravity course taken by rainfall and snowmelt, which would carry it through the Wallula gap and down the Columbia, past Portland, to the Pacific. Geology favored Portland over Puget Sound. The lowest proposed railroad route through the Cascades called for a climb of three thousand feet, but the Columbia emerged onto the tidal plain only seventy-five feet above the level of the Pacific. Puget Sounders argued that Portland was a river port with dockage made difficult by annual variations of thirty feet or more in the level of the Willamette; that the hundred-mile channel to the sea was shallow and shifting and climaxed by the menace of the Columbia bar. But Portlanders pointed out that not only did they have gravity going for them, but their city was older, more populous, better known. Washingtonians knew, too, that Oregon was represented in Congress by senators and representatives who could vote and trade votes while the territory sent east a mere nonvoting delegate. Portland was a threat to Tacoma's hold on the terminus, and Henry Villard was Portland incarnate.

Born in Bavaria in 1835 to a family that for six generations had been producing pastors for the Reformed Church and bureaucrats and jurists for the government, Henry at eighteen quarreled with his father, changed his name from Hilgard to Villard, and ran off to America. He could speak no English when he arrived but learned it well and quickly, becoming one of the best newspapermen of his day, distinguished not only for the accuracy of his reporting but for an extraordinary ability to get copy back to his paper from difficult areas. After the Civil War, in which he had several exclusives on major battles, Villard married the daughter of the great abolitionist editor,

William Lloyd Garrison, and in 1868 became secretary of the American Social Science Association, a position he used to promote the idea of a civil service system.

Ill health led Villard to return to Germany to rest. While recuperating he was recruited by a group of German investors who were concerned about some American bonds they had purchased. Would Villard see what could be salvaged? He would. The assignment led the thirty-eight-year-old reporter into the field of high finance, and into combat with the flamboyant Ben Holladay, a transportation tycoon Mark Twain had admiringly nicknamed "King Hurry."

Lank, ill-educated, shrewd, unscrupulous, and grasping, Holladay had parlayed a knack for barter and bluff into control of five thousand miles of western stagecoach lines. These he sold to Wells Fargo before completion of the Union Pacific took most of the profit from long-haul horsepower. Holladay invested his profits in low-price, high-risk steamships (the risk was to the passengers and crew), which he put on the run between Portland and San Francisco. He took an even longer shot on a mining claim in Nevada. The Ophir turned out to be the greatest silver producer in the Comstock Lode.

Holladay's steamship operations drew him into a fight with the well-established Oregon Steam Navigation Company. Through its control of the passages around the rapids of the Columbia, OSN dominated transportation in the Pacific Northwest. Holladay and the OSN each sought to lay rails from Portland to the Golden Gate. More was at stake than transportation: there were land grants totaling 4,300,000 acres, much of it heavily forested with enormous trees. In the course of the contest Holladay bought up a big chunk of Portland: wharves, warehouses, a streetcar system, newspapers, newspapermen, the state legislature, some judges, and at least one United States senator (John H. Mitchell) who let it be known that "whatever is Ben Holladay's politics is my politics, and whatever Ben Holladay wants, I want."

Not even the outpouring of the Ophir could pay for all this corruption and construction too. There had to be bond sales. Holladay raised more millions with a bit of Gilded Age sleight-of-hand that was considered wizardry at the time, and would be illegal today. He created something called the European and Oregon Land Company and assigned to it the land grants due his Oregon and California Railroad if and when the line was completed. As president of the land company he gave himself a contract promising payment of $1.25 an acre for the land by 1889. This contract he assigned to his bankers, the London and San Francisco Bank of San Francisco, as security for an Oregon and California Railroad Company bond issue. By 1873 more than $11 million of these bonds were in the hands of

German and English investors. The Oregon and California tracks had been laid from Portland to Roseberg, but ahead was the difficult terrain of the Umpqua Mountains. Then came the Panic of 1873, and the London and San Francisco Bank suspended payment of interest on the Holladay bonds. It was at this point that Henry Villard agreed to return to America to see what could be saved for the German investors.

Villard and Holladay met in Manhattan in April of 1874. Each was a self-made man and proud of his handiwork. Villard was solidly built, already thin-haired and graying, with dark, wide-set eyes and a down-swept mustache. He dressed somberly and was given to long silences and short questions. Holladay was loud and garrulous, a back-slapper, angular, full-bearded. His vest was a lattice-work of gold chains, his fingers a showcase for jeweled rings. He clanked when he walked.

Holladay arrived at the conference accompanied by an attorney and his pet senator; Villard, by a professor of law from Harvard. According to one account, Villard took a seat on the far side of the room from Holladay but the promoter carried his chair over, placed it beside Villard's, draped an arm over Villard's shoulder, and began spinning frontier yarns. Villard was so proper he had found himself unable to forgive even Abraham Lincoln for the barnyard humor with which he interlarded interviews. He edged his chair away. Holladay followed. In the course of the day's negotiations they made a complete circuit of the room.

"A genuine specimen of the successful Western pioneer of former days," said Villard of Holladay later. "Illiterate, coarse, pretentious, boastful, false and cunning. His reputed great wealth was fictitious and he was, on the contrary, in financial extremities. That a man of such character should have found it so easy to command millions of foreign capital was quite a puzzle and a shock."

For all his unadmirable attributes, Holladay proved no match for the urbane Villard. Within two years Villard forced King Hurry to abdicate power in Oregon. Villard took control, first on behalf of the German bondholders, subsequently on his own. He took over the Oregon and California Railroad, the Oregon Steamship Company, and the Oregon Central Railroad. He bought Holladay's wharves and warehouses and some of his Portland real estate. Then in 1879 he bought the Oregon Steam Navigation Company, which after laying tracks along the south bank of the Columbia River through the Cascades had renamed itself the Oregon Railroad and Navigation Company. The purchase consolidated his command of existing transportation in the area. Though he lived in New York, Henry Villard was now the most important man in the Pacific Northwest.

The key to Villard's power lay in his control of the gravity route through the Cascades. Only two transcontinental railroads had been chartered by Congress, the Union Pacific–Central Pacific and the Northern Pacific. He could sell out to either.

The Northern Pacific had resumed construction on its main line but the gaps were lengthy, money short. In 1881 Villard approached President Frederick Billings with an offer the NP could not resist: the right to lease the existing tracks along the Columbia at a favorable rate in return for waiving any claim to damages for the Oregon Railway and Navigation Company's operations in their chartered area and an agreement to divide the territory they would serve along the Snake and the Columbia, except for a feeder line Villard would be permitted to run into the Palouse wheat country.

The lease served the Northern Pacific's immediate needs, but it scared hell out of Tacoma. It meant that when the transcontinental was completed it would funnel traffic through the Wallula gap, down the Columbia, and past Portland. Tacoma would be isolated, at least temporarily, at the north end of the Kalama spur. With his interests in Portland and Oregon, Villard would obviously try to make the Oregon city the metropolis of the West, no matter what the NP called Tacoma.

Trepidation in Tacoma increased when Villard created the Oregon Improvement Company to handle industrial developments and assigned his cousin, Dr. E. W. Hilgard, a professor of geology at the University of California, to study Cascade coal deposits. It was an article of faith in Tacoma that the Carbonado-Wilkeson deposits on the upper Puyallup drainage system meant that Tacoma would become the great coal-loading port of Puget Sound. But Professor Hilgard reported that although the deposits near Tacoma were superior in quality, those at Newcastle in the foothills behind Seattle were more plentiful and more accessible. Tacomans scoffed, but Villard acted on his cousin's recommendation. He bought the Newcastle coal field, bought two steam colliers to carry coal from the Sound to San Francisco and Portland, and bought the old Seattle and Walla Walla railroad (which actually ended at Newcastle). He restyled it the Columbia and Puget Sound. The articles of re-incorporation spoke of extending the line through Snoqualmie Pass to Walla Walla, though this was more a warning to the Northern Pacific that Villard could compete for the mountain traffic than an actual plan to build.

Villard had the Oregon Improvement Company reorganized with power "to build, purchase, own and run steamships between Portland, Astoria, Seattle, Victoria, Sitka, San Francisco or any other port in the North Pacific, and to build, purchase and own docks, piers, warehouses, locks, ferryboats, stages and other means of transportation." Tacomans noticed the absence of specific mention of Tacoma. In every move by Villard they saw menace. The kindest word for Villard in Tacoma's thin newspapers was *villain*.

The leasing arrangement between Villard and the Northern Pacific for use of the tracks on the south side of the Columbia was a truce, not a peace. The NP retained the right under its charter to build a competing line down the north bank. Villard doubted the NP could afford such a fight and he did everything he could to make the attempt costly. He instructed an agent to buy up rights-of-way guarding the approaches to the Wallula gap: "Wherever physical conformation confines location to narrow limits, buy only as much as may be necessary to give us control; wherever the road broadens out, buy full sections and even more. . . ."

On the political front, Villard gave quiet support to moves in Congress to declare the Northern Pacific land grant forfeit. Senator Mitchell, whom Villard had taken over from Holladay along with that worthy's other investments, thought there was a reasonable chance of getting Congress to withdraw the grant for construction on the Washington side of the Columbia.

Villard's moves could be interpreted as invitations to be bought out. One of his most trusted advisers wrote him to say, "Our true policy is . . . to be in a good position to be gobbled up. The Union Pacific being much the stronger, I should prefer to cultivate an intimacy with it." Villard entered into discussions with Sidney Dillon of the Union Pacific about construction of a line from Baker, Oregon, to Ogden, Utah, which would give the UP direct access to the Pacific Northwest.

At this point, the Northern Pacific counterattacked. President Frederick Billings, who like Villard was more a money man than an engineer, arranged the sale of $40 million in first mortgage bonds to a syndicate headed by J. P. Morgan. That looked like enough money to permit the completion of the main line. Villard, writing of himself in the third person, admitted that "he perceived at once distinctly what damaging consequences the great financial strength thus secured to the other company might have for the interests represented by him. The fear, indeed, was justified that his company would be struck in its vital part by the continuance of the NP main line down the Columbia. The mere threat would greatly affect the market value of his company's securities."

His response was startling. He would not sell, he would buy. In his own words, Villard "formed the boldest resolution of his whole business career. It was nothing less than the acquisition of a sufficient amount of Northern Pacific shares to influence the direction of Northern Pacific affairs . . . so as to insure lasting harmony between the two corporations." Quietly he began to buy Northern Pacific stock. When he reached the limit of his personal resources without having obtained enough stock to achieve his purpose, he staged Wall Street's most famous maneuver, the Blind Pool.

In February of 1881, Villard sent a prospectus to fifty wealthy men offering a chance to subscribe to a fund of $8 million which would "lay the foundation for an enterprise the exact nature of which cannot be disclosed until later." Their only security would be his reputation. It was enough. Villard was Wall Street's reigning wizard. Oregon Railroad and Navigation stock that had been given as a bonus in bond sales two years earlier was selling at 185.

"The effect of the circular was astonishing," Villard recalled. "The very novelty and mystery of the proposition proved to be an irresistible attraction. One third of the persons and firms appealed to signed the full amount asked for before the subscription paper could reach the other two-thirds. A regular rush for the privilege of subscribing ensued, and within 24 hours of the issue of the circular, more than twice the amount offered was applied for. . . . The subscription commanded a 25% premium at once, which rose to 40 and 50%; that is people were willing to pay 15 hundred dollars for every thousand they were permitted to contribute."

Villard went aggressively after the remaining NP stock he needed to win control. Billings fought back. The NP abruptly issued 180,000 shares of common stock that had been held in reserve since the reorganization following the line's bankruptcy. It was sold to 242 persons allied with Billings and favorable to his policies. Villard went to court, charging fraud and asking an injunction to block the issue. The Billings people compromised. They conceded Villard a controlling interest on the board.

In July, Villard incorporated the Oregon and Transcontinental Company under the laws of Oregon. It was created to hold a majority of stock in both the Northern Pacific and the Oregon Railway and Navigation Company, and to supply funds for the completion of the main line. Villard was elected president of the NP. Two of his closest associates, Thomas Oakes and Anthony Thomas, were elected first and second vice presidents.

The man Tacoma considered its worst enemy was now in control of the railway that was Tacoma's reason for existence.

The conqueror made a triumphal tour of Puget Sound immediately after he became president of the railroad in September 1881. Tacoma civic leaders were uncertain how to greet him. They decided to appear friendly and hope for the best.

The town band was at the platform when the special from Kalama pulled in shortly after dark on the evening of Tuesday, October 4. Kerosene lamps illuminated a banner bearing the legend WELCOME TO VILLARD AND PARTY, which stretched across Pacific Avenue between Halstead House (Room and Board, $1.50 a day. Rates by the Week) and the Bostwick and Davis Drug Store (Dr. Bridgman's Electro-Magnetic Ring Cures Rheumatism).

The visitors were taken to the residence of General J. W. Sprague, general superintendent for the Northern Pacific, who lived at the spot on the bluff later occupied by the Tacoma Hotel (and now by a parking lot). The biggest house in town was none too big. The party included H. Thielsen, engineer; J. C. Ainsworth, superintendent of the River Division of the Oregon Railway and Navigation; J. Kohler, manager of the Oregon and California; C. F. McKinn, a New York architect; and George Pillsbury of Minneapolis, who was identified in the papers the next day simply as "the greatest miller in the world."

The next morning they were taken to the division headquarters of the Northern Pacific, the coal bunkers where the S.S. *Great Western* was loading, and the dock where the ship *Dakota*, just in from New York, was discharging railroad iron. To the delight of Villard's hosts, she was preparing to take on sacked wheat, the *Dakota*'s master having declined to risk his vessel crossing the Columbia River bar. Tacomans hoped Villard would be impressed. Indeed he was; no sooner was he back in Portland than he launched a campaign to have the Columbia channel improved.

At noon Villard was escorted to Cogswell's Hall. Another banner proclaimed him welcome. Red, white, and blue bunting masked the raw boards of the second floor hall. A bouquet of late-blooming roses from local gardens was placed before the guest of honor. The Honorable Elwood Evans had been drafted as master of ceremonies. He was the town's most distinguished attorney, a pioneer who had crossed the plains in 1851, a politician who, as an anti-slave Whig, bolted to the Republicans early and in consequence served as speaker of the territorial house of representatives. Corpulent now and full-bearded, Evans made an imposing figure on the platform. His eloquence was usually high flown and all but interminable. But in introducing Villard he chose his words of welcome with painful caution.

"The Board of Trade of the city of New Tacoma, having been advised that official business has occasioned your presence in this city, deem it their duty to tender you their respects. . . ." Gradually Evans warmed to the task. "In some parts of the world, countries build railroads, but you have reversed that doctrine. Here railroads build countries. . . . Here abound coal, iron, lime and timber. Across yon mountain chain are wheat fields of unbounded area, of almost fabulous yield. We need the railroad to facilitate the profitable utilization of those products. From those eastern granaries, if you give us transportation to the sea, the world may be supplied with bread. From our mines and forests we will supply the interior with fuel and lumber. . . ."

Villard arose, a tall, solid man in dark broadcloth, his yellow-white mustache neat, his dark eyes stern. He expressed pleasure at his reception, then reached into an inside coat pocket and brought out a sheaf of clippings, glanced through them, and reminded his audience that "efforts have been made in this town to abuse, slander and vilify me to an extent that pained and surprised me." After letting Tacomans know that he remembered, he assured them that "neither the slander nor the abuse affected me any more than the wind which blows across your bay." He promised that in the future as in the past neither compliments nor vilification would keep him from his duty as president of the railroad. "That duty," he continued, drawing the first hearty applause of the afternoon, "I am free to say I consider to a great extent identical with the interests of your town."

The Northern Pacific, he pointed out, was the largest shareholder in the Tacoma Land Company and "hence more largely interested than any of you individually in the fate of this town. The Northern Pacific will do whatever can be done legitimately, with due regard to its other interests as a transportation line, for the development of this place. . . . We shall certainly do nothing to hurt your town."

In spite of the qualifications, his listeners seemed relieved. At least he was not declaring war.

The Cascade Division, the line across the mountains, would be built. But he could not say when. He implied it might not be for years. He cited the high cost of bridges and tunnels. He pointed out that the area was so undeveloped that it would for some years yield little freight. Nor would he say through which pass the rails would run. Glumness settled back on the audience, to be lifted somewhat when he promised that the Oregon Improvement Company would build a large warehouse to store wheat at Tacoma: "It will be the first means of making Tacoma what it has not been so far—that is, a wheat shipping port."

Villard concluded with the announcement that the Northern Pacific would as quickly as possible build a line from Portland to Rainier, across from Kalama. If Tacoma's estimates about the greater ease of shipping wheat from Puget Sound as compared to shipping it across the Columbia bar were correct, the farmers of Walla Walla would route their grain north from Kalama. This was not what Tacomans wanted. They wanted rails across the mountains, by-passing Portland. Subdued applause and stiff handshaking followed the speech. Villard was escorted to the waterfront, where the *George E. Starr* had steam up. "The Tacoma band performed several airs as the boat swung out from the wharf and headed for her destination," said the next day's *Ledger,* failing to mention that the destination was Seattle.

In Seattle, Villard again promised that the Cascade Division would be built, sometime. He delighted his audience by adding that it would use "the most feasible pass and if that proves to be Snoqualmie [the pass most advantageous to Seattle, and the one recommended in 1841 by Wilkes] I would welcome the fact." He promised that Seattle would be given adequate rail service to Portland.

Villard was received in Portland not as conqueror but as savior. He assured the Portland Board of Trade that the Northern Pacific would reach that city, the Oregon and California would be extended southward, feeder lines would be pushed into farmlands and mineral areas, and within three years Portland would be the nexus of a railroad system of two thousand miles or more.

"It is no extravagance," declared the *Oregonian,* "to say that Mr. Villard has organized and combined interests which, in their detail and entirety, form the most stupendous scheme yet undertaken on the American continent." Nor was Villard unimpressed by the enormity of it all. "No man in this country," he wrote, "had ever before at one time had supreme charge of such gigantic operations, extending from the upper Mississippi to the Pacific Ocean, and from Puget Sound to the northern boundaries of California."

Villard had 25,000 men, 3 out of 5 of them Chinese, working laying tracks. He was spending $4 million a month. He also financed a major publicity campaign in Europe to lure immigrants to Washington and Oregon. In 1883 the Northern Pacific employed 831 agents in Great Britain and 124 on the Continent, mainly in Scandinavia and Germany, to distribute pamphlets about the glories of farming in the West and to pass out samples of Washington-grown wheat. California papers complained that more than half of the foreigners who reached San Francisco by train were on their way to Washington and Oregon.

The Northern Pacific had cash flow problems. After Cooke's failure, Congress had tightened the regulations on railroad finance. Government inspectors were slow to report completion of the twenty-five-mile sections of line, and Villard was forced to juggle funds, at times extending his personal credit, to see that bills were met. But only four hundred miles of track remained to be laid and everything seemed manageable when he left for New York after a visit to Portland in May of 1883. He promised the Portland Board of Trade that when he returned in the fall it would be as the first passenger on the first through train from St. Paul.

In New York Villard received a staggering report from his chief engineer. Costs were running $14 million above estimates. Villard felt betrayed by his bookkeepers. But there was nothing to do except finish the main line.

Work continued on the final section in the western Rockies. Crews put together a jack-straw pile of timbers 112 feet high, 1,800 feet long to form a trestle across O'Keefe's canyon, and another 226 feet high and 860 feet long over Marent's gulch. They tunneled under Mullen Pass and Bozeman Pass. When outlaws led by a trio known as Dick the Diver, Ohio Dan, and the Barber levied tribute on the construction camps, vigilantes rounded them up, lynched them all, and buried them in a mass grave, using the Barber's crutches as a cross. Nothing was going to stop them. In August the east and west crews sighted each other fifty-five miles west of Helena, Montana.

Villard invited the entire Washington diplomatic corps, the governors of all the seven states crossed by Northern Pacific rails, former President Ulysses S. Grant, the Cabinet, General William Tecumseh Sherman, assorted senators and representatives, and a tribe of Indians to the driving of the final spike. So many accepted that it took four trains from the east and one from the west to bring everybody to the confluence of Gold Creek with the Clark Fork of the Columbia in Montana where the last thousand feet of track awaited laying.

Late on the afternoon of September 3, the celebrities seated themselves in a gaunt grandstand decorated with fir branches. As the sun sank behind the brown hills, they listened to introductions and orations that threatened to last longer than the construction period. In the lavender twilight the last rails were pulled out onto the ties by Old Nig, a veteran workhorse. The Fifth Infantry Regimental Band played a march. Artillery thundered. A picked team of construction workers drove the spikes into place until only one was left.

The last spike was steel, not the traditional gold. It was the same spike that had been set at Thompson's Junction in Minnesota fourteen years earlier when construction began. A Mr. Davis, first name not listed, had swung the sledge at the start and he was on hand to finish the job. He tapped it gently and handed the hammer to Villard, who passed it to Billings, who gave it to Secretary of the Interior Henry Moore Teller, who turned it over to General Grant. Each tap was recorded by telegraph in New York, St. Paul, Portland, and

Tacoma. At last the sledge was returned to Davis. With a full swing he set the spike firmly. East and west were properly joined.

Villard continued west for ceremonies in Tacoma, Seattle, and Portland. Tacoma celebrated the completion of the main line but with less than total enthusiasm. The trains reached the terminus by way of Portland. Construction of the Cascade tunnel through the mountains was not mentioned in the speeches by company officials.

Portland stood triumphant and gave Villard a hero's welcome when, as promised, he was first to disembark from the first through train. "I still see as clearly and as inspiringly as though it were yesterday the beautiful decoration of the city with triumphant arches of flowers and evergreens, bunting and emblems, the great street procession, the splendid evening concert and reception at the Mechanics' Pavilion," he recalled shortly before his death seventeen years later. "It all marked the height of my power and leadership—which immediately began, however, to recede with such speed that I was compelled to resign from three of my companies by December 17, 1883."

Villard tried to raise money to pay for the cost overrun on construction by placing a second mortgage on the Northern Pacific, but the move drove down the value of existing NP shares and those of the Oregon and Transcontinental. His reputation for genius withered as had Cooke's. "The throng of people which follows with alacrity the man who leads them to profits will desert him just as quickly when he ceases to be a money-maker for them," Villard noted sadly. He had discovered "downright treachery" among his confidential advisers, two of the Oregon and Transcontinental directors having used their private knowledge of the condition of the company to make money selling its shares short.

On December 16, three friends who had audited the books told Villard he was personally all but insolvent and the Oregon and Transcontinental on the verge of bankruptcy. They formed a syndicate to advance him, on pledge of all his real and personal property, a sufficent amount to meet his individual liability and save the Oregon and Transcontinental. But they forced him to resign the presidency of the Northern Pacific, the Oregon Railway and Navigation Company, and the Oregon and Transcontinental.

"His fate was certainly tragic," Villard said in a third-person autobiographical note. "Within a few years, he had risen from entire obscurity to the enviable position of one of the leaders of the material progress of our age . . . and received on his transcontinental journey such homage as few men have ever received in this country. But his fall from might to helplessness, from wealth to poverty, from public admiration to wide condemnation, was far more rapid than his rise, and his brief career was everywhere used to point a moral."

Villard had filled the gap. The tracks ran from the Mississippi to Puget Sound. Control of the transcontinental passed back to the Charles Wright faction of the Northern Pacific board, whose interests centered on Tacoma and the completion of the Cascade Division.

"Bore, Bennett, Bore"

ON December 27, 1880, a stocky, dark-haired engineer reported to the Northern Pacific headquarters in Tacoma for orders. Virgil Bogue, a graduate of Rensselaer Polytechnic Institution and a one-time associate of Frederick Law Olmsted, had just come from eastern Washington where, among other things, he suggested the name for Pasco. (Conditions at the juncture of the Columbia and Snake rivers reminded him of the heat, dust, and sand storms he had experienced in the Andes at the silver-mining town of Cerro de Pasco.) The instructions given Bogue in Tacoma called for a considerable change in climate. He was to assemble a survey party with all possible speed, ascend the Green River to its headquarters, and locate a pass for rails through the Cascade barrier. It was dead winter. Rains were falling heavily at sea level. On the rare moments of clearing in Tacoma, snow could be seen fresh and deep far down the mountainside. That was the point: a winter survey would include snow depths.

With the aid of NP Commissary Officer John McAllister, a nephew of the James McAllister killed in the area during the Indian War, Bogue rounded up some experienced woodsmen, equipped them with axes, brush-hooks, saws, snowshoes, sleds of a type used by prospectors in British Columbia (an experiment), camp equipment, and a pack train of cayuse ponies. The party assembled at the McClintock ranch near Buckley. By the time Bogue came up from Tacoma on January 17 they had cut trail several miles eastward toward a low mountain that had been named Enumclaw, "the place of bad spirits," by Indians who had been caught on it during a lightning storm.

Bogue selected the route toward the Green with the rest of the party following, widening trail and laying corduroy across the worst bogs. "We soon found that exploration for this trail was a serious matter," Bogue reported to the American Geographical Society.

Swamps and hollows impeded our progress. We had to force our way through fir thickets and over fallen tree trunks of great size. There were many places where the undergrowth had been bent down by snow to a nearly horizontal position, forcing us to a choice between scrambling over or crawling under on all fours. We had many falls. . . . At night, worn out by a day of such toil, bruised, scratched and sore, soaked to the skin, our reflections were such as would hardly bear publication. As usual in winter, the rain fell in torrents much of the time, forming morasses. After having cut trail through masses of forest debris, our party was frequently obliged to return and lay corduroy or build rough bridges of cedar puncheons to afford footing for the ponies.

After ten days in the thicket they reached the Green, forty-four miles from Tacoma as the railroad eventually ran, sixteen miles from McClintock's ranch. They expected to move faster along the stream but found themselves in a gorge whose rocky walls resisted trail making. Snow or rain fell daily. Men sickened and were sent back to Tacoma, or simply became sick of the job and quit. But times were tough. There were more recruits where they had come from.

On February 8 the party emerged from the Green River canyon into a forest of good timber but also into snow waist deep on level ground. They built up the site of an advance base, Camp Seven. Some of the forty men began to hollow a dugout, but reconnaisance showed the river upstream too rough and the project was abandoned. The half-finished dugout gave its name to the stream which empties into the Green at the campsite, Canoe Creek.

After a week at Camp Seven, Bogue and a party of nine pushed ahead on snowshoes. His men hauled the British Columbia sleds, but they proved ill-suited to the forest and often had to be carried. A storm broke on February 20. They were pinned on a ledge while the Green rose over its banks "to a height I had not supposed possible." Not for four days could they escape. They moved out through flowing fog; and when it lifted "we caught sudden sight of a large eagle flying in widening circles, directly over our heads, a good omen." Eagle Gorge had its name.

The party remained earthbound. They floundered forward through drifts, sometimes plunged into shallow pools of snowmelt. On March 2 they camped at Smay Creek, sixty miles from Tacoma, short of supplies, exhausted, and discouraged. Ahead lay more miles, more weeks, of tilted snow and tangled forest leading toward the sawtooth ridge of the barrier range. Where they had been, could rails go?

Bogue sent five men back for supplies. He pushed ahead with two Indians, Peter and Charley, and Joseph Wilson, a Canadian voyageur and prospector who, at the age of fifty-five, was reputed to be tough as a smoked horseclam. "Our outfit, light as we dared make it, consisted of one or two blankets each, besides our rubber blankets, a small fly tent, a frying pan, tin kettle and coffee pot, and a few provisions, principally flour, baking powder, beans, bacon and coffee."

A ridge they followed in hope it would parallel the Green wandered south. They climbed down, found the Green again near Hot Springs, and debated what to do. His supply party not having returned, Bogue sent the Indians back for supplies and with Wilson pushed upstream. When the Indians failed to rejoin them by March 7, Wilson volunteered to make a forced march alone to Smay Creek for food.

Bogue, camping alone, crossed the fresh trails of a wolf and a bear while gathering firewood. "In the lengthening shadows that evening I prepared a solitary supper and ate it without my usual appetite, and as quietly as possible," he confessed. His revolver had not been fired for months and he doubted a handgun would discourage a bear. Tired but sleepless that night, he heard a sudden loud snap, painfully audible in the stillness. Moments later there was a scratching at the tent. The fly parted. Wilson asked cheerfully, "Boss, you asleep?" He had met the Indians on the trail, shouldered most of their supplies, and, sending them down for more, returned under doublepack to the tent.

A change of luck came with Wilson. The weather cleared. They found the main stem of the Green and on March 17 crossed what is now called Tacoma Pass (too high to be helpful) and made camp on the east side. A few days later, when supplies had been brought up, Bogue set out with James Gregg, Andy Drury, and Mattew Champion to follow the height of the land northward in search of a better pass.

They followed a tributary of Cabin Creek to its source on a spur, elevation forty-four hundred feet, and camped in deep snow among balsam, within a short distance of the main divide. In the morning they climbed to the top. The range was sharp and well defined and ran nearly due north. They made good progress until afternoon, when the ridge curved to the northeast and a mountain confronted them, forested to the peak. As they worked east, the ridge dropped rapidly. One of Andy Drury's snowshoes caught in the other. He plunged headlong down the slope and was almost buried in a drift. Drury was unhurt but they made camp, and named the mountain Snowshoe Butte.

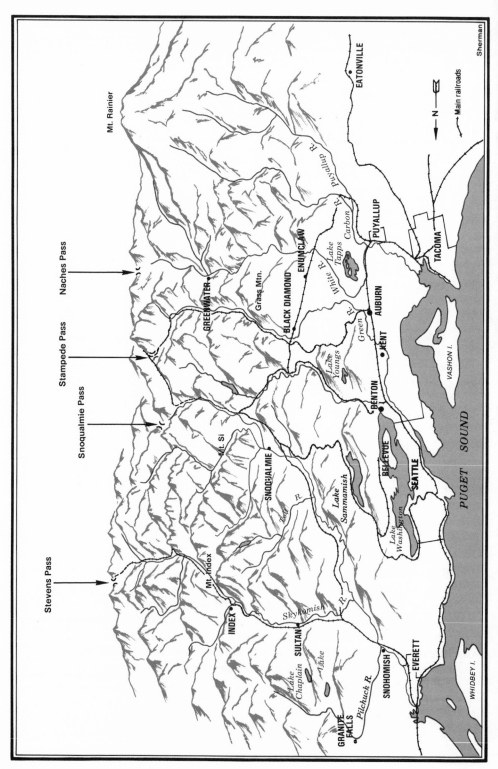

Possible rail routes through the Cascades

"For several days we had been blessed with fairly good weather," Bogue reported,

but the next was one of the most dismal I remember. It blew a gale and was severely cold. With the wind came thick fog which, added to the gloom of the balsam forest, made our movements groping and uncertain. The moisture seemed to congeal in small, sharp crystals which found lodgment in every wrinkle or fold of our clothing, and made it difficult to face the wind. Making for the highest ground we did our best to follow the divide, whose crest was no longer clearly defined. It soon changed its course from easterly to southeasterly and fell off rapidly in elevation. As we felt our way along, the constantly descending course of the ridge led us to conclude that since morning we had, somehow, missed the main range and must be following a spur which would lead to the Yakima River.

Brief explorations only added to the uncertainty. We spent a whole day crawling about the northerly slopes in our endeavor to find a ridge so decidedly bearing north as to give assurance it was the main divide. At night we brought up near our previous night's camping place, annoyed at the loss of time, but now quite certain that our morning journey was in the right direction and that if we had pursued the ridge further we should have come to a bend to the north, an indication that it was none other than the main range.

Starting early on March 19th, with our route for the morning at least settled upon, and with favoring skies that lighted our hearts, we made excellent progress. A little after nine o'clock appeared a sharp bend in the ridge to the north, as anticipated. We descended along a well-defined crest so rapidly that in less than an hour the barometer marked only 3,495 feet elevation at a point where for a little distance about us there were no trees. It was evidently one of the lowest points of the divide.

Bogue had found a pass you could drive a train through:

To the east a spur cut off much of our view but facing west we looked down on Sunday Creek. Beyond its confluence with the Green were the mountains to the south, covered with dark fir forests, and back of them the great snowy mass of Mount Rainier sharply defined against the blue sky. It was a beautiful scene, so impressive that for a moment all were silent. Thence we continued our trip northward, finding several other depressions in the range, but none as promising as the one just described.

Bogue called his discovery Pass No. 1 and rather hoped it would someday bear his name. Instead Northern Pacific officials referred to it as Garfield Pass, honoring the president who was assassinated that year. But that name did not stick either.

While Bogue's men were cutting trails in the area a few weeks later so that instrumental surveys could be run across the divide, Bogue became dissatisfied with a group camped by a little lake at the head of Sunday Creek, a few hundred yards below the pass. He dispatched a foreman notorious as a slave-driver to get some work out of them. The foreman showed up, and the men threw down their tools, rolled up their blankets, and took off for Tacoma, all except young Johnny Bradley of Puyallup. He stayed. When a new crew arrived they found he had nailed a board to a tree and printed on it, in pencil, "Stampede Camp." Usage transferred the name to the little lake nearby, then to the pass.

Stampede Pass it still is.

Stampede Pass proved higher than Bogue thought; its elevation as determined by an aneroid barometer was 3,725 feet. That was some 700 feet higher than Snoqualmie, a few miles to the north, the pass Governor Stevens had recommended as the best. From the standpoint of the C. B. Wright group, who sent Bogue into the field, Stampede had one decisive advantage: it came through the mountains directly east of Tacoma, whereas Snoqualmie debouched close to Seattle. But Bogue's discovery coincided with Villard's take-over of the Northern Pacific, and while Villard controlled the transcontinental no effort would be made to bypass Portland by laying track through the mountains to Puget Sound.

When Villard lost power, a decision to construct the Cascade Division again became possible. But there were complications. Villard had been president of the Northern Pacific, the Oregon and Transcontinental holding company, and the Oregon Railway and Navigation Company which controlled the Columbia. In 1884, Robert Harris, a friend of Wright's, became president of the NP, and Elijah Smith of Boston, president of the O & T and the ORNC. Each preached the paramountcy of the whole region, each played for parochial advantage.

Harris saw the benefit in expanding the coal operations in the Wilkeson-Carbonado area and completing the Cascade Division, if money could be found. Smith, who as president of the O & T still controlled a large block of NP stock, did not oppose the Cascade construction directly but emphasized the high cost of such a project and urged fiscal caution. At the same time Smith as president of the ORNC served notice of intention to cancel the NP lease for use of the tracks along the Columbia, but offered to negotiate a new lease, at a favorable rate, for a long period.

Harris was in a bind. The NP needed the use of the tracks for the time being but Harris wanted the railroad to have its own line to the coast. Entering a new lease agreement with ORNC would undercut his argument for pushing ahead with the Cascade Division. Failure to negotiate with Smith for a new lease might cause Smith to turn to the Union Pacific, which would bring a rival transcontinental to the area. There was also the question of the land grant. Villard's failure, like that of Jay Cooke a decade earlier, had helped trigger a recession which added to the growing hostility toward the railroads. Yesterday's empire builder, today's robber baron.

In 1884 a bill calling for forfeiture of all unearned land grants west of the Mississippi was introduced in the House of Representatives on a Monday, cleared by the House Committee on Public Lands with a do-pass resolution on Friday, and overwhelmingly adopted only two weeks later by the full House. The Senate killed it, but 1884 was a presidential election year. Land grants became a campaign issue. The Democratic platform called roundly for the return to the nation of all unearned land grants and denounced the stranglehold of grasping monopolies on the public domain. The Republicans more tolerantly asked forfeiture only of those grants where there had been no attempt in good faith to fulfill the conditions of the grant.

In Washington Territory the cleavage over forfeiture was sharper. Elisha P. Ferry, territorial governor from 1872 to 1880, after that an attorney on retainer for the NP, dominated the Republican convention, which rejected forfeiture and nominated an antiforfeit candidate for delegate to Congress. The Democrats were breathing fire; their plank declared "the government should now avail itself of the breach of condition and resume control of granted lands, thereby closing for the future forever the open gateway through which a system of landlordism, now bringing such sorrowful and calamitous fruition in the fairest portions of Europe, is affecting an entrance into our free republic." They nominated Charles S. Voorhees of Walla Walla to carry the message to Congress. (When it was revealed during the campaign that as a lawyer Voorhees had once contended that land grants were forever, and irrevocable, the Democrats explained that a lawyer's brief was not to be equated with his belief.)

Robert Harris tried to soothe territorial antagonisms to the railroad. In March he authorized James McNaught, head of the law firm representing the Northern Pacific in Washington, to announce that the Cascade Division would be built "at once." But no rails were laid. The natives remained restless; they wanted steel and smoke, not words.

In July, Harris came in person to Seattle to explain delays and promise better things. He was a practical railroad operator of long experience, an urbane and well-intentioned man, but he underestimated the hostility of Seattle to the railroad that had jilted it in favor of Tacoma and for which the government was holding off the market, as potential land grant, vast areas in the Cascades which the Seattle people believed to be rich in minerals that would assure prosperity.

Harris' pleasantries and promises were met with sarcasm and blunt questions. He was baited by two adept attorneys. Judge Thomas Burke, a stumpy little Irish orator, believed Harris' speech to be "such as the Indians would call *cultus wah wah,* which translated from the Classic Chinook means worthless, good-for-nothing talk." John Leary, a New Brunswick lumberman turned lawyer, who was the town's leading businessman, demanded to know not *what* Harris hoped to do but *when.* Harris might not be able to convince them, but they could make him mad. After all, he represented investors who had put up more than $90 million to bring transportation to the region. He had not come across the continent to this wooden town above a clam beach to be told how to manage his railroad. When a Seattle spokesman warned that the townsfolk might lay their own line to Walla Walla, Harris dared them to try: "Sometimes there is a little difference between planning a railroad and putting it into operation."

Seattle complaints led Harris to take one definite action. He had ridden up from Tacoma on a special train along the track of the Puget Sound Shore Line, an NP subsidiary. John Leary, who accompanied him, moaned all the way through the valley about the service given Seattle. Bulk freight shipments were broken up in Tacoma and forwarded piecemeal. The schedule of the only daily train was so arranged that passengers arrived at 2:00 A.M. Harris fixed that. He cut off service entirely. Cows grazed undisturbed on the tracks of the Orphan Line through the Duwamish valley.

Tacomans gloated at Seattle's discomfiture. But in November, Charles Voorhees, the anti-NP Democrat, carried King County by enough votes to assure his election as delegate to Congress from the territory. And Grover Cleveland, running on a platform that included land grant forfeiture, became the first Democrat to win the presidency since the Civil War.

With his negotiations over a new lease on the ORNC track bogged down and the threat to the land grant rising, Harris decided early in 1885 that the Cascade Division must be rushed through at all costs. His engineers told him that Stampede Pass was too steep for efficient rail service. There would have to be a tunnel. They recommended it be dug at the 2,880-foot level, which meant a very long tunnel, almost two miles. Harris feared the cost would give his opposition on the NP board a persuasive argument against the project. He finessed objections by winning the board's approval of a vaguely worded statement about future plans for the Cascade Division, which he then interpreted as giving him authority to call for bids on what would be the longest and most difficult tunneling operation attempted up to that time in America.

On January 22, 1886, Captain Sidney Bennett, temporarily resident in Yakima, received a telegram from his younger brother Nelson, then visiting in Philadelphia. The wire said the Bennett brothers had won the contract to drive a tunnel 16 feet wide, 22 feet high at the crown, 9,850 feet long through the north shoulder of Mount Rainier. "Get going," said the kid brother, who was boss.

Sidney Bennett needed no urging. Haste was imperative. He and Nelson were not only undertaking an assignment of formidable difficulty, but they were betting more than they possessed that they could finish the job in twenty-eight months. Their contract pledged a one-hundred-thousand-dollar performance bond plus 10 percent of the contract price if they failed to have trains rolling under the Cascades by May 22, 1888. Back in Philadelphia where the bids had been opened, the defeated contractors, who numbered a dozen, were predicting that the Bennett brothers' victory would not make them but break them. Their bid had been so low—less than half that by some of their more experienced rivals—that even if they beat the deadline they could still lose a fortune. But if anyone could get the job done on time, it was agreed, the Bennetts were the ones.

Nelson Bennett was forty-three years old, five feet nine inches in height and almost as wide: put a mustache and goatee on a bulldozer and you would have a reasonable facsimile. Born in Canada, left fatherless at six, Nelson quit school at fourteen to work on a farm. He came to the United States during the Civil War, helped build Army barracks for a time, then caught on as a brakeman on the Dixon Air Line.

Nelson was in Detroit in 1864 when he received a letter from one of his brothers in Pennsylvania: "I have found the Eldorado. Come at once. I am boring for oil and we can slip into a fortune as easy as eating mince pie." Nelson could not draw his railroad pay until the end of the month, so he got himself fired on his next run. He arrived in the oil fields with two dollars, worked four weeks as a day laborer, then passed himself off as a contractor and agreed to bore a six-hundred-foot well ("I hired a competent man to manage, then stood round looking wise until I learned something"). He sank twenty-seven wells before the boom tapered off. He took a small fortune west but lost it in land speculation in Missouri and Iowa. Next he taught school in Missouri (he had gone through the sixth grade), fought Indians (twenty personal acquaintances were killed in the race wars of the West), prospected in the Dakotas, organized a mule-train freight service in the Southwest. He was in Salt Lake City, broke again, when the copper rush to Montana began. Bennett contracted to move a quartz mill from Ophir, Utah, to Butte, six hundred miles, on muleback, and did it. He put the profits into building Butte's first street railway and the profits from that into moving a steam sawmill into the Lost River region of Idaho. He was rich again.

His Rocky Mountain activities brought Bennett into contact with Washington Dunn, who was building the Utah and Northern for Jay Gould. Bennett teamed up with Dunn, doing the outside work while Dunn hustled contracts. They undertook to dig a thirty-five-mile irrigation ditch in Idaho to carry Snake River water to 270,000 acres. The job required six hundred men, twelve hundred horses, and an arsenal of drilling and blasting equipment. On this project Sidney Bennett, Nelson's leaner and meaner older brother, a cavalry captain in the Civil War, demonstrated what an admirer called "a peculiar genius for slave-driving." Dunn died, and Nelson Bennett went into the negotiating end of the business, leaving Sidney to direct field work. The Bennetts won the contract for the first 134 miles of the Cascade Division, Pasco to Ellensburg, before securing the Stampede assignment.

A human bulldozer and a slave-driving genius were needed on the Stampede. Just getting men and machines to the worksite required prodigious effort. Nelson shipped west five engines, two water wheels, five air compressors, eight seventy-horsepower boilers, four large exhaust fans, two complete electric arc-light plants, two miles of six-inch wrought-iron pipe, two miles of water pipe, two fully equipped machine shops, assorted tools, thirty-six air-drilling machines, several tons of steel drills, two locomotives (named "Sadie" and "Ceta" after his daughters), sixty dump-cars, two sawmills, and a telephone system.

On the east side of the Cascades, the rails toward the mountains ended just beyond the village of Yakima; on the west they had been run from Tacoma through Buckley to Eagle Gorge. Beyond the railheads only vague pack-trails twisted through the forests, up to the mountainsides, to the portals. An even sketchier path went up through the pass to connect the east and west worksites. It was so indistinct that the veteran John McAllister and a companion lost their way and their horses in a snowstorm, and survived for a week on nothing but boiled oats. When a search party reached them McAllister was shoveling a path down the mountain through ten feet of snow.

"Have you any grub?" McAllister asked his rescuers.

"Yes."

The old settler sat down and wept.

Through such country, in the dead of winter, Sidney Bennett had to move an industry, a work force, and living facilities, against a deadline. The first wagons started from Yakima only eleven days after the contract was signed. In the dry, rocky hills around Yakima the crews chipped away at the road with picks, but as they approached the mountains they came to a stretch of fifteen miles where a warm Chinook wind had melted the snow. The wagons sank above the axles. So they built a moving roadway of planks. Boards were laid end to end across the bog, the rear boards being hand-carried forward as soon as the back wheels of the wagon cleared them. It proved impossible to keep the wheels on the planks with the horses hitched in the normal way. They rigged block and tackle, fastened one end of the rope to the wagon tongue, the team to the other end, and drivers slogged ahead of the wagon shouldering the tongue to guide it. When all went well they could make a mile a day.

Things were worse in the mountains. The trail led along gorges five hundred to a thousand feet deep; it crossed creeks and rivers; it threaded through a tangle of forest. Where the grades were steepest and not even double-teaming could move the wagons, the block and tackle was rigged from trees to allow the horses to pull downhill. In some stretches the machinery was put on scows that could be skidded across the frozen snow. The weather was awful, alternating rain and snow. The winds could knock down a horse.

An advance party under Master Builder W. H. Buckner reached the east face on February 9. "Before we could get to the portal," he reported, "we had to shovel a road through snow 800 feet long and eight feet deep. At the face of the tunnel there was 200 inches of water falling from the top of the bluff 170 feet, which had to be turned. There was ice eight to ten feet deep across the cliff. We made a cut through snow and ice twenty feet wide, eight to ten deep and 150 feet long just to get at the portal at the east end. In order to reach the west portal it was necessary to shovel a trail through snow four to ten feet deep, four feet wide, and four miles long."

Hand-drilling on the approach to the east face began February 13. Entries in Sidney Bennett's work journal are laconic:

Feb. 15. Work on excavation on approach to tunnel will be prosecuted until point of heading is reached.

March 15. 36 inches of snow fell within the last 36 hours.

March 21. Rained for last 24 hours.

March 27. Began work on the "bench" inside east portal.

March 31. Commenced timbering; put 12 setts in—the first used.

April 1. Sixty men worked in east end. Completed excavation of the approaches to the heading at west end.

April 2. Commenced running the heading of the west end. The extent of the day's work was 5½ feet by hand drills. The excavators at the east end have made to this date 200 feet.

April 6. Harder rock—blue trappite in the west end.

May 1. Snow retarding the work in the east end.

May 5. The first man injured. It was by falling rock.

On the trail, organization replaced improvisation. A hundred wagons were moving men and machinery up the roads. Stations had been built every twelve miles. These were "rag shows"—tent camps—where teamsters could get food and sleep. It had been found that sleds that worked on the slanted snowfields could be hauled across mud as the freezing line rose with the temperature. At the portals the men lived in real houses, though on the east side workers had to shovel away fifty feet of snow to reach solid ground for the foundation of what was called Tunnel City.

The first compressor boiler left Yakima on February 22. It was eight weeks reaching the portal but on June 19 the equipment was assembled. Sidney's notes say triumphantly, "Two Ingersoll drills started in the east end—the first machinery that started."

If the Bennetts were to beat the deadline, it would be with the help of technology. They planned to attack the rock with six Ingersoll Eclipse drills at each end of the tunnel, the power to be generated on the east side where six large boilers were installed to supply four 480-horsepower compressors. A pipe 12,500 feet long was run over the pass to carry air to the drills at the west face.

Captain Sidney hoped to drill 400 feet of rock a month when under full steam. More than 122,000 cubic yards of rock were to be chipped out of the mountain. Just finding a place to put the debris was a problem. On the west end the rock was run down a spur for a quarter mile, then dumped into a ravine that was eventually filled and used as roadbed for the track. A visitor who rode one of the dump trucks reported that it went downhill "with a speed that made a person's hair rise like the quills of a fretful porcupine."

Reporters trooped "to the front." Those from Tacoma tended to be enthusiastic, those from Seattle and Portland dubious. A favorite rumor was that there had been an engineering miscalculation and "when the east side and west side meet in the middle they'll be a mile apart." Tilton Sheets, a civil engineer and surveyor, visited the digs in

July to assure readers of the Tacoma *Ledger* that all was well. His tone was that of a recruiting sergeant:

Any man who will work can find employment and command from two dollars all the way to three per day according to how he can work. If he is worth three he can get it.

How do the men live—their board and all that? Very well—as cheaply and well as they could live in Tacoma. The contractors have built camps and the men are well fed—plenty of beef and good food otherwise, for all of which they pay $4.50 a week. Of course it's roughing it a little—that's understood. Every man provides his own blankets. Good meals can be obtained at points along the road towards Ellensburg at two-bits, but up towards the summit they come higher, naturally enough—say four-bits. For parties visiting the scene on a flying excursion it is advisable to take provisions along.

Saloons? Oh, yes—too many of them. That's one trouble. Many of the men get caught by them every pay day and don't work till they have to.

Another *Ledger* reporter met a professional gambler coming down from the west portal. He was in complete agreement with Surveyor Tilton about the opportunities for diversion on the mountainside:

His smile was contagious even across a hundred feet of space. He carried only a little hand satchel such as ladies affect. Shaking this and smiling over the clash of ivory and what-not within, he asked: "Poker? Roulette? Chuck-luck? Try your hand. Anything you wish." Pleased at the reception of this sally, he continued. "What's your racket? I can tell you, it's no good up there. I've been all through it, from Ellensburg to the Gorge, all through. It's worked out. There's saloons and restaurants every fifty feet. You can get a good meal for two-bits—as good as you can at Tacoma. There's nothing left in it for us. What's your game? Whiskey?"

Such prosperity and luxury proved more than some men could stand. The week that Tilton Sheets's effusion appeared in the *Ledger,* Captain Sidney penned an unusually long entry in his daily journal:

About 150 men in east end struck for nine hours as a day's work. [They were working twelve-hour shifts, seven days a week.] It lasted two days but did not prevail. In this matter the sheriff of [Yakima] county was called upon the ground to prevent disorder and injury to persons or property. One man was shot by him in his attempt to escape arrest on a criminal charge.

In a letter to Nelson, who was at company headquarters in Tacoma, Sidney remarked that they were using three crews at all times, "one coming, one drilling, one quitting." But the work went on.

August 9. Electric lights were extended in the west end, having previously been placed in the east end. The rock in the east end is getting so hard it has to be blasted with No. 1 Giant Powder.

August 18. One man killed and another injured by blasting.

Sept. 1. Three Ingersoll drills started for the first time in the west end.

At this point Sidney added up progress and estimated what remained to be done to meet the deadline. They would have to average 13.58 feet a day through May 21, 1888. The crews had yet to make as much as 13 feet on any day.

Sept. 5. Work was advanced so far that the smoke and gas incident from blasting had to be remedied, and the steam fans were applied, which helped clean the tunnel thereof.

Sept 25. Drilling delayed because of the breaking of rock above the face of the tunnel caused by blasting shots. Five days to remedy.

Oct. 1. The end of this month found us 33 feet short of the daily average required.

Oct. 15. Air boxes were extended 265 feet in the west end.

Oct. 29. The tunnel is in bad shape. The roof is cracking and rock is falling, which causes delay.

Oct. 31. This month showed a gain of 17 feet over the daily average required.

Nov. 1. A Foreman and five men have quit because of some grievance and left camp.

Nov. 15. Snow sheds over the dump track to be built.

Nov. 29. A land slide into the crib became so extensive we had to stop work in the east end for a week, which delays progress.

Nov. 30. This month work fell behind 23½ feet.

Dec. 1. Work delayed by rain which caused east end of tunnel to be flooded.

Dec. 31. There was a loss of the required average in December of 9 feet. Five months of machine work in tunnel during year. 48 feet behind schedule.

The delays in construction and the increasing stridency of the campaign in Congress for forfeiture of the unearned land grants caused NP President Harris early in 1887 to decide to lay a temporary switchback track through the pass. That way train service could begin before the tunnel was complete.

A thousand more men were hired in March to shovel snow off the mountain above the tunnel so that rails could be zig-zagged over the summit. With the realization that they would have a direct connection with the east a year ahead of schedule, Tacomans were caught on a rising tide of enthusiasm. Tourist excursions were organized to visit the end of the line and applaud the workers as they marched off to the front, shovels on their shoulders.

"Beyond the end of the track," wrote the *Ledger*'s front line correspondent,

a clearing very like a new country road extends along the edge of the river and fringes the hill and is soon lost at the turn. A few men may be seen lifting and letting fall their shovels here and there where the road leads over into full view. Columns of blue smoke rise above the trees at irregular intervals. A few workmen are building a footbridge across the river back of the station. The large tents are in the midst of a partial clearing and about 30 horses and mules stamp and whinny under the trees while packmen are binding to their backs bales of hay, barrels and bundles of every description, while for every switch of the tail or misstep of the burdened animal his heart is sent to perdition forty times in the loud prayers of the drivers.

They are leaving now, as late as 11 A.M., starting away by the trail, which, a mere pathway, begins at once a precipitate ascent of the mountain. They go in single file, the drivers or packmen more noisy than before, keeping the horses in line. A few laborers have just come in and are directed on toward the picks and the new dirt and the smoke in the shadowy gap further along.

A sound, as of distant cannonading, seems to shake the earth as it rolls down from out of the mysterious shadows of the gulch and beyond. Every few moments a thunder and crash through the woods tells of the blasting rocks and the fall of giant trees.

And this is the front.

By March 28, 1877, the shovel brigade had cleared enough roadbed for the start of track-laying above the tunnel. The rails sashayed up the slope in a series of three switches on each side of the mountain. At each switchback the train would run up to a dead end and back onto the track climbing to the next switch. This Z-route reduced the grade to 297 feet per mile.

The last spike on the switchback was driven at two minutes past six on the afternoon of June 1. Assistant General Manager J. M. Buckley (for whom the Northern Pacific named the town of Buckley) served as master of ceremonies. Mrs. H. S. Huson, wife of the assistant project engineer, made the final tap on the spike with a bottle of champagne. An experimental first train—two locomotives, a baggage car, caboose, and a wooden-seated coach—was sent from Yakima to Tacoma on June 6. The route having been tested, Charles Wright was carried over it in triumph the next day in his private parlor car.

Scheduled traffic over the Stampede began July 3. The first regular overland train to the east—four coaches, with twenty passengers—left Tacoma at 1:45 P.M. The first westbound passenger train arrived at 7:15—seven hours late.

On the Fourth of July Tacoma for the second time celebrated the completion of the transcontinental. President Cleveland was invited to speak but the celebrants had to settle for lank, scruffy Eugene

Semple, the governor. A grandstand was built at the present site of Stadium High School. The papers claimed that eighteen thousand visitors came to town, which would have been more than the combined populations of Seattle and Olympia. Festivities lasted three days, marred only by a dispute in the hose-laying contest between the Seattle and Tacoma fire departments. Somebody recognized one of the Seattle volunteers as a professional sprinter who specialized in running at carnivals with the handicap of a fifty-pound flour sack on his shoulders.

The switchback served more as a symbol of the Northern Pacific's intention to complete the route than as a serviceable means of transportation. The track had been laid so hastily on frozen ground that much of it had to be replaced after the first thaw. The grade was too steep to permit heavy freight. Crews drew hazard pay for running the huge decapod lokeys that were hooked fore and aft to trains of five passenger coaches or five light-loaded freightcars for the eight miles between Martin on the east side and Stampede on the west. There was a brakeman for every two cars.

Notwithstanding the precautions there were accidents. Engineer J. Harvey Reed was taking a decapod over the pass with a load of heavy bridge timbers. The engine broke down. Reed tried to jockey the load over the top with a little Baldwin, Engine 457. He pushed the freightcar up the first leg of the switchback but, as he backed up the second leg, snow jammed into the sand pipes. When he called for sand, none spilled onto the track. The wheels of the Baldwin began to spin on slick steel. Engine and car slowed, halted, and, after a desperate wheel-spinning pause, slipped backwards, slowly at first, then faster and faster. Reed and his firemen jumped, landing safely in snowdrifts. Engine and car sped down the slope, rocking around curves until they came to a curving trestle where two men were working. The engine struck one man killing him instantly. His companion dropped face down on the ties. Just as it reached him the engine jumped the track, hurtled over the side without touching him, and plunged into the ravine.

Engine 457 was restored to service, as was Engineer Reed. He was at the throttle of the little Baldwin three months later when it was overtaken and rammed from behind in a tunnel. The coal tender was knocked loose but there was enough water left in the boiler for Reed to get back to Martin. For years old-timers yarned about the arrival of the bob-tail lokey.

While the trains ran the slalom course over the summit, Captain Sidney's work gangs moled below, none too expeditiously. There were slides, strikes, cave-ins, deaths from blasting, and some mayhem at management level. Sidney persuaded Nelson to persuade President

Harris to remove the project engineer, with whom Sidney did not see eye to eye. And somebody, somewhere along the line of authority, decided to furnish slave-driver Sidney with a carrot as well as a club. A bonus was offered. Each month, for every foot gained over the necessary average of 13.58 feet a day, laborers doing continuous duty were paid twenty-five cents extra, drill men and expert workmen, fifty cents. The pace increased phenomenally. On September 1, 1887, a year after the Ingersolls were put at both faces, work was 410 feet behind schedule. In the next eight and a half months they made up 454½ feet—132½ in April alone. It cost the Bennetts thirty-three dollars extra for every man who had worked steadily that thirty days—and it saved the performance bond.

Moving into May, when each blast might mean open space ahead, the Bennetts offered a thousand dollars to the first man through the bore with the fringe benefit of a steak dinner and whiskey for the side he represented. Each team picked a tough little powder-monkey who could wiggle and struggle. Foremen had problems keeping the chosen men out of the area of flying rock when shots were touched off.

Shortly after noon on May 3, 1888, the men who rushed into the smoke and rock dust after a blast felt a draft. The west side representative wriggled into the hole and collided, head-on, with the eastern representative. As the delegates butted each other, their constituents pushed in behind, heaving and struggling, until at last the man from the west was shoved through—skinned, bleeding, triumphant. For the west this offset the statistic that through the long campaign the east had moved more rock.

Captain Sidney's wife had long insisted she would be the first person to walk under the Cascade range. She at least was the first of her sex. On her first crawl, Mrs. Bennett, a lady of heroic proportions, became stuck. The eastern team managed to pull her back by her ankles. Chagrined but determined she went down the tunnel, shed some undergarments, and, according to legend, sent out for a bucket of lard to coat her shoulders and hips. This time the men of the west gallantly pulled her through. She arose, her dark hair powdered with blasted basalt, and uttered the immortal words, "The drinks, gentlemen, are on my husband."

In Tacoma, along Cliff Avenue, the cannons thundered again. For the third time the Northern Pacific had been completed, this time for real.

"The Chinese Must Go"

FOG hung over the bay and rolled in drifts through the Tacoma business district on the evening of February 17, 1885. A small group of business and professional men were gathered in B. R. Everett's saloon, which, since its opening a month before, was being described locally as "the finest place on the Pacific Coast, outside San Francisco." Mr. Charley Lamson—he insisted on the "Mister"—presided at the solid walnut bar, longest north of San Francisco, and kept polished the most varied collection of colored glasses north of San Francisco. (Seattle was not on Tacoma's list of comparatives.) The group was composed of John S. Baker, a young grocer; Horace Wintermute, physician; James Chamberlain, town alderman; and Joseph Dieringer, a hay dealer. They knocked back a few drinks as they waited, not sure what the night would bring, for the invitations from the Chinese community had been as indefinite as they were ornate.

Shortly before ten o'clock, Charlie, a Chinese waiter from the nearby San Francisco Chop House, came in. Carrying a kerosene lamp, he escorted the little party down the slippery board sidewalk to the waterfront. Across the tracks, half extended over the water on pilings, stood the maze of buildings that made up Tacoma's main Chinatown. Charlie suddenly blew out the lamp and disappeared, leaving his entourage in damp darkness. Not for long. Whistles shrilled, gongs clanged, rockets whizzed up through the murk to explode in red streamers. A delegation of robed Chinese, escorted by aides bearing candles, crossed the tracks. It was Chinese New Year. In a time of racial tension in Tacoma, the Chinese merchants sought to build a bridge to the Occidental community.

The businessmen were led through shops specializing in porcelains, rice, dried foods, work clothes, teas. They were offered cigars and drinks of *no moi ju*, a rice brandy. They were bowed into a banquet room above a dry-goods store and served a ten-course Chinese dinner. The comestibles had been carefully selected to give the least possible offense to an Occidental palate. Drinks were served during courses and between courses. Dinner over, the Chinese competed in expressions of humility and gratitude for the presence of their guests, in expression of wistful hope that the little dinner might strengthen the bonds of friendship and commerce that bound east and west. And so forth, and so forth.

The businessmen responded with good humor broadened by much *no moi ju*. Dr. Wintermute paid tribute to the niceties of Chinese medical science, observing that "nothing could be more scientific and effective than the Chinese treatment of a tumor by rubbing it with an oyster shell, since that treatment means the last of the tumor, as well as the last of the patient."

Another round of *no moi ju*.

John Baker revealed that the skill he showed in operating Tacoma's S. Baker Wholesale Grocery stemmed from an apprenticeship in Canton where he had been in the ginseng, seaweed, and dried cat business.

More *no moi ju*.

Henry de Rasloff, who arrived late, essayed a speech in Chinese but was shouted down by his fellows who chanted, "Allee Samee, Me No Savee."

Still more *no moi ju*.

Joe Dieringer did homage to Chinese cuisine. After regretting the absence from the feast of shoulder of fricasseed rat, he discoursed on the delights of "parboiled mouse, two months old, its teeth extracted, its tail pomaded with glue, its ears nicely set, the whole immersed in a sputtering, crackling lake of dragon's lard, dotted like an archipelago with ambrosial isles of waxed insects, tanned sealskins, swans' rudders, cormorant filets and jackass corns."

Back to the rice brandy.

It was in this tone that the Tacoma *Ledger* reported one of the few efforts to create understanding between the white and Chinese communities on Puget Sound in the 1880s. The gap was deep and dangerous.

The question of the Chinese in Tacoma was nearly as old as the town. The first topic debated at the first meeting of the first literary society on January 25, 1875, was "Resolved: That Chinese Immigration has been an injury to the United States." W. J. Fife, W. H.

Leeds, and Francis Cook upheld the affirmative; W. E. Dingee, J. S. Howell, and a Mr. Young, the negative. As Herbert Hunt reports in his *History of Tacoma,* "The affirmative won. It always did."

Tacomans were not entirely of a mind about the undesirability of the Chinese presence. For some years Chinese were accepted quietly, though unenthusiastically (*tolerated* would be the precise word) as a work force. They did the town's washing, waited table, cleaned house, handled lumber on the green chain at some mills. The town's garbagemen and sewage disposal force, they carried off slops from homes, restaurants, and hotels in pails hung on poles balanced across their shoulders. Most of the garbage they collected was fed to their pigs. The fact that Chinese kept pigs under their houses, and sometimes inside, was held against them by barroom sociologists of the day, though the custom was by no means unknown among the whites. (A merchant named Graham tethered an insatiable swine known as Graham's Hyena outside his store on St. Helens. It charged at anyone carrying a bucket. After the Hyena mistook a few shopping baskets for garbage pails, the town council adopted an ordinance prohibiting the leashing of hogs on downtown sidewalks.)

Most Chinese lived along the waterfront on the outboard side of the Northern Pacific tracks on land leased from the railroad. (They were not permitted under law to buy real estate.) A few kept garden plots on the hillside. There was a handsome vegetable garden on the site later occupied by Rhodes Department Store at Eleventh and Broadway. They supplemented the truck from their plots and the catch from the bay—whites ridiculed their preference of bottomfish to salmon—with rice, steamed bread, and skunk cabbage.

Drawing from chapter opening in Oregon och Washington *by E. T. Skarstedt*

They kept apart. Most dressed in blue blouses, blue cotton pants, and sandals. They wore their hair long and queued. Few spoke good English; whites dismissed their language as bird chatter. Sometimes they held parties at which it was rumored that much gin was drunk and opium smoked. There was also talk of the kidnaping of white women, but on the one recorded occasion that police investigated the report that a Caucasian ingenue was suffering a fate worse than death in an opium den it was found that the lady in question had suffered the same fate professionally many times before. The police put her on a boat to Seattle.

Nearly all the Tacoma Chinese had come as railroad laborers from Kwantung Province whose capital, Canton, was the first and for many years the only port where foreigners were permitted to do business. It was one of the most overpopulated, poverty-ridden areas in the world, a place where millions lived at the edge of starvation, where a young man with three hundred dollars could contemplate retirement. There was no problem finding men willing to work abroad. Hiring was done through the Six Companies of Kwantung, licensed by the Chinese government. Company agents gathered gangs of workers who agreed to pay the company 2½ percent of their wages, plus a forty-dollar deduction to cover the cost of passage across the Pacific. The Six Companies negotiated the workers' contracts with their American employers and represented the workers' interests in the United States not only as laborers but as residents in a foreign land. They acted as unofficial consuls. The system worked reasonably well as a way of bringing in mass labor to build railroads, especially during the Civil War period when much of the American work force was under arms, but it created problems when some of the Chinese chose to stay on after the tracks were laid. They competed with white immigrants and with emancipated blacks for the work available to the unlettered newcomer.

Job competition was fiercest in the city, especially competition between the Chinese and the potato-famine Irish. San Francisco, which had the greatest concentration of Chinese in the 1870s, gave rise to several Irish orators of influence, the most notorious being Dennis Kearney, a teamster who honed class hatred on racial hatred. Kearney denounced the nabobs of Nob Hill for planning to reduce white workmen to the status of coolies; he ended every speech with the cry, "The Chinese Must Go." Less well known but more effective as a tiller in the fields of racial hate was Frank Roney. Setting aside his socialist-egalitarian convictions, he cold-bloodedly used anti-Chinese prejudice as a device for getting whites to join trade unions. A white label on a cigar meant it had been wrapped by union workers, all white. No Chinese spit in your smoke. Sinophobia was midwife at the birth of the San Francisco Central Labor Council. Some nationals, too, most notably the Knights of Labor and the International Workingman's Association, used opposition to the Chinese as an organizing principal.

If labor organizers were sometimes callous in their exploitation of the Chinese Question, they had the excuse of economic interest. It is harder to understand the shift of American intellectuals from an early awe at Chinese civilization to acceptance of Chinese inferiority. As early as 1824, young Ralph Waldo Emerson was writing in his journal, "They are tools for other nations to use. Even miserable Africa can say I have hewn the wood and drawn the water to promote the civilization of other lands. But China, reverend dullness! hoary idiot! All she can say at the convention of nations must be—I made the tea."

By 1842 Americans could read in the article on China in the *Encyclopedia Britannica* that "The Chinese is cold, cunning and distrustful; always ready to take advantage of those he has to deal with; extremely covetous and deceitful; quarrelsome, vindictive, but timid and dastardly. A Chinaman in office is a strange compound of insolence and meanness. All ranks and conditions have a total disregard for the truth."

Horace Greeley assured readers of the New York *Tribune* that, "the Chinese are uncivilized, unclean and filthy beyond all conception, without any of the higher domestic or social relations; lustful and sensual in their dispositions; every female is a prostitute of the basest order." And in the rival New York *Herald,* James Gordon Bennett defended the opium wars with the argument that "lusty boys are not worth over four dollars at the [Chinese] sea ports, and good looking girls three. When material is so plentiful and so cheap a little of it may be wasted without much injury. If the great rivers are opened by such a war, it is a worthy investment."

An article in the *Anthropological Review* stated that "as the type of the Negro is foetal, that of the Mongol is infantile. And in strict accordance with this we find that their government, literature and art are infantile also." Edwin Meade, in an address to the Social Science Association of America, told the assembled scholars, "It is true that the ethnologists declare that a brain capacity of less than 85 cubic inches is unfit for free government, which is considerably above that of the coolie as it is below the Caucasian." And on February 14, 1879, Senator James Blaine, who the following year became secretary of state, said, "There is no comparing European immigration with an immigration that has no regard to family, that does not observe the tie of parent and child, that does not have in the slightest degree the ennobling and civilizing influences of the hearthstone and the fireside."

In the great discussion of the Chinese Problem, the only ones who defended the Chinese and suggested there might be a white problem were the newspaper humorists. Peter Finley Dunne's comic character, Mr. Dooley, observed "Th' Chinymen have been on earth a long time, an' I don't see how we can push so many iv thim off iv it. Annyhow, 'tis a good thing f'r us they ain't Chrstyans an' haven't larned properly to sight a gun."

The United States was committed by a treaty negotiated with China in 1846 to protect Chinese visiting or resident in this country. In theory they possessed the same rights as other foreigners and could come and go freely, engage in any occupation. In 1868 a new treaty, known as the Burlingame Treaty, was negotiated. The preamble stated that the contracting parties "cordially recognize the inherent and inalienable right of man to change his home and allegiance and also the mutual advantage of the free migration and emigration of their citizens and subjects from one country to the other." Each nation pledged to protect the persons and property of visitors from the other but neither conferred the right of naturalization to the visitors.

Governments may pledge high ideals but if the citizenry, grubbing for a living, finds the ideals burdensome, adjustments are probable. In 1880 the State Department persuaded China to concede permission to the United States to regulate, limit, or suspend immigration, but not absolutely to prohibit it. Congress, reacting to anti-Chinese agitation in the West, passed an exclusion act in 1882 which suspended immigration of Chinese laborers for ten years but did not restrict entry of students, merchants, travelers, and government officials.

The Chinese Exclusion Act coincided with the completion of the Northern Pacific main line, on which Villard had employed some seventeen thousand Chinese, and with a national slowdown in construction. Chinese contract laborers, laid off by the railroads, flooded into the cities. To white workers in railroad towns like Tacoma it appeared that the Exclusion Act was a fraud. Organizations and individuals who had a stake in the anti-Chinese movement—racist politicians, labor organizers, demagogic editors, enforcement agencies seeking larger budgets—claimed that for the benefit of corporations seeking to depress the wage scale, Chinese by the thousands were being smuggled into the country, especially across the British Columbia border.

There are no reliable statistics on the number of Chinese in Tacoma in the 1880s and little information on how long individual Chinese stayed. Newcomers moved in with their countrymen, moved on when jobs were available elsewhere. There seems to have been a high turnover. But some Chinese who arrived early, during the construction of the Kalama-to-Tacoma line, had stayed to grow up with the community. Among the Celestial old settlers were Sing Lee, who said he came in 1872; Kwok Sue, who arrived in 1873; Lum May, who opened a store in 1874; and How Lung, who went into business in 1875. Each apparently began by selling Oriental goods to his countrymen, then branched into operations that brought him into association with the white business community. All became labor contractors. They learned English, wore business suits by day, kept books, paid taxes. Some attended Christian churches, though there is no record of their becoming communicants. They tried to serve as bridges between the cultures. And eventually they were all walked over.

In 1881 Tacoma's population almost doubled from the 1,098 whom federal census takers counted the previous year. Among the arrivals was Jacob Robert Weisbach, heavy-set, humorless, a modestly successful merchant and failed revolutionary.

Weisbach was born in Worms, on the Rhine, on November 14, 1832. As a young man he fell under the influence of Giuseppe Mazzini, the Italian revolutionary who founded Young Europe, an underground organization that recruited antimonarchial idealists "believing in a future of liberty, equality, and fraternity for all mankind, and desirous of consecrating their thoughts and actions to the realization of that future." Young Robert—he did not use the Jacob—was consecrated enough to shelter Mazzini after he fled Italy in 1853, and to write essays in defense of the anarchistic theories of Pierre Joseph Proudhon, activities for which he was eventually sentenced to prison for five months, but released on condition he leave Germany. He went to China, where, like McCarver with the blacks during his stay in the South, he came to blame the laboring poor for their poverty. In 1859 he left China for America.

New York not proving to his liking, Weisbach moved on to northeastern Kansas where, in Marysville, he entered the mercantile business and the Republican party. Abraham Lincoln appointed him postmaster of Marysville in 1862, his neighbors elected him to the state legislature, and the governor made him quartermaster of the Second Brigade of the Kansas State Militia during the Indian troubles of 1864. In 1867 he was elected county commissioner. The following year he helped found a new town, the largely Germanic community of Frankfort, which elected him its first mayor. Disillusioned by the Grant administration, he left the Republicans for the Greenback Labor party in the 1870s, and, disappointed by the pervasive farming depression and the slow growth of Frankfort, he decided at the age of forty-nine to move to the Pacific Northwest.

Weisbach set up shop in a two-story frame building between Fifteenth and Seventeenth on Pacific Avenue. The family lived upstairs. Gold lettering on the street-level windows proclaimed "J. Robert Weisbach. Groceries, Provisions, Furnishing Goods, Clothing, Glassware." Politics, too. Germanic names were second only to Anglo-Saxon in Tacoma. There were enough Germans to support a German-language weekly, a German Methodist Church, a German choral society, and a German-American Association of one hundred members, of which Weisbach was president. When in 1883 the legislature gave permission for the towns of New Tacoma (estimated population 4,000) and Old Tacoma (400) to merge, an election was scheduled for December to choose a mayor and nine aldermen who would steer the combined communities through the first six months of union. Weisbach was nominated for alderman from the Third District, the downtown area, by the People's party.

Town politics were more personal than partisan. Cleavage of opinion was deepest over the railroad and the land company. With the completion of the main line all the towns in the territory were gaining population, but Tacoma, with the greatest expectations, had not caught Seattle, much less Portland. The faction calling itself the Businessman's party argued patience, Tacoma would realize its destiny now that Villard was losing power; those who called themselves the People's party argued that the Northern Pacific and Tacoma Land Company officials were more interested in the stockholders back east than the citizenry on Commencement Bay.

Weisbach was not antibusiness, he was anticorporation. A small businessman himself, he helped organize the Tacoma Chamber of Commerce. When workers digging a well on Kay Street swore they smelled petroleum, Weisbach joined in organizing the Mutual Oil Company to exploit the oil. He was not opposed to being rich. But he shared the farmers' suspicion of bankers, retained his old Proudhonian suspicion of the power structure, and as a former political prisoner felt government tended to protect the powerful against the weak.

The election proved to be a test of familiarity, not philosophy. After two years in town, Weisbach had been there longer than half the residents. He was part of the downtown landscape, a familiar figure, bearded, balding, dressed in broadcloth, a picture of probity, the embodiment of the burgher, an old-timer at fifty-one, not yet gone to seed. He was elected, as were most of the men on the People's party ticket, but hostility toward the Establishment was not overwhelming. General John Sprague, the manager of the land company and former superintendent for the Northern Pacific, was elected mayor. With more than a thousand ballots cast, Sprague got all but two votes.

In May of 1884, when Tacoma was to elect officials for full two-year terms, Sprague declined to run. At a meeting open to all males Weisbach was nominated as candidate of the Citizens Ticket. He beat out Walter J. Thompson, a young banker, 302 votes to 200—a margin that would have been more impressive had not Thompson told the assemblage he would not run if nominated nor serve if elected.

Opposing Weisbach in the final was E. S. "Skookum" Smith, the engineer who had brought the rails into Tacoma in 1873. Smith was an Establishment figure long associated with the railroad and the land company, but he ran under the colors of the Tacoma Temperance Voters League and the Women's Christian Temperance Union. Thus saddled, he crossed the finish line thirty-nine votes behind Weisbach, the German having nothing against an occasional schnapps.

The old revolutionary was in charge of the Northern Pacific's new town.

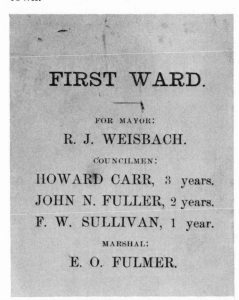

Election ticket, 1884 Courtesy of Rick and Francie Carr

Weisbach's term as mayor coincided with a turn-down in the national economy that limited the benefits completion of the Northern Pacific main line might have brought Tacoma. Population expanded at the terminus, as it did throughout the territory, but wheat prices were low, construction was slow in California, the major market for Puget Sound lumber, and the forest of masts at dockside in Commencement Bay was largely stationary. The migration to the cities of Chinese laid off from railroad projects was a complication resented by white job-seekers.

The Carpenters' Union, Tacoma's first labor organization, its membership proudly lily-white, expressed the mood of the day when it voted unanimously to condemn Alderman John E. Burns for employing Chinese to lay pipe for his water company. Burns reacted by firing the Chinese, hiring Indians to take their places, and lecturing the populace on the threat of coolie labor to the dignity of the white worker. Burns became one of Tacoma's most active agitators against the Chinese.

The most virulent propaganda against the Chinese appeared in the Tacoma *Ledger* under the by-line of its editor. A lean, tense, dramatically handsome young man from Philadelphia, Jack Comerford ("Jim Jams Jack" to the boys in the city room) detested Orientals with a passion as unfettered as his prose.

In January of 1885 two patrons of a Pacific Avenue brothel got in a fight, knocked over a lamp, and burned the place down. A Chinese merchant leased the property for a laundry. Comerford was aghast that the town's main street should be defiled by a washhouse. Under the headline CHINESE INVASION OF TACOMA, the *Ledger* outlined the clear and present danger: "Allow Chinese twenty feet on any prominent street in any city with a future to it, and like the speed of atmospheric pestilence they spread the contagion of their filthy numbers so rapidly that in a brief time they will occupy the whole street." Tacoma was warned of the sad fate of San Francisco, where

block after block was deserted by the citizens. They fled from it as a pest, as a charnal house, as a ghostly morgue; as a free and open school for the debauchment of their sons and daughters. . . . The Chinamen swarmed in like rats, where the original rat had piloted the way and let them in. Hundreds of these creatures were crowded into these filthy tenements; packed in their sleeping apartments and in their noisome dens of opium joints and pestilent prostitution, like decaying dog-salmon boxed up for shipment. Why permit an army of leprous, prosperity-sucking, progress-blasting Asiatics to befoul our thoroughfares, degrade the city, repel immigration, drive out our people, break up our homes, take employment from our countrymen, corrupt the morals of our youth, establish opium joints, buy or steal the babe of poverty or slave, and taint with their brothels the lives of our young men? . . . If no other method of keeping them at a distance from our people can be found, let the citizens furnish them with lots on the waterfront, three fathoms below low tide.

Press discussion of the Chinese presence was one-sided. The only published response from the Chinese community to all the abuse was a letter to the editors of the *Ledger* and the *News* from Mark Ten Suie and Un Gow. They asked plaintively why they were called heathen after they had been baptized Christian. The most polite of the published replies was that a Christian Chinese was a contradiction in terms.

On a Saturday night in February 1885, in the lumber town of Eureka in the heart of the northern California redwood country, two rival groups of Chinese got into a fight. Eureka was crowded with loggers laid off for the winter. The whole town turned out to watch the fun. The Chinese were armed, and in the course of shooting at each other they shot a white youth in the foot and a councilman through the head. Law-and-order loggers thereupon assembled in Eureka's largest hall, declared the Chinese a menace to the community, erected a gallows at the entrance to Chinatown, and recommended that the Chinese depart within twenty-four hours.

Among the visitors in Eureka that weekend was William Christie, a carpenter by trade, a member of the Tacoma school board and a political associate of Mayor Weisbach. He and the mayor were charter members of a short-lived secret society known as the New Era Brotherhood, the aims of which were never made public. Christie was impressed with the simplicity and effectiveness of the Eureka solution. Returning a few days after the dispersion, Christie met with Mayor Weisbach and a small group of anti-Chinese in a room above the Weisbach store. No records were kept of what was said, but rumors spread through town that direct action was contemplated against Tacoma's Chinese.

Some business leaders and churchmen, who styled themselves "The Better Element" and feared that forcible expulsion would give Tacoma a bad name, suggested that Weisbach call a public meeting to consider ways of solving the Chinese Problem without violence. Weisbach agreed, setting the time as 7:30 on Saturday, February 21, the place as the Alpha Opera House.

It was the largest indoor assemblage Tacoma had known, though some picnics and horse races had drawn more. The county assessor estimated the town's population that month as 6,936 (including 532 Chinese). About 900 persons crowded into the hall. They were nearly all male, white, and of legal age, which meant about half of the town's registered voters were present. Eli Bacon, a fireman, was chosen as chairman, and Albert Whyte, the feisty little United States marshal, served as secretary.

The question before the house was not whether the Chinese should leave Tacoma but how they should be persuaded to go. Those who spoke against the use of force went out of their way to deplore the Chinese presence; they agreed the aliens were unsightly, ill-smelling, untrustworthy, dirty to the point of leprosy, immoral, and unassimilable, but argued that their presence, however awful, was legal. That was the extent of the defense. The other speeches dealt with ways and means of forcing them out.

Former Alderman Burns agreed that they could not be chased away simply because they were Chinese but suggested that the town council adopt health and sanitation ordinances that would make it possible for the city to burn down Chinatown, after which the Tacoma Land Company could furnish land for a Chinese colony well removed from the rest of the community, or "we could ship them 250 miles due west."

The Reverend J. B. Thompson, Methodist, said he was conservative about what he liked and radical about what he didn't. He didn't like the Chinese but demurred at the idea of dumping them in the ocean. Segregation seemed the answer. A fellow member of the cloth, the Reverend J. A. Ward, thought that responsible property owners could be persuaded to restrict sales and rentals to whites. H. K. Moore, an attorney, warned that five thousand Chinese prostitutes in California were infecting the sons of the very best people. He also deplored what a Chinese in the block did to property values.

The *Ledger,* which described the speeches as "mild, void of bitterness, responsible but firm," was charmed by the words of the mayor. They were met, said the paper, with "distinguished approval." Weisbach allowed that talk about the rights of the Chinese to be in town was well and good but what was being overlooked was the right of self-preservation. (Applause.) The community had a right to protect itself. (Applause.) He did not know who should be punished most, the corporations or the Chinese. (Applause and suggestions.) "They came here to steal your cream and on their return to China to laugh at your folly." (Groans.) He was not here to incite violence "but it behooves us to rid ourselves of this curse." (Footstamping.) "If the people are in earnest, if they are Free Americans in fact, they will not yield up their homes and businesses to the filthy horde." (Distinguished approval.)

Weisbach's harangue was followed by adoption of a resolution which said that Chinese should be excluded from Tacoma and that it was the duty of every good citizen to discourage the employment of Asiatics. Chairman Bacon appointed two doctors, a lawyer, a banker, and five workingmen as an action committee. They drew up for circulation throughout the city an agreement pledging to boycott Chinese as employees or tenants. "Full publicity" was promised anyone who refused to sign.

This was hardly what the Better Element had in mind when they asked the mayor to call a public meeting. For the first time they seemed to realize how limited was the authority of the educated and the well-to-do in a mushroom community of strangers, where indeed one man's opinion was as weighty as another's and the moderating influence of church and social groups not well established. They decided to hold another meeting, attendance by invitation only, to discuss alternative things to be alarmed about.

Theirs was a more genteel gathering marked by the familiar complaints of the upper class against the way things worked. W. J. Fife, "Old Billy," said the real problem in Tacoma was "dilly-dallying by the city council." J. A. Banfield thought there ought to be a law against Chinese living where they were not wanted. The Reverend Mr. Ward, muting his anti-Chinese sentiments in deference to the congregation, declared that Tacoma was "an eastern city set down in the west." An easterner himself, he meant this as a compliment. He explained that Tacoma's eastern qualities were not its saloons (one for every seventy two adult males) or brothels (no statistics available) but "the businessmen, the enterprise, the virtue and purity of the domestic fireside." The Reverend Mr. Thompson added that, as the anti-Chinese said, a Chinese brothel was no asset to the community, but that neither were white brothels, of which there were lots more, not to mention saloons, and gambling joints, and places that stayed open on the Sabbath.

The Better Element had found its theme: Tacoma had nuisances in more urgent need of abatement than the presence of Chinese. A sense-of-the-meeting resolution cited the report of the most recent Pierce County grand jury, which had held "that saloon-keepers are almost universal violaters of the law by selling liquors to minors and permitting gambling on their premises. By general report we find houses of prostitution in conspicuous places, near the business portion of the city. The impunity which these dens of vice seem to enjoy can result only from criminal negligence on the part of city officers." They added that if city officials wanted to remove obstacles to progress they might busy themselves getting the stumps out of downtown streets. They then organized themselves into the Tacoma Law and Order League, a title suggesting that the laws should be obeyed in dealing with the Chinese and order maintained by more circumspect conduct in the business area, especially on Sundays.

Their reward was to find themselves described in the *Ledger*, in prose unmistakably Comerfordian, as

a group so small as to be almost intangible . . . without influence, attractiveness, cohesion . . . so weak numerically and so wanting in public notoriety that it recalls Mark Twain's good Indians, who are now an extinct tribe because luckily they never existed. . . . For the most part cranks, busybodies, officious small committees, a cackling sisterhood of impractical reformers in the van, with a hen-pecked, submissive, tongue-driven confraternity of suppressed manhood always in their rear. . . . A little band of silly detriments who, for some inscrutable reason, are permitted to disorganize churches, annoy society and by their cant and ridiculous conduct attach a bad reputation to every community which is too wise to be controlled by them. They are anything but a Vigilance Committee. They have too little at stake and are too much unsexed and emasculated to form themselves into a determined body of that kind.

After receiving that broadside the Law and Order League sank from the public record without trace. It was the anti-Chinese, incited by the press, encouraged by the mayor, who organized. William Christie headed a committee that gathered hundreds of signatures on petitions promising to boycott stores that employed Chinese. Merchants found it advantageous to emblazon their advertisements for shoes and shirtwaists, soap, cigars, even funerals, with the slogan "The Chinese Must Go."

A local of the International Workingman's Association was formed and claimed (but did not necessarily have) sixty members. The IWA had no connection with the earlier organization of the same name, the first Marxist international. This one was the brainchild of Burnett Haskell, a left-wing California lawyer much given to creating revolutionary organizations that existed mainly as letterheads. Haskell proclaimed the IWA an umbrella for radicals of all types. The Tacoma chapter seems to have attracted mainly the physical. Its most notorious members were Mike Ward, who impressed companions by biting chunks out of his whiskey glasses; Jacob "Big Foot" Ralph, an oversized Nova Scotian who was said to have decked John L. Sullivan in a barroom, and Dennis Nearney, who did not mind being confused with Dennis Kearney, the San Francisco agitator. Nearney had been jailed for, among other things, beating his wife and threatening to blow up the houses of Northern Pacific officials when the NP sought to remove his shack from company right-of-way. A perennial candidate for town marshal, he offered himself unsuccessfully for the presidency of the IWA local.

More genteel in make-up was the Tacoma Anti-Chinese League. It grew out of a meeting called by Mayor Weisbach on June 9 to orchestrate the activities of the various organizations committed to getting rid of the Chinese. The league drew representatives not only from the IWA, the New Era Brotherhood, and the Carpenters' Union but from the Typographical Union, the fire department, the Independent Labor Party, and such ethnic organizations as the Turn-Verein, the Germanic Society, and the Hibernians. Weisbach was elected president; B. W. Coiner, an attorney, vice president; and M. P. Bulger, a sewing machine salesman, secretary.

The city council responded to the pressure. They adopted an ordinance recommended by the mayor which required five hundred cubic feet of air space per individual in sleeping rooms. Weisbach and the Reverend Mr. Ward then toured the Chinese houses to see if city requirements were being met. Of course they weren't. The report was read at an anti-Chinese mass meeting in the Opera House and sections describing shanties noisome with hog slops and human excrement, redolent of dried fish, dead chicken, and opium, with buckets overflowing with garbage and laundry were printed in the *Ledger*.

The anti-Chinese could now argue that the Chinese were a health menace.

As violence in Eureka preceded the anti-Chinese agitation in Tacoma, violence in Wyoming preceded bloodshed in Washington.

On September 2 white and Chinese coal miners working in a shaft operated by the Union Pacific at Rock Springs, Wyoming, got into a brawl. That night white miners attacked the houses of the Chinese workers, setting the buildings on fire and shooting at the inmates as they fled. Authorities found twenty-eight bodies. Five days later Chinese were murdered in the hop fields of western Washington.

The cultivation of hops on Puget Sound was begun in the 1860s by the ubiquitous Ezra Meeker, but the crop did not become commercially important until the early 1880s when a blight all but wiped out the vines in Europe. Prices soared, acreage expanded, and for a time finding pickers was a problem. The recovery of European fields, the larger Northwest crop, and the business recession led to lower prices in 1885, which in turn led to wage cutting. Hops were usually harvested by Indians with a few white workers included in the crews to serve as pace-makers. The Indians received seventy five cents a box, the whites a dollar a box. In August, Lars and Ingebrigt Wold, the largest hop producers in Squak Valley (today's Issaquah) decided to use Chinese labor and pay them ninety cents a box, a rate offensive to both white and Indian pickers.

At ten o'clock on the night of Monday, September 7, a party of whites and Indians climbed the fence surrounding the field where the Chinese were camped and began shooting into the tents. Two men, Fung Wai and Mox Goat, were killed in their beds. A watchman, Ying Sun, was shot in the back as he ran and died the next day. Three others were severely wounded as they fled to the woods. The raiders pulled down the tents. One was set ablaze by a candle inside. Clothing, bedding, and personal possessions from the other tents were piled on the fire. The next day all the Chinese were gone except for two who volunteered to look after the wounded and bury their dead.

Later that week a Chinese work force at the Oregon Improvement Company mine on Coal Creek, not far from Squak Valley, was attacked. Forty-nine Chinese were employed there, most of them as coal pickers in the bunkers; they were paid $1.25 for a ten-hour day spent separating rock and slate from the coal. The mine superintendent told protesters that whites would not work for that pay, that the price of coal was so low the company would shut the mine rather than use white pickers. If necessary, guards would be hired to protect the Chinese. No guards were present on the night of September 11 when a band of masked men carrying rifles kicked in the door of the barracks where the Chinese roomed, routed them from bed, drove them into the woods, and burned the dormitory and cook-house. Shots were fired but no casualties were reported.

Terrorism achieved the result the night-riders wanted. Chinese fled the hop fields and the coal fields. One of them was quoted in the Seattle *Post-Intelligencer* as saying, "White man much too bad. Too much make-um fire. Me no catchum clothes, no catchum lice, no catchum anything. Me no go back, too muchee flaid." Refugees from the upper valleys converged on Tacoma and Seattle, replacing the Chinese who had been intimidated into leaving the towns by earlier threats. They were not welcomed.

On the day of the Squak Valley massacre, a local of the Knights of Labor was organized in Tacoma. The Knights had been established in 1869 by a handful of garment workers in Philadelphia who hoped to improve the estate of the working man by reforming society through rhetoric and cabalistic ritual. The national regarded strikes as "a relic of barbarism." More a lodge than a union, they attracted little attention until 1883 when some runaway locals ad libbed a successful strike against the Union Pacific, which had proposed a wage cut. That victory, coinciding with the recession, led to a spectacular though short-lived spurt in membership, six hundred thousand in 1885.

Mayor Weisbach was on hand for the investiture of the Tacoma local, but he was upstaged by Charles Voorhees, the territorial delegate to Congress, who not only appeared but petitioned for membership, though he was a lawyer and Knighthood was not to be granted to Chinese, saloon keepers, or attorneys. Dan Cronin presented the charter to the Tacomans. A small, husky Irishman with an arm crippled from an accident in the woods, Cronin had been present at Eureka when the Chinese were chased out; a few months later the national sent him to Washington Territory to organize. Cronin had a well of bitterness, a gift for words, and a knack for arousing anger. His rhetoric, heavy with implied threats of things to come, ran counter to the Knights' claim that they opposed violence, but it attracted the discontented who wanted action. From Tacoma, Cronin moved on to Seattle, where he played a pivotal role in the first anti-Chinese rally there.

The meeting, called by a group styling itself the Liberal League, was held in the bleak, plank-seated Yesler Hall on Sunday, September 20. It attracted a large audience of working-class males, many of them unemployed. The scenario followed that of the first Tacoma meeting seven months earlier: uncomplimentary descriptions of the Chinese; expressions of hope that if they were made to feel unwanted they would leave; cautious expressions of concern from political figures (James Hamilton Lewis, a young lawyer noted for pink whiskers and sartorial splendor, starting on a career that would carry him to the Senate, ducked the question of expulsion but assured the audience that he loved them and would look out for them); then, a fighting speech, with Cronin playing the role of Weisbach at the Tacoma gathering.

"Taffy," Cronin called what had gone before. "Action," was what he demanded. When Cronin was through those assembled voted to convene a Puget Sound Anti-Chinese Congress in Seattle on Monday, September 28, to plan the immediate departure from western Washington of The Yellow Menace.

As in Tacoma, the Better Element of Seattle countered with an assemblage of their own. Establishment figures such as Judge Orange Jacobs, County Prosecutor J. T. Ronald, Territorial Governor Watson Squire, Assistant U.S. Attorney Cornelius Hanford, and Northern Pacific Attorney James McNaught graced the platform. Mayor Henry Yesler presided. (Jim Jams Jack Comerford sarcastically described the speakers as "horny-handed, leather-palmed sons of toil.") While some speakers said they would not mind seeing the Chinese go back where they came from, all urged patience lest violence besmirch Seattle's reputation and impede capital investment. These were arguments the unemployed and poorly paid found less than persuasive. The Anti-Chinese Congress was held as scheduled.

Tacoma sent the largest delegation, one-third of the total of sixty-nine delegates. Mayor Weisbach, Deputy Pierce County Assessor Alex Macready, and A. U. Mills, a contractor, were chosen at a mass meeting to represent the city. Twenty other delegates were sent by labor, fraternal, ethnic, and political groups. The party took the Sunday evening steamer to Seattle, where they were met at the dock by a brass band and a reception committee of anti-Chinese who escorted them in a torchlight parade to the Occidental Hotel.

"Every socialist and anarchist who could walk or steal a ride to Seattle was a self-elected but nonetheless welcome delegate," grumbled retired Colonel Granville Haller (the same Haller who had been ambushed by the Yakima at the start of the Indian War). "Long-haired men and short-haired women were noticeable by their numbers and their noise." Haller thought he saw in the congress the end of the Republic.

Weisbach was the unanimous choice of the congress for president. "You curse the Chinamen for coming here," he told the cheering delegates in his acceptance speech. "They are not to blame. You ought to take the men who brought them here by the neck and choke them. In this crusade you have the united capital of the coast against you—a hard fight. I have been engaged in this work for years. Chains and prisons have been my portion but I believe there is an eternal justice."

Weisbach served, too, on the resolutions committee, which hammered out the plan of action. Delegates would go home and call mass meetings in each community for October 3. At these meetings expulsion committees would be elected to visit all Chinese in each town and warn them they must leave by November 1. What would happen if they refused was not mentioned. But the final resolution adopted by the congress declared, "We hold ourselves not responsible for any acts of violence which may arise from non-compliance with these resolutions."

In a concluding speech, Attorney George Venable Smith summed up the mood of the congress: "The Chinese must go at all hazards, peacefully if possible, but they must go."

Some five hundred anti-Chinese paraded through downtown Tacoma to the Alpha Opera House on October 3. Colonel J. M. Steele, a portly, much-wounded Civil War hero now dealing in real estate, presided as an expulsion committee, the "Committee of Fifteen," was elected to carry the word to the Chinese. The time had come. Get out of town. Don't be here after November 1.

Many Chinese left quietly. More than a hundred were reported to have caught the train to Portland or the boat to Victoria. Others had no funds to buy tickets anywhere. And some, especially those who had been in town for years, who had jobs, or businesses, who felt they had friends, stayed on, unable to believe force would be used against them. They were encouraged by men like former Mayor Sprague, who assured the Chinese who consulted him that this was the United States, they were in Tacoma legally, their rights would be protected.

Sun Chong, one of the more prosperous merchants, called on E. W. Taylor, a lawyer who served part time as a deputy prosecuting attorney. Sun wanted legal advice on ways of resisting expulsion. Taylor said he could not take the case and added that it was his personal opinion the townfolk meant business. The Chinese would be well advised to leave.

Sun said it would be difficult for the merchants to go. They had made improvements in their stores, which they could not sell at a fair price under existing circumstances. Could the City of Tacoma indemnify them for their losses if they were forced out? Taylor told him to see Mayor Weisbach.

The merchant from Canton and the merchant from Heidelberg faced each other that afternoon across the mayor's desk. The Chinese asked if it were true his people would have to go.

"It is," said Weisbach. "The firm determination is that you must and will have to go."

"We will have to go?"

"Yes."

Chong asked, merchant to merchant, if the city could not pay for the improvements the Chinese had made in their buildings. Weisbach said he would see what could be done.

There was no legal precedent for such payment. Nothing could be done. Weisbach could be a stickler for some rules.

The Committee of Fifteen, having given the Chinese notice of the deadline, began to call on employers. Most found it expedient to fire their Chinese employees, but H. S. Ferguson, proprietor of a barrel factory outside of Puyallup, faced down a delegation with a brace of pistols. A bomb exploded one night outside his plant. He let his Chinese go.

George Atkinson, manager of the Tacoma Mill, was affronted by having a group of workmen tell him whom he could employ. He demanded that those of his visitors who owed him money, and there were several, repay him on the spot. The anti-Chinese accused him of intimidation.

The Reverend W. D. McFarland, pastor of the First Presbyterian Church, a gaunt, red-haired Scot, came home one evening to learn that his family had been waited on by three members of the expulsion committee and warned to fire their Chinese servants. They had no Chinese employees but McFarland was outraged. He let it be known that his sermon the following Sunday would be on the Chinese Question.

The pews were packed, anti-Chinese showing up as well as those who opposed the expulsion. United States Marshal Albert Whyte, commanding officer of the Home Guard, sang the solo, "Holy Father, Thou Hast Taught Me." McFarland then lectured his congregation on law and order and the obligations of citizenship. He described the committee's visit to his house and said that had he been home he'd have kicked them into the street.

T. L. Nixon, an attorney, secretary of the YMCA, stood up and walked out. Others began to follow him.

"That's right," shouted the minister, "if you can't take the truth about yourselves, get out. Go! Go! I will preach on till the benches are empty."

Some of the congregation stayed, but reaction to the sermon was so adverse that McFarland visited Captain Whyte at the Home Guard headquarters and said that for the safety of his family he needed a weapon. Whyte showed him boxes of Army .45s which the territorial adjutant general had sent to Tacoma for distribution to the guard in case of trouble. "Help yourself. There are a hundred of them."

"In that case I'll take two," said the minister. For the next month he made pastoral rounds with the butts of the revolvers bulging under the tails of his Prince Albert.

As tension in the town mounted, Jim Jams Jack Comerford interviewed Albert Whyte of the Home Guard to see if force would be used to block eviction of the Chinese.

"Al, you don't mean you'd really try to carry out orders to stop us?"

"I am a soldier. When I get orders I intend to obey them."

"But we'll have 600 men with Winchesters opposed to you and they mean to fight."

"What's that to me. I am a soldier. I obey orders."

"You and your men will be killed."

"What's that to me. I am a soldier. I obey orders."

"Captain, what you are is a damned fool."

The orders to defend the Chinese never came.

Resistance in Tacoma to the anti-Chinese movement was crumbling. The last public debate on the subject was held by the members of the Tacoma Chamber of Commerce on October 8.

A committee chaired by George Fuller, the city attorney, presented a resolution which in its preamble conceded that the presence of the Chinese was injurious to the interests of the white laboring man and favored all lawful means of getting them out of town, including direct negotiations with the Emperor of China, but which concluded with a demand for law and order:

We absolutely disapprove of the use of any coercive measures looking to the expulsion of the Chinese, excepting those of a negative character, of refusing to employ them or rent them buildings . . . ; we denounce all attempts at inciting violence or the commission of any unlawful acts for the purpose of effecting their removal as highly injurious and prejudicial to the welfare of our city and especially to the welfare of the workingmen dependent upon capital for employment; and we call upon the officers of the law of this city and county to preserve order throughout the present anti-Chinese agitation, and to hold all persons using language calculated to incite to violence primarily responsible for all unlawful acts which may grow out of the same, and to prosecute them to the fullest extent of the law therefore.

Former Alderman Burns moved a substitute resolution "cordially and fully endorsing the actions of the so-called workingmen's movement for the expulsion of the Chinese, save and except only so much thereof as may contemplate unlawful violence." Whether there was in his mind violence that might be lawful, Burns did not say.

Ezra Meeker arose. He was one of the best-known men on the Sound, tiny, spry, and obstinate. He had held out to the end against the conviction of Leschi when he was young and poor and new to the community. Now he was a major figure in the hop industry, and he was the most articulate of the defenders of the Chinese against violence. He had written a long letter to the *Ledger* denouncing the hysteria and warning "the better part of the community [that] so long as we keep silence, and neither by word or action, say or do aught to counteract the pernicious effects certain to follow in the wake of this agitation, our silence will properly be construed as an endorsement of the cry, The Chinese Must Go." He had warned the mayor that his actions tended to incite lawlessness, riot, and bloodshed.

Now Meeker addressed the Chamber, his pale eyes fixing on those most hostile to the Chinese:

Among you I know I have many friends. You all know that I spring from and am of the labor class; that my sympathies are with them; that my every action has been to favor our own people. Yesterday I had 730 people in my employ, out of which 28 only were Chinamen, and these only in an out-of-the-way place where it was not easy to get others to go.

I am not in favor of the Chinese coming. I am in favor of the restriction act, but that is a very different question from that which you propose, a very different matter from saying in an unlawful manner "You must go" to a person who is here under our laws, entitled to the protection of our laws, entitled to the rights guaranteed to all living under our laws. I say this intimidation movement is a very different question as to whether any of us favor the Chinamen coming among us.

Many of you will live to see the day that you will look back upon our actions with amazement and wonder, and regret that the recollection of this period should not be forgotten under the pressure of a busy life. I say, let us respect our laws, enforce their provisions, make them better if they are not good enough, deprecate lawlessness, place ourselves aright in the eyes of our nation and the civilized world, and we need not fear the result.

Meeker moved a compromise resolution to set up an investigating committee to see how many illegal Chinese there really were, but "condemning the popular cry that the Chinese Must Go" as "revolutionary in character, unlawful in intent, harmful in result, and if persisted in certain to lead to bloodshed and riot." Meeker's resolution concluded with a call for "enforcement of the law to protect every individual in his rights under the law."

John Arthur led the attack on Meeker's proposal. He was an attorney from Philadelphia, married to the daughter of a major Northern Pacific shareholder. He had come to Tacoma as attorney for the Tacoma Land Company but quarreled with the local manager, Isaac Anderson, and lost his job. Now, turning to Anderson, General Sprague, Skookum Smith, and other mainstays of the company he accused them of perpetuating the Chinese presence by giving the Chinese secret assurances they would be protected. This, he said, must stop. There was no room in Tacoma for a Mandarin class. "The time has come when you can no longer be allowed to run this city."

Meeker's resolution was rejected. The Chamber of Commerce then voted, forty-one to twenty-two, to adopt Burns's resolution supporting the anti-Chinese movement "except where it might contemplate violence." Nobody defined violence.

If anyone was to block the expulsion, it would have to be the United States government.

As a frontier governor, Watson Squire had many disadvantages. He was an easterner. He was strikingly handsome. He dressed elegantly and spoke Ivy League English. He was rich; his beautiful wife, Ida, had inherited much of the Remington Arms fortune. He was resented as an appointee—all territorial officials were appointed and resented—but he was something especially resented, a Chester Arthur Republican holdover in the first Democratic administration since the Civil War. Democratic newspapers in the territory wanted him removed, if only for the patronage, but what they complained about in print were his dude clothes, his lah-de-dah manners, and the pneumatic cushion with which he protected his bottom from the governor's chair. Squire remained in office mainly because many influential Democrats disliked him less than they disliked the leading Democratic aspirant for the office, Eugene Semple. Asked by President Cleveland what he thought of Semple, a Seattle businessman called the candidate "a drunken, drooling fool without the capacity for office beyond that of a poundmaster." So Squire lingered on in Olympia, the axe poised over his neck. He was as quiet as he could be.

Governor Squire's immediate problem was to seem to meet the federal government's obligation to protect the Chinese nationals against violence without having to call on the United States Army to confront citizens of the territory. It is uncertain whether he arrived at his course of action by inadvertence or by guile. What he did was accept the word of the local elected officials that they could protect the Chinese from violence. There was a semantic catch: the federal government considered the threat of force to be an act of violence, while local officials felt that if the Chinese left without being physically abused the expulsion was nonviolent. Squire may not have realized that as the representative of federal law, the Constitution, and the guarantees of United States treaties he was applying different meanings to such words as *force, violence,* and *lawful* than did the elected officials interpreting the will of their local communities.

On October 14, as the Committee of Fifteen called on the Chinese and their employers to announce deadlines and the anti-Chinese groups paraded the downtown streets, Squire wired Sheriff Lewis Byrd of Pierce County to remind him that it would be very humiliating for both of them if the Army had to be called in. The governor asked whether the sheriff could deputize "enough reliable men to over-awe any turbulent element." Byrd replied that though the people seemed determined to get rid of the Chinese, he could "safely say we have a sufficient number of good substantial citizens among the businessmen of Tacoma who will stand ready and willing to assist me in the preservation of peace and the protection of the property and rights of the Chinese should occasion require their aid." The sheriff did not mention that there were even more members of anti-Chinese groups who stood ready to be deputized as well and that their interpretation of what constituted violence might be exceedingly narrow.

On October 20, Secretary of State Thomas Francis Bayard wired Squire from Washington to say the Chinese ambassador had asked protection of Chinese nationals in Washington Territory. Bayard said that "every power of law should be lent to secure them from assault." The governor wired the sheriff saying, "I trust you will make your arrangements so perfectly no assault will be attempted. Do not fail to secure a positively reliable *posse comitatus* in sufficient numbers to insure protection against disturbances of the peace." He also sent a letter to Mayor Weisbach which concluded, "The great question with me is the preservation of order and thereby the preservation of the good name of the Territory. I trust that I may depend upon your cordial support in carrying out the instructions of the authorities in Washington, that 'every power of law should be lent to secure the Chinese from assault.' "

Weisbach did not answer directly but instead called to his office a number of business leaders. After the Chamber of Commerce resolution urging the departure of the Chinese, most of the town's businessmen were resigned to the expulsion and concerned with preventing bloodshed and property damage and with minimizing adverse publicity. Thirty signed a letter to the governor assuring him that "there will be no occasion whatever for the presence of troops or the employment of an organized force under the sheriff," and that "the sheriff will be able to preserve the peace and enforce the laws. He will be supported in this by the citizens generally. We hold ourselves responsible for these assurances."

The governor wired General Sprague for his estimate of the situation. "Order will be preserved by sheriff," Sprague wired back. "If necessary five hundred deputies will support him. There will be no disturbance. Will write."

In a covering letter on October 23 Sprague said: "It looked at one time as though there might be some trouble, but that is passed. I am not surprised that people at a distance who read Tacoma papers conclude that there is danger of mob violence; but the papers, strangely enough, do not represent public sentiment here. A vast majority of people here desire to have the Chinese go and many are willing to utter incendiary language to frighten the Chinese away but will not countenance unlawful acts. . . ." Sprague added that the sheriff was quietly deputizing a *posse comitatus*, and that "I expect to be a deputy sheriff myself, an honor that I never expected to attain." Sprague did not say, and probably did not know, that the sheriff was issuing badges to five anti-Chinese for every law-and-order man who received one.

Only minor events disturbed the surface calm of the week before the deadline. The publisher of the *Ledger,* R. F. Radebaugh, ordered Comerford to stop writing about the Chinese and Jim Jams Jack resigned loudly. The Tacoma Ministerial League, made up of eight Protestant ministers out of the town's twenty-seven, issued a manifesto including the Chinese in the human race and asking conciliation of differences. Governor Squire came to town and made an all-things-to-all-people address to the Chamber. "The Chinese should go," he said, "but they should be made to go legally."

No attention was paid to a new group, the Committee of Nine, which had been established in great secrecy by the anti-Chinese. Its members were A. U. Mills, contractor; M. P. Bulger, sewing machine salesman; William Christie, carpenter; Frank McGill, street commissioner; W. H. Hunter, house painter; John Budlong, carpenter; W. H. Rapier, Sr., and W. H. Rapier, Jr., plasterers; and Chancellor Graves, the janitor at the Central School. Each man was committed to recruit nine others who would be known only to him, each of whom would recruit nine others, and so on, chain-letter fashion, ad infinitum. Such an organization could not meet to make policy but it could serve as apparatus for assembling a large body of men at short notice at a pre-arranged signal.

On Halloween, which was also the eve of the expulsion deadline, a delegation of anti-Chinese from Seattle arrived by steamer and marched solemnly through light rain to the Alpha, where the Tacoma Anti-Chinese League was holding a rally. George Venable Smith congratulated the people of Tacoma on having declared their independence from the Northern Pacific. There was no discussion of direct action against the Chinese.

Deadline day dawned clear. About 150 Chinese, some from Tacoma but many others from outlying communities where expulsion committees were active, such as Black Diamond, Carbonado, Sumner, and Puyallup, boarded the steamer *Southern Chief* for Victoria. A few took the train south. About two hundred remained in town.

November 2 in Seattle three men charged by the government with murder for their part in the Squak Valley massacre were acquitted by a King County jury which deliberated only half an hour over evidence that included a confession from one of the accused. The message was clear. It was open season on Chinese. That night in Tacoma both the Committee of Fifteen, which had been selected to tell the Chinese they must go, and the clandestine Committee of Nine held meetings. A. U. Mills, the contractor, shuttled back and forth between the groups. There was no announcement of what was decided.

Shortly before dawn Tuesday morning, November 3, the southwest wind strengthened and the rain turned into a downpour. The steamer *Bob Irving,* coming south from Seattle, was forced to take shelter in Quartermaster Harbor. Work was suspended on the *North Pacific,* which was getting new machinery. The *Lottie,* discharging oats from the San Juans, chaffed at the mill dock as gusts rocked her. Men trudging to work that morning found Pacific Avenue, Railroad Street, and C Street deep in mud. The hill streets, Ninth and Eleventh, flowed like the Puyallup, too thin to plow, too thick to drink. Delivery wagons making their morning rounds sent mud squirting across the plank sidewalks. A miserable day.

Between 8:30 and 9:00 A.M., Sheriff Byrd encountered Mayor Weisbach on Pacific Avenue and asked if he knew what the Committee of Fifteen had decided. Weisbach answered somewhat evasively that as far as he knew nothing was to be done that day, the sheriff could relax. Byrd said that as he saw things, he and the mayor had the same obligations and ought to keep each other informed. They parted, Byrd heading for the post office, Weisbach for his store.

Exactly at 9:30 the whistle shrieked at the Lister Foundry, its sound heavy in the rain-thick air. Other factory whistles joined the ululation. Suddenly the streets were full of grim-faced men moving to a point of assembly on Pacific. When between two and three hundred had assembled they formed a line and slogged up the hill to Seventeenth and C (today's Broadway) where an isolated Chinese house stood.

The main body of marchers waited in the street, sullen and menacing, while a small group—never positively identified—pounded on the door. There was no response. A frightened young Chinese was pushed forward through the mob and ordered to tell his countrymen that if they opened the door they would not be harmed. The door opened a crack. Through the translator they were told that the time had come to go. Chinese were not welcome. Tacoma could wait no longer. They must leave today. Pack their belongings. A wagon would come at 1:30 to take them out of town. Those who were ready to leave then would not be harmed. Remember: 1:30.

The ultimatum delivered, the spokesmen and their silent escort, a mob in raincoats, orderly but ominous, moved northward along C Street toward the next Chinese house.

Sheriff Byrd was on Pacific Avenue when he heard the whistles and saw the marching men. He asked a passerby what was going on. "They're removing the Chinese," the man said. A moment later an undersheriff brought Byrd the same information. Byrd sent him back to the courthouse on C Street to tell the staff "to do what they can." He then walked to Weisbach's store at Seventeenth and Pacific.

The mayor was inside. Byrd told him there was "a body of men marching along C street and going into the China Houses for the purpose of driving the Chinese out." Together they left the store and went up the hill. They caught up with the marchers at Ninth and C. The anti-Chinese were marching in files, two or four abreast.

"Do you consider this a mob?" the mayor asked the sheriff.

"No, they're too orderly to be a mob."

Byrd approached some of the leaders. Later he could not remember who they were but he remembered asking what they were doing.

"Nothing."

"Well, what does this mean?"

"Nothing in particular."

"What are you going to do?"

"Just find out how many Chinese there are in the city."

"Well, keep the peace and don't interfere with anybody."

They promised not to and went on their way, down C Street to Seventh, down the hill to Railroad Street (today's Commerce), and back south along Railroad. Several Chinese shops and houses stood between Seventh and Ninth. The largest belonged to Lum May.

To Lum it seemed there were a thousand white men in the street in front of the Chinese shops. "When the doors were locked they broke forcibly into the houses, smashing in doors and breaking in windows. Some of the crowd were armed with pistols, some with clubs. They acted in a rude, boisterous, threatening manner, dragging and kicking the Chinese out of the houses. My wife refused to go and some of the white persons dragged her out. She lost her reason and has ever since been hopelessly insane," he said in an affidavit later.

Lum, who had been in Tacoma since it was a village, recognized Mayor Weisbach in the crowd and appealed to him for help. "I told him that Mr. Sprague had said the Chinese had a right to stay and would be protected. He answered me, 'General Sprague has nothing to say. If he says anything we will hang him or kick him. You get out of here.' "

Lum began to cry. Weisbach told him that he was a baby to cry over the loss of property, that he had been warned earlier that he must leave and now the time had come: "I mean my word shall be kept good."

The strike force moved on down Railroad. Albert Whyte, the captain of the Home Guard, was watching from the window of his office at Ninth and Railroad. He had encountered City Attorney Fuller a few minutes earlier and Fuller warned him that he was looked upon as an enemy by the Committee of Fifteen. If he were seen on the street it might touch off a riot. To keep the peace he kept out of sight.

To Whyte it looked as if the leaders of the march were Dolph Hannah, a member of the city council, Probate Judge James Wickersham, and Fire Chief Jacob Ralph. "Weisbach was with the crowd as they passed up Railroad and while they were in front of the China Houses and stores. I should think there were several hundred persons in the crowd and Sheriff Byrd was with them."

After the crowd had passed, Whyte talked with Prosecuting Attorney Fremont Campbell, who asked if he had telegraphed the governor. Whyte explained that he had nothing directly to do with the governor because Squire had put him under the orders of the sheriff. Campbell asked if he wanted to talk to Byrd. Whyte said yes. Campbell said he would go get the sheriff. He left and did not come back.

Sometime that morning a Chinese got to the telegraph office and paid for a wire to the governor. MOB DRIVING CHINAMEN OUT OF TOWN. WILL YOU NOT PROTECT US. There was no answer.

Meanwhile the marchers continued the length of Railroad Street, descended Seventeenth to Pacific, and started north along the avenue. At Fifteenth, where Schoenfelds now stands, they encountered resistance. When a delegation went to the porch of the Ezra Brown house to say their Chinese servant must leave, Mrs. Brown shooed them off with a broom. Later, at the residence of Mrs. Byron Young, the widow of a former sheriff, the mistress of the house greeted them with a shotgun. "You want China Joe," she said. "All right, come and get him. But before you get him, you get this." They didn't press the matter. Nor did they even approach the residence of Isaac Anderson, the manager of the Tacoma Land Company, who had let it be known that he had hired sharpshooters and promised them five hundred dollars for each trespasser wounded, a thousand dollars for each body.

The Reverend Mr. McFarland, the pistol-packing Presbyterian, had been in Puyallup that morning. He returned to find the march under way and went at once to the office of the Home Guard. He found Whyte looking out the window at the marchers who were crossing Ninth, headed north.

"My God, captain, is this America?" cried the minister. "Why do we stand and do nothing? I must do something." He started for the door.

Whyte caught him. "Just a minute." He pointed out the window. "See that man. He's the mayor, remember? And that; he's a judge. And that one; he's on the council. And that one; he's sheriff. And most of the rest of them have been deputized. You've already made yourself disliked for trying to prevent an illegal procedure. Every man out there would just love to have you start something. Don't matter what you do, you can't stop this thing. You can only make it worse."

McFarland sagged against the window frame. "Perhaps you're right," he conceded. They watched the anti-Chinese move on to the bluff leading down to the waterfront where the main Chinese settlement stood. A flight of stairs led to the tracks. The houses were across the tracks, the front side on land, the rear on pilings over the water. These were substantial buildings, some of them three stories high, and interconnected.

How Lung, who had come to Tacoma in 1875, owned nine of the buildings. Six he rented to other Chinese, three he used himself, one as a family residence, one as a store, and one as a warehouse. When he saw a mob of several hundred men in front of his store he bolted the door. "They came to my store and kicked off the door. They took hold of the Chinese that were in these houses, some of whom were Chinese women, including my wife, and pulled them out of doors. Some persons in the mob pointed pistols at the Chinese but did not fire. The Mayor of Tacoma, Mr. Weisbach, was there with the mob. He came to my house and said I must go. The mob forcibly took some of my goods away."

From Chinatown under the bluff the marchers set off down the beach road toward Old Tacoma. Sheriff Byrd hurried ahead; he wanted to caution the hot-tempered George Atkinson, manager at the Tacoma Mill, against resisting the expulsion of the Chinese who worked there, but Atkinson had already left for Little Canton, where most of the men lived.

Little Canton—Old Town Chinatown—was a line of thirteen houses standing between the mill and Old Tacoma on the outboard side of the tracks. It was very Chinese in appearance, with pastel-colored paper curtaining the windows, bamboo furniture, and narrow gardens paralleling the rails. All the houses had been built on leased land by Sing Lee, a fifty-one-year-old Cantonese who had come to Washington Territory from California in 1858, and to Tacoma in 1872. He had lived in Tacoma longer than all but a handful of the whites, and was probably the most prosperous of the Chinese. Besides brokering contract labor, he chartered ships for voyages to China, ran a store dealing in rice, clothing, and herb medicines, operated a brickyard, and grew vegetables on a 160-acre farm he leased east of town. Sing Lee was out of town on business the day he lost it all.

George Atkinson witnessed the arrival of what he called "the crowd from New Tacoma," led, he thought, by Judge Wickersham, Councilman Hannah, and Fireman Ralph. Weisbach was present but took no noticeable leadership role. "The crowd went into the houses. The Chinamen had no time to get together their belongings but were compelled to leave everything which they could not carry away in their hands. Some asked permission to remain long enough to sell or get rid of such stuff as they could not pack but the crowd said they must go that day. They were herded and driven away like cattle over to New Town by the beach road. I should think the crowd were about an hour and a half getting the Chinamen out and marching them off."

It was 1:30 when the mob, herding the Little Cantonese ahead of them, got back to New Tacoma. The strike force split at the Half-Moon yards, one group escorting the Chinese up the slope to Pacific Avenue, the rest moving on Chinatown below the bluff to round up the Chinese they had warned earlier. "They broke open the houses where the doors were locked," said Kwok Sue, who had arrived in Tacoma the same year as the Northern Pacific. "Some of the mob were armed with pistols. The Chinese became thoroughly frightened. Some of the mob went upstairs and broke the windows and destroyed furniture. My house being on the waterfront some of the rioters came in a boat, invaded my house, took a great many of my goods and carried them into the boat."

Resistance was feeble. Charles Joles said later that when he and Renwick Taylor were hunting for hideaways, an old Chinese threatened them with an enormous pistol of ancient design. Taylor turned his back and the Chinese started to pull the trigger. Joles knocked away the gun and the hammer fell on his thumb. It was the only injury to a white man during the expulsion.

Sheriff Byrd said he saw no sign of violence except a plank knocked off the end of one of the buildings below the bluff: "I was unable to find the party who did the damage and was informed that he had left. I went up the steps leading to Pacific Avenue and again demanded of the crowd that they keep the peace and use no violence and violate no law in any manner."

While the sheriff was preaching law and order, one of his staff arrived with word that the prosecuting attorney would like to see him at the courthouse. It was 2:30 in the afternoon, five hours after the signal whistles had blown for the expulsion, when the two officials most responsible for the rule of law in Pierce County met to discuss what should be done. "We came to the conclusion that it would be useless to telegraph for troops as none could arrive in time to be of any service," Byrd swore later. "We then discussed the idea of calling my deputy sheriffs together. I said I thought we had so few upon whom we could rely that any attempt to do anything would be fruitless and would probably lead to a collision in which many, both of the whites and the Chinese, would lose their lives." So they did nothing.

The Chinese, numbering between 125 and 200 by various estimates, were herded together in front of the Halstead House on Pacific Avenue between Eighth and Ninth. They were allowed to put such baggage as they had salvaged onto a flotilla of delivery wagons which stood waiting in the mud, the horses steaming in the cold rain.

A few of the merchants were given forty-eight-hour reprieves to supervise the packing of the goods. Kwok Sue was one. He returned to his waterfront store to find the safe open and empty, much of his merchandise gone. While he was packing the remainder a gang of whites stormed in and demanded to know who was owner of the place. "I told them I was," Kwok testified later. "Four or five of them pulled pistols out of their pockets and said, 'You are a son of a bitch. You must get out of the house.' I told them, 'Gentlemen, give me the time the sheriff has allowed me, the 48 hours.' They said, 'We have no time to give you. You should have gone at half-past one.' I became frightened, left and went away. I went out into the country about a mile and a half to the Indian agency."

Up on the bluff, shortly after three o'clock, somebody gave the order to march, south to Lake View. Teamsters cracked their whips, the wagons lurched forward. The elderly and the sick Chinese were permitted to ride. The rest trudged after the wagons, wrapped in blankets against the cold rain, duffle slung on poles over their shoulders or in laundry bags on their backs. Their sandals sucked mud; some took them off and went barefoot. Many were crying. Armed whites on horseback rode beside the refugees, herding them like cattle, and a guard of club-carrying whites brought up the rear, urging on the stragglers. They marched down Pacific Avenue to Seventeenth, then turned south along the tracks toward Lake View, the first station outside Tacoma.

Mayor Weisbach watched the departure of the dismal procession from a distance. Standing beside him at Seventh and Pacific was B. W. Coiner, an attorney.

"Do you see any disturbance of the peace?" Weisbach asked Coiner.

"Why do you ask?"

"I'm the mayor. It's my duty to preserve the peace. I want to know if I am doing my duty."

"I'm inclined to think there is a disturbance of the peace, Mr. Mayor."

"Well," said Weisbach after a pause, "I don't agree with you." He walked off.

About five o'clock the last few Chinese to have been located around town were dispatched under escort. Only then did Sheriff Byrd send a telegram to the governor: A LARGE BODY OF MEN AS-SEMBLED TODAY AND MOVED ALL THE CHINAMEN OUTSIDE OF THE CITY.

Squire wired back: TELEGRAM RECEIVED. I REGRET TO HEAR OF ANY VIOLENCE IN YOUR COUNTY. CAN YOU PRESERVE CHINESE FROM ASSAULT WITH THE FORCE AT YOUR COMMAND? IF NOT I WILL SO INFORM THE GOVERNMENT AT WASHINGTON. ANSWER IMMEDIATELY.

Byrd replied: MOST OF CHINAMEN HAVE BEEN REMOVED BEYOND CITY LIMITS. NO PROPERTY DESTROYED. THOSE REMAINING WILL BE REMOVED TOMORROW. NOBODY INJURED BODILY. NO GOVERNMENT FORCE COULD REACH HERE IN TIME TO PREVENT REMOVAL TOMORROW.

Squire answered: LEND EVERY POWER OF LAW TO SECURE CHINESE FROM ASSAULT AND REPORT RESULT TO ME.

That evening Squire also received a desperate telegram from Puyall-lup: PEOPLE DRIVING CHINAMEN FROM TACOMA. WHY SHERIFF NO PRO-TECT? ANSWER. GOON GAU.

Squire answered Goon: TELEGRAM RECEIVED. I HAVE TELEGRAPHED FACTS TO THE GOVERNMENT AT WASHINGTON.

It was dark by the time the column of refugees reached the Northern Pacific station at Lake View, a small frame building that served as waiting room, ticket office, warehouse, and living quarters for the stationmaster. As many Chinese as could get in huddled around the potbellied stove in the waiting room. The rest took shelter under the roofs of three partially open freight sheds. The merchants who had been permitted to stay behind sent a wagonload of food and blankets to their countrymen, and some whites contributed provisions.

The Chinese with money were told they could buy tickets on the morning train to Portland. W. H. Elder, the stationmaster, sold seventy-seven tickets that night, some at the group rate of thirty for $120, the rest at the regular fare of $6. It was the largest number of tickets ever sold in a day at Lake View.

At three in the morning a southbound freight was flagged to a stop. "Load 'em aboard, I'll haul 'em," said Engineer Jack Hawkins. Those Chinese who could not afford tickets climbed into the boxcars with such of their possessions as they had saved. The remaining Chinese boarded the morning train for Portland. After the train pulled out, Stationmaster Elder looked through all the buildings. No Chinese remained.

"GONE!" exulted the *Ledger* headline the next morning. "Two Hundred Chinese Leave the City—How the People's Request was Enforced."

After detailing the day's events, the story concluded:

The last of the stray sheep were seen wending their way along the avenue shortly after five o'clock, and with the exception of about twenty-one China-men in the stores, including two or three Chinese families, and several others employed at white residences, the city is free of Chinese. The work had been conducted swiftly, surely and without any trouble. No Chinese had been abused, and no violent deeds committed. The Chinese had been quietly requested to go, and they had peaceably and quietly complied.

Sheriff Byrd wired the governor: ABOUT TWO HUNDRED CHINESE MOVED OUT YESTERDAY. THINK THERE ARE ABOUT FORTY CHINESE LEFT IN THE CITY AND THEY ARE BEING PACKED TO LEAVE.

Goon Gau wired from Puyallup: I AM NOTIFIED THAT AT THREE P.M. TOMORROW A MOB WILL REMOVE ME AND DESTROY MY GOODS. I WANT PROTECTION. CAN I HAVE IT?

Squire did not answer Goon but did telegraph the secretary of the interior: SHERIFF AT TACOMA HAS NOT PROTECTED CHINESE FROM IN-TIMIDATION AND FORCIBLE REMOVAL. ABOUT TWO HUNDRED WERE EX-PELLED YESTERDAY AND TODAY. SHERIFF INFORMS ME NOBODY INJURED BODILY SO FAR. I HAD INSTRUCTED SHERIFF TO LEND EVERY POWER OF LAW TO SECURE THE CHINESE FROM ASSAULT. THE CHINESE ARE IMPLOR-ING ME FOR PROTECTION. HAD I NOT BETTER ISSUE PROCLAMATION, WARNING AGAINST RIOTING AND ASSAULTS, ON PENALTY OF THE LAW AND UNITED STATES INTERFERENCE?

While the telegrams were ping-ponging across the country, fire broke out in Little Canton, the line of houses Sing Lee had built be-tween the Tacoma Mill and Old Town. The hose company was slow in arriving. The houses were destroyed.

That afternoon Mayor Yesler wired Squire from Seattle: IN VIEW OF WHAT HAS TAKEN PLACE AT TACOMA, A NUMBER OF CITIZENS HAVE REQUESTED ME TO ASK YOU FOR TROOPS IMMEDIATELY. ANTICIPATE TROUBLE VERY SOON.

King County Sheriff John M. McGraw wired: HOPE TO BE ABLE TO PRESERVE ORDER WITHOUT AID OF TROOPS BUT THINK IT BEST THAT YOU

BE PREPARED TO SEND THEM AT A MOMENT'S NOTICE. WILL KEEP YOU ADVISED.

In the evening Governor Squire issued a warning against participating, or inciting others to participate, in any riot or breach of the peace, and calling on all sheriffs and law officers to secure all Chinese residents from assault:

Fellow-citizens, I appeal to you! Array yourselves on the side of the law! This is the time in the history of the Territory for an intelligent, law-abiding, and prosperous community who love their country and their homes, who are blessed with boundless resources of forest, field and mine, and who aspire to soon become a great self-governing State, to assert their power of *self-control* and *self-preservation* as against a spirit of lawlessness which is destructive alike to immigration, to labor and to capital.

If you do not protect yourselves, you have only to look to the step beyond; which is, simply, the fate of Wyoming and the speedy interference of United States troops.

The next morning, Thursday, Frank Wilson, a Tacoma policeman, was on guard in front of Chinatown-below-the-Bluff. His instructions were to keep everyone out of the buildings. Three men from the Committee of Fifteen approached and said they had been told some Chinese were hiding in the buildings. Wilson let them pass. They were inside only a few minutes. "All right, Frank," one said to the guard as they left. "I guess they've all gone." A few minutes later Wilson saw fire erupt at the rear of the building they had been in.

How Lung was in his office packing his business records when the fire started in the building next door: "Many persons came to see it and some tried to keep the fire from burning the railroad timbers by making connection with the water pipe by means of a hose. I did not see any fire engines nor firemen on the ground at any time. No one tried to put out the fire in my houses."

The railroad trestle was saved. Chinatown burned to the pilings. "The houses were of no value," said the *Ledger,* "except to the Chinese."

Ah Chung Charley, who had been carting up merchandise in Kwok Sue's store, was charged by Tacoma police with setting the fire "for revenge." Nobody believed that, not even a Tacoma jury. Ah Chung was acquitted of arson and put on a train for Portland.

Assistant United States Attorney C. H. Hanford, who was in Tacoma when Chinatown was destroyed, wired the governor: CHINESE HOUSES HERE BURNING. YOU OUGHT TO DO SOMETHING FOR SEATTLE QUICK.

From Seattle Sheriff McGraw begged: ORDER TROOPS AT ONCE. DELAY IS CRIMINAL. . . .

Friday, November 6, the governor wired the secretary of the interior: IT IS EVIDENTLY IMPOSSIBLE TO PROTECT CHINESE AT SEATTLE WITHOUT UNITED STATES TROOPS IMMEDIATELY.

Ten companies from Fort Vancouver arrived in Seattle by train at two o'clock Saturday morning. That noon President Cleveland issued a proclamation declaring that "domestic violence exists within the Territory of Washington . . . which justifies and requires . . . the employment of military force to suppress domestic violence and enforce the faithful execution of the laws." The president warned and commanded "all insurgents and all persons who have assembled for the unlawful purpose aforesaid to desist therefrom and to disperse and retire peaceably to their respective abodes," and admonished "all good citizens . . . against aiding, abetting, countenancing, or taking any part in such unlawful acts or assemblages."

That night in Tacoma the Turn Verein honored Mayor Weisbach and the Committee of Fifteen at a ball celebrating what the *Ledger* called "this glorious victory—this peaceful and successful culmination." Even Captain Whyte of the Home Guard described the expulsion as "the most orderly disorderly proceeding in history."

A federal grand jury was sitting in Vancouver at the time Tacoma chased out the Chinese. United States Attorney William H. White sent an agent to gather information. He subpoenaed fifteen Tacomans who had opposed the expulsion, including General Sprague, Ezra Meeker, the Reverend Mr. McFarland, and Captain Whyte of the Home Guard (himself a deputy United States marhsal), and took them to Vancouver to appear before the grand jury. Their testimony persauded the jurors that the departure of the Chinese had not been voluntary but the result of a conspiracy against the laws of the United States amounting to insurrection. While the mayor and the Committee of Fifteen were being lionized at the Victory Ball in Tacoma they were being named in secret indictments issued by the jury in Vancouver.

The Justice Department was seriously concerned that the arrest of the leaders of the expulsion might lead to an armed uprising in Tacoma. They asked the Army for help. All was quiet in Seattle since the troops had appeared. On Monday, November 9, four of the ten companies garrisoning that city were ordered to Tacoma. When the troop train reached Tacoma at noon some of the residents, thinking they were en route back to Fort Vancouver, were waiting at the station to wave them on. To the Tacomans' amazement the men of Companies E, F, G, and H of the Fourteenth Infantry, 125 strong, disembarked and made camp at Seventeenth and Pacific. Downtown was occupied by the Army.

In the afternoon United States Marshal J. W. George and Deputy Marshal Whyte arrived with the warrants for the arrest of the twenty-seven alleged conspirators. Whyte persuaded Marshal George that they would not need a military guard as they served the papers. He was correct; there was no trouble. Many of the wanted men turned themselves in voluntarily. By evening twenty-six of the twenty-seven, everybody except Jim James Jack Comerford, who was rumored (falsely) to be in South America, had been placed under arrest and taken to the little wooden courthouse at Ninth and C streets.

Whyte proposed letting everybody go home for the night. Marshal George would not hear of it. These men were charged with conspiracy, riot, and insurrection. He was worried that the Tacoma populace might rise, storm the building, and free the political prisoners. He favored stationing troops around the courthouse to keep the townsfolk at bay.

"You've got some of Tacoma's best citizens under arrest," Whyte protested. "They're not going to run away, I'll guarantee that. Everyone will still be here in the morning. I'll guard them myself."

The Tacoma Twenty-Seven were indeed an unusual collection to be facing felony charges. They included the mayor, two city councilmen, the probate judge, the fire chief, and the president of the YMCA. They ranged in age from twenty-seven to sixty-four years, averaging forty-seven. All but two were family men; collectively they boasted sixty-four children and eleven grandchildren. Sixteen had been born in the United States, five in Germany, four in Canada, one in Sweden, and one in Ireland. Those naturalized had spent on the average of twenty years in the United States, seventeen as citizens. Eleven had served in the United States Army. None had previously been charged with a crime in this country, though Weisbach had been convicted of political offenses in Germany. There were six carpenters, three blacksmiths, three merchants, three journalists, two butchers, two plumbers, and a draughtsman, photographer, brick mason, civil engineer, boat builder, molder, farmer, and shoemaker. The county assessor valued their property at two hundred thousand dollars. They were not run-of-the-mill troublemakers. Still there was tension when Whyte went into the courtroom where they were to be confined for the night. The deputy marshal was met with cold silence from his fellow townsmen. Whyte unbuckled his two-gun belt and dropped it on the floor.

"Let's send somebody over to Wintermute's store for boxing gloves," he suggested. "I'll box anybody in the house."

Not a word.

"Well, we've got to do something to keep warm. Wrestle, anybody?"

Jack Forbes, the biggest man in the room, stepped forward. Whyte was outweighed by fifty pounds but he had been a gymnasium instructor in the British Army. He soon had Forbes up on his shoulders. Forbes grabbed Whyte by the hair. Whyte yelped and shifted his grip to a full nelson. Forbes pulled harder on the hair and said, "What are you going to do about that?" "Break your neck," said Whyte, gaily. Forbes let go, Whyte let go, and the rest of the night passed in conversation.

A large, sullen crowd watched in the morning as the prisoners were formed into a column of twos and paraded to the station at Seventeenth and Pacific. Whyte and Weisbach marched at the head, Marshal George brought up the rear. Some of the spectators cheered the prisoners, some muttered threats against the authorities. "California Jim" Steele, the real estate dealer, helped change the dangerous mood. He had been shot through the throat in the Civil War and his voice was a high falsetto, especially curious from a man who weighed nearly three hundred pounds. "Say, Weisbach," Steele piped as the heavy-set mayor and the little deputy marshal passed, "has Whyte got you or have you got Whyte?"

Exactly a week after the Chinese were driven from the town, the leaders of their expulsion were put aboard a train and taken south along the same route. In Vancouver they were brought before District Judge John P. Hoyt. The United States attorney read the indictments. There were two counts. The first charged conspiracy to deprive certain subjects of the Tai Sing Empire (China) of equal protection under American law; the second charged conspiracy to make an insurrection against the laws of the United States, assembling and making a riot, and insurrection during which the accused broke open houses and shops in Tacoma, drove the Chinese from the city, and by threats prevented their return, all of which denied the Chinese immunities and privileges guaranteed by treaty.

The Tacomans all indicated they would plead not guilty. Since the trial could not be scheduled for several months, the United States attorney suggested they be released on small bonds. Judge Hoyt, calling the crime charged "one of the gravest known to American law," said that bail had to reflect its seriousness. He set bail at five thousand dollars each but allowed them time to raise it and agreed it could be posted in Tacoma.

Tacoma greeted the accused as heroes when they returned on Friday evening. The Steilacoom town band serenaded their train as it passed through Lake View. Cannons boomed to herald their approach to the city. A welcoming procession set out from Eleventh and Pacific to meet them at the station. Thirty-two women bearing torches led the way, followed by the fire department in uniform, the Turn Verein in German national costumes, then between five hundred and eight hundred men, women, and children in street clothes, with a torch-bearing delegation from the Anti-Chinese League bringing up the rear. Business houses along the line of march were decked with flags and illuminated with lamps. Bonfires burned at the street corners, the flames reflected against the low clouds.

At the station the accused men were put into individual carriages. They were driven to the Grand Army of the Republic Hall and served a banquet, then driven along a parade route to the Alpha Opera House for a civic reception. John Burns, the master of ceremonies, offered "heartfelt thanks to these brave and noble men, so unjustly accused." Rose Stannus undertook to speak for the women of Tacoma. She expressed female gratitude "to you citizens who have heard and listened to the voice of labor, you fellow citizens who have cleared this city of slave labor. . . . These noble men have borne the brunt of condemnation and suffered from treachery but they swept away the slaves that had taken the bread from the people's mouths and from their children's mouths. . . . Our eyes no more meet the unclean Chinamen; our nostrils are no more offended by the vile odors from Chinese wash-houses. . . . To Tacoma have you given the distinction of being the first city in this country which has solved the Chinese problem without violence."

After other effusions every bit as hyperbolic, Burns declared, "The court of last resort, to whom appeal is taken, is now in session. The prisoners have been called before the bar. The prisoners will now plead to the indictment." (Laughter and applause.)

Mayor Weisbach arose. He had come a long way in the thirty years since his belief in "a future of liberty, equality, and fraternity for all mankind" led to his exile from his native land. As he saw it he was still fighting the good fight. He "could find no language expressive of my feelings of gratitude. . . . A victory has been achieved with a little sacrifice but it is worth many times the sacrifice. . . . The people have pledged new allegiance to the banner which has been unfurled and that banner is the banner of humanity." (Cheers.) "That noble banner has been raised and manful has been the rally to its support. This unanimity of sentiment in the cause of humanity is not everywhere found. . . ."

And indeed it was not. Tacomans, even those who had opposed the expulsion, were shocked and dismayed by the reactions in out-of-town papers.

"The Chinese have been driven out of Tacoma by methods that

would disgrace barbarians," said the *Oregonian*. "The act is a crime against civilization and mankind, on the level with the expulsion of the Jews and Moors from Spain and the Huguenots from France. Such a thing would not be possible in any community governed by the principles of justice and civilization. It is characteristic of a mushroom railroad town." Ah, that was it: the *Oregonian* was a Portland paper, unhappy about loss of the terminus.

Seattle, too, was understandably envious. After all they still had their Chinese. "It appears two of the Chinamen driven out of Tacoma were British subjects," reported the Seattle *Chronicle*. "They have appealed to their government for redress. The Tacoma papers are not cracking so many horse jokes about the affair as formerly, and they will very shortly awake to the sober fact that an international question has arisen which cannot be lightly tossed aside."

The *Ledger* answered that one for Tacoma: "We have whipped England twice and if necessary can do it again. There is, however, no likelihood that England will trouble herself about two miserable Chinamen. . . . A civilized nation that will permit Chinese to become citizens or subjects is not so high toned that it cannot brook insult."

The editorials that hurt were those in distant cities, especially in the East, which inveighed against "the Tacoma Ruffians," and spoke darkly of anarchy, of a city "in the hands of reckless elements."

The New York *Times* declared, "It is clear that the lives and property of the Chinese residents in this country are to be protected at all hazards, and that the reckless, worthless agitators, who are a far greater curse to the community which they infest than the other class of people, will subside."

The New York *Herald* editorialized, "A dispatch from Portland gives a list of the hoodlums who have just been indicted at Vancouver. Prominent upon it are the names of the mayor and the president of the Y.M.C.A. What probability is there of an honest verdict by a petit jury drawn in the neighborhood where the principal civil magistrate and chief professing Christian headed the anti-Chinese mob?"

The New York *Sun* demanded stronger federal action against Tacoma: "The dispersion of the Tacoma people, therefore, is not enough to prove that no federal interposition is required. A violation of a treaty is a continuous violation of the law of the land."

The New York *Tribune* agreed that the federals should be more firm with Tacoma: "No reason has been given, or assuredly no sufficient reason, for the inaction of the government on this occasion."

The community drew together in defense of what had been done.

The Anti-Chinese League passed a resolution introduced by John Burns calling for the names of all those who had given information to the grand jury, "thus traitorously combining with the Chinese Six Companies," to be preserved forever on a blacklist of dishonor. Men who had opposed the expulsion tried to get right with the town by appearing at the courthouse to put up bail for the twenty-seven defendants. When the *Overland Monthly* carried a favorable article about "The Tacoma Method" of solving the Chinese Question, Tacomans had it reprinted and widely distributed.

In the spring election, an Anti-Chinese Ticket, campaigning in defense of the expulsion, won every seat. Mayor Weisbach did not seek re-election, but candidates who defended the Tacoma Method ran first and second in a three-man field, between them polling 72 percent of the vote. Five years passed before any candidate known to have opposed the expulsion won office in Pierce County.

The effect of all this was to fix in the public mind the image of Tacoma as a place beyond the rule of law.

The mills of federal justice ground ever more slowly and finally shuddered to a complete stop. After a year's delay the trial of the indicted leaders was transferred from Vancouver to Tacoma. Then the original indictments were dropped on technical grounds. The United States attorney immediately presented evidence to a new grand jury, but only ten of the original defendants were re-indicted. In February 1887, after another year had passed, these second indictments were dismissed because there had been women on the grand jury which returned them and the territorial supreme court had ruled the Territorial Woman Suffrage Act unconstitutional. On March 4, 1887, another grand jury, all male, again heard the evidence but refused to indict anyone. The case was closed. The anti-Chinese were home free. The Tacoma Method appeared vindicated.

But Tacoma had placed in the hands of her competitors for eastern capital investment and the trade of the Far East an effective weapon.

Mayor John W. Linck, who served from 1908 to 1910, deplored the effect of the expulsion on the city's business. He claimed that the loss of just one trans-Pacific line which refused to consider Tacoma as a terminus meant millions of dollars annually.

"It was wrong," said M. P. Bulger, one of the Committee of Fifteen, shortly before his death in 1917. "We were young and hotheaded. We defied the law. We were inflamed over an evil condition. It was a condition which the town had to get rid of and it was a good thing when the riddance was made. But we went about it in the wrong way. I would not now take part in any such proceeding. On the other hand, I would oppose it most strenuously."

Ezra Meeker was correct when he told the Chamber, "Many of you will live to see the day that you will look back upon our actions with amazement and wonder, and regret that the recollection of this period should not be forgotten. . . ."

Instant Tacoma

THE ill effects of the expulsion of the Chinese were not felt in Tacoma for several years. The indictment of the city leaders and the national editorial disapproval of the Tacoma Method were overshadowed locally by the Northern Pacific's decision to bore the Stampede Tunnel. Construction of the Cascade Division was the kiss of the fairy prince; the boom that had gone comatose at birth in 1873 stirred and took new life. Tacoma awoke.

It was a time when dreams came true, the dreams of those old-timers and true believers like Carr and McCarver who looked at the bay in the forest and saw a city, the dreams of money men who waited until the rails were laid to the chosen site before coming west in parlor cars to get in at the second floor, the dreams of the drifters who happened to have floated nearby when somebody else laid track through the mountains, by-passing geology and Portland, and made Puget Sound one of the continent's outlets to the Pacific.

Masonry replaced wood along Pacific Avenue. The business district climbed the hill. Streetcars, horse-drawn at first, then powered by steam, nosed into the woods, opening residential areas. Three-story houses of no little elegance blossomed on the hill between New Tacoma and Old Tacoma, and on the downtown bluff between Ninth and Tenth on A Street arose the Tacoma Hotel. The brilliant young architect Stanford White, of the New York firm McKim, Mead, and White, designed it when his inspiration was fresh and the NP's money flowing free. It reflected with calm assurance the Victorian assumption of man's control of the world about him. More than the industry at water's edge, the great brick building on the hill dominated the Tacoma scene and symbolized a dream made manifest.

From the waterside rooms one commanded a view of the lovely curve of Commencement Bay, the pastels of the tideflats sweeping off and up into dark forest toward the serrated barrier of the Cascades, above which floated the ethereal bulk of the sleeping volcano. One saw the rails reaching eastward across the marsh, into the mountains, toward the farms and industries of the nation; over the tip of Browns Point the salt waters of the East Passage opened to all the seaports of the world. Ships were many. They were tied three deep at the docks, anchored out in the stream awaiting berthage, setting out for Australia, Chile, Liverpool, San Francisco. One could watch them standing southbound, windborne, or trailing opalescent plumes of smoke as they headed for the coal bunkers, grain elevators, and sawmills below the bluff. It added up to a vision of the future, the realization of the dream that land and opportunity and the enterprise of free men would create a new and better society, a community where all could live in harmony amidst splendor. Why, down in the kitchen the world's biggest steam-driven potato peeler could handle a ton of spuds an hour.

Everybody benefited. General Matthew Morton McCarver was in his grave, but his stepson-in-law, C. P. Ferry, was hustling real estate with such success that he gloried in the nickname "the Duke of Tacoma." Howard Carr was on the city council. Will Blackwell had a hotel of his own, was a founding father of the Chamber of Commerce, a director of the Carbon Hill Coal Company, and (to his eventual distress) was on the boards of two banks; he was building for his beloved Alice a mansion on Cliff Avenue, overlooking the glorified shed on the NP docks that had brought them to Tacoma in 1873.

In this game of sudden affluence anybody could play. The cards seemed stacked for everyone to win, even an impoverished intellectual like Allen Chase Mason.

Mason was from Illinois, a young man of charm, education, and taste—but no money. He had a bachelor of science degree from Illinois Wesleyan, had read for the law, taught school, and written two textbooks, *Mason's Problems in Arithmetic* and *One Thousand Ways of One Thousand Teachers*. His wife, Libbie, had also graduated from Wesleyan. For all their education they had not prospered. In 1882, Mason's attention was attracted to Tacoma by an article planted in the Chicago *Times* by the indefatigable NP flak, Sam Wilkeson, and the following year he came west on the Union Pacific–Central Pacific, then up the coast on the S.S. *Dakota*, a trip that left him, after paying a month's rent in advance, with $2.85.

Mason caught on with a real estate company, earned a $2 commission on his first sale, $10,000 more that year, and in 1884 built gas and electric plants in Olympia, foresightedly incorporated the Shore Line Railroad and laid enough track from Old Tacoma toward Point

Defiance to make it necessary for the Northern Pacific to buy him out, and joined Nelson Bennett in a company that obtained the first franchise for a Tacoma street railway. He founded an irrigation company in Yakima, financed extensive farming operations in the Palouse country, became a director of banks in Tacoma, Bellingham, and Yakima, a stockholder in the Tacoma Hotel and the largest stockholder in the Tacoma Theater Building. In less than a decade he ran his $2.85 up to $10 million.

Most of his profits Mason put into land development, promotion, and speculation. Publicity had drawn him to Tacoma, and he counted on publicity to attract others. He spent up to $5,000 a month advertising in papers around the country; his messages were not of his company but of the town. What was good for Tacoma was good for Allen C. Mason. His letterhead bore at its top Tacoma's Star of Destiny, a map he drew of the Northwest with Tacoma at the center and such lesser entities as Seattle and Portland consigned dimly to the rays. At the bottom of the stationery was a quote from a newspaper about the high cost of keeping the Columbia River channel partly safe.

Mason knew the power of suggestion and the power of slogans. "Keep in view of the water," was his motto as he opened areas for development. On some view property he not only sold lots; he built houses and sold them on the installment plan. He was willing to risk money to make money. When the gulch on north I Street blocked residential development, he built a bridge to city specifications and presented it to the City of Tacoma, cost-free. Beyond that gulch lay another and deeper one. So Mason spent $12,000 on another bridge at Thirtieth and Proctor, improved the gulch as a park, and presented them both to Tacoma. The bridge opened up the north end as far as the Smelter, and Mason was the developer.

Since Allen and Libbie loved to read, he gave the city six thousand books and wrapped them in a handsome wooden building with an auditorium for public meetings and a wide porch with a view of the water. When Mason built for his own family it was a house all Tacoma boasted of, a Victorian mansion of thirty-six rooms, including a shooting gallery, bowling alley, pool and billiard room, and banquet hall. He insisted on local materials. The foundation stones were quarried at Wilkeson, the rooms paneled in the best Nisqually oak and Vashon madroña. Balustrades were of vine maple, structural timbers of knotless fir and cedar. You could roast an ox in any of several fireplaces. Tacomans boasted that the whole shebang cost $86,000 to build and gained in value every day. Why, sir, that front doorknob just by itself cost $150.

The boom in real estate fed on a boom in industrial development, especially in the lumber industry.

The completion of the Northern Pacific coincided with the application of steam power to logging. Mills, of course, had long been using steam, but in August 1881 John Dolbeer, working along Salmon Creek near Eureka, California, experimented with a six-foot-long spool of Manila rope attached to the drive-shaft of a steam-engine. When the spool turned it wound in the rope and moved a log toward the machine. Dolbeer's first steam donkey engine was weak and cranky—the jogs jammed into soft spots or mounds; the ropes stretched in wet weather, frayed in dry—but the concept was sound, the technology matured, and the glory days of the skidroad bullwhacker who guided and goaded eight to ten brace of oxen along the corduroy skid roads were over. Machines could move logs faster and farther and opened new areas to exploitation.

At this same time rails replaced water as the favored means of moving felled logs to the waiting saws. In the early days, lumbermen either dropped trees directly into the Sound or cut stands that were so close to shore that the logs could be rolled or dragged to water and floated to the mills. After loggers peeled the forest back from the shore for two or three miles, they pursued it up such streams as were large enough to float logs—and some that were not. On creeks too shallow for logging they built splash dams, and impounded a head of water and supply of logs which, when released, charged down the streambed sweeping everything before them (and ripping out the spawning beds on which the salmon runs were based). Only a few streams were suitable for such destructive drives but soon their banks were bare.

In 1881 a stretch of narrow-gauge track was laid from Tenino to Olympia, the first railroad in the Northwest built specifically to haul logs. By 1884 lumbermen were telling reporters that logs could be moved ten or fifteen miles by rail more swiftly and at no greater cost than one or two miles with oxen. Rails ran deeper into the woods.

Railroads are expensive. An operator was reluctant to build a line to stumpage he did not control; even if he would take the risk his bank probably would not. In the 1860s and 1870s, mills sawed logs brought in by private operators who took them from land they might not own; by the 1880s, skinning the timber off a tract was no longer regarded as doing the owner a favor. Mill owners began buying stands of timber in workable blocks before building railroads. The scale of operations was increasing.

Mills were becoming larger, faster, and more expensive. The band saw was introduced. It wasted less power, made less sawdust, and further speeded the process. The largest and oldest trees could now be brought to market.

New markets opened around the Pacific rim, in Australia, China, South America, especially in connection with railroad building and mining enterprises. Ship design evolved to handle the special needs of lumber freighting: the lumber schooner, single-decked, broad of beam, long in the bow, square in the stern, with oversized hatches that permitted easier stowing of long timbers; the great schooners that reduced the number of crewmen needed on the long hauls; the barkentines with square sail forward, schooner rig aft, to take advantage of the trades on the runs to Australia and China.

All these trends in technology, industry, finance, and freighting coalesced in the emergence of the St. Paul and Tacoma Lumber Company as the world's largest sawmill operation.

Back east on the Great Lakes, forests were running short on old growth, lumbermen were looking for still-green pastures. Among those checking the possibilities for mill-site acquisition and stumpage purchase on Puget Sound were two groups from St. Paul, one headed by Henry Hewitt, Jr., and his brother-in-law, Charles Hebard Jones; the other by Colonel Chauncey Wright Griggs and a long-time associate, A. G. Foster. Though they were from the same area, they did not know of each other's presence in Tacoma until Thomas Fletcher Oakes of the Northern Pacific, in conversation with Colonel Griggs at the Tacoma Hotel, mentioned Hewitt and Jones. The conversation turned to the advantages of one huge, first-class, fully financed company instead of two rivals. It was an idea whose time came almost immediately.

After visiting Minnesota to confer with other backers, the St. Paul men returned to Tacoma together in a private railroad car named the Glacier. There was nothing glacial about their actions. Arriving on the afternoon of June 4, 1888, they hurried up the hill to the courthouse and filed articles of incorporation for the St. Paul and Tacoma Lumber Company, with a capital stock of $1,500,000, hurried back to the Tacoma Hotel for dinner, then gathered in the office of George Browne, a Tacoma real estate and streetcar promoter, for a business meeting. Acting as the board of the new corporation, they elected Colonel Griggs, president; Foster, vice president; Hewitt, treasurer, and Browne, secretary.

Griggs and Hewitt were the key figures. The colonel, a Connecticut Yankee, left home at seventeen years, knocked around for a time as grocery clerk, school teacher, bank teller, and dry-goods salesman until in 1856, at twenty-four, he moved to St. Paul. He teamed up with a young Canadian, James Jerome Hill, in the wood and coal business. It prospered, as did they, though Griggs and Hill soon went separate and unfriendly ways, Hill to become creator and president of the Great Northern, Griggs, after service in the Civil War, to become an important figure in coal, wholesale groceries, contracting, and transportation in the Red River region.

Henry Hewitt, Jr., was a knobby, dour Englishman whose parents moved to Wisconsin when he was a boy. He quit school at sixteen to work as a teamster, but at twenty was an independent contractor. He made considerable money building dams, then branched out into freighting, banking, lumber, and targets of opportunity. His success, he liked to say, rested on two principles: "See what the people are going to need, see it first, then get it—the market will follow," and "Admit nothing. Make them prove everything."

The St. Paul and Tacoma bought from the Northern Pacific some ninety thousand acres of timberland, all but six thousand of it in Pierce County—the largest single private land deal in American history until Frederick Weyerhaeuser bought ten times as much from Jim Hill. The NP also tried to sell the St. Paul men a mill site on the south side of Commencement Bay, out beyond Old Town. Hewitt and Jones would not hear of it: not enough back-up land between water and bluff to store the lumber and marshal the fleet of flatcars that would be needed whenever rail rates came down and the interior market opened up. Jones, who had grown up working in his father's sawmill in Vermont and since had made, lost, and made again a small fortune in Michigan and Wisconsin lumber, was the most experienced lumberman in the group. He defied the conventional wisdom and insisted on building out on the tideflats.

The Army Engineers had yet to impose their will on the Puyallup. There was no industry on the tideflats. The river split into several channels some distance up the valley and oozed through cattails and swamp grass to merge almost imperceptibly with the bay. Much of the land was awash at high tide. The area that remained above water, an off-again on-again island called the Boot, squished when stepped on. A couple of cabins had been built out there and remained above ground, but waterfront opinion in Tacoma was that anything heavy as a mill would require waterwings.

Jones designed a small sawmill to cut the lumber needed for building two huge mills on the flats. His log pond leaked, the water rising and falling with each tide, but Jones managed to caulk it with sawdust and soon the pilot plant was cutting construction timbers for the larger mills.

A dozen timber cruisers picked out the sections of timberland St. Paul and Tacoma would buy out of the NP land grant. (They chose townships 16 and 17, range 5 east; 16 and 17, range 6 east; 18, range 5 east; and 20, range 7 east.) As part of the sale, the Northern Pacific required St. Paul and Tacoma to lay standard track in the woods, the first full-sized logging railroad. Six miles were spiked down the first year; eventually the tracks stretched 120 miles before logging trucks put the Tacoma Southern (later known as the Tacoma, Orting, and Southeastern) out of business.

The first of Charles Hebard Jones's twin mills started cutting on Monday, April 22, 1889. The main building was nearly the size of a football field, with a shingle mill alongside. The foundations rested on fifteen hundred pilings driven into the silt; masonry was set atop the pilings, the floor and machinery on that. The mill did not submerge. Jones also defied custom by installing band saws, the first to be used in a mill handling Douglas fir. Experienced sawyers warned that the thin blades would hang up in the huge logs, perhaps even in small ones if they were pitchy; but when the boilers were fired and the carriages moved the logs to the head rigs, the steel sliced evenly through and the new mill turned out a quarter million board feet of lumber a day.

There were other mills abuilding. Pacific Mill was the largest rival for St. Paul, with a half-million-dollar plant out beyond Old Town, on the site where John Swan, the pioneer salmon fisherman, had built a cabin. At night the southern shore of the bay could be traced by the glowing cones of the slash burners. Cyrus Walker, the shrewd superintendent for Pope and Talbot, complained that "lots of people are going crazy on the mill question." Certainly some of the mills were marginal, but St. Paul and Tacoma for years was not only the largest but the most innovative and most influential. Its presence on the tideflats started industrial expansion there. It pioneered the shipment of lumber by rail to new markets in the Midwest. It helped draw to Tacoma the great schooners and brigantines that made the waterfront "a forest of masts."

On a summer evening in 1889, Thea Foss, blonde and Norwegian and new to the Pacific Northwest, the bride of an immigrant carpenter, sat on the porch of a houseboat on the Tacoma waterfront. Her husband, Andrew, was up the valley for a few days building a shed. A fisherman rowed past the houseboat, cursing his luck.

How'd you do?

Nothing but goddam dogfish. Why he'd sell the damn boat for ten bucks.

Five, said Thea, her peasant computer assessing the cost of the boat against the daily discomfort of carrying waterbuckets on a yoke from the pump a quarter mile away.

Agreed. And the Fosses became boat owners.

Thea soon learned there were more fishermen than boats. She sold her rowboat for fifteen dollars one morning and bought two more from men unhappy after a day of bare hooks and blistered hands. She began renting the boats at a dime an hour, fifty cents a day. By the time Andrew finished his shed and came home with thirty-two dollars, Thea had forty-one dollars in a cookie jar.

Andrew thought a while and decided to build rowboats. Before long he and Thea had nearly two hundred boats, a few of them skiffs but most sturdy, clinker-built craft capable of surviving when the winds rose and the bay got lumpy. These the Fosses rented to fishermen, duck hunters, and picnickers. Sometimes sailors, longshoremen, or harbor officials wanted a rowboat to take them out to ships at anchor, or workmen needed rides to mills that could not be reached on foot at high tide. Such customers usually did not want to row, they wanted to be taken. Rowboats were all right to rent for sport but made slow taxis. Andrew began to ponder power.

A venerable steamship called the *St. Patrick* had been abandoned at the head of the bay after going aground. Andrew built a hull and with the help of relatives newly arrived in Tacoma from Norway by way of Minnesota he transferred her engine and boiler to his new craft. The resurrected *St. Patrick* ran so well a buyer made an offer Andrew could not resist. He sold her and with the proceeds bought a second-hand steamer, the *Lizzie A.*

The *Lizzie A.* was the most unprofitable craft the Fosses ever operated. She was small but she was slow. Unreliable, too. Andrew improved her looks with paint and putty but she remained raffish rather than rakish, and there was not much he could do about her performance, putter as he might. One day when he was away Thea sold the old clunker for five hundred dollars and a pair of horses. Andrew grumbled but out of the proceeds bought the *Hope,* a naphtha launch.

Naphtha was one of the shortcuts to the future that wound up a dead end. It is a colorless, flammable liquid derived from crude petroleum and now used as a solvent. In the 1890s it was a fuel for low-power engines, a rival of gasoline. Unlike the steamer, a naphtha launch had no boiler to explode; unlike the gasoline-powered boat of the time, it usually started.

Foss's two-horsepower *Hope* proved as rewarding as she was reliable. For years she carried people and provisions from shore to ship, from ship to ship, and back. Harbor traffic in Commencement Bay was building up. It was not just the lumber trade. Grain ships from

Tacoma now rivaled Portland's. In 1885 Tacoma had loaded only 19,000 bushels of wheat to Portland's 4,600,000; by 1892, thanks to the Cascade Division, Tacoma loaded 4,200,000 bushels to Portland's 5,000,000. Twenty-one ships cleared the harbor with grain that year, seventy-four with lumber.

Nor was the Sound any longer a one-way street. The bark *Isabella* sailed into Tacoma from Japan in August of 1885 with two million pounds of tea, the first Oriental cargo to appear on customs house records in Washington State. In June of 1892 the British flag *Phra Nang* arrived from China, the first steamer to carry a payload across the Pacific to Puget Sound.

The *Hope* called often at Quartermaster Harbor on Vashon Island, where the Puget Sound Dry Dock Company of Tacoma installed a floating dock that had been built up near Port Townsend. It was 102 feet wide, 315 feet long, the best marine repair facility this side of San Francisco, and it gave Dockton its name.

The naphtha launch went putt-putting among the steamers that came off the ways of Commencement Bay yards—the *Mogul* in 1885, the *Henry Bailey* in 1888, and in 1889 the *State of Washington*, the *Skagit Chief*, and Nelson Bennett's *Fairhaven*, named for the town he was promoting in opposition to Tacoma. Tacoma loved them all, even the *Fairhaven*, for any Tacoma-built craft posed a challenge to Seattle's dominance of the mosquito fleet, the flotilla of small boats that served western Washington as highway before the road system developed.

The marine highway was lengthening. Alaska was considered almost local waters. The Puget Sound and Alaska Company of Tacoma sent ships on schedule to the Panhandle and Cook Inlet, occasionally to the Bering. In 1892 the British North Pacific Company, which had ties to the Northern Pacific Railroad, promised regular service to the Orient.

As the maritime world opened out before them, Andrew and Thea bought more launches and a steamer or two. They catered to the passenger trade, carrying workmen and supplies, but they took the president of the United States through the Narrows when he visited, and their green and white boats were familiar as gulls. They styled themselves the Foss Launch Company and did not plan to compete with the long-established tugboat companies in moving barges and log rafts, and towing sailing vessels in from the strait. But their shallow-draft launches could approach the sawmills when they were left high and little more than damp by low tides. Servicing the mills was part-time work, dependent on tides, unprofitable for the heavy-duty tugs of the established companies. The Fosses were willing to try when asked. Their launches, though underpowered, could handle most of the work assigned them. So Thea and Andrew changed the name of the company to Foss Launch and Tug, and registered the trademark that is still on the funnel of the Foss fleet, "Always Ready."

The naphtha-craft could not handle the work of rafting booms when the largest Douglas fir logs hit the water. So Andrew designed and built new boats for the purpose, squat, snub-nosed, round-sterned craft of a design still seen butting waves on the Sound. Diesel was coming in; it had the quick-start, no-boiler advantage of naphtha, was less dangerous, more economical. The Foss Company was one of the first tugboat operations to go diesel. Andrew and Thea skipped the gasoline generation and became the major mover of deadweight on the Sound, always ready.

Some men dreamed impossible dreams. A company was formed to meet Tacoma's warm-weather needs by sliding blocks of ice down a sixty-mile chute from Nisqually glacier. Nothing came from that idea except cartoons. But other visions, like that of Dennis Ryan for a smelter, though too much for the man who dreamed it, came true later.

Dennis Ryan was a minor league St. Paul capitalist who visited Tacoma in 1887 to see what lay at the far end of the new rails. He saw Commencement Bay as a possible assembly point for the raw materials used by the lead industry: coke was available in the Cascades, lime had been found at Roche Harbor in the San Juans, iron flux could be brought down from Alaska, the Coeur d'Alenes were producing high-grade ore. San Francisco would be the market.

Ryan put together the Tacoma Milling and Smelting Company and raised enough money to buy fifty acres between Old Town and Point Defiance, hard by a favorite clam bed of the Puyallup Indians. He built a small smelter in 1888 which produced more smoke than profit, a deficiency soon to be corrected by William R. Rust.

The son of a failed grain dealer, Bill Rust left college to look after the family business, left the family business for the Colorado gold fields in search of a quick financial fix. He found no gold; instead he found himself working as a day-laborer, twelve-hour shift, in a stamp mill crushing ore. Rust, who had run stationary engines in the family warehouse, became an engineer, then foreman. Having learned the stamping trade, he found backing and organized the Black Hawk Public Sampling Works and the Denver Public Sampling Works. Both companies did well. In 1887 Rust visited Tacoma but decided the time was not ripe. In 1889 he returned to Commencement Bay with thirty thousand dollars of his own money and organized the Tacoma Smelting and Refining Company, which bought out Ryan's Tacoma Milling and Smelting. He shut down the Ryan smelter and completely rebuilt it.

Rust's roasting furnaces were fired on September 2, 1890, and the fires started in the crucibles of the first stack on September 15. Tacoma was proud as the pollution plume of the new plant rose above the Indians' place of the maples and drifted north toward Seattle. On September 27, the *Queen of the Pacific* sailed for San Francisco with twenty-three tons of processed bullion, each ton showing $228.25 worth of silver, $91.57 gold, and $100 lead. Billy Rust had a paying proposition.

Other entrepreneurs met other needs. Harry Morgan drifted into Tacoma in 1884 from Maryland, or so he said, and quickly established himself as Boss Sport, the fellow in charge of the community's illicit entertainment activities.

He was in his mid-thirties, a compact, dark-haired man with a big dark mustache and ill-fitting dark suits, the prototype of the boomtown gambler: friendly, Republican (the Republicans were in local power), generous to the needy—especially to those he had helped become needy, provided they did not complain to authorities—and reputed to be a man of his word in business dealings, though this was hard to prove since he seldom signed papers. The gambling games that Morgan ran were, if not honest, at least open: there was little excuse for not knowing what you were getting into. Morgan was loud in defense of vice as a civic virtue:

"What do you want to blast us for?" he asked a reporter from the *Ledger,* which showed an unfavorable interest in his Board of Trade Billiard Hall when it first opened. "You never saw a religious town in your life that was worth a damn."

"If it comes to that," one of his henchmen added, "we and our friends have more influence in the town than all the church people. The refined element ain't any good. They don't build up a town because they ain't got enterprise."

"I tell you," Morgan concluded in a classic apologia, "a town without saloons and gamblers ain't worth a damn. Look at Seattle. Everything is open there and strangers say it's a good place because things are lively and men spend their money. If you break up this game you are only driving money out of town."

There was no question that Morgan's activities brought money into town, though the prosecuting attorney on occasion raised difficulties about the methods employed. There was, for instance, the Livensparger case.

The J. C. Livensparger family of Minneapolis was among the thousands lured west by the completion of the Northern Pacific. In the spring of 1886 Livensparger sold his livery stable, withdrew his life saving from the bank, and with wife and young daughter took the train west. They arrived in Portland looking for a new life, but first a place to spend the night.

Under the gaslights outside the station, Livensparger fell into conversation with Jeffson J. Harland, who directed the newcomers to a rooming house nearby. The accommodations proved unsuitable. Occupants in adjacent rooms changed every half hour or so, and between times were noisy. In the morning the Livenspargers found more decorous lodging, and in the afternoon Jeff Harland, heavy with apology, found them. He said he should have realized the rooms would not be to family taste, but he had been preoccupied with business problems. He was developing a new town, Coal Harbor, and the work was almost more than he could handle. So many details; so much for one man to do. Here he was, a sure-fire millionaire in the making, sole owner of an enterprise that was a key to the mint, and he had to scrabble for cash. Why, he was going to take time off from the really important things to go up to Seattle and collect money. Not that those people up there were deadbeats, just slow to pay if you didn't put a hand on their shoulder and look 'em in the eye. After all, it was only a few thousand dollars. A year from now they'd all be bragging they'd been in business with Jeff Harland and might have gotten in on the ground floor of Coal Harbor.

Livensparger got in at the basement. He not only went north with Harland to scout out the Puget Sound area for investment, but he bought Harland's ticket and loaned him money to get his watch out of hock. The NP schedule was rigged so that travelers to Seattle had to spend the night in Tacoma. The men took a room at the Blackwell. Harland went for a stroll and returned to say he had bumped into an old friend, George Williams, a very shrewd fellow, very farsighted, knew everybody and everything in Tacoma, exactly the fellow to give Livensparger good advice on business opportunities. Williams would be at Harry Morgan's Board of Trade that evening.

Torches set in iron stands guttered on the board sidewalk outside the Board of Trade. A barker sporting a derby and checked vest described the opportunitites for judicious investment.

"Come on now, any gentleman with half a dollar and a whole heart. Tempt the Goddess of Fortune. If you have half a dollar don't squeeze the coin till the Bird of Freedom farts and the Goddess of

Liberty faints. Invest it here. Throw the dice and see what you draw. Everybody has a chance. If you're lucky you win, if you ain't you lose. The smallest prize is a dollar bill."

Inside the swinging doors the visitors found themselves in a big room with a bar along one wall, a small stage alongside it. Waitresses took turns singing and dancing. The stage faced a line of curtained boxes where in obscurity the girls could hustle drinks, at the very least. Harland and Livensparger went to the gaming rooms on the second floor. George Williams was rolling dice in a game called Twenty-One, or Bunco. He was doing so well Harland joined him. He invested the last of the money Livensparger had loaned him in Portland, lost it, borrowed more, lost that. Harland was no quitter. He kept trying as long as Livensparger had anything left to loan. On their way back to the hotel, Harland assured his patron that he had no cause to worry about the $610 they had left at the Board of Trade. He would pay it back out of the money he was going to collect in Seattle next morning.

Next morning Harland was gone. So was Livensparger's watch. Livensparger became suspicious. He told his story to Prosecuting Attorney Fremont Campbell, who had heard similar tales. Harland and Williams had both worked in the past as dealers for Morgan, and Campbell suspected were now employed as bunco-steerers who hung around railroad stations and saloons and improvised free-lance swindles.

A grand jury indicted Harland for swindling and theft, Williams for helping. Morgan hired the veteran, respected, and expensive Elwood Evans to defend the con men. He got Williams off, but the jury found Harland guilty as charged and the judge sentenced him to eighteen months in the new territorial prison at Walla Walla. Evans appealed. His brief cited as error the fact that women served on both the grand jury and superior court jury that convicted his client. The territorial supreme court sustained the appeal; the legislative act giving women of Washington Territory the right to vote and serve on juries was ruled unconstitutional. Harland was free to go about his business.

Knocking out woman suffrage was a bonus to Morgan, who, like most sporting men, disapproved of females having the franchise, the theory being they would favor prohibition. The publicity resulting from the trial, as well as the continued attacks by the *Ledger*, helped Morgan considerably. Tacoma was growing fast, but every newcomer to town soon learned where Morgan operated and the recreation he offered.

In 1888 the Boss Sport opened a new joint, Morgan's Theater (later called the Comique), at 817 Pacific Avenue, where the

Olympus Hotel now stands. The *Ledger* implied that Sodom and Gomorrah would have rated PG to Morgan's X. They blamed the Morgan Theater for every Tacoma shortfall from stumps in the street to the murder of a young man on a somewhat distant downtown street. But the paper did offer a convincing diagnosis of the myopia among policemen visiting Morgan's establishment and the prevalent vertigo among magistrates dealing with offenses committed on the premises: money impeded vision.

Once some patrons of Morgan's place were brought before a municipal justice unaccustomed to encountering as defendants those who had not yet been victimized. It dislocated him so much that he imposed fines of only ten dollars, which the prosecutor felt obliged to note was only half of the minimum required by law. Adjusting admirably, the judge raised the fine by ten dollars—and suspended half the imposition. Such adumbrations eventually led the city council to revoke Morgan's license, a defeat he calmly circumvented by transferring the license to a buddy.

In time the *Ledger*'s carping annoyed Morgan sufficiently to cause him to bankroll the transformation of his theater program bill into a daily paper. It was called the *Daily Globe* and employed as its editor J. N. Frederickson, a desk man whose memory lingers in the Valhalla of Journalism as perpetrator of the headline, over the story of a hanging, JERKED TO JESUS. Editorship failed to inspire Frederickson further, and Morgan lured from the *Oregonian* William Lightfoot Visscher, a Civil War cavalry colonel of impetuosity and pungent prose. Visscher was disenchanted with a community which relied on gravity to pull riches past it. He did not want to become a freshwater barnacle. He responded to Morgan's blandishments to come to Tacoma and say something nice about vice.

Direct endorsement of sin Visscher avoided, at least as far as one can tell from surviving issues of the *Globe*. But sinners he tolerated as he did Masons, Democrats, Englishmen, and Socialists not opposed to hard liquor.

Tacoma journalism could be rough. Sam Wall of the *Evening Telegraph* disagreed so strongly with an eight-line comment on his character that he walked into the *Evening News* city room and told Herbert Harcourt, who had emitted the offending opinion, that it was his intent to kill him. He then shot Harcourt through his tie-pin, a target that deflected the bullet from fatal course. Wall was captured but not brought to trial. Harcourt found employment elsewhere.

Visscher avoided such excesses of expression. He contented himself with giving good coverage of community affairs and parodying the *Ledger*'s former anti-Chinese theme by running edits headed THE LEDGER MUST GO. The *Globe* scored points, gained circulation, lost advertisers, and, after two years of understated vindication of vice, went under.

Morgan, too. The Boss Sport died unexpectedly in April of 1890, aged forty, to the relief of the *Ledger* and the benefit of the Pierce County legal profession. Morgan left no will. He was reputed wealthy, and court records showed him possessed of papers for considerable real estate, much of it gained on double-or-nothing bets lost by patrons who had blown their cash. Included in his inventory were a shingle mill at Buckley, a sawmill on Boise Creek in King County, and two thousand dollars in IOU's from Pierce County Sheriff Lewis Byrd, which might have come in handy. But Morgan's list of creditors read like the city directory, and as word of his intestate state spread, heirs sprouted. One styled herself Lena Morgan and produced three little Morgans alleged to be issue of Harry. Others claiming descent or blood ties included an Edwin C. Morgan, Marty Morris, Mary Barry, and three people named Hampton. Litigation dragged on for more than a decade. By the time the estate was settled the lawyers had the money and the Tacoma Boom was hardly an echo. Morgan's property was auctioned at ten dollars a lot, the shingle mill for one hundred dollars, and the theater for fifteen hundred, including *Ledger* ill will.

Dora Charlotta Morgan, whom the courts held to be Harry's one and only widow, was left with nothing except his bouncer, Frank "Jumbo" Cantwell, whom she had married.

It was a time when even the domestic difficulties of private citizens might work out to the benefit of the community.

C. P. Ferry came to Tacoma only a few months after Matthew Morton McCarver. He built a house near that of the old boomer in Old Town, served for a time as McCarver's private secretary, correcting the general's inspired spelling and eventually marrying a daughter of McCarver's second wife, which made him McCarver's stepson-in-law, though he preferred to be called the Duke of Tacoma.

A man of imposing presence, big-nosed, long-jawed, loose-framed, he was hard-working and intent on money. Ferry served as agent for the Tacoma Land Company, handled McCarver's estate after his death, and managed his own property well. He pioneered the development of South Tacoma and the papers guessed he was worth a million or two. After his first wife died, Ferry courted and won a vivacious, auburn-haired divorcee, Cynthia Trafton, who of course was considerably younger than he. He was very proud of her. Jealous, too.

In 1889 Ferry's contributions to the Republican party were rewarded with an appointment as United States commissioner to the Paris Exposition. It seemed the perfect honeymoon: Paris, visits to the 984-foot tower Alexandre Gustave Eiffel had built for the event, a suite in the best hotel, a government carriage for rides on the Champs Elysée, diplomatic status. What more could a girl ask? Well, Cynthia wanted to learn French. Ferry hired as tutor a champagne salesman who claimed noble connections. Cynthia's efforts were assiduous, her accent improved steadily, but Ferry's enthusiasm for bilingualism lessened. He found the tutor to be more than efficient, he was also young and handsome. A story in the Tacoma *Ledger* quoted a story in a New York paper to the effect that the Duke of Tacoma was going about with his hand in a cast because Cynthia had broken his forefinger when he waved it under her nose during a discussion about elisions in latinate derivatives.

Ferry decided it was time for them to return to Tacoma with the objets d'art they had collected for the new house Cynthia was planning. She wouldn't go. Ferry agreed to stay in Paris a while longer if she would promise not to admit the tutor to their suite nor recognize him on the street. She kept her word. She met him at a hotel. Ferry and a detective interrupted one of the French lessons. During the explanations that followed, she bit a chunk off her husband's nose. He demanded, unsuccessfully, that Parisian authorities jail her as "a common woman."

When the Duke of Tacoma returned to his home turf, his patrician nose appeared intact but Mrs. Ferry was not with him. She was no longer Mrs. Ferry. He was accompanied, however, by the collection of art they had purchased for the new house. Most of it Ferry gave to the city's new museum, which he helped finance and which was named for him. Some he gave to the city for its parks. The two maidens guarding the Division Avenue entrance to Wright Park are mementos of the Duke of Tacoma's time in Paris.

Out of personal misfortune, civic amenities.

In the closing years of the decade even the seagulls were losing sleep. They rose in clouds as the thunder of blasting rolled across the bay. New additions were announced weekly, and black-powder men were in such demand they could charge twenty dollars a day to blow up stumps on land being cleared for development as Tacoma climbed its

One of Allen Mason's real estate promotions Courtesy of Rick and Francie Carr

hills and spread south across the glacial plain. Houses correctly called "grand" were being built as far away as American Lake.

Downtown had firmed into masonry. The biggest theater north of San Francisco, designed by J. M. Wood in a style emulating that used by Stanford White for the Tacoma Hotel, was playing to standing-room-only audiences whether its attraction was the J. C. Duff Comic Opera Company in *Paola*, the San Francisco Opera Company in *Little Red Riding Hood* with a real wolf in the cast, Polar Bear Sam's Alaska Indian dancers with "eight braves, eight squaws," or James O'Neill, later to father the playwright, as *The Count of Monte Cristo*.

Sectarian, ethnic, and commercial publications sprouted like crab-grass. Between 1887 and 1890 there were founded the *Baptist Sentinel, Temperance Echo, Epworth Budget, Real Estate Journal, Northern Light* (a labor publication), *Northwest Horticulturist, Puget Sound Lumberman, Real Estate and Court Index, Washington Investment Journal, West Coast Lumberman,* the *Budstikke* (Danish-Norwegian), *Tidende* (Danish), *Wacht Am Sunde* (German), and the *Folkeblad, Westra Posten,* and *Tribunen,* all Swedish. Puget Sound University, Whitworth College, and the short-lived Washington University competed for students.

Industry continued to expand. Not only were four steamships launched in one year, but the engine for one of them was built in Tacoma at the expanded Lister Foundry. Billy Rust had his smelter going full blast. The Puget Sound Flouring Mill was grinding wheat; the grain coming over the mountains was now creating jobs beyond those for warehousemen and longshoremen. The Tacoma and Southeastern, incorporated by the St. Paul and Tacoma interests, had started draining the forests from the Cascade foothills.

A Businessman's Ticket swept the city council elections on a platform pledging an effort to rid the city of the stigma of being "in the hands of lawless elements," which had hung over Tacoma since the expulsion of the Chinese. Agents said to represent the Union Pacific were in town taking options. A rumor that the UP planned to make Tacoma its terminus was repeated often enough to become an article of faith. Allen Mason built a warehouse complex at the head of the city waterway to accommodate the new line when it arrived. George W. Vanderbilt, son of the old Commodore who had growled about Jay Cooke's folly in running railroads from nowhere to nowhere, let it be known he had invested three hundred thousand dollars in Tacoma. Tacomans forgave the Vanderbilts' past error and welcomed George to the ranks of true believers.

Anything was possible. Why even Henry Villard had belatedly seen the light. The old wizard had recovered his health, some of his fortune, and his magic touch. In 1887 he returned from self-imposed exile in Germany and with the backing of the Deutsche Bank bought his way back onto the board of the Northern Pacific. By 1889 he was again chairman of the board. But it was too late for him to interfere with the construction of the Cascade Division: Villard saw his task now as making profitable the track he had once opposed. Events, and the rivalry of the Union Pacific, which leased the tracks along the Columbia from the Oregon Railway and Navigation Company, turned Villard into a defender of Tacoma's interests against those of the Columbia ports.

Villard bought out Nelson Bennett's Tacoma Street Railway Company and announced that the horse-drawn trams and even the "modern" steam dummies would be replaced with Edison's electric trolleys. Everything up to date in terminus city! There was even talk of paving Pacific Avenue.

Some had doubts. In the fall of 1889, twenty-four-year-old British journalist Rudyard Kipling, on a tour of America, came up from California to take a look at what he had been told was a classic example of town-booming. "Tacoma was literally staggering under a boom of the boomiest," Kipling reported in *Coast to Coast*, his book on American travel:

I do not quite remember what her natural resources were supposed to be, though every second man shrieked a selection in my ear. They included coal and iron, carrots, potatoes, lumber, shipping and a crop of thin newspapers all telling Portland that her days were numbered.

We struck the place at twilight. The crude boarded pavements of the main streets rumbled under the heels of hundreds of furious men all actively engaged in hunting drinks and eligible corner-lots. They sought the drinks first. The street itself alternated five-storey business blocks of the later and more abominable forms of architecture with board shanties. Overhead the drunken telegraph, telephone and electric-light wires tangled on tottering posts whose butts were half whittled through by the knife of the loafer. Down the muddy, grimy, unmetalled thoroughfare ran a horse-car line—the metals three inches above road level. Beyond this street rose many hills, and the town was thrown like a broken set of dominoes over all.

We passed down ungraded streets that ended abruptly in a fifteen foot drop and a nest of brambles; along pavements that beginning in pine-plank ended in the living tree; by hotels with Turkish mosque trinketry on their shameless tops and the pine stumps at their very doors; by a female seminary, tall, gaunt and red, which a native of the town bade us marvel at, and we marvelled; by houses built in imitation of the ones on Nob Hill, San Francisco, after the Dutch fashion; by other houses plenteously befouled with jig-saw work, and others flaring with the castlemented, battlemented bosh of the wooden Gothic school.

The hotel walls bore a flaming panorama of Tacoma in which by the eye of faith I saw a faint resemblance to the real town. The hotel stationery advertised that Tacoma bore on its face all the advantages of the highest civilization, and the newspapers sang the same tune in a louder key. The real estate agents were selling house-lots on unmade streets miles away for thousands of dollars. On the streets—the rude, crude streets, where the unshaded electric light was fighting with the gentle northern twilight—men were babbling of money, town-lots and again money. . . . I think it was the raw, new smell of fresh sawdust everywhere pervading the air that threw upon me a desolating homesickness.

Kipling's companion came back from a ramble, laughing noiselessly. He proclaimed the Tacomans mad, all mad. "Young feller," he warned, "don't you buy real estate here." Nor did he. Kipling took the *Flyer* to Seattle. It was a memorable trip, "the water landlocked among a thousand islands, lay still as oil under our bows, and the wake of the screw broke up the unquivering reflections of pine and cliffs a mile away; 'twas as though we were trampling on glass." It brought Kipling to a city which that summer had been swept by fire: "In the heart of the business quarters there was a horrible black smudge, as though a Hand had come down and rubbed the place smooth. I know now what being wiped out means."

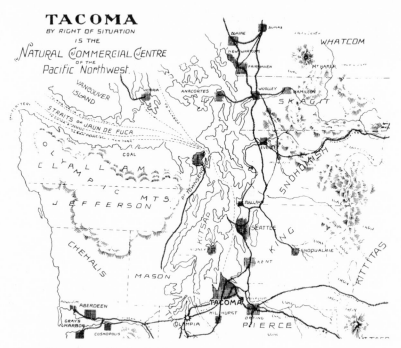

TACOMA

BY RIGHT OF SITUATION
IS THE

Natural Commercial Centre
OF THE
Pacific Northwest.

From West Coast Trade, *1892*

"Seattle, Seattle! Death rattle, death rattle!" chanted Tacoma school children. Businessmen, too, at luncheon meetings.

"Tacoma, a railroad promotion," sneered Seattle newspapers.

"Seattle, flea-town on the sawdust."

"Tacoma, village of density."

The high school tone of the jibes overlaid hatred. Antagonism lay deep. Fortunes were at stake. Men had bet their futures, and dominance in the region remained in doubt.

Seattle had some advantages. It was older, had second-generation leadership, lay nearer the open ocean, fronted the lowest mountain pass. But Tacoma was the designated terminus, had backing from eastern capital, and by 1890 seemed to be closing in fast on a rival with a thirty-year head start.

When the census takers made their decennial rounds in 1870 they listed 23,955 residents in Washington Territory, of whom 1,107 were in Seattle. Tacoma did not exist as an entity recognized by the government. Ten years later the territory had more than trebled in population: the count stood at 75,166. Seattle's population had also trebled and was now 3,533. Tacoma appeared for the first time as a community of 1,098. Seattle chose to note that it was three times larger in spite of Tacoma's designation as NP terminus in 1873. Tacomans chose to point out that starting from nowhere they were only 2,435 residents behind an older, better-established rival. Either way, the race was not over.

The completion of the main line of the Northern Pacific in 1883 spurred rapid growth throughout the territory. Both cities gained population, Seattle more rapidly than Tacoma. But with construction of the Cascade Division, Tacoma surged. School figures indicate the rapid growth. In 1886 there were 964 pupils and 18 teachers in Tacoma; in 1887, 1,111 pupils and 20 teachers; in 1888, 1,401 pupils and 23 teachers; in 1889, 2,294 pupils and 31 teachers. Whereas growth was slight between 1886 and 1887, in the next two years the school population doubled.

In 1889, Tacoma claimed more than half the telephones in the state: 492 out of a total of 940. Seattle had 280. Six steamships hit the water from Tacoma yards that year, and 130 sailing vessels with a tonnage of 111,086 operated through the port. Tacoma's manufacturing industries represented an investment of $5,190,417, employed 3,484 persons, paid $192,579 in wages, and produced goods worth $5,844,185. The St. Paul and Tacoma Lumber Company's mill was the largest, with an investment of $1,500,000. Its 700 employees earned a monthly payroll of $35,000. Most of Tacoma's industries had been operating less than a year, many for less than six months.

Tacomans could hardly wait for the 1890 census, but it showed them still somewhat behind Seattle. Washington was a state now, not a territory. The state population was 357,232, Seattle's was 42,837, Tacoma's 36,006. Boosters in both cities interpreted the statistics to hometown advantage. Seattle was not only larger but had almost trebled the margin of lead, from 2,435 to 6,831. Tacoma pointed out that while Washington's population had increased 3½ times in the decade and Seattle's 12 times, Tacoma's was nearly 34 times larger in 1890 than in 1880—and booming.

The excitement of the race, and the ingenuity of the statisticians, continued to build. There were no federal enumerators to make an official count, but Tacomans estimated their over-all population by counting the names in the Polk directory and multiplying by a factor of 2½ to account for dependents and persons overlooked. That gave Tacoma an estimated population of 45,080—up 9,074, or 25 percent, in a year. Then growth began to slow, but in 1892 Tacoma multiplied listings by 2¾ instead of 2½ and claimed a population of 49,761, up 10 percent. In 1893, still using the 2¾ multiple, the gain was 5 percent and Tacoma claimed to have 52,329 residents.

Then suddenly, with the Panic of 1893, the excitement died, the flow reversed. When the census was taken in 1900, Seattle had nearly doubled in population, going from 42,837 to 80,676. Tacoma, which had 36,006 in 1890 and claimed 52,329 in 1893, showed only 37,714.

The Uses of Adversity

"Adversity makes men wise, not wealthy." OLD ENGLISH PROVERB

LAYING rails from nowhere to nowhere in an effort to unlock grainfields, timberlands, and mineral deposits was an undertaking by no means unique to the United States in the last quarter of the nineteenth century. Similar enterprises were underway in Canada, Chile, Peru, Argentina, Russia, Australia, and China. Expansion outran distribution, especially in agriculture. Production grew, prices fell, credit tightened. As early as 1890, the more foresighted of the railroad promoters sensed danger. Edward Henry Harriman warned other members of the board of the Illinois Central that "it would be unwise to pass any resolutions adopting a policy for a large expenditure of money." James J. Hill told his son-in-law, Sam Hill, that the nation was headed for "a panic that it will take five years to get over."

The economy slowed in 1891; the crash came in May of 1893. There was a classic run on the banks, with depositors en masse withdrawing their savings, putting the money into gold when possible, and burying the hoard in the backyard or stashing it in mattress or cookie jar. Credit dried up as though a spigot had been turned. Construction stopped, services were cut, men were laid off by the tens of thousands. Banks insisted on mortgage payments, foreclosed when debtors could not meet their obligations, but found few buyers for the property claimed, and went broke themselves. By the end of the year sixteen thousand businesses across the nation were bankrupt; 20 percent of the labor force, between two million and three million men, were out of work; five hundred banks had locked their doors on depositors.

In Tacoma, things were worse. There were twenty-one banks in the city in May of 1893, many of them little more than store-front operations held together by public confidence in men who wore dark suits and celluloid collars and could count. After a year, only seven survived.

275

First to go was the Merchants National. TEMPORARY SUSPENSION said the headline in the *Ledger* on June 1, 1893, but the *Ledger* was then owned by Nelson Bennett, who was also president of the stricken bank, and the headline was overoptimistic. The suspension stretched into permanence. The Traders Bank was next, closing July 21, three days ahead of the Tacoma National. Then State Savings failed, its chief depositor the City of Tacoma. Payment was suspended on city bonds; employees were paid in scrip that cashed at discounts of up to 60 percent. Each failure led to runs on the remaining banks. Crash followed crash. Institutions with British connections were more trusted, and the Bank of British Columbia became recipient of many transferred accounts before it too went under.

The Northern Pacific again went into the hands of receivers. So did the Tacoma Hotel. So did the Tacoma Land Company. Work stopped on the huge Tourist Hotel the NP was building alongside Old Woman's Gulch at the head of Cliff Avenue. The building stood empty until gutted by flames. Later the shell was transformed into Stadium High School.

The movers and shakers of the community found themselves shaken. Consider William Blackwell, the popular hotelier. When the opening of the Tacoma Hotel led to the closing of the Blackwell Hotel on the wharf, William and Alice moved into a house at Eleventh and A streets, where the Judsons had raised oats and where the post office now stands. Blackwell joined General John E. Sprague in founding the Tacoma National Bank, of which he served as vice president until Sprague's death, then as president. He was elected to the territorial legislature, helped organize the Tacoma Board of Trade and later the Chamber of Commerce, and was a major stockholder in the Tacoma Theater as well as in one of the street railways and a wharf.

When he became wealthy, Blackwell built a handsome house on view lots he had purchased for twenty-five dollars apiece at the head of Cliff Avenue, next to Old Woman's Gulch. Before the place was complete the Tacoma Land Company offered him forty thousand for the land, which they coveted as site for the chateau-like Tourist Hotel. Blackwell accepted, bought a smaller lot at South Fourth between Broadway and Cliff Avenue, and had the dream house rebuilt there. It was one of the marvels of the town, commodious and gracious, looking down at the wharf, where they had started in Tacoma, and out at the Mountain. The staircase and hall, paneled in Minnesota white oak, were especially admired. Will gave Alice a quit claim deed for the place in her own name when they moved in.

The crash came soon after. When the Tacoma National closed, Blackwell felt personally responsible for his friends' deposits. He mortgaged all the Blackwell property except Alice's house. His holdings were considerable—they included the sites later occupied by the Winthrop Hotel and the National Bank of Washington—and he raised enough to reopen the bank. Then he went to New York to try to borrow more. While he was away a new run on the Tacoma National wiped out the stop-gap and left him broke. Cashier Herbert Fishbach in tidying up the office after the money ran out found in a desk a few torn bills that had been set aside for return to the Treasury. He took them to Alice, and they provided just enough to get Will home from the East.

The Blackwells were suddenly penniless in their mansion with a view. City officials let Alice grow vegetables at the edge of Cliff Avenue so there would be food on the Blackwell table. Will dug clams. (It was of this period that Congressman Cushman spoke when he said his constituents did not starve but they ate so many clams their stomachs rose and fell with the tide.) They took in boarders. Alice's two nieces, whom the Blackwells had adopted as daughters, baked cookies and peddled them door to door. Will tried prospecting for gold without finding more than a show of color. The family income totaled twenty dollars a month. Blackwell was considering shipping out as a common seaman on an Oriental steamer when the Provident Company, which had taken over the Tacoma Hotel on a mortgage foreclosure, hired him as manager at one hundred dollars a month. Part of each month's pay he gave to those who had lost money in his bank.

Another riches-to-rags story was that of Henry Mahncke. In February 1893 Mahncke completed the Berlin Building at Eleventh and Pacific. His principal tenant was the ill-fated Merchants National, first to fail. By December Mahncke was working in the Berlin Building as his own janitor and furnace-stoker. To meet payments on two earlier mortgages he borrowed twenty-five hundred dollars from G. A. Worden, who represented the Otis Elevator people in the Northwest, then, unable to repay Worden in cash, he leased him the building. In effect he was now working for Worden, who was also broke and ran the Berlin Building elevator. They called themselves the Millionaires Club. Grimly they hung on, awaiting the return of good times.

Some let go, among them the manager of the Northern Pacific's Land Division, Paul Schulze. German-born, handsome, well-educated, a protege of Henry Villard, Schulze was a man of affairs (not all of them business). He was financially involved with the NP, the Yakima and Kittitas Irrigation Company, the Tacoma Grocery Company, the Tacoma Railway and Motor Company, and the Traders Bank—every one of which went into the hands of receivers during the Panic. Schulze's house at 601 North Yakima was mortgaged beyond its worth. He owed thirty-five thousand dollars alimony. His debts exceeded three hundred thousand, not counting the more than a million it was later discovered he had embezzled. His assets were about five thousand.

Schulze solved his problems by withdrawing thirty-five thousand dollars from an account he did not have in San Francisco. After a last spasm of affluence, he returned from the University Club to the big house that dominated the double block on Yakima Avenue, dined alone by candlelight, burned his private papers in the kitchen stove, stirring gently, said ambiguous goodbye to his Chinese cook ("I am going on a long trip"), wrote a letter to his mistress, and shot himself through the temple.

Paul Schulze's last wish was that his ashes be sent to Germany but he was buried in Tacoma.

Others got out of town. They fled by the thousands. Abruptly the tide of westward migration, which had reached flood in the late 1880s, reversed in Tacoma. Population ebbed eastward. The little wooden station at Seventeenth was full of people spending their last cash on one-way tickets back to where they came from.

Those without money or work hung around for a time, subsisting on clams, berries, charity, and editorials in the papers which recommended that the unemployed prospect for gold, oil, or other improbable geologic possibilities on nearby streams. There were no provisions for state or federal aid to the destitute, no emergency credit to businesses in trouble. The Cleveland administration and its Republican opposition agreed that although the depression was deplorable the people at risk to its rigors were not the responsibility of the United States government. Local governments sometimes instituted public works projects—road-building and drain-laying, for the most part—during hard times, but the City of Tacoma and the County of Pierce were broke too. Churches and ethnic clubs exhausted their resources. The poorhouse was so overcrowded that it closed. When the berry bushes were picked clean and only the clams were left to be gathered, many who had come looking for a new life were ready to settle for the old. They left on foot. They stole rides on trains.

The railroads gave new mobility to the needy as well as to the affluent. For those without tickets, there was the boxcar; and if the side-door Pullman, as they called it, was locked or guarded, the more daring decked the box (climbed to the roof) or rode the rods. On passenger trains the baggage cars had closed forward compartments (blind baggage), but getting into them might involve a bribe to the crew or stationmaster.

One way or another, singly or in groups, the unemployed took off down the tracks. As winter and the depression deepened, the exodus became organized. The migrant unemployed formed into groups— "tramp gangs," to the townsfolk who feared them; "industrial armies," they called themselves—and sent representatives to petition authorities for food and the railroads for transportation to some place where there might be work. The armies camped at the outskirts of the railroad towns, pooled their food, agreed on a destination, and issued tickets to their members, the tickets entitling each man to an equal portion of any necessities the group could beg, scavenge, or liberate.

"We intend to go where we can get work," the captain of one group which came down the tracks from Tacoma told a reporter in Portland in December of 1893. "In our party are thirty-one loggers, fifteen miners, a railway ticket agent, two cooks, a waiter and seven brakemen. Most of us came here from the Sound. We are honest men and want work. We can't get employment here and do not want to impose on the good nature of the Boards of Charities any longer. Some of our party may be bad men, but I promise no one will violate the law. Most of our men are well educated, and I myself am a college graduate." His group was given a supply of flour and permission to occupy a boxcar headed for California.

Such organized bodies of unemployed men moving about the West, under discipline, living off the land, posed an unspoken threat to established order. There was talk that the industrial armies might take over idle factories. What many of them did, instead, was follow one of the most improbable of political pied pipers, Jacob S. Coxey, of Massillon, Ohio, in his march on Washington, D.C.

A prosperous businessman, forty years old, with a handsome second wife, a stone quarry, a stable of prize thoroughbreds, and sympathy for the less fortunate, Coxey thought he knew the way to end the depression. The federal government should put people to work building an interstate highway system. He proposed that it be financed by issuing $500 million in paper money, which the secretary of war would spend at the rate of $20 million a month by hiring the unemployed at $1.50 for an eight-hour day to build roads. Since the roads would mainly benefit rural areas, Coxey added a plan to permit other governmental bodies to construct public works: the key to his proposal was the non–interest-bearing bond. He proposed that any state, territory, county, or municipality be permitted to issue bonds worth up to one-half the value of its assessed property. These bonds could be deposited with the United States Treasury as security for interest-free loans of paper money which, though legal tender, could only be used for public improvements. The principal was to be repaid the Treasury out of local taxes at the rate of 4 percent a year for fifteen years with the paper money issued at the time of the loan retired as payments were made.

A soft-spoken man with a trim mustache and rimless glasses, Coxey looked more like a prosperous farmer than an economic messiah. He proved ineffective at publicizing his proposals until he teamed with Carl Browne, a hustler whose faults did not include a lack of flamboyance. Browne had been a house-painter, cartoonist, theosophist, snake-oil salesman, and private secretary to Dennis Kearney during that demagogue's anti-Chinese agitation. A big fellow, notoriously reluctant to bathe, with long graying hair and a beard worthy of a prophet, Browne decked himself out in buckskin coat, fringed, of course, and with buttons made of Mexican half-dollars. His ensemble was completed with high boots, sombrero, a fur coat of dubious derivation, and a necklace of amber beads. His vocal range was from foghorn to buzz saw. As an attracter of attention, Browne was a triple threat, combining visual, vocal, and odoriferous pollution. He was also imaginative.

Browne and Coxey decided to send Congress "a petition with boots on." The unemployed would march on Washington to demand passage of a Good Roads Bill and a Non–Interest-Bearing Bond Bill. Coxey took credit for the idea of the march, Browne for calling the marchers "The Commonweal Army of Christ." Browne painted a remarkable banner for the army to march under. It bore a picture of Christ which critics felt looked suspiciously like a Browne self-portrait, and it was captioned "Peace on Earth, Good Will to Men, He Hath Risen, but Death to Interest on Bonds."

The first battalion of the Commonweal Army started for Washington from Massillon on Easter Sunday, 1894. A color-bearer with Browne's banner led the way, followed by General Coxey in a piano-box buggy drawn by his forty-thousand-dollar pacer Acolyte, and, in a separate carriage, the second Mrs. Coxey, who held in her arms their infant son whose baptismal certificate read, no mistake, Legal Tender Coxey. Marshall Browne rode a spirited stallion. The others walked. Among those in the ranks were Cyclone Kirtland, an astrologer who claimed that according to the stars the army would be "invisible in war, invincible in peace"; Unknown Smith, who had earlier been known as ringmaster for a disbanded circus; David McCallum, author of an economic treatise which sold under the title *Dogs and Fleas, by One of the Fleas;* Christopher Columbus Jones, a five-foot apostle of reform who marched under a silk hat; and Jones's private secretary, who "sustained a plug hat with impressive dignity."

The Commonwealers numbered only two hundred by the most favorable count, but they were accompanied down the glory road by forty-three reporters, four telegraph operators, and two linemen. Carl Browne had done his public relations work well. Though the stories the reporters filed were heavy with ridicule, they were numerous. Coxey's tatterdemalion troops captured the national imagination as they traipsed south. Others followed.

Tacoma and Seattle organized separate contingents in April, Seattle first. On the afternoon of Saturday, April 8, some two hundred men gathered in a skid road hall furnished with only two chairs and a card table. Harry Shepard, a soft-spoken engineer, made a quiet speech that called on "the respectable unemployed" to unite for the amelioration of their condition. He urged order, discipline, and self-reliance in gathering food and funds for a protest march across the continent. The seventy-two who signed the muster roll the first day pledged themselves "to uphold the constitution, recognize only honest workmen, assist any officer in the lawful discharge of his duty, repudiate all connections with drunkards, thieves and convicts, and to protect life, liberty and property." They elected Shepard their general.

Tacoma organized a week later. The unemployed and their sympathizers gathered in the National Theater, a run-down hall at Twelfth and A streets. After considerable speechifying, the mantle of leadership settled not on a quiet engineer like Shepard but on one of Tacoma's loudest personalities, Frank P. "Jumbo" Cantwell, long-time bouncer for Harry Morgan, occasional prize fighter, and current husband of Morgan's common-law widow, Dora Charlotte—usually called Charlotta. Not for Jumbo a tone of respectability or a demand that his followers eschew association with thieves and drunkards. Cantwell himself was not unknown in police court. Respectability he could do without. Notoriety was the spur.

Cantwell told the would-be marchers that they could hire a train at cut-rates to carry them to Washington. How to pay for it? "Every feller who follers us from Tacoma, we'll make him dig up ten cents— militia, police, I don't care who he is—we'll make him dig up. Then we'll use the money to pay our way. But when we come back to Tacoma, we won't hang out at the Old National. Oh, no. We'll go to the Tacoma Hotel and be the elite."

Or so said the *Ledger* in a report on his speech. The *Ledger* complained that Jumbo's followers were "the best dressed, best fed lot of unemployed to be found on the Coast," and disapproved of "emi-

"Jumbo" Cantwell Courtesy of Photo. Coll., UW Library

grants going not west but east, with no purpose but to present a demand that the government shall help them, shall take them in its charge and provide for them. . . . The Army is marching to the unknown in search of the impossible and the impractical." The paper suggested that the government simply draft the unemployed, ship them out of the country to Nicaragua, furnish them with pick and shovel, and set them to digging a canal.

The Commonwealers were not to be dissuaded by such suggestions. They organized into companies, or "cantons," of sixty men, drilled at marching by morning and in the afternoons rustled provender for the mess. "General" Cantwell helped out by boxing an exhibition and turning over his purse to the commissary. Two meals were served daily. They were long on clams, crab, salmon, and beans, short on meat and bread.

Cantwell and Shepard arranged that their Tacoma and Seattle armies would meet at Puyallup at the end of the month. They would then ask the Northern Pacific for train service east. While preparations were being made for the Puyallup encampment, a Commonweal contingent from Butte, Montana, flagged down a freight train, piled four hundred men into fourteen empty boxcars, put an unemployed engineer at the throttle, and headed east. The Coxeyites regarded this as hitching a ride, the NP as stealing a train. Railroad officials obtained a court order forbidding anyone to deprive rightful owners of the use of their boxcars. Fifteen deputy marshall were hastily sworn in. They caught up with the train at Billings, where a crowd had gathered to wish the Butte army godspeed. The deputies started shooting and several by-standers were wounded before the engine was uncoupled from the freight and the engineer arrested. The townsfolk sided with the unemployed. They helped the army liberate another engine and supplied the Commonwealers with food. The train pulled out for the East with flags flying and a live rooster perched on the locomotive. President Cleveland called out the United States Army. Regulars from Fort Koegh found the freight parked on a siding at Forsythe, Montana, the engineer catching some sleep. The Industrials surrendered without resistance.

A reporter asked Jumbo Cantwell his views about commandeering trains. Cantwell at the time was trying on a uniform that had been presented him by fellow members of Tacoma's gambling fraternity: a long-tailed coat with epaulets, dark pants with blue stripes down the leg, a broad-brimmed black hat heavy with braid. "We'll get back there one way or another," he promised, admiring his finery in a mirror. "We ain't too proud to steal a train. Them fellers in Congress has broke the law. Why can't we?"

United States Marshal James C. Drake began swearing in deputies to guard railroad property. Deputies were easy to find: why, the pay was five dollars a day, and room and board. Drake dispatched a dozen to Puyallup where the Commonweal armies were to rendezvous; others patrolled train yards in Seattle, Ellensberg, Yakima, and Spokane. They were armed with .45s and Winchester rifles requisitioned from Tacoma sporting-goods stores, and they carried copies of a restraining order isued by United States Circuit Court Judge C. H. Hanford of Seattle. It prohibited any action which would deprive the receivers of the bankrupt Northern Pacific from the regular use of the line's locomotives, cars, and equipment.

The Seattle Commonwealers under "General" Shepard started for Puyallup on April 28, Jumbo's Tacoma troops a day later. A light drizzle was falling as the unemployed marched down Pacific Avenue that Saturday afternoon, through a thin line of spectators on the plank sidewalks. A guard of honor carried a flag presented the Commonwealers by the local post of the Grand Army of the Republic. It hung limply. General Cantwell, his uniform partly concealed by a macintosh, followed the flag. He kept the Colonel, his pet Saint Bernard, on a long leash. Some four hundred Coxeyites marched after him. They sang as they went down Pacific to Puyallup Boulevard then over to the river, Civil War songs, and "Good Night, Ladies," and, to an old tune, the new words of "Coxey's March":

> Come now, you sons of labor, and join the noble cause.
> It's time I'm sure for something to be done
> For bread and meat is very scarce because of their cruel laws.
> We'll pack our traps and March to Washington.
>
> So sing along, march along,
> Come along, march along.
> While the air is pure and balmy
> And every mother's son
> Will march to Washington
> And join General Coxey's army.
>
> Now we're all honest toilers
> But can't get work to do.
> From honest work we ne'er were known to run,
> So help us Grover Cleveland
> The times look very blue.
> We'll pack our traps and March to Washington
>
> Dish out a little silver.
> We hear you've got too much
> We'll try and help you spend it, just for fun.
> Yes, silver's good enough for us,
> For gold we'll ne'er touch.
> We'll pack our traps and move to Washington.

It was evening when they reached Puyallup. They moved into two empty buildings their scouts had spotted and began steaming out shoes and bedrolls. The Seattle army, already encamped in an unfinished hotel, had commandeered a deserted cafe. The coffee was already hot.

A United States marshal served General Cantwell with Judge Hanford's order prohibiting interference with Northern Pacific trains. Jumbo accepted the document, glanced at its index of things not to be done, folded the injunction, and pocketed it, remarking enigmatically that the Commonwealers had lost some property and would reclaim it wherever they found it. At a joint rally in the Puyallup

Opera House later that evening Jumbo was the most frequent speaker, and less obscure.

"I'm a gambler," he said in introducing himself to the Seattle army. "I'm not looking for a job, but I'll lead you to work and to victory. We're like Christ. If they strike us on one cheek, we'll turn the other. But then we'll give 'em one." He shadow-boxed about the stage to thundering applause.

The next morning's papers brought news that Coxey's original band from Massilon had reached the outskirts of Washington. The Associated Press described them as "350 miserably dressed, woe-begone, grumbling, out-at-the-elbows and down-at-the-heels specimens of humanity," but the Tacomans were cheered by the story: it could be done. And the story said Coxey was calling for reinforcements.

Cantwell and Shepard agreed to let Jumbo's wife do much of the negotiating with railroad officials for the rent of a train. Charlotta Cantwell was a handsome woman in her mid-twenties, well spoken and well dressed, fond of diamonds and seal-skin. The NP men were impressed enough to be very polite but not enough to reduce fares or rent her twenty boxcars to carry the Commonwealers as far as St. Paul. Their position was full fare in passenger cars, no people in box-cars.

Jumbo sounded out the federal marshals on their interpretation of the judge's restraining order. What would they do if the unemployed hopped freights in twos or threes, or even by the dozen? When they gave him no encouragement he asked, "Well, what if one of us should hire a few cars and an engine for the purpose of transporting freight say, to Spokane. What if he ran it into Puyallup and said, Hey, these are my friends and I am going to give them a pull across the mountains, what would you do?" The marshals shrugged off the question.

With other deputies, Cantwell took a different line. "Now you fellers are getting a good thing, $5 a day and keep. There are upwards of a hundred of you and your job is easy. It costs our gang about $25 a day to live here. If you contribute $25 to our support, we'll stay three or four months, till the railroad gets tired of putting up your pay and gives us a ride back east."

Such talk was probably aimed less at the deputies than at the people of Puyallup, who were nervous about all the strangers. In mid-week there was word from Washington that Coxey, Browne, and little Christoper Columbus Jones had been jailed on charges of illegal assemblage on the Capitol grounds. The *Ledger* headline read: COXEY WAS CRUSHED. Puyallup might well wonder what would happen if the march were abandoned and the army remained in camp. They did not care whether the Commonwealers made it to Washington but they wanted them out of town. They wired the governor for help.

Governor John H. McGraw showed up in Puyallup ready for almost anything. A feisty little man with a bald head, waterfall mustache, and rimless pince-nez, McGraw had made his political reputation when as sheriff of King County he stood up to the mob that attempted to chase the Chinese from Seattle three months after the Tacoma expulsion. The Puyallup brass band met him at the depot, and a mass meeting was arranged at the Robinson Opera House. A meeting suited the Commonwealers fine. They had nothing else to do. They packed the hall.

The chairman explained that Puyallup had a problem, or rather from eleven hundred to thirteen hundred uninvited problems. The governor was introduced and said he was there to listen. Ezra Meeker said that what the Puyallup people wanted to hear was what the Commonwealers intended to do. They brought Jumbo lumbering to the podium.

Cantwell said his men didn't want to be in Puyallup, they wanted to be with Coxey in Washington. They were not thieves or hobos. Not a chicken house in Puyallup had been disturbed. They would not steal from people as poor as themselves. They weren't even stealing rides. They were ready to pay a thousand dollars for boxcars but the railroads wouldn't let them go even for money:

"These men came to this state through fraud and misrepresentation on the part of the railroad corporations and a rotten, lying press. Now for God's sake let them go. The Northern Pacific is owned in Germany, and all the money of this country has been sent to Europe, and these men have none. We won't disband here, and when I say we won't, I speak for the Seattle contingent as well as my own."

Jumbo started to tell of finding powder buried along the track near Orting. He suspected the railroad intended to blow up the train if the Commonwealers seized one. The chairman ruled him out of order. When the shouting died down, Cantwell was saying, ". . . the highest men in this country don't want us to get back to Washington but we'll get there and get justice."

E. J. Jeffries, a tall, thin attorney who espoused Populist causes, made his way from the audience. "The governor, I believe, will come to our rescue and enable us to leave the state . . ."

McGraw stood up. "I am not here for any such purpose." The light from the bare bulbs shone off his skull; his cascading mustache was dark against his pale face. "I am not in sympathy with this march or this movement." There were gasps in the audience. "As governor of this state I owe a duty to the state and the nation. I came here solely to consult with the citizens of the town, and if they will appoint a committee of ten, or fifteen, aye, of twenty-five to go to Washington and present your petitions, I will do all that I can to secure transportation for them. More I cannot do."

There was a tumult of boos, hisses, and groans. Jeffries turned to McGraw, who had resumed his seat. "It is said we should go home. We have no homes. Where is it we should go? Back to Seattle, where the judge would vag us in twenty-four hours? No, we want to go east, and there demand redress of our wrongs from the chief executive of this nation. Can you not, Governor McGraw, go to the courts and induce them to give us transportation, even in cattle cars, to the end of the line at St. Paul?"

The uproar in the hall drowned the words of Jeffries and the chairman. Eventually McGraw signaled that he would like to speak. The room quieted. The governor rose to dead silence; not a cheer, or handclap, not even a boo greeted him. He said quietly that he had already talked to officials of the Northern Pacific and, since the railroad was in the hands of receivers, to agents of the Justice Department. The government did not want the marchers back in Washington, and the NP would not carry the unemployed east without compensation.

The audience was no longer quiet. McGraw raised his voice against the rising murmur, and his speech took on the tone of a political statement. "I look on this movement as wholly unwise. That men are out of employment is a matter to be deplored. I know what it is to work myself, and I know what hard labor means. This is a country of magnificent resources and in this great nation, I believe, there is room and opportunity for all . . ."

An attorney in the audience shouted that the governor was not speaking to the question. The Chair ruled that he was but amid howls and hisses the governor said that the gentleman's position was well taken and sat down.

When order was restored, a committee of Puyallup citizens was named to discuss with the railroad people the question of getting the Coxeyites somewhere else. The meeting adjourned. Outside it was raining hard.

During the night, the leaders of the Seattle and Tacoma armies agreed on a new strategy. They would break camp, cross the mountains in small groups by any available means—which meant walking or stealing rides on trains—and reassemble at Spokane where a new attempt would be made to hire boxcars.

Throughout the following day the men trudged out of town, singly, in pairs, in groups of a half dozen. The rain soaked their bed-rolls, ran in rivulets down the greasy frying pans strapped to their packs, squished in their shoes. Only a few turned back toward Ta-coma or Seattle, though "General" Shepard gave up; he had been deposed by his men and replaced as general by Jeffries, the attorney. Most of the Industrials headed eastward along the tracks leading into the cloud-hidden Cascades. As freights chuffed past up the grades or stopped at stations and watering tanks, some of the men swung aboard. The crews made no effort to dislodge them.

At 5:00 P.M. a special freight left Tacoma for Spokane: fifteen cars, five loaded with shingles, two with lumber, and eight cattle cars, empty. As the freight came into Alderton just east of Puyallup, a company of the Seattle army climbed into the cattle cars, and as the lokey struggled up the grade toward Buckley, the men already aboard helped marchers along the track to climb in. When they reached Buckley there were about 120 Commonwealers aboard, much given to song.

The stationmaster wired Tacoma that "the Industrials" had seized the train. United States Marshal Drake sent out a call for all available deputies and commandeered a locomotive and passenger car to give chase. Then came a corrective wire: the train had not been captured. Its engineer, still in control, had pulled onto a siding at Palmer, un-coupled the locomotive, and raced back down to Buckley, leaving the stranded Commonwealers to keep warm cursing him.

Marshal Drake canceled his call for a special and bought tickets for himself and twenty-six deputies to Palmer on the regular Ta-coma-to-Spokane night train. At Puyallup, who should join the party with a first class ticket but Jumbo Cantwell. It was a strange trip the marshal, the general, and the deputies made through the storm. At every stop a few Commonwealers tried to climb into the baggage car. Jumbo busied himself boosting his boys in, while the deputies helped the conductor and brakemen put them off. As the train pulled away, Jumbo would shout back to his water-logged troops, "Spokane or bust, boys, Spokane or bust. I'm with you."

Between stations he joshed with the deputies. When he displayed a Colt .45 and boasted of his ability with it, Deputy Jack Jolly, who claimed to have been a lawman in the Southwest, took him up on it. "I don't want to fight in this car because there are ladies present, but if you'll step on the platform at the next station, or come to the smoking room, I'll give you first draw."

"Well, now," replied Jumbo, "tell you what I'll do. I'll shoot at a mark with you for two-bits a shot, or spit at a crack, or run you a footrace. Come on. Where's your sporting blood?" No blood, sport-ing or otherwise, was shed.

At Palmer they found members of the sidetracked army shivering under wet blankets in the cattle cars or huddled around a bonfire in the lee of the water tank. The marshal assigned Jolly and six deputies "to keep order," then went on with General Jumbo to spend the rest of the night at Hot Springs Hotel, which beat Palmer all hollow for comfort.

The men they left behind quickly found common cause in denouncing the privileges of the elite. A camaraderie developed between guards and guarded. The deputies unlocked the depot and allowed the Commonwealers to bed down with them around the potbelly stove. The next morning they shared breakfast. The Northern Pacific had ordered the Stampede Tunnel closed to men on foot. A few Commonwealers climbed the old switchback trail over the pass, but the deputies allowed most of them to walk the tunnel, and sometimes furnished escorts with lamps.

Public sympathy was on the side of the unemployed. Wherever parties camped—Orting, South Prairie, Buckley, Palmer, Hot Springs, and in the towns across the mountains—well-wishers brought food. When Jumbo disembarked at Ellensburg ahead of his troops, two butchers donated a side of beef apiece, a Chinese loaned his restaurant, a baker turned over the use of his ovens, the town provided flour, and that evening the general presided over a banquet for two hundred marchers.

On May 9, there was violence. About 150 Commonwealers were on a freight which was shunted onto a sidetrack two miles from North Yakima. Marshal W. C. Chidester of Tacoma, a local politician of considerable popularity, arrived with a dozen deputies but could not persuade the riders to disembark. He walked to Yakima, wired for reinforcement, and returned to the train at the head of a forty-eight-man posse. Chidester ordered the engineer to back down the hill onto a bridge over the Yakima River. The Commonwealers set the handbrakes. When the deputies tried to release the brakes, fights broke out atop the boxcars. Half of Yakima had turned out to watch the excitement. Fights broke out among the spectators too. Shooting started among the spectators, though who was being aimed at by whom was never determined. Three Industrials suffered flesh wounds, Marshal Chidester was shot through the leg and Deputy Jolly through the lung. Jolly was quoted as saying Chidester wounded himself trying to get his revolver from his pocket, then shot Jolly while hopping around in pain. Both survived but their friendship did not.

The wounding of United States deputies in the course of duty led Judge Hanford to order the arrest on contempt charges of all Industrials who defied his injunction and boarded trains. One hundred fifty-three alleged free riders were rounded up at Yakima along with five local citizens (an attorney, a former policeman, a former town marshal, a saloon keeper, and a barber) sympathetic to the Coxey movement. They were loaded into boxcars, shipped to Spokane for safekeeping, then back to Seattle for trial. Thirty were sentenced to sixty days at McNeil Island penitentiary.

The disorganized remnants of the Tacoma and Seattle armies kept on the move toward Spokane. They had no place else to go, no place to stay. One group stole a flatcar from a siding, pushed it onto the main line, and coasted twenty-five miles down the mountainside to Ellensburg without meeting a train coming the other way. Less lucky was a party that built a scow from lumber donated by an Ellensburg mill. She was twenty feet long, six feet wide, flat-bottomed, ugly, and unstable. They named her *The Pride of Ellensburg*, shoved off into the swift-flowing Yakima, and overturned. Four of the men were drowned; eleven were rescued after clinging to a fallen tree for nine hours.

Most of the men walked. About half of those who had camped at Puyallup joined Jumbo at Spokane, but no boxcars were to be rented there either. Cantwell took the train to St. Paul to see if anything could be arranged. His men set out along the tracks through the Bitterroots and the Rockies, stealing rides when they could, slogging it when necessary. They crossed the mountains through passes still clogged with a record snowpack and came down onto the plains just in time to catch the floods.

Jumbo Cantwell's command straggled into Great Falls, Montana, with gunnysacks wrapped around ruined shoes, clothes in rags, food gone, energy gone, hope gone. There Charlotta Cantwell, returning from the reconnoitering trip to St. Paul on which she had accompanied her husband, found them. She turned herself into a one-woman USO. She rented vacant houses, borrowed furniture, and found shelter for 1,260 men in all. She rustled food from bakers and butchers, shoes and clothing from church groups. By night she took over the Salvation Army headquarters, which stood across from a line of saloons and dance halls, and staged fund-raising rallies that emptied the rival night-spots. Her act was something to see. So was Charlotta: young, blonde, with blue-gray eyes and a figure always described by reporters as "fine." She was traveling with her six-year-old daughter by her previous marriage. For protection they had the family Saint Bernard, Colonel. Mother and daughter sang the songs of the Coxey movement, most of them new words to familiar tunes, and pretty awful. "Only Last Fall," a ballad of bad times, was done to the music of "After the Ball":

Bright were the prospects, clouds not in sight
Happy your homes were, from morn to night
Then came the office sharks, spoke soft and low
Fooled you poor workmen. How, you now know.

You knew the reason, after it was done.
You helped close all the factories that run.
That's why you're idle, no work at all.
Voted your jobs away, only last fall.

After each number the Colonel would pass through the crowd, a basket in his mouth, and fix each man with mournful eyes until he contributed. If anyone reached in the basket for change, a growl changed his mind.

While Mrs. General, as the men called her, shook down the business community for contributions, the daughter of the regiment, chaperoned by the Colonel, made the rounds of the saloons, selling copies of Coxey songs, pictures of the General and Mrs. Jumbo, and poems confected by her mother. Their best-seller was the lachrymose "Over the Dam":

'Tis hard looking up the bright river
And seeing where I might have turned back.
To think that I took things so easy
Letting everything go to the rack.

But I'm here now just as you find me.
And I'm—well, you can see what I am.
I drifted too long with the current
And of course I went over the dam.

Charlotta not only managed to feed and clothe her men and get them back on the road, but she left behind in Fort Worth a Home Guard of the Industrial Army to take care of any Commonwealers who came through later. She preceded the troops down the line to St. Cloud, Minnesota, where on the Fourth of July she addressed a huge crowd at a picnic sponsored by the American Railway Union. She raised enough to hire a freight to carry the party on to Minneapolis. Charlotta rode in the caboose with her daughter and the Colonel, while the troops filled the boxcars. Now they were writing poems about her, such as the toast proposed by Edward J. Clark, the Coxey movement's poet laureate:

You may drink to the trade
  And the creatures of fame

But I raise not my glass
  'Til I hear her sweet name. . . .

'Tis to her I will drink—
  Our companion in life
God's great inspiration
  General Jumbo's wife.

At Minneapolis the army split into smaller groups. The main body headed for Washington; others drifted off toward their home states, or pursued rumors of jobs. Mrs. Cantwell went to Chicago and there she collapsed. Doctors told her she probably was suffering from dropsy and would have to rest. She returned to Tacoma arriving, she told a reporter, with $1.15, "so you can see we're not broke."

But the Coxey movement was broke—and broken. Its treasury was empty, and it had drained to the dregs the manpower available for a march. Of thousands who started, hundreds arrived; of them few stayed. Congress ignored them and they drifted away. Coxey went back to Ohio to run for Congress. Carl Browne followed a lady to Atlantic City. Only the die-hards stayed.

Jumbo Cantwell stayed. He established a small camp for his Puget Sound constituents and managed to see that his men had two squares a day. He joined eight generals in drafting a Petition of the Unemployed and a proposed Bill to Provide Work for American Citizens. The petition was a catch-all of demands from "millions of unemployed or partly unemployed and underpaid workingmen who have naught but their ability to labor to provide themselves and families, and whose average wealth would not purchase a decent coffin." The bill proposed a work relief project under which the secretary of war would hire any man who had been out of work thirty days or more and employ him on public projects at a minimum wage of two dollars for eight hours. A Populist senator from Kansas presented the petition to his colleagues and introduced the bill, which disappeared into committee and never emerged. The Industrial Army disbanded and drifted out of town. Coxey was defeated for Congress. Jumbo Cantwell returned briefly to Tacoma, then dropped out of sight. When he was next heard of he was an alderman on the Chicago council. Charlotta stayed in Tacoma until the probate of Harry Morgan's estate was completed in 1902. By the time the lawyers were paid there was nothing left for her. This fascinating lady disappears from the records at this point.

Coxey's proposals foreshadowed actions taken by the federal government to combat later depressions, but all the Petition on Boots accomplished as far as Tacoma was concerned was to drain the town of at least four hundred men, 1 percent of the population.

There were other losses: Seattle stole Mount Tacoma. At least that is how Tacoma looked on the decision of the United States Board of Geographic Names labeling the dominant peak of the Cascades *Mount Rainier.*

The dispute over the Mountain was slow to develop. The men of the Vancouver expedition were the first whites to see the peak—that was in May of 1792—and George Vancouver named it for his naval friend, Peter Rainier. Mount Rainier was used as the name by all American as well as British map makers, though settlers sometimes used the Indian word *Tacoma.* Dr. Tolmie, the first European to visit the Mountain, was the first to put the Nisqually word in writing. On October 15, 1833, six weeks after he had visited the Mountain with a small party of Nisqually and Puyallup, the Hudson's Bay Company physician noted in his journal, "Had a fine view of Tuchoma or Mt Rainier, appearing in relief against the cloudless firmament."

Theodore Winthrop's posthumous account of travel in the Pacific Northwest brought the word into print in 1863, and in 1868 the settlers on Commencement Bay commenced calling their town *Tacoma.* There was no argument. The Seattle *Intelligencer* referred to *Tacoma* as the Indian name for the Mountain; Tacoma papers called the mountain *Rainier* without quotation marks or apology. In conversation the whites seem to have used the names interchangeably; a few old-timers preferred to call the peak *Old He.* For many it was simply The Mountain.

During the period of Villard's control of the Northern Pacific in the early 1880s, a young geologist named Bailey Willis was assigned to scout the Wilkeson area for coal deposits the railroad could claim. Willis pointed out to authorities the possibilities of the Mountain as a tourist attraction, and was given permission to cut a trail into the Spray Park area, where Dr. Tolmie had gone on his 1833 climb. The NP already was emphasizing the scenic grandeur of the Pacific Northwest in its national advertising. Now the company saw an opportunity to connect the natural feature most symbolic of the region with the terminus of their railroad. The March 1883 issue of *Northwest Magazine,* which the NP controlled, contained the announcement:

"The Indian name Tacoma will hereafter be used in the guide books and other publications of the Northern Pacific Railroad Company and the Oregon Railway and Navigation Company instead of Rainier which the English Captain Vancouver gave to this magnificent peak when he explored the waters of Puget Sound in the last century."

Seattle took it as a declaration of war. Seattle papers, citing the right of discoverers to name things, accused Tacoma of attempting "an historical robbery." Tacomans asked who was Peter Rainier, and answered that he was an enemy of the United States. Seattle warned that if Tacoma got away with renaming the mountain they would try next for the territory. Tacoma thought that a fine idea. They induced Territorial Representative Thomas H. Brents to submit a bill proposing that when Washington became a state the state be called Tacoma. Seattle papers described Brents as a pettifogger, a tool of the Northern Pacific, and a third-rate lawyer to boot.

Papers in both towns carried on the controversy with enthusiasm. Seattle denied that *Tacoma* was an Indian word, or at least that it was a Salish word, or that if it was it meant *Rainier;* at most, it was as Winthrop had said, a generic word for all mountains. Tacoma papers asked, who had ever heard any other Cascade mountain called *Tacoma.* After 1883, Tacoma papers always referred to *Mount Tacoma,* Seattle papers continued to say *Rainier.* With the great boom in population following completion of the NP main line, most residents of Tacoma were newcomers who had never heard "Mount Rainier" except in scorn or jest. In Seattle, just the opposite.

In 1890, the question was referred to the United States Board of Geographic Names, which was composed of men representing the scientific and professional services of the government, such as the Corps of Engineers, the Post Office, the State Department, the Navy Hydrographic Office, the Coast and Geodetic Survey, and the Lighthouse Board. They voted unanimously to retain *Rainier* as the official name.

The NP people sighed and went along. Not Tacoma. A delegation of Tacomans waited on Charles Fee, the general passenger agent for the line, and urged resistance. C. T. Conover, an apologist for the Seattle point of view throughout the controversy, quoted Fee as telling them, "Gentlemen, we have carried this farce as far as we are going to for advertising purposes. The name has been officially declared to be Rainier and that is what we shall call it. You can call it what you please."

That they did. Tacomans continued to call it *Mount Tacoma* and kept up the fight officially for thirty-five more years. No issue in the city's history had such whole-hearted support as the campaign to reclaim the mountain from Rear Admiral Rainier.

The question of the name took on added importance when

Congress began serious consideration of proposals to create a national park at the mountain. The idea had first been proposed in 1883 by James Bryce, the British historian (*The American Commonwealth*) and diplomat, and Karl Zittel, a German geologist. They had been invited by Villard to witness the driving of the final spike on the Northern Pacific in Montana, and came afterward to Tacoma. Bailey Willis, the NP geologist, took them along his trail to Spray Park. In a joint letter of appreciation to Villard they said they could think of nothing more beautiful in Switzerland or the Tyrol, in Norway or the Pyrenees, and expressed the hope that "the suggestion will at no distant date be made to Congress that Mount Rainier should, like Yosemite Valley and the geyser region of the Upper Yellowstone, be reserved by the Federal Government and treated as a national park."

Villard lost power soon after and was not in position to push the project, but after Washington became a state in 1889, the congressional delegation deluged House and Senate at each session with bills proposing a park on the mountain. It was an issue Tacoma and Seattle could both support—except that Seattle wanted the park to be named *Mount Rainier National Park* and Tacoma was only reluctantly willing to compromise on *Washington National Park.*

A Tacoma Academy of Science was created to gather data unfavorable to the name, career, and personality of Peter Rainier and supportive of the use of Indian nomenclature for natural objects in general and for the Mountain in particular. Affidavits were sworn and less formal statements taken in which Indians testified they called the peak *Tahoma,* or *Tacobet,* or *Tuwouk,* or *Tacoba*—even in some instances, *Tacoma.* Some said the word meant "snowy mountain," others "mother of waters" or "full breast." Old settlers claimed to have heard Indians speak of "the mountain that was god." Indian legends were created in the best Victorian tradition. Poems proliferated.

A Justice to the Mountain Committee formed itself around the person of Sam Wall, the Tacoma newspaperman who once had shot a rival editor for suggesting in print that he might be partial to Seattle. The committee won support in far and sometimes improbable places. Colonel John Puget, the explorer's great-nephew, wrote that he favored *Tacoma* over *Rainier.* So did the historian Bryce in a missive flowery as Paradise Valley in the fall. The governor of Massachusetts, the mayor of Boston, the editor of the *Archeologist,* none of whom had seen the Mountain, expressed preference for having it called *Tacoma.* Even Princess Angeline, daughter of Chief Seattle, came down from Seattle to say that in her family it was always called *Tacobet.*

But when Congress created the nation's fourth national park in 1899, they called it *Mount Rainier National Park.*

In the meantime, Seattle had captured Alaska.

In August of 1896 three weary prospectors in the Yukon Territory of Canada made camp on a small stream called the Rabbit. Among the rocks of the stream bed they detected the glint of gold. The first gravel they swirled in a pan yielded grains worth about four dollars—and ten cents a pan was enough to make a claim worthwhile. By nightfall they had washed out enough gold dust to fill an empty shotgun shell, and had found several sharp-edged nuggets, a find hinting at the presence nearby of a motherlode. The next day one of the prospectors chopped a blaze on a spruce and pencilled on the clear wood:

To Whom It May Concern

I do, this day, locate and claim, by right of discovery, five hundred feet, running up stream from this notice. Located this 17th day of August, 1896.

G. W. Carmack

An American who had prospected unsuccessfully in the Canadian North for ten years, Carmack and his Indian companions, Skookum Jim and Tagish Charlie, had made the richest strike in the history of prospecting.

The news was slow to trickle Outside. It was men already in the Yukon Territory who raced to the Rabbit and took up claims the length of the creek. They were richly rewarded for their presence, and they renamed the Rabbit, *Bonanza.* Through the long, subarctic winter they labored; they hauled wood and brush from the hills, thawed the ground with bonfires, dug and scraped through the permanently frozen undersoil six to eight inches a day until, if luck was with them, the candles strapped to their foreheads shone on the glitter of the thin, elusive pay-streak, the scatter of gold spread by the wash of an ancient flood and buried under the debris of centuries, then twisted by the movement of drifting continents.

There was much gold. By the time the Yukon thawed in the summer of 1897 most of the old prospectors were rich, if not beyond the dreams of avarice, at least temporarily beyond expectation. Not a claim on the Bonanza was valued at less than a million. The jubilant sourdoughs boated down the Yukon to the Bering Sea where, at St. Michael, they found a pair of superannuated steamers, the Alaska Commercial Company's *Excelsior,* and the North American Trading Company's *Portland,* a rusty relic of contraband runs and frequent confiscation. The Bering Sea was the last place a shipowner thought of before scuttling. Ships sent there carried supplies nobody else would buy and returned with prospectors whose last hope had failed and who paid their passages in IOU's Pollyanna would have discounted at 90 percent. Not this time. "I was struck with their air of exuberance," said the skipper of the *Excelsior,* "and impressed with their prosperity."

That was after the *Excelsior* put in at San Francisco, with fifteen new millionaires and a thousand pounds of gold. Everybody who was interviewed said the best was yet to come, that the *Portland* was bringing out a ton of gold. They were wrong. When the *Portland* showed up in Seattle two days later, she carried two tons of gold, and the stuff of legend. To the Puget Sound communities paralyzed by depression the *Portland* seemed a fairy prince with the kiss of life. Every town could boast some frog transformed by the alchemy of gold dust. Seattle had sent north a YMCA secretary distinguished only by the prodigious number of push-ups he could perform; he returned with thirty-five thousand dollars in gold—some said eighty-five thousand—and laughed at offers of a half million for his claim. In Anacortes they talked of the day laborer who, finding no labor, found his way to the Yukon; wired from San Francisco telling his wife to stop taking in washing and picking berries and to start buying finery. A teamster from Buckley had parlayed four horses into two hotels. Two sisters from Winlock were said to be making ninety dollars a day sewing, just sewing. A skid-road greaser from Whatcom Bay got four thousand dollars by auctioning off a case of champagne he had won in a spitting contest. And Tacoma boasted Jack the Diver, a young man from Old Town, who came back from two years in the North and learned that in his absence his wife had divorced him. The next day he showed up at the marriage license desk in the courthouse with a girl on each arm.

The Panic was over. The stampede was on. Tacoma failed to get moving and Seattle seized the opportunity to meet the needs and desires of the tens of thousands who joined one of the strangest mass migrations since the Children's Crusade.

Seattle was the older city. Although its forced growth in the 1880s had been as rapid as Tacoma's, making it too a city of strangers, community roots went deeper and suffered less damage in the sudden chill of the Panic. A second-generation city, Seattle had survived the tests of the Indian War, the doldrums of the Civil War in the West, the shock of the NP decision to put its terminus elsewhere. During the anti-Chinese agitation, Seattle drove more Chinese out of town than Tacoma did—but the town leadership rallied to prevent the expulsion of the final few, and Seattle did not have to live down a reputation back east of being in thrall to lawless elements. The great fire that gutted the business district and wharf area in the summer of 1889 had permitted the building of downtown Seattle in brick and stone, the realignment of streets, the creation of a more rational waterfront; reconstruction provided jobs even during the depression years. City directories indicate that many workmen who fled Tacoma during the Panic, especially men in the building trades, went no farther than Seattle.

But of all Seattle's blessings, the greatest was Jim Hill: "the empire builder" to admirers; "the barbed-wired, shaggy-headed, one-eyed old son-of-a-bitch of western railroading" to biographers like Stewart Holbrook. Jim Hill brought to Seattle in July of 1893, just as the depression started, the Great Northern, and the arrival of the transcontinental on Elliott Bay kept Seattle from suffering the full impact of the Panic. The Great Northern gave Seattle not just its long-sought transcontinental connection but the terminus of a railroad more efficient and better financed than the Northern Pacific (which was, indeed, again bankrupt). The Great Northern was shorter; its grades were less steep and the heavy grades were close together so that the use of extra locomotives could be concentrated in short stretches. The NP had been built with the idea of real estate promotion; Jim Hill thought in terms of freight volume, not the quick profit of a one-shot land deal but the continuing profits of accreted development. When the courts gave Hill the rights to a land grant claimed by a line the Great Northern had absorbed he agreed not to disturb squatters who had settled on the area; instead he accepted western timberlands in lieu of the farmlands originally promised. These he sold at bargain rates to lumbermen whose operations he calculated would supply the Great Northern with freight for decades, and he lowered the freight rates to make wider markets available for them in the Midwest. He could be petty, vindictive, stubborn, but he could be far-sighted and sudden. It was Jim Hill who, acting on information passed on casually by a sea captain he met on one of his trains, was able to persuade the major Japanese steamship line, Nippon Yusen Kaisha, to make Seattle instead of San Diego its port of entry. When the green and black *Miiki Maru* steamed into Elliott Bay on August 31, 1896, with a cargo of silk and tea, the whole town turned out to watch her tie up. The city council had declared the day a holiday. Well they might, for this linkage of regular rail service across the continent with regular steamer service across the North Pacific established what nature had failed to provide: the Northwest Passage to the Orient.

When the news came from San Francisco that gold had been found in great quantities up north, Seattle moved swiftly to exploit the opportunity. Even before the *Portland* tied up at the Schwabacker Dock, every Seattle ship scheduled to go north that season was booked full, arrangements were being made for additional vessels, and Seattle was advertising itself as the gateway to the Klondike. The Seattle Chamber of Commerce set up a publicity committee and chose as its director an unemployed editor, Erastus Brainerd.

A cultivated chap from the East who had proved an ineffectual newspaperman, Brainerd chanced to be a genius at publicity. He wrote articles for national magazines, planted quotes from the articles with the wire services, then used extracts from the wire stories in advertisements which proclaimed Seattle the Emporium to the Klondike, the Gateway to Gold. Repetition was the key: Seattle and Alaska, Seattle and the Yukon, Seattle and gold.

Before Tacoma awoke to the full possibilities of the rush north, Seattle was synonymous with Alaska. Reports about the Yukon in Tacoma papers usually carried Seattle datelines. So swiftly did Seattle establish itself as the take-off place for the Yukon that Charles Mellen, then serving as president of the Northern Pacific, arranged for the NP steamships to leave not from the company dock at Tacoma but from commercial docks in Seattle, where they had to pay rent. The only ship that sailed regularly between Tacoma and Alaska in the first months of the rush was named, oh bitterness!, *The City of Seattle.*

"The principal thing for Tacoma to do just now is advertise," a businessman warned his fellow Tacomans a few weeks after the rush began:

Pick up any of the eastern newspapers today and you will find just how much this town is losing by not keeping to the front as a starting and outfitting point for miners bound for Alaska. Syndicates and trading companies are advertising in the east that large stocks of supplies can be purchased at Fort-Get-There and Hamilton on the Lower Yukon, but we who read letters and know the experiences of men already in the Yukon Country know of the high prices paid there for provisions. All the men who know what they are about buy their supplies before they start. Groceries and necessary hardware and clothing can be bought cheaper here than at any eastern point, and far, far below Alaska prices. Tacoma needs to make this known, to advertise in every eastern paper, to establish a bureau of information and furnish all the most reliable news of the new land that can be obtained, to send out her prices and to use the present unprecedented opportunity to make her advantages as a supply station generally known.

It was not done. The Tacoma city government was in more than usual disarray, bitterly divided over a mayoralty election that had been decided by two disputed votes. A recount was not possible because the ballot boxes were stolen from the city clerk's office. At a time when speedy action was imperative, Tacoma had two mayors and two civil service commissions and the question of who was in charge rested with the courts. The Chamber of Commerce was split three ways over the question of who should be publicity director for a campaign to attract Alaska trade. The Northern Pacific was again being reorganized; its directors were too involved with deciding who was running things to run anything. The Tacoma populace, still numbed by the collapse of the dreams of the 1880s, surrounded by buildings incomplete or partially empty, remained suspicious of promotions and calls to civic greatness.

Individuals responded. Tacoma's West Coast Grocery went quietly about its business of supplying the merchants of Southeastern Alaska and firmed up a relationship with the area that endures after eighty years. But many of the Tacoma endeavors in the Gold Rush seemed less like Seattle's than like Charlie Chaplin's.

Most of those who rushed to the Klondike went by water to the head of Lynn Canal in Alaska, then struggled over the mountains to the Yukon River. The most immediate problem to be solved was getting across Chilkoot Pass into the Yukon Territory. On this aspect of the rush, Tacoma focused its attention.

Nelson Bennett and Hugh Wallace, men of vision, experience, and money, financed construction of a cable system to lift freight over the Scales, the last steep slope before the summit of the Chilkoot. They were able to get the towers in place, the cable strung, the power equipment and the fuel up into the mountains, and engineers willing to operate the machinery instead of joining the rush. It worked. But completion of the White Pass and Yukon Railway made the high-strung contraption obsolete long before it was amortized.

James Knox of Puyallup sailed north with a hundred goats which he proposed to rent as pack animals on the Chilkoot. The goats were uncooperative. They wound up as stew.

Jefferson Dorsett, a Chicagoan visiting Tacoma, solicited funds for the construction of a flotilla of hot air balloons, "each of sufficient amplitude to support a ton." These would be carried folded to the base of White Pass, inflated over bonfires, and attached by hawsers to slings holding a ton of cargo. "The unencumbered argonaut can gaily climb the pass," said the Dorsett prospectus, "towing his gear and duffle as a boy might fly a kite." Nothing was said of what would happen if the balloon lifted the argonaut off his feet, or if the wind were blowing from the north, which was not improbable since

Skagway is an Indian word for "north wind." Dorsett drifts off from the records, his mission unfulfilled.

Seattle prospered in part by providing passage. Tacoma tried. A Tacoma group resurrected the bark *Shirley,* which was rotting away in Quartermaster Harbor on Vashon Island. They caulked her spread seams, renamed her *Clondyke,* sold passage for eighty passengers on a hull designed to sleep twenty, and sent her north under tow of the tug *Defiance.* A passenger wrote back cheerfully from Comax on Vancouver Island that all was well since among his shipmates were three good fiddlers, a banjo player, and the dirtiest cook on the Pacific, "and the captain is still partially shober." The *Shirley* got through to Skagway, where she was abandoned. Hers was almost a success story. Compare it with the tale of the *Edith.* She had been condemned as a passenger vessel, so some Tacomans chartered her, loaded her with horses, hogs, and sheep, and made it to Dyea, only to find there was no dock. They drove the livestock over the side and, riding herd in rowboats, managed to get most of the animals ashore. The money they made from selling meat they lost at faro.

That most perennial of Puget Sound pioneers, Ezra Meeker of Puyallup, rushed north to found a bank. It failed. All he salvaged was some stationery embossed with pure gold.

The workbook of the Tacoma local of the International Longshore Workers Union has only one entry for 1887. "Nothing worth noting took place during this year with the exception of the Klondike Rush."

In Seattle gold spurred growth, and growth battened on growth. Bank deposits surged from $4.6 million in 1897 to $7 million in 1898 and $12.3 million in 1899; bank clearings in the same period went from $36 million to $92 million. Shipments to foreign points rose from $2.8 million in 1897 to $4 million in 1899; imports more dramatically from $1.1 million in 1897 to $5.3 million in 1899.

When the federal census was taken in 1900, the state had grown from 357,232 to 518,103—an increase of 44 percent. Seattle's population had jumped from 42,837 to 80,676—an increase of 98 percent. Tacoma's had increased from 36,006 in 1890 to 37,714—only 4.7 percent. Worse, Tacoma had dropped 14,615, or 24 percent of its estimated population, at the peak of its growth just before the Panic.

The race for dominance on Puget Sound was over. Tacoma was the second city. Its struggle in the next years was not for triumph but for survival.

Absentees
and Hometowners

AT the turn of the century most of the important decisions about Tacoma were still being made in distant places, either in the board rooms of corporations or the drawing rooms of tycoons.

In 1893 Frederick Weyerhaeuser, the quiet, industrious German-American burgher who had unobtrusively become the most formidable lumberman in the United States, bought a mansion at 266 Summit Avenue, the fashionable residential street in St. Paul. Legend has it that when he moved in he did not know that his next door neighbor at 244 Summit was James Hill, who had just completed the Great Northern and was moving toward dominance of the Northern Pacific. The two empire builders hit it off. Before long they were exchanging visits, though Weyerhaeuser was a shy, undemonstrative man who liked to retire early and be at his desk by 7:15 in the morning, while Hill was a fountain of energy who spewed ideas and conversation long after midnight, then slept in.

A biographer tells of Weyerhaeuser dozing before the fireplace in the den at Hill's place a few years later while the burly, one-eyed Canadian discoursed about the vast stands of timber in the Pacific Northwest and the low rates the Great Northern would charge for shipments east. It is hard to imagine F. W. drowsy when timber was the topic. As well as anyone he knew that the virgin forests of the Great Lakes area, on which his fortune and his empire were based, would soon be gone. As early as 1885 he had considered timberland in the Northwest. The Northern Pacific had offered some of its land grant in western Washington and a mill site on the Tacoma waterfront, but Weyerhaeuser had decided the time was not right. (His frequent associate in lumber deals, Peter Musser, did take an option on eighty thousand NP acres the following year, but never exercised it.) In 1891 Weyerhaeuser had another opportunity to consider the possibilities of Puget Sound when he passed through Tacoma on his way to Alaska, but again he did not buy.

In 1898 Weyerhaeuser was among a group of midwestern lumbermen who formed the Coast Lumber Company to take advantage of seasonal rates offered by the Great Northern in the spring when cars were not in great demand. They began to import cedar shingles to St. Paul from Puget Sound for distribution throughout the upper Mississippi area. The following year, Weyerhaeuser invested six hundred thousand dollars, which was matched by the Lindsey and Phelps Company of Davenport, Iowa, for the purchase of a stand of fir along the Skagit and Sauk rivers in the North Cascades. They formed the Sound Timber Company to handle the tract. Then Weyerhaeuser took the great plunge.

In the first week of the twentieth century, on January 3, 1900, to be exact, the talks that had started between Hill and Weyerhaeuser in front of the fireplace at 244 Summit reached their climax in the greatest purchase of timberland known at that time. Weyerhaeuser and William H. Phibbs, the land agent for the Northern Pacific, which Hill now dominated, signed papers calling for the purchase of nine hundred thousand acres from the NP land grant at six dollars an acre. Hill had begun by asking seven dollars an acre, Weyerhaeuser by offering five—they were an evenly matched pair.

Of the $5,400,000 purchase price, $3,000,000 was to be cash on the barrelhead, and the remainder paid over a four-year period in eight installments of $300,000 plus interest at 5 percent. Weyerhaeuser and his partner, Frederick C. A. Denkmann, agreed to put up $1,800,000; William Harris Laird and Matthew G. Norton and associates, $1,200,000; O. H. Ingram, Robert Laird McCormick, and S. T. McKnight, $350,000 each; and nine others, smaller amounts.

They called their new company the Weyerhaeuser Timber Company. When the directors gathered in the Tacoma Hotel for their first meeting early in 1900 they had no definite idea of the extent of the forest they had purchased. One-fourth of the timber had not been cruised. Spot checks on the three-fourths covered by cruisers for the Northern Pacific some years earlier indicated that cruising had been casual and perhaps optimistic. Nonetheless Frederick Weyerhaeuser could assure the directors with regard to the timber, "There is a great lot of it, in every conceivable direction." Some years later it was estimated that they had paid ten cents a thousand board feet for what could be used from the original purchase.

Timber prices were rising, pushed upwards in part by publicity about the Weyerhaeuser purchase but also by the decimation of virgin timber across the continent, the warnings by such public figures as Theodore Roosevelt and Gifford Pinchot that the end was nigh, the continued railroad building which not only absorbed vast amounts of lumber in bridges and ties but created new cities and industries, thus accelerating the westward movement of the American people and stimulating the inflation that followed the long depressions and deflation of the last quarter of the nineteenth century.

It was soon apparent that the Weyerhaeuser Timber Company would in the long run benefit by holding its trees while others cut theirs. But Jim Hill's sale from the land grant had been based on the promise that it would create eastbound freight for his railroads. Weyerhaeuser's solution to the dilemma was to sell some of its timber to other mill owners and to invest the profits, which were considerable, in yet more stumpage. The new purchases were chosen to fill in gaps in the original holdings and block the land into the bold, simple patterns advantageous to large-scale logging and enormous mills which permitted the Weyerhaeuser Company to skip at least a generation in the vertical organization of the lumber industry. "Not for ourselves, not for our children, but for our grandchildren," said Frederick Weyerhaeuser of his Northwest forest. And so it was to be.

To manage and enlarge this forest empire the Weyerhaeuser Timber Company imported a lank, stretch-necked Hoosier who signed himself Geo. S. Long and whose experience had been in lumberyards and mills, not forests. George Long confessed that on arrival in Tacoma he "had no conception of even what townships and ranges meant, had never been in the woods in my life, did not know how to find a section corner, had never attempted to estimate a quantity of timber, did not know anything about its value, why one tree might be worth more than another, and absolutely knew nothing about logging." But he was a quick study, and Weyerhaeuser's odd choice proved to be a stroke of genius.

Long did not mind asking questions that made him sound dumb; he just didn't want dumb answers. He questioned everybody he met who knew anything about the lumber business and he forgot nothing. He went out into the woods to see for himself, a city-looking fellow who wore a mackinaw as if it had a celluloid collar but who, to the surprise of many a logger, could climb a hill covered with vine maple without drawing a deep breath. He could outwalk a camel on a hot day. "Hell," grumbled an old timber beast who escorted him through the pine country of eastern Washington, "you might as well expect to get sweat outa a soupbone."

In Tacoma, Long operated out of a warren of small, cabinet-stuffed offices in the handsome Northern Pacific headquarters building at Seventh and Pacific Avenue. F. S. Bell, the son-in-law of one of the directors (W. H. Laird), had given him a crash course in keeping logging records, and eventually Robert Laird McCormick, the company secretary, a man as hulking in build as Long was spare, came west to help run things, but for two years Long's total office staff consisted of a man who kept books and a woman who typed, filed, and drew maps. In 1902 he expanded his office staff 50 percent, hiring an abstracter of titles. The four of them supervised the expansion of the Weyerhaeuser timber holdings to 1,500,000 acres by 1905.

Weyerhaeuser cut no lumber in Tacoma. Their first mill in the Pacific Northwest was at Everett, where in 1902 the company bought a run-down rig from the Bell-Nelson Mill Company. It produced only twenty-eight million board feet the first year, a figure that rose steadily as new equipment was installed and Long found out about machinery and production and the delegation of authority. He still looked like a dehydrated deacon, but he was an all-around lumberman now, and recognized as such by his peers. Stewart Holbrook, the logging historian, tells of the time Long gazed severely at a hooting, howling motley of mill owners, all convention-drunk, and admonished them, "Loggers, when you are sober I admire you. But when you're drunk, God damn you, I love you."

They loved him back. Not so, the men in the woods. At Weyerhaeuser camps, no conversations were permitted at meal times, no thermometers were kept in the bunkhouses, and men were fired arbitrarily in groups as warning against undue independence.

If Long was very much a man of his times in labor relations, he was ahead of his time in forestry practice, especially with regard to fire prevention. The great summer fires of the Pacific Northwest, a phenomenon which preceded logging but was increased by it, horrified him as well they might horrify the man in charge of hundreds of thousands of acres. He instituted fire protection measures on company lands, led in the organization of industry-wide efforts—and asked the legislature for tax concessions to companies practicing good management. Long phrased his request to the senators with effective earthiness: "There's honey in a dunghill, but it takes a bee to get it."

By 1914 the Weyerhaeuser Timber Company had hived up 1,982,000 acres (1,514,000 of them in Washington), containing more than forty-one billion board feet, acquired at an average cost of $8.80 an acre—$17,500,000 in all. The Panama Canal was open, taxes were rising, lumber prices were rising too. It was time to start cutting on a grander scale. Weyerhaeuser still did not build a mill in Tacoma, but the company joined the Tacoma Commercial Club in erecting a $300,000 office building overlooking the bay between Tenth and Eleventh on A Street. Eventually the staff would number in the hundreds. Tacoma had become headquarters for the world's largest timber operation, a place where decisions were made that affected other communities.

At the Tacoma Smelter, control flowed in the other direction, eastward.

After acquiring Ryan's smelter in 1889, Billy Rust was hard put to keep the furnaces warm during the long depression. With the return of prosperity in the late nineties, he enlisted the support of the octogenarian Darius Ogden Mills, a power in mining finance ever since the California gold rush half a century earlier. Mills became the largest stockholder in Tacoma Smelting and Refining. From his Manhattan office he was able to secure much business for the Smelter from other companies in which he was influential. Ore concentrates moved south by ship from the great Treadwell mine at Juneau, westward by rail from the Bunker Hill and Sullivan mines in the Coeur d'Alenes. Profits from this work made it possible for Rust to install new copper furnaces and converters in 1902 and, three years later, an electrolytic copper refinery, the first on the Pacific Coast.

With this modern plant, the Tacoma Smelter became a key piece in the high-stakes game being played on Wall Street for control of the metals industry, especially in the rivalry between Harry R. Rogers and the Guggenheim brothers in lead and copper. As a young man Rogers had worked for a statewide grocery wholesaler in Massachusetts. He was impressed with the advantages of large-scale operation over fragmented businesses. Rogers began putting rival companies together in one package, ending cut-rate competition and permitting price fixing. After he helped John D. Rockefeller assemble Standard Oil, the papers began calling him the Trust Builder. He created a copper trust that dominated the industry and then in 1896 set out to merge all the major lead producers. That led to a confrontation with the Guggenheim brothers—Daniel, Murry, Isaac, Solomon, and Simon—who had important holdings in lead. They refused to enter the trust. Rogers went along without them; the prospectus for his new octopus, the American Smelting and Refining Company, declared it would combine "all the principal smelting works in the United States, except the Guggenheims." The Guggenheims were up to the challenge. After a series of dazzling maneuvers they wound up with $45 million in ASARCO stock, enough to give them effective control.

As part of their war with Rogers for lead, the Guggenheims became increasingly interested in copper. They signed the world's most glamorous mining engineer, John Hays Hammond, to a seven-year contract which called for him to receive the unprecedented salary of $250,000 a year, plus a quarter interest in all properties the Guggenheims purchased on his recommendation. Hammond began exploring for copper and gold, and shopping for smelters.

It was through Hammond that the Guggenheims became interested in the Tacoma Smelter. He pointed out that with its tidewater location it had obvious advantages as a concentration point for ores from around the Pacific rim. Hammond approached Mills to learn if the plant might be for sale; Mills talked to Rust, who had known Daniel Guggenheim in Colorado; Rust came to New York and discussed a deal with Guggenheim, then president of American Smelting and Refining. Dan offered a million. Billy laughed and said if he heard four million he might start listening. Dan laughed. Neither man was amused. They parted coolly, Rust saying he realized he had made a mistake—it would take five million to catch his attention.

The Guggenheims really wanted the Smelter, not only for their own purposes but to keep it out of the hands of Rogers or the Rockefellers. Dan decided to try through an intermediary. He summoned to his seventeenth-floor office Bernard Baruch, a thirty-four-year-old attorney and speculator who was accorded wizard status on Wall Street; Baruch's father, a physician, had treated Meyer Guggenheim, the founder of the dynasty, and the younger Baruch had accumulated a considerable amount of ASARCO stock. Dan explained that he wanted to negotiate for the Tacoma Smelter and one in San Francisco owned by the Selby Smelting and Lead and Mining Company without alerting Rogers or the Rockefellers. If Baruch could buy them, the Guggenheims would meld the properties into a new corporation in which Baruch would be given a block of stock.

Baruch decided the best place to start would be with Darius Mills, who had not only the largest block of Tacoma Smelter stock but a chunk of Selby as well. As he walked from his office at 111 Broadway to the Mills Building at 21 Broadway, he wondered what stories he would have to sit through before getting down to business. The venerable Mills made all supplicants who came before him listen to tales of his youth. Baruch sometimes found the old gentleman's accounts of men and money and market maneuvers to be fascinating, but this time Mills stroked his mutton-chop whiskers and tapped his bare chin and yarned on and on about the joys of poverty and about the great old days out in California when he slept under the wagon when it rained and gnawed old salt pork when he couldn't start a fire. Baruch finally got a chance to ask if he could get options to purchase Mills's stock in the Tacoma and Selby smelters. No. But at least Mills promised that he would not make a deal with the Rockefellers or Rogers while Baruch negotiated with Billy Rust and other stockholders for their shares.

Baruch enlisted the help of a brokerage-house friend, Henry C. Davis, who as a young man had worked on a Northern Pacific construction crew and knew Billy Rush, and of an attorney, A. E. Jopling, who had helped Baruch on an earlier assignment in which he purchased the Liggett and Meyers Tobacco Company for Thomas Fortune Ryan, outbidding the Duke tobacco interests.

The Guggenheim team arranged a secret meeting with Billy Rust. They met in a warehouse on the Everett waterfront where they were not likely to be recognized. The negotiations were anticlimactic. Baruch simply made an offer Rust couldn't resist—$800 a share for the common stock. That came to $5 million for original stock and invested capital of about $500,000. Offered eleven times his investment (and a total that exceeded the $5 million he had told Guggenheim it would take to make him listen), Rust gave Baruch a forty-five-day option on his own holdings and agreed to persuade enough other stockholders to sell to provide a controlling interest.

Baruch hurried to San Francisco for talks with the Selby people. Word of his presence, and his connection with the Guggenheims, leaked out. Daniel wired from New York to close the deal without delay, lest the Rockefellers enter the bidding. "As if that wasn't exactly what I've been trying to do," Baruch said in reply. But he succeeded in arranging that purchase, too.

The $5 million for the Tacoma Smelter was paid in cash. Daniel Guggenheim changed his mind about creating a new corporation for the Tacoma and Selby operations and instead absorbed the plants into the ASARCO complex. That made it impossible to reward Baruch with the promised block of stock in a new corporation. Samuel Untermeyer was told to negotiate a cash settlement with the negotiator. Baruch told the attorney that he had anticipated his stock would eventually be worth a million dollars, so he should be paid a million for putting the deal together. Plus expenses.

"Are you trying to hold up American Smelting and Refining?"

"No, Mr. Untermeyer. I had not thought of that—until now," Baruch replied, and walked out.

The impasse was taken to Dan Guggenheim, who shrugged slightly, smiled slightly, and said, "If Bernie says he ought to get a million dollars, give Bernie a million dollars."

The check, including expenses, was for $1,106,456. On receiving it, Baruch wrote out checks for $300,000 each to Billy Rust and Henry Davis for their help. "There were not two more surprised men in America than Davis and Rust when they got those checks,"

Baruch wrote of his voluntary kickback. "Both protested against receiving them. I told them they had to take the money because they had earned it. Without their help I could never have closed the deal."

Rust spent most of the windfall on building and furnishing a handsome colonial style house of hand-dressed Wilkeson sandstone at Tenth and I streets.

With the Smelter situation under control, Dan Guggenheim went to Alaska in 1906 to see if prospects were as promising as scouts reported. Indeed they were. He was shown ore samples from Bonanza Mountain in the Wrangell Range where, according to Alaska legend, a pair of prospectors named Tarantula Jack Smith and Clarence Warner got lucky. They were looking for a spot to graze their packhorses when one of them saw, high on the western slope, a patch of green.

"Could that be grass?" one asked.

"No. No. It's got to be malachite chalcocite. Copper. A mountain of it."

Not a mountain but good enough, a vein of chalcocite 180 feet wide and 80 feet high. The samples Guggenheim examined assayed as high as 70 percent pure copper. Engineers said it could be delivered to Tacoma for less than five cents a pound if a way could be found to bring it down from the seven-thousand-foot level in the tumult of mountains.

Guggenheim enlisted J. P. Morgan as an ally. They formed the Alaska Syndicate to exploit the mineral discoveries. They bought coal fields and the Kennecott copper claim. They built steamship lines. And they ordered a railroad built into the mountains to bring out ore. The first terminus site washed away the first year. Morgan and Guggenheim met in New York to decide what to do. It is said that as far away as Prince William Sound you could hear J. P. pounding the table and shouting, "Whatever the route we've got to bring that copper and coal together."

The syndicate bought out a right-of-way that had been surveyed and sketchily started by Michael J. Heney, an Irish adventurer and engineer who had previously rammed the White Pass and Yukon Railway from Skagway to Whitehorse. Then they hired Heney as project engineer, and he created the fantastic Copper River and Northwestern. It included caissons sunk 150 feet into the beds of mountain rivers, a four-span bridge across the face of a moving glacier, and other engineering improbabilities. It cost $23 million and it quickly paid for itself.

The first shipment of Kennecott ore to Tacoma in 1911 was laid down at the Smelter at a cost of four and one-half cents a pound. It smelted out to a value of a half million dollars. The next year the houses of Morgan and Guggenheim divided three million dollars as the first annual dividend from the Kennecott mine.

By 1916 Billy Rust's Smelter was too small and too old for the tasks at hand. A new reverberatory process was introduced. A new stack, at the time the tallest in the world, rose beside the bay, its plume of pale, arsenic-laden smoke a symbol of enterprise, profit, and a special way of looking at the world.

In 1905, the year the Smelter passed into control of the Guggenheims, the Wall Street wars of the railroad kings touched off a new burst of real estate speculation in Tacoma.

Eleven years earlier, Jim Hill had put together an alliance, amounting to an illegal trust, of the three transcontinental railroads serving the Pacific Northwest. The Great Northern, he had created; the Northern Pacific, he captured after a wild bidding war in which the price of its stock was driven up from eighty-seven dollars a share to almost a thousand a share; but the Union Pacific was controlled by his greatest rival, E. H. Harriman, who had the support of the Rockefellers, and with the UP Hill had to compromise.

The accommodation reached between Hill and Harriman involved creation of a holding company, Northern Securities Company, Ltd. Capitalized at $400 million, it held controlling blocks of stock in each of the railroads. Its board included six representatives from the Great Northern, four from the Northern Pacific, and three from the Union Pacific, a composition that made Hill top dog. But as part of the deal, Hill acknowledged that not only would Harriman's UP be left unmolested in its control of Oregon but that the line, which reached Portland from Salt Lake City on other people's tracks (the Oregon Short Line and the Oregon Railway and Navigation Company), would be allowed to serve Puget Sound by way of the Northern Pacific's line north from the Columbia.

This deal, however rational it seemed to the proprietors as a means of providing service without the disorder of cut-throat competition between themselves, was in violation of the Sherman Anti-Trust Act of 1890. The Supreme Court so ruled, though only five to four. In 1905 Hill and Harriman went back to war for control of the Pacific Northwest.

Hill set out to ram a line of his own down the north bank of the Columbia, thus breaking through the bottleneck formed by the Oregon Railway and Navigation Company's control of the river route and permitting him to serve the Vancouver-Portland area. In a follow-up maneuver he sent the brilliant engineer John F. Stevens (who had found the Great Northern's route through the Cascades, Stevens Pass), disguised as a millionaire sportsman, into central Oregon; Stevens located and bought a right-of-way for a line to Bend, which would not only raid Harriman territory but threaten an advance south to San Francisco. And in a speech to the Lewis and Clark Exposition in Portland, Hill made the challenge to Harriman overt. He told the Portlanders that it was his intention "to help with the development of this great state of Oregon."

Harriman counterattacked. He announced his intention to extend the Union Pacific northward from the Columbia to Puget Sound, thus helping with the development of the great state of Washington.

At this point, a fourth transcontinental entered the scene. The land-locked Chicago, Milwaukee, and St. Paul decided to break across the barrier of the Rockies and reach the Pacific at Tacoma. Lucius R. Manning, a Tacoma real estate dealer, was secretly commissioned to acquire property. He obtained a handsome stretch of waterfront before rumors of the Milwaukee's plans leaked out. When hints of a major development began to drive up prices, Milwaukee agents indicated they were interested in land on the developed side of south Twenty-fifth, while new agents bought sites to the east. Even so the asking price for the land on which the Milwaukee Station was built rose in a day from five thousand to forty-nine thousand dollars. The necessary land was blocked up, a bond issue was floated for construction, and $2.5 million was set aside for construction of warehouses on the waterfront where the Osaka Shoshen Kaisha steamships had agreed to pick up wheat for the Orient. The Milwaukee secured a right-of-way through Snoqualmie Pass, and construction started.

With the assurance that a second transcontinental was headed Tacoma's way, civic confidence returned. Land speculation began again. An ebullient developer named William J. Bowes, later to become a media celebrity as master of ceremonies on the Major Bowes Amateur Hour, drew attention to himself and his projects by presenting Tacoma with two enormous sphinxes for Wright Park. They were of plaster of Paris and disappeared in the Puget Sound rains, as did Bowes himself. But they were nice while they lasted. So were the Regents Park development financed by the Narrows Land Company, a San Francisco group, and assorted other dream suburbs.

On an unseasonably clear day in November of 1905, while the Milwaukee excitement was rising, a stranger walked into the Morrison and Balkwill real estate office at Tenth and Pacific and told portly Sam Balkwill that he would like to look at property along lower Pacific. Balkwill suggested a carriage, but the stranger wanted to hoof it. All through the afternoon Balkwill panted after the customer along Pacific, up Jefferson, back along Broadway, down Commerce, down the hill to the waterfront, up the hill to Market. It was worth it. In the cool of the evening, the stranger revealed himself as agent for a railroad. He deposited five hundred thousand dollars to Balkwill's account for him to draw on in lining up property. The Union Pacific, too, was coming to town.

Harriman's plans, as officially announced later, were grandiose. The tracks would enter downtown by a tunnel from the lower reaches of what is now called Nalley Valley. There would be a freight station at Seventeenth and Broadway, a passenger station at the intersection of Jefferson and Pacific. Elaborate viaducts would carry the tracks across the downtown streets. Bridges would span City Waterway to the developing tideflats.

The Tacoma business community was so enthusiastic at the prospect of a third terminus that they raised $100,000 in forty-eight hours to help Harriman acquire needed property. In all, the Union Pacific spent $2 million on Tacoma real estate and at least $100,000 on the tunnel toward downtown. Yet doubt persists that Harriman ever meant to make Tacoma a terminus. The buying and the digging may have been a bluff, a feint to force Jim Hill to open the NP's tracks from Seattle and Tacoma to Kalama as a common carrier, thus avoiding an expensive battle. At least that is what Hill offered and Harriman eagerly accepted, along with joint use by the Union Pacific of the massive, copper-domed station the Northern Pacific was building in Tacoma at a cost of $650,000. Work stopped on the tunnel and, when the streets above began to sag, it was filled in. Bottomless holes and rumors of Chinese hideaways remain a legacy from that enterprise.

"Today the Union Pacific has closed the biggest deal it has ever made," said Harriman in summing up his compromise with Hill, "and Tacoma has got the blackest eye she will ever get."

It wasn't all that bad. Tacoma did not get the Union Pacific terminal facilities but did receive UP train service from Portland and Great Northern service from Seattle down the NP tracks. The Milwaukee came in on its own, the first freight arriving in the fall of 1910, the first passenger train in the spring of 1911. And in 1912 the Northern Pacific started building a water-level route into the city. It followed the shoreline from south of Steilacoom, ran under Point Defiance through a 4,400-foot tunnel dug by and named for Nelson Bennett, and by-passed the Smelter through a shorter bore.

Completed in 1914, the water-grade route marked the end of the railroad construction era. During the second coming of the transcontinentals to Tacoma, the lines spent some $20 million on property acquisition and improvements. Real estate values reflected the impact. The Tacoma Land Company's property was appraised at about $1 million in 1905. During the next ten years the company sold $3 million worth of land and in 1915 its remaining holdings were still appraised at a million.

Nonetheless, the second cycle of land speculation and false hope left the townsfolk suspicious of promoters' promises, uneasily aware of how little control they had over their economic destinies, and willing to experiment instead with public ownership in many fields.

Among the oddities of Tacoma history, none is greater than that it was Charles Wright, capitalist, banker, railroad president, major stockholder of the Tacoma Land Company, who put the town on the path to municipal socialism through his sale to the city (at no little profit) of the Tacoma Light and Water Company, which he had formed in 1884 immediately after regaining control of the Northern Pacific from Henry Villard.

Water, Tacoma always had plenty of. It fell from the sky, it seeped from the ground, it lay around in lakes and ponds and puddles. But delivering water to houses was something a man could make money doing. In 1873, as New Tacoma was taking shape, Tom Quan began hauling barrels of drinking water from a spring by the Commercial Dock up the hill to Pacific Avenue in a mule cart. Quan and Long-Ear Nellie remained the town's only public utility until 1877 when Billy Fife dug holding pits on the west side of Ninth Street at Broadway, channeled water into them from a nearby stream, and, using logs that had been bored into pipes by an Olympia manufacturer, ran the water to the corner of Ninth and Pacific, where it could be picked up by the bucketful. Later Fife laid a hundred yards or so of pipe to business establishments and residences.

Demand was not great. The Tacoma hillside overflowed with springs and the water table was easily reached by well diggers. Several early office buildings had springs in their basements, most notably the Fidelity Building, which covered what was known as the Presbyterian Font, whose waters were reputed therapeutic until condemned as a health hazard.

Population growth in the early 1880s brought the danger of contamination and increased the need for fire protection. John E. Burns and Philip Metzler were first to organize a water company. In 1883 they dug a tunnel that tapped several streams behind a house Burns owned at Thirteenth and D (Market) streets. They diverted the flow through a flume to a hundred-thousand-gallon reservoir from which a four-inch main ran down to Pacific near Eleventh Street, where it branched—a three-inch pipe taking water south to the main business area, a two-inch pipe running north and dropping to one inch along Whiskey Row, as Pacific from Ninth to Seventh was called. Water pressure was low, but bathing, like clothes washing, was a once-a-week matter and the system seemed adequate, at least to Captain Burns.

Not so to Charles Wright. Visiting Tacoma in July of 1883 to help dedicate Saint Luke's Church, to the construction of which he had contributed thirty-five thousand dollars, and to lay the cornerstone for a girls' school (contribution, fifty thousand) named for his daughter Annie, Wright saw need for and opportunity in a more adequate water system. After Villard's failure returned the Wright interests to control of the railroad which could so greatly influence Tacoma's growth, Wright asked the city council for a franchise. In June of 1884 the Tacoma Light and Water Company was incorporated with a capitalization of three hundred thousand dollars. Wright named General John Sprague, who had recently retired as NP superintendent, to be president and hired Isaac Smith, who had "corrected" Olmsted's dream of Tacoma, as engineer.

Smith recommended bringing in water from a pond called Tule Lake so named because of its luxuriant cattails, but Spanaway Lake and Clover Creek were tapped instead. The water was brought to town in broad wooden flumes which emptied into a 2.5-million-gallon reservoir at Hood Street, a site still used by the city water division. While the flume was being built, other water was taken from Tacoma Eastern Gulch and Galliher Gulch. The first delivery was made from the Galliher facility to the Puget Sound Transfer Company at Thirteenth and Pacific in January of 1885. Water from Spanaway reached downtown Tacoma in August.

The "Light" aspect of Tacoma Light and Water was subsidiary. Electric lighting came to Tacoma in 1882 when the Tacoma Mill installed a generating plant in a clapboard barn on the waterfront and reduced fire danger in night operations by lighting the sawmill with sixteen-candlepower bulbs. Oil and gas remained the favored means of illumination in home and office for several years. In 1885 Wright's engineers used water flowing from the Galliher Gulch to turn the paddles of a small dynamo and offered electric service to anyone brave enough to use it. The city became the main customer. On the day after Christmas 1886, the first electric street lights were switched on. They cost the city twelve dollars a month each. Though service was spasmodic, Tacoma was proud of its occasional incandescence, especially since Seattle was still stuck back there in the oil age. In January of 1888 a new generator went into operation and arc lights of sixteen candlepower cut the gloom along Pacific Avenue, Tacoma Avenue, and D Street and in Old Town from sundown until midnight—except on the three nights a month when the moon was considered full.

Even so, some people were not satisfied with Tacoma Light and Water's performance, especially Captain Burns of Burns and Metzler, whose company it drove out of business. An imaginative and hot-tempered Irishman, Captain Burns first attracted attention in the 1850s when he chartered his schooner to the War Department during the Indian troubles. In later years when in his cups Burns was wont to lament that he and the U.S.S. *Decatur* had, alas, saved Seattle from the siwash.

Burns nursed a Celtic passion for grievance and bore Charles Wright no good will at all. Elected to the first city council of the combined new and old Tacomas, he introduced an ordinance awarding the water franchise to his own shoestring company. When it was turned down in favor of Tacoma Light and Water, Burns fulminated against the Railroad Crowd, Philadelphia Nabobs, and the Dogfish Aristocracy, finding them impediments to civic progress, enemies of the working man, and dangers to the purity of drinking water. He carried in his pocket a bottle of pickled salamanders he claimed to have retrieved from the Wright water supply.

Burns waged war on the Wright interests in ways that were as ingenious as they were unsuccessful. When he learned that the Tacoma Land Company contemplated building wharves on the tideflats facing the city, Burns formed a syndicate to head them off by driving pilings along the mud bank and claiming the waterfront as improved property. The Land Company, learning of the scheme, rented all available pile drivers and tried to corner the local supply of piling. Burns located a pile driver and operator in a back water up by Port Townsend and brought them to Commencement Bay, but when his machine went into action the Land Company's fleet of pile drivers surrounded it and, for each pile Burns set, they set several of their own. Townsfolk lined Cliff Avenue to root for the pile driver of their choice. The great pile-driving war ended with Burns, who had been smart enough to see the value of the tideflats, regarded as the town crank while the Land Company had established a winning claim to much of the future industrial area.

Burns's attacks on Tacoma Light and Water could be laughed off. Not Nelson Bennett's. In 1890 the hero of Stampede Pass bought the

Tacoma Hotel from the Land Company. In the next three months the hotel's water bill went up from the $75 a month the Wright water company had charged the Wright land company to $502. When Bennett complained, the bill at his residence was almost doubled. Bennett complained to the city council and filed suit in superior court, eventually sustained, against arbitrary rate increases. The council complained to Wright about citizen reaction to rates and service under the franchise. Wright complained right back. He wrote from Philadelphia to say that Tacoma had grown faster than anticipated, that higher rates were needed to pay for intended improvements, and that "if the council is going to show an antagonistic feeling to the company and a disposition to deprive the enterprise of a reasonable revenue from its investment, I shall not be able to raise money to go on with the work and therefore will not undertake any further expenditure." Perhaps, he suggested, the time had come for Tacoma to control its own water and gas.

If Wright meant that as a threat, others saw it as opportunity. The Chamber of Commerce, alarmed by several deaths in Tacoma from typhoid, including two members of the Chamber, commissioned a study of the purity of Tacoma Light and Water's water. A University of Minnesota chemist gave Spanaway Lake a clean bill of health but warned that the delivery system was suspect. Indeed it was. The Chamber report noted that the flumes bringing water to the Hood Street reservoir were uncovered and unguarded; children swam in the drinking water, workmen washed clothes in it, cows luxuriated in it.

For his part, Bennett welcomed the word that Wright wanted out of the water business. He offered to set up a new company, capitalized at $1,500,000, to build a water system with the city supervising construction and retaining the right to buy him out at any time at cost, plus 8 percent. Colonel Chauncey Griggs of the St. Paul and Tacoma Lumber Company made a somewhat similar gesture. The council passed an ordinance referring a $1,500,000 bond issue to the electorate, the money to be spent either on buying out Wright or building a new water system. When the public indicated deep doubt that the council was capable of making a $1,500,000 decision, the councilmen rescinded the ordinance and created a water commission to study the problem. The commission brought in an outside expert at $50 a day, plus expenses, and learned that it would cost from $1,800,000 to bring in water from nearby springs to $2,950,000 to get it from the Green River, with the other possible sources—the Mashel, the Green, and the South Fork of the Puyallup—lying between those extremes. It seemed cheaper to buy out Tacoma Light and Water. By a margin of ninety-two votes more than the necessary

60 percent majority, the voters approved a bond issue for the purchase of the system.

Negotiations began. The council suggested a price of from $1,350,000 to $1,500,000. Wright asked $1,850,000, then dropped to $1,800,000. The council said $1,500,000 was the limit. Wright said $1,800,000, at once, or he would refuse to sell at all. The council sent a three-man committee, headed by Council President Harris A. Corell, back to negotiate. Wright came down to $1,750,000. The deal was closed. Tacoma was in the light and water business.

There proved to be less to the purchase than met the eye—and more. Somehow Wright's gas works had been left out of the transaction, though the electric plant was included. Tacomans learned that the company engineer had warned against further use of Spanaway water and the company had been dipping into Clover Creek for its supply. A property owner had a court order blocking that practice. Wright had sold the city two undeveloped springs which he said could be brought into use for $400,000, but a city survey indicated they were smaller and more distant than indicated—in fact, "totally useless." A supply of pipe that came with the purchase proved to be smaller than represented.

Shortly after taking over the water system, Tacoma had to call out the firemen to pump emergency supplies from nearby streams until a deal could be worked out with property owners for temporary use of Clover Creek. The bond issue for purchase had put the city $300,000 over its legal debt limit. No money was available for improvements of the water system.

Superior Court Judge John C. Stallcup, acting as a private citizen, brought suit to invalidate the bond issue. He lost. But when a suit involving the validity of some city warrants came before him on the Department Two bench, Judge Stallcup extended his opinion to let the town know what he thought of the purchase of Tacoma Light and Water:

For lawless and void debt-making, no community of English speaking people of like population can show a parallel to our city officials. It appears that this C. B. Wright water involvement hangs like a millstone around the neck of the city, holding the city not only in shameful disgrace but in the deplorable condition of no water supply, and at the same time bereft of the means and power with which to acquire one. . . . The city acquired no water or water supply; the water which the said company had been running through their wooden flume, mains and supply pipes, and selling to the city and citizens, was water which they were lawlessly taking from the farmers of Clover Creek, so that . . . the city has been perpetually enjoined from taking water therefrom, and the property left in the possession of the city by the iniquitous transaction is an affliction simply. . . . No greater hurt can be done our institutions than by giving judicial cloak to such villainies as are disclosed by the records in this case.

A judge making a political speech from the bench in the guise of a judicial decision on another matter was no more unusual than the situation in the Tacoma city attorney's office, where James Wickersham served without confirmation by the city council.

Wickersham—"Nimble Jim" to his detractors—was a small man with great visibility. Coming to Tacoma in 1883 from Illinois, he was elected probate judge the following year. Twice indicted for helping to organize the Chinese Expulsion, he was never tried on the charge. But in 1889, while still on the probate bench, he was indicted, tried, and convicted of the charge that he seduced a nineteen-year-old door-to-door book peddler and arranged for her to have an abortion. The girl later recanted her testimony, a development that would have created a greater sensation had it not occurred in the week of the great Seattle Fire. Wickersham survived the scandal and won appointment as city attorney in 1894, but when Mayor Edward S. Orr renominated him in July of 1895 the council failed to act on the appointment, Orr refused to name anyone else, and Wickersham stayed on as a lame duck.

Some duck, some limp. Wickersham filed suit against Tacoma Light and Water, claiming Wright's company had misrepresented its assets in a way that constituted fraud. He asked damages of one million dollars. The move made Wickersham an instant hero to many, though some businessmen objected that the case would damage the city's credit (of which Tacoma had none to spare), some thought the suit could not be won, and some thought Wickersham had nimbly maneuvered himself into a position from which the city council could not dislodge him, especially since he charged the council president, Harris Corell, with being under the corrupt influence of the company.

The trial in Judge Hugh Pritchard's court lasted eighteen days in December. Testimony and evidence did nothing to increase the popularity of the water company. The company's property had definitely been overvalued, though the defense produced some evidence that it was by city officials in their attempt to make the bond issue palatable to the voters. Wickersham showed that Council President Corell, as a partner in the law firm that represented Tacoma Light and Water, received 30 percent of the legal fees paid by the water company to the firm, including 1 percent of the $1,750,000 sale price he helped negotiate with Wright. Corell saw no legal or ethical problem in the arrangement.

The jury was not out long. They returned with a verdict for the city and set damages at $787,500. The verdict was greeted with cheers, as was Wickersham's appearance in court. (The following week the city council confirmed his appointment as city attorney.) Speaking from the bench, the judge said that as far as he was concerned Corell had done nothing wrong and no investigation of his actions would be recommended; he added that while it seemed to him the damages set by the jury might be too high by half, he would not substitute his personal judgment for that of twelve men.

A year later the state supreme court reversed the jury's decision, finding, so they said, no evidence of misrepresentation or fraud. Two Tacoma editors were jailed for contempt of court after commenting on "vicious and vacillating decisions" by "supreme simpletons." Wickersham won a rehearing, and the court, still vacillating, not only decided there had been fraud and misrepresentation but added $10,000 costs to the damages, making the total $979,500.

Charles B. Wright died in Philadelphia in March of 1898, aged seventy-six, disillusioned with the city he had helped create and which he had indeed loved, though perhaps as he might have loved a prize milch cow. Five months after Wright's death the city council accepted a compromise settlement with the executors of the estate. Tacoma was dropped as defendant in a series of countersuits that had been filed by the Philadelphian's lawyers, and the city received $100,000 damages, $25,000 in court costs, and possession of the property and franchise of the Commercial Electric Light and Power Company in which Wright had sequestered some of his Tacoma assets.

Though the city now owned the light and water facilities, cows continued to luxuriate in the flume that brought Clover Creek water to the reservoir. There was no money to repair the run-down system, especially after the council cut rates. After a decade of public ownership, the National Board of Fire Underwriters noted that "the effluent, as observed, shows no conspicuous clarification." Tacoma's water might be dirty but in summer it was also not abundant. But in the early years of the twentieth century, new, deep wells were dug in South Tacoma, tapping the aquifer below the clay and gravel. The new wells yielded water of exceptional purity, but it was not cheap. The water had to be pumped to the surface and the cost of power was high.

The electric generating facilities Tacoma acquired from Charles Wright proved inadequate for the city's needs; dilapidated, too. The community bought most of its power on contract from private utilities. They were not in business to make publicly owned utilities look good; there were no regulatory agencies; and the price charged for the power Tacoma needed to pump water from the new wells made officials think about producing more electricity of their own. Steam generation was expensive, but the area was rich in mountain streams; it turned out, however, that the best sites were controlled by private power companies.

Tacoma's city attorney was gaunt, gray-haired Theodore L. Stiles, a specialist on constitutional law. Stiles had helped write the state constitution in 1889 and served four years on the state supreme court. He assured the city council that Tacoma could condemn land for public use outside the city limits, an opinion shared, when the test came, by five of the nine supreme court justices. That was enough. The way was cleared for Tacoma and other municipalities to exploit for community benefit the hydro-power potential of the Cascades and the Olympics.

After Tacoma had established its legal right to build distant dams, Stone and Webster, the ringmasters of private power in the Pacific Northwest, offered to guarantee the city power at less than the estimated generating cost of the proposed dam. The offer was denounced as a bribe. Tacoma voters answered a call to declare their independence from outside corporations. They approved a bond issue for a dam and powerhouse at La Grande on the Nisqually.

The dam, built at a cost of $2,354,985, came on the line in August of 1912. Officials celebrated by cutting electric rates, and in 1915 cut them again by adopting a combination cooking and lighting rate of one cent a kilowatt hour, the start of penny power.

While the La Grande project was being put together Angelo Fawcett, who had been out of office for a decade, resurfaced as mayor— and as champion of public ownership of almost anything. Fawcett was a man who got things done, though not always by the rules. Powerful looking, with broad shoulders, broad forehead, wide-set eyes, sweeping mustache, and a geyser of hair, Fawcett for more than thirty years was Tacoma's most flamboyant and resilient politician.

Born in Ohio of Irish-German stock, educated in Illinois, wounded in a Civil War battle that claimed the lives of forty-four of the sixty men in his company, Fawcett later supported himself as a horse trader, telegrapher, and traveling salesman. He came to Tacoma in 1883 with his third wife shortly after his second wife divorced him (the first had died), and opened a store for wagons and plows on Pacific Avenue. He helped found the Chamber of Commerce (from which he soon dissassociated himself) and joined an array of fraternal organizations from the Maccabees to the Tribe of Ben Hur. Politics clearly lay ahead.

Fawcett was elected county commissioner on the Democratic ticket in 1892. In 1893, during the Panic, he combined sympathy for the distressed with political shrewdness by hiring Germania Hall for Christmas Day and offering a free turkey dinner to any child between the ages of three and fourteen. They could not vote but their parents could. Fawcett fed two thousand people that day and won a nickname that he flaunted the rest of his life, "Turkey." The Democrats at once nominated him for mayor, and though he ran behind both Republican and Populist candidates he was only 559 votes behind the winner.

Two years later, as the candidate of both the Democrats and the Populists, he overwhelmed the incumbent mayor, Edward Orr, by two votes, 2,683 to 2,681, in an election that provided the town with arguments and attorneys with fees for two years. Orr secured a court order mandating a recount. When the city councilmen appointed to check the ballots unlocked the vault in the new City Hall, they found someone had punched a hole in the wall and made off with the returns from several disputed precincts. Republicans argued that the theft, which occurred after Fawcett's inauguration, constituted misfeasance or malfeasance, and they demanded his resignation. Fawcett refused to quit. A woman spread the rumor that the mayor had hired her son to steal the ballots and gave him three hundred dollars to go to Canada. The young man got as far as Bellingham, where he burned to death trying to rescue a girl from a fire. Fawcett denied everything. A superior court judge ruled the mayoralty election invalid and ordered Fawcett to turn the office back to Orr. He did, but appealed to the state supreme court, which made him mayor again.

The mystery of the missing ballots was not the only problem involving Fawcett with the courts. The voters had adopted a charter amendment setting up a Tacoma Civil Service Commission with stringent rules designed to control political patronage. Fawcett stuffed the commission with Populist friends. A superior court judge invalidated the election establishing the commission, but the board refused to leave office and were upheld by the supreme court. By the time the commission's legitimacy was established, its desirability seemed doubtful to Fawcett. Forgetting who had appointed them, the commissioners were cramping his style in further appointments. Chairman Govnor Teats raised objections when the mayor went outside the civil service list to appoint a female friend to be assistant city librarian with offices in the City Hall. Fawcett charged the chairman with "prostitution of a public trust" and the city council dismissed Teats from the commission. Mrs. Fawcett sued for divorce, and won. The assistant librarian subsequently became the mayor's fourth wife.

Some fun and games at City Hall involved public policy. The Commercial Electric Light and Power Company, in which Charles Wright held the utility properties he had not unloaded on Tacoma, held a contract that permitted it to use the city's utility poles. Fawcett told the company to remove its wires. Commercial Electric replied that they didn't have to. So one night Fawcett led parties of city linemen onto the streets and pulled down the wires, to the outrage of the company and the inconvenience of citizens who awoke power-less. Commercial obtained a court order prohibiting the city from in-terfering with company crews when they replaced the wires. Fawcett went to a different judge and secured an order restraining company linemen from climbing city poles. Lawyers prospered. In the end the supreme court ruled that the company had a valid contract and Ta-coma taxpayers were stuck with the costs incurred by Fawcett's charge on the light brigade.

When Fawcett came up for re-election in 1898 he was renominated by the Democrats, but this time the Populists ran a candidate of their own. The Republicans offered the electorate not one but two can-didates, one favoring the gold standard and the other free coinage of silver—though what impact the mayor of Tacoma might have on na-tional monetary policy the subsequent debate did not make clear. In a broken field, the incumbent's chances of holding on seemed good, but both Republicans finished ahead of Fawcett. His political career seemingly at an end, he went back to the wagon business.

1910 was a year of change. The automobile was making the wagon obsolete and the voters of Tacoma adopted a new city char-ter, which established a commission form of government and in-creased the power of the mayor. Fawcett decided the time had come to re-enter politics. The city's population had more than doubled since he left office, and all that most voters remembered of his mayoral and marital difficulties was that he had fought the private power company and the woman he married in 1898 was still his wife.

Although the populists who had helped elect him had faded from the political scene, the Teddy Roosevelt Progressives were in good odor. Describing himself as "a former Democrat who since Theodore Roosevelt has voted Republican in national elections," Fawcett filed as an Independent. His platform was equally eclectic: he stood for an open town, which the business community favored; open govern-ment, which the press spoke well of; and municipal ownership, which the voters had overwhelmingly approved a year earlier. The combination proved unbeatable. Fawcett was elected in the primary, polling more votes than the combined total of six other candidates.

When it came to municipal ownership of utilities, Fawcett was bet-ter than his campaign promise. Not only did he support public power, but he joined with Utilities Commissioner Nicholas Lawson in a campaign to secure a municipal water supply from the Green

River. Fawcett and Nicholas chose a site for the headworks and, without getting approval from the city council, purchased it. Their tactics were of dubious legality, the price paid for the land unnecessarily high—or so it was argued—but Fawcett and Lawson secured for the city an abundant supply of mountain water which remains one of Tacoma's greatest assets.

Early in his new term, a delegation of businessmen visited Fawcett to complain that the old dock below Cliff Avenue was distant and dilapidated. The time had come to get rid of the notion that Tacoma benefited by making it difficult to get to Seattle. The mayor threw city support behind a campaign to acquire the waterfront north of Fifteenth Street and to build a municipal dock. While they were at it, they built a new Eleventh Street bridge and authorized a municipal tramline to serve the tideflats.

The enthusiasm for civic amenities was catching. The school board was pressured by the newspapers into approving the construction in Old Woman's Gulch, a deep ravine alongside the high school, of a concrete stadium. The construction was slipshod, the concrete seats fundamentally numbing, but the view was superb and the Stadium a source of pride for years to come.

It would seem that in a time of do-it-yourself euphoria, when civic projects were completed nearly as quickly as they were conceived, a mayor with Fawcett's capacity for identifying himself with popular causes would be unbeatable. But, as the philosopher A. J. Liebling points out in his second law, "A man may be smart enough to pick himself up by the seat of his pants and throw himself out the front door." This Fawcett accomplished. A year after he was sworn in, he was thrown out.

Fawcett's problem, shared by many a later mayor, was the town's vigorous but squalid night life. The existence of box-houses and brothels was more than tolerated by a majority of males in the sawmill and seaport towns of the western frontier, and no politician intent on office risked overt opposition to commercial sex. But in 1910, that year of change, Tacoma's Emma Smith DeVoe brought to climax the drive for woman's suffrage in Washington. Fawcett was made mayor in the spring by an all-male electorate, but in the fall women got the vote. The rules had changed. Fawcett was suddenly called to explain himself to a new and suspicious constituency. It was not easy.

Before woman suffrage, Fawcett had been asked by businessmen to do something about a house of prostitution on Pacific Avenue. He had arranged a trade with the whoremonger, yielding city property on A Street for the brothel on the main drag. From the point of view of a frontier male this was a pragmatic solution. To the newly enfranchised females it was an endorsement of Sodom, Gomorrah, and the Seattle Skid Road.

Fawcett set out to finesse the threat by establishing his puritan bona fides. The papers had been harrumphing about the sad fate of some poor souls who wandered into Tacoma saloons and after entertainment by resident sharpies invested most unwisely. Fawcett proposed that the city council adopt an Anti-Treating Ordinance, which would make it illegal for anyone to buy anyone else a drink in a public place. In all probability he looked on this as a proposal certain to be rejected by his fellow councilmen. He would propose, they would oppose, and he could say he had broken his lance tilting with sin.

The other councilmen were not strangers to the game. They resented the mayor's frequent raids into their territory. They were not inclined to play patsy. They debated the Anti-Treating Ordinance long enough to establish it as Fawcett's brain child and then, after a show of reluctance, unanimously adopted it, leaving Fawcett and Tacoma the butt of vaudeville jokesters along the coast, and the mayor the target of every saloon keeper's wrath.

Along with woman suffrage, Washington adopted the "Oregon System," which gave voters the right to petition for new legislation, to reject by referendum laws adopted by the legislature or city council, and to recall officers. Fawcett, everybody's favorite in 1910, found himself in 1911 the object of a recall in which he had to defend himself simultaneously against charges that he was pro-pandering and anti-saloon. Out he went, replaced by an amiable Republican reformer of utmost good intention. A few weeks later, Tacoma recalled the public utilities commissioner and the public works commissioner.

The spasm of righteousness soon passed. In 1914 Fawcett, pledging a town of undefiled purity, campaigned for mayor as a reform candidate. His opponent, the Reverend C. F. W. Stoever, spent all his time explaining the inexplicable rumor that he was a tool of the liquor interests.

Back in office, Fawcett concentrated on helping the workingman by building payrolls. He won approval of a public market on Market Street, and championed the extension of public streetcar service on the tideflats, but the great triumph of his third term was Camp Lewis.

In September of 1916 Steve Appleby, a cashier at the National Bank of Tacoma, attended an encampment of the Northwest Businessmen's Preparation League at American Lake. From the military grapevine he picked off the rumor that the War Department had sent a Captain Richard Park to Seattle to study sites in the Pacific Northwest for an army encampment, but that nothing near Tacoma was under consideration. No banker could fail to see the injustice of such an oversight. He alerted his peers, who descended upon Captain Park in sufficient strength to force him to tour the encampment area at American Lake. He was as impressed as Dr. Tolmie had been, and Lieutenant Wilkes. His report brought the commanding general of the Western Department up from San Francisco. General J. F. Bell inspected the National Guard facilities at Camp Murray and the land nearby at American Lake and found it good but sadly expensive. He let it be known, without making any commitment, that if the Army could get, say, 30,000 acres without cost they might establish a post. He did not need to add that the post would require construction from local materials and would meet a payroll.

The Washington State Constitution prohibited governmental bodies from giving land or extending credit to private industry in order to win payrolls. The prohibition did not extend to courting Uncle Sam by similar lavishments. When the generals found Tacoma-Pierce eager, they raised the asking price to 110,000 acres, then compromised at 70,000.

In December of 1916, Mayor Fawcett proclaimed Tacoma's need for the military presence. He sponsored a drive by local businessmen to raise funds to help pass a bond issue under which the citizenry of Pierce County would pledge $2 million to condemn and buy land which they would then give to the federal government for use by the Army—land, ironically, that had been given by the federal government to Washington to parcel out to private citizens.

The bond proposition carried, six to one, and in the weeks before the United States entered the war to end wars, the land needed for armies to practice upon was taken back from unhappy settlers, willing speculators, and, of course, powerless Indians.

The military became, as it remains, Pierce County's basic payroll.

One Man's Tacoma

I WAS born in Tacoma in 1916, the year the Smelter was rebuilt and Pierce County began commandeering land to present to Uncle Sam in return for the Camp Lewis payroll. The room in which I was born looks out over the gulch that Allen Mason bridged to open the North End to residential development. From that room one sees the bay, the Cascades, the Mountain. The enclosed world of the ravine with its singing stream (now buried as part of a storm sewer project), the expanse of salt water leading off to every seaport in the world, the ethereal bulk of the Mountain sometimes manifest on the eastern horizon still mean, to me, living in Tacoma.

One of my first memories is of being held up to look over the railing of the balcony on the second floor of the house to watch a long line of great gray warships steam down the East Passage, round the point where George Vancouver dined with the Puyallup, and anchor in the bay Charles Wilkes named Commencement. The war to end wars—the first war of my lifetime—was over, though children still sang, "Kaiser Bill went up the hill to take a look at France; Kaiser Bill came down the hill with bullets in his pants." The visit of the Pacific fleet marked victory. Marked, too, Tacoma's linkage with the military, a growth industry more reliable than railroads.

From our house on north Thirty-first Street on quiet nights one could hear the trains clanking along the waterfront on track laid by the old tunnel builder, Nelson Bennett; hear, too, the long whistles, mournful and romantic. We used to play by the tracks, though we were not supposed to, and the great game was to put a penny on the rail, then retrieve it after the train had passed. The penny would be paper thin, misshapen, and almost too hot to touch. The money from the railroads was thinning out too. Tacoma's romance with rails was fading.

In 1920 the Northern Pacific moved its traffic department to

Seattle; soon afterward the rest of the western headquarters went north. The Tacoma Lumbermen's Club telegraphed a complaint that this was "like throwing over an old love for a new." But the NP left its shops and their payroll in Tacoma as a sort of alimony, and the city acquired the graceful old Headquarters Building at Seventh and Pacific Avenue as an auxiliary police station.

Tacoma's affair with the Union Pacific had ended in a breach of promise. As for the Chicago, Milwaukee, and St. Paul, it had found little profit in reaching the Pacific. That railroad managed to go broke during the great twenties boom. Sold at courthouse auction it passed into the hands of Wall Street receivers who had no sympathy for Tacoma. When Osaka Shoshen Kaisha, the Japanese shipping line which gave the Milwaukee Line considerable business, shifted its terminus to Seattle, the Milwaukee's western headquarters went too. Tacoma, a railroad creation, was left as a way station. Only the Union Depot and streets bearing the names of NP officials—Wright, Villard, Oakes, Ainsworth, Wilkeson, and Sprague—recall the days when Tacoma had a special relationship with its rails.

As children we didn't care about the loss of the termini. What bothered us was the loss of our Mountain. Tacoma had never acquiesced in the decision by the United States Geographic Board that the great peak was *Mount Rainier*. We called it *Mount Tacoma* and wanted the world to do likewise. In the twenties, Tacoma created another Justice to the Mountain Committee to get the bureaucrats to give us back our Mountain.

The committee marshaled considerable support. Theodore Roosevelt, Ambassador James Bryce, Mary Roberts Rinehart, Amelita Galli-Curci, and Will Rogers were among those who favored *Mount Tacoma*. Tacomans combed the records for proof that Theodore Winthrop knew what he was writing about when he said the Indian name was *Tacoma*. Others researched Peter Rainier and announced triumphantly that he was fat, myopic, funny-looking, foreign, and had fought against the United States in the Revolutionary War. Tacomans persuaded a national convention of Indian leaders "to pray to the Great Spirit Kitchemanitou to restore to the Indians Tacoma, meaning Nourishing Breast." School children wrote essays, local historians wrote letters to editors, and everybody wrote poems. My father wrote one of many poems called "The Mountain That Was God," the title deriving from a highly suspect "Indian" legend, and my mother, part-Indian, wrote "The Mountain That Was Ours." And they lost again. The Geographic Board clung to *Rainier*.

Tacomans then petitioned Congress for relief from the intolerable burden. The Senate, in its wisdom, passed a bill on April 21, 1924, declaring *Mount Rainier* to be, henceforth and forevermore, *Mount*

Tacoma. But the Public Lands Committee of the House of Representatives failed to report the bill to the floor. So Mount Rainier it remains, except in Tacoma, where we usually refer to the ethereal presence simply as The Mountain.

Tacoma hasn't even had good fortune with nicknames. Back in the 1880s the eccentric eastern promoter, George Francis Train, saddled the community with the sobriquet "City of Destiny." That one went sour during the Panic of Ninety-three. When the Milwaukee Road and the Union Pacific rekindled civic expectations early in the twentieth century, the Chamber of Commerce came up with the slogan "Watch Tacoma Grow." That proved to be about as exciting as watching coral accrete. Tacoma grew by only 16,000 between 1910 and 1920, achieving a population of 96,965. Seattle during the same ten years gained 127,000 inhabitants.

Tacoma then styled itself the Lumber Capital of the World. So, for a time, it was. Logging trains continued to roll in from the mountains, bearing to the saws the carcasses of giant trees. The ships of the world came to the wharves below the bluff to pick up lumber from mills that lay like beached sea-mammals at the tideline. By night one could trace the curve of the harbor by the ruby glow of the screens atop the waste burners. Few questioned the practice of discharging industrial waste into the sky for all to share. Particulate matter from the mills, like the chemical exhaust of the Smelter, smelled like dollars in a community anxious for payrolls. Nevertheless the old-fashioned sawmill was an endangered species.

Costs rose as lumbermen chased the virgin forests deeper into the surrounding mountains. Distances were greater, the slopes steeper. The cream had been skimmed. There was decreasing profit in the simple geometry of transforming round logs into rectangular planks. A new technology arose, more sophisticated and more capital intensive. Logs were not merely sawed; they were broken up by machines and chemicals to be reassembled as plywood, fiberboard, cardboard, and newsprint. St. Regis Paper Company bought the land where the great pile-driving war had been waged in the 1880s between John Burns and the Tacoma Land Company. They built the kraft mill which has helped to stabilize the economy while making its contribution, too, to what is known as the aroma of Tacoma. West Tacoma Newsprint was built at the mouth of Chambers Creek not far from the site of Andrew Byrd's grist mill, where Job Carr found occasional employment while waiting for the city of his dreams to materialize.

One by one the waterfront sawmills I knew as a boy disappeared, usually in a burst of flame, a rain of cinders, and an investigation by the insurance company. Tacoma's publicly owned power system, part of the heritage of the Angelo Fawcett period, lured electrochemical industries such as Penn Salt (now Pennwalt), Hooker Chemical, and Ohio Ferro-Alloy to the tideflats to replace the lost payrolls. They were most welcome. But they made Tacoma, increasingly, a community in which the basic economic decisions were made in distant board rooms.

Tacoma's struggle long since had become not to surpass Seattle but to survive as something other than suburb or satellite to the metropolis, to remain a community with a distinct economic base and personality. During the Depression, survival was all. Any activity that kept people in town was welcomed. Banks might fail and mills might close but the oldest profession flourished in Tacoma with a vigor unsurpassed since Harry Morgan was blindfolding the police department with dollar bills.

During the Thirties, Tacoma received more national headlines than at any time since the great boom of the Eighties—most of them inadvertent and unfavorable. It was the city's misfortune to be the scene of two kidnapings at a time when the murder of Charles and Anne Lindbergh's son made kidnaping the most newsworthy crime. Charles Matson, the young son of a prominent Tacoma physician, was taken from his North End home by a gunman, sexually assaulted, and murdered. The manhunt went on for years—the FBI file on the case remains open—but the killer was never caught, or identified. George Weyerhaeuser, scion of the timber family (and now president of the Weyerhaeuser Company), was pulled into a car as he walked home from grammar school. He was released unharmed after several days, and his kidnapers were captured and convicted; but though the story had a happy ending, it helped fix on Tacoma the reputation of being kidnap capital of the West.

Even successes went quickly sour. In 1940 Tacoma realized an old dream of direct connection with the Kitsap Peninsula. The Narrows Bridge was opened to traffic fifty-one years after George Eaton, a clerk in the NP Land Department, proposed a Tacoma to Port Orchard railroad to link the terminus of the transcontinental with the proposed Puget Sound Naval Shipyard. But Galloping Gertie, as the slender, swaying suspension bridge was nicknamed, went into the Sound almost before the echoes of dedicatory speeches died down, the victim of design changes brought about by demands for economy in government—including bridge construction. It was not to be rebuilt until 1950.

The New Deal, American re-armament which followed the rise of

Nazi Germany, and World War Two lifted Tacoma out of economic stagnation. During the war, everything Tacoma produced was in demand, especially soldiers. Fort Lewis, Madigan Army Hospital, and McChord Air Field, which had been acquired by the War Department in 1938, expanded hugely, while the tideflats sprouted shipyards. Not since the days of Stampede Tunnel construction had Tacoma shared so fully the heady excitement of common purpose and overtime pay. But with the outbreak of peace it was back to the same old problems in the same old city.

The generation that had been off to the wars returned to a town strangely unchanged. Tacoma had won its fight for survival, but Downtown was a relic of the nineteenth century. It was like a pressed flower, a memory of when Tacoma had been invited to the dance.

City government, too, was something out of the past. Tacoma voters adopted the commission form of government in 1910, when that was the latest municipal style, like the grid pattern on streets. For a time the system of elected department heads who sat as a council to make policy energized municipal affairs. The combination of legislative and administrative authority allowed able men, like Ira Davisson, the utilities commissioner, to sell their plans to the public and carry them out. Tacoma's light and water departments provided electricity and water to the citizenry and industries at rates as low as could be found in the nation. The public works department, too, was innovative and efficient. But inevitably innovation settled into routine. Time-servers became policy makers. Vision perished. Municipal politics became largely a question of who ran the police department, because that's where the money was.

The mayor might be titular head of Tacoma but he had direct control only of the garbage department while the commissioner of public safety appointed the chief of police. The mayoralty race drew two or three candidates at most; the line-up in the public safety commissioner primary usually looked like the start of the Boston Marathon.

Tacoma had an open town tradition. There had been a "crazy house" on the hill above Old Town before the village was incorporated. New Tacoma was not far behind in providing commercial sex as an amenity. Harry Morgan gave gambling a good name. Prohibition brought the speak-easy. Night life in Tacoma meant bookie joints, slot-machine and pin-ball routes, unlicensed drinking spots, and an abundance of brothels, most of them in Opera Alley, between Broadway and Market Street. They offered all the glamour of a fast-food franchise, but the operators paid high rent. Reform advocates were assured that Seattle was worse—and more prosperous.

Control of night life in Tacoma centered on two local organizations that grew up during Prohibition. Sometimes they shared, more often they competed. There was little rough stuff, just politics and corruption. Each side financed one or more candidates in the quadrennial election of safety commissioner. The side that won the election got to run things without raids while its rival planned better precinct organization.

Change came, surprisingly enough, from within the police force. Some idealistic young men returning from military service objected to selective enforcement of the vice laws. Styling themselves a Vigilance Committee they raided some joints that had paid their dues. The safety commissioner was embarrassed. His embarrassment increased when other cops with ties to the out-of-power organization began making raids too. The commissioner suspended several policemen for excessive diligence. The Civil Service Board, after a prolonged hearing, ruled that a policeman could not be suspended for enforcing the law, no matter on whose behalf he was enforcing it.

In the ensuing uproar a reform candidate for safety commissioner, backed by church groups, won election. Unfortunately between the night of victory and the day of inauguration he made a tour of inspection of the places he was pledged to close and was tape-recorded in intimate conversation with a charmer of no discernible virtue. His reform administration thereafter labored under difficulty. Whenever enforcement became onerous to the forces of the night somebody would phone the commissioner, play the tape-recording, and suggest the virtues of moderation in all things. Moderation became so rampant that the military threatened to put the town off limits. The American Social Hygiene Association sounded the alarm on venereal disease. National magazines ran articles deploring "Seattle's Dirty Back Yard." A legislative committee headed by State Senator Albert D. Rosellini held the town spellbound with a televised investigation of Tacoma vice that made city officials look, if not wicked, awfully silly.

Tacomans had had enough. A charter proposing a council-manager system of municipal government was drawn up by a freeholders committee. It won adoption at the general election of November 1952—the one in which General Eisenhower was elected president. Tacomans went on to elect an elitist city council, perhaps the best-educated city council in the history of American governance. Its nine members averaged six years apiece of college education. In their collective wisdom they hired a city manager of rigorous honesty, who appointed an old-shoe chief of police competent and content to live on his salary. The climate changed. Tacoma won a Municipal League rating as an All American City, night life disappeared as a serious political issue (and almost disappeared altogether), and the populace had time to address more important problems, such as Tacoma's role as second city—and worry about law enforcement in surrounding Pierce County.

The City of Destiny remains unsure of what its destiny should be. The land is much changed from that which George Vancouver called "the most lovely country that can be imagined" where "the labour of its inhabitants would be amply rewarded in the bounties which nature seems ready to bestow on cultivation." Few would care to depend on cultivation of the land today. Nor will Tacoma ever be the metropolis of the Pacific that Job Carr envisioned that Christmas Day when he stood in his canoe and shouted "Eureka." It is unlikely to become, as Allen Mason hoped when his earlier dreams of greatness had faded, a Philadelphia to Seattle's New York, though the possibility remains that it will be, as R. F. Radebaugh of the *Ledger* once predicted, a Liverpool to Seattle's London.

The Tacoma of today, 187 years after Vancouver's visit, 128 years after Delin started his mill among the skunk cabbages, 115 years after Job Carr exulted in his first sight of the Sheltered Place, 106 years after the Northern Pacific chose Commencement Bay as its terminus, 81 years after Nelson Bennett undercut the Cascades, 76 years after the crash stilled the great boom, remains a city set in beauty, a city small enough for people to say hello on the downtown streets, a city where it is safe to walk at night and a morning's drive takes you to mountain or ocean, a city of easy access to parks and playgrounds, and to the more metropolitan delights of Seattle: in short, a pleasant place to live.

An anonymous visitor to the Pacific Northwest, quoted in the January 12, 1894, issue of *Harper's Weekly,* had it right: "Well, gentlemen, if I were a man of wealth seeking a home and investments on Puget Sound, I would live in Tacoma and invest in Seattle."

Acknowledgments

Writing a book about one's hometown and region means being in debt to more people than can be remembered, let alone acknowledged. Who first took me into the Job Carr cabin and talked about the Civil War veteran who with ax and saw and hammer shaped it from material at hand? Who made me wonder what it must have been like to be in Peter Puget's rowboats as they moved up a waterway toward the unknown? When did I think of what it meant to those whose roots were a thousand years deep when they were asked to give up the land and streams that nurtured them?

Some old debts I remember. My older brothers took me first into the woods and it was they whom I first heard speak the Chinook jargon, though they had picked it up late from Indians working in the lumber camps. Miss Chesney at Jason Lee Junior High School and Miss Burgess at Stadium High turned history into people. Mr. Bonney (W. P. Bonney, for twenty-six years secretary of the Washington State Historical Society) let noisy boys roam between the displays of Egyptian mummies and stuffed oxen and arrowheads at the Ferry Museum. I wish I had known then that his father was in the first party of pioneers to reach Puget Sound through Naches Pass, but I might not have appreciated that contact with adventure. Certainly as a boy I did not appreciate my casual encounters with little old Ezra Meeker. He was an acquaintance of my father and occasionally stopped by for a chat, sometimes in the company of Oscar Brown, the keeper of the Brown's Point lighthouse (which I wrongly supposed had been named after him). As best I remember, Meeker was always talking about Progress and the Future of Puyallup, and I got as far away as possible. I didn't know that he had sat on the jury that tried Leschi of the Nisqually and had held out against that legal lynching, nor did I know that his had been the strongest voice raised against the expulsion of the Chinese from Tacoma. Had I listened in those old days in my father's study under the picture of Carlyle, I might have learned a lot. But at least I remember Meeker as a man, not a statue.

There are so many others, but I must try to limit myself to acknowledging the help of those who made specific contributions to this book. I am indebted to the Howard Carr estate for a bequest that made possible more extensive research than I could have otherwise undertaken, and to Rick and

Francie Carr for use of the Carr family diaries, letters, and pictures. Gary Reese of the Tacoma Public Library has been unfailingly helpful in research, and his published studies of Pierce County history have deepened my understanding of the pioneer period. Frank Green and Jeanne Engerman of the Washington State Historical Society Library, Nancy Pryor of the Washington State Library in Olympia, Desmond Taylor of the University of Puget Sound Library, and Robert Monroe and Dennis Andersen of the University of Washington Library responded thoughtfully to every query. Eric Groves of the British Museum (Natural History) put in my hands specimens collected by Archibald Menzies during Vancouver's exploration of Puget Sound, and explained their botanical importance. Lorraine Barker Hildebrand of the Tacoma Community College Library had gathered an extensive collection of documents on the expulsion of the Tacoma Chinese and offered helpful suggestions as to their significance.

I have also drawn on the resources of the Oregon Historical Society, the Provincial Archives of British Columbia, the Fort Nisqually collection at Point Defiance in Tacoma, the Huntington Library, the Library of Congress, the National Archives, the National Maritime Museum at Greenwich, the British Library, and the Steilacoom Library, as well as the morgues at the Tacoma *News Tribune,* the Seattle *Post-Intelligencer,* the Chicago *Tribune,* the New York *Times,* and the Portland *Oregonian.*

Dr. Norman Clark of Everett Community College and Dr. Charles Pierce LeWarne each read the manuscript in two different versions. Their valuable suggestions supported those of my wife, Rosa, and led to substantial rewriting and improvements. Rosa also went over galley proofs and page proofs, did the indexing, and joined in the research.

Finally, I must mention the students in my classes at Tacoma Community College. During the past ten years they have written some three thousand research papers. Many have taken seriously the task of educating me, and their labors are reflected in this book.

To all, my deep appreciation.

Murray Morgan
Trout Lake
June 1979

Notes on Sources

There are certain basic works that must be consulted by any historian interested in this area. Primary among these for the early history of the area are Hubert Howe Bancroft's *History of Oregon, History of the Northwest Coast, History of British Columbia,* and, most important, *History of Washington, Idaho, and Montana,* all published in San Francisco by the History Company between 1884 and 1890. For the material on Tacoma, my most frequently used published source was Herbert Hunt's *Tacoma: Its History and Its Builders: A Half Century of Activity* (3 vols.; Chicago: S. J. Clarke, 1916). Hunt is also the source of most of the photographs not otherwise acknowledged. Other frequently used sources are William Pierce Bonney, *History of Pierce County, Washington* (3 vols.; Chicago: Pioneer Historical Publishing Co., 1927); Clinton A. Snowden, *History of Washington: The Rise and Progress of an American State* (6 vols.; New York: Century History Co., 1909); and Glenn Chesney Quiett, *They Built the West: An Epic of Rails and Cities* (1934; reprint ed., New York: Cooper Square, 1965).

Subsequent references to these works in the essays that follow will be cited in abbreviated form.

The Eyes of Discovery . . .

The documented history of the Puget Sound region begins with the visit of the Vancouver Expedition in 1792. The original documents I consulted were in the new Public Records Office (PRO) at Kew and the old Public Records Office at Chancery Lane, London; the British Library (BL); the Linnean Society (LS); the National Maritime Museum (NM), Greenwich; the British Museum of Natural History (BMNH), London; the Royal Botanic Gardens archives (RBG) at Kew; the Royal Scottish Botanical Society library, Edinburgh; and the Museo Naval, Madrid.

Most important were Peter Puget's journal, vol. 1 (PRO Adm 55/27), and Puget's rough journals and notes (BL, Add MSS 17541–17552); Archibald Menzies' journal (BL, Add MSS 32641) and Menzies' letters to Sir Joseph Banks (BMNH, Banks Correspondence, vols. 7–9; RBG, Menzies Correspondence, 1.163, 1.175, 1.1221, 1.356, 1.358, 2.150). Banks's instructions to Menzies are to be found in Banks Correspondence, vol. 7, BMNH. The Oregon Historical Society in Portland has an unfinished, unpublished biography of Menzies by Norah Gourlie (MS 1524). Personal relics of Menzies are in the Provincial Archives of British Columbia. Specimens he brought back from the Northwest Coast are preserved in the British Museum of Natural History, and descendants of some of the plants he collected in this area are growing at Kew and Edinburgh. The Linnean Society in London has a few of his sketches. (He was no artist.) The Museo Naval in Madrid has copies of information Vancouver gave Juan Francisco de la Bodega y Quadra concerning his charting of Puget Sound and the Strait of Georgia.

The most useful general books on the expedition are the official account by Captain Vancouver, *A Voyage of Discovery to the North Pacific Ocean and Round the World* (London, 1798); Edmond S. Meany's copiously footnoted *Vancouver's Discovery of Puget Sound* (New York: Macmillan Co., 1907); Archibald Menzies' *Journal of Vancouver's Voyages April to October 1792,* edited by C. F. Newcombe, British Columbia Archives Memoir no. 5 (Victoria: W. H. Cullin, 1923); and Bern Anderson's thorough *Surveyor of the Sea* (Seattle: University of Washington Press,, 1960).

Henry Wagner's *Cartography of the Northwest Coast of America to the Year 1800* (Berkeley: University of California Press, 1937) sets the Vancouver voyage in perspective. Robert B. Whitebrook's *Coastal Exploration of Washington* (Palo Alto, Calif.: Pacific Books, 1959) and his "Vancouver's Anchorages on Puget Sound," *Pacific Northwest Quarterly* (PNQ), 54 (July 1953): 115–24, are especially valuable for explaining the methods of the survey.

No full studies of Puget and Menzies exist, though both are covered in the *National Dictionary of Biography.* C. F. Newcombe has a profile of Menzies in his edition of the *Journal,* cited above.

See also: Erna Gunther, "Vancouver and the Indians of Puget Sound," *PNQ,* 51 (January 1960): 1–12; F. W. Howay, "Notes on Cook's and Vancouver's Ships," *Washington Historical Quarterly,* 21 (October 1930): 268–70; F. Bruce Sanford, "In the Wake of Captain Vancouver," *Northwest Magazine,* March 23, 1969; Adrien Mansvelt, "The Original Vancouver in Old Holland," Vancouver *Sun,* September 1, 1973; Marion H. Johnson, "The Last Search for the Northwest Passage," *Oceans,* 9, no. 5 (September 1976): 30–37.

The Eyes of Exploitation . . .

Most of this chapter derives from published sources, although I consulted the original copies of the journals of John Work and William Fraser Tolmie, and Tolmie's unpublished "History of Puget Sound and the Northwest Coast, 1878," all of which are at the Provincial Archives of British Columbia in Victoria; the H. H. Bancroft file of "Miscellaneous Correspondence concerning Oregon" and the Frances Fuller Victor file of "Correspondence and Notes concerning Oregon" at the Bancroft Library, Berkeley; a photocopy of A. C. Anderson's manuscript on "The Origin of the Puget Sound Agricultural Company" at the University of Washington Library; and the typescript of George Traill Allan's "Reminiscences of Fort Vancouver, as it stood in 1832" at the Fort Vancouver Historical Site.

Of published sources, Bancroft's histories form the Old Testament for this period of Puget Sound history. The account of Oskonton, How-how, and the closing of the Cowlitz River is drawn from his *History of the Northwest Coast* and from Washington Irving's *Astoria: or, Anecdotes of an Enterprise beyond the Rocky Mountains* (1836; reprint ed., Norman: University of Oklahoma Press, 1964).

George Simpson is profiled in the *National Dictionary of Biography;* by E. E. Rich in *Part of Dispatch from George Simpson, Esqr.,* Publications of the Hudson's Bay Record Society, vol. 10 (London, 1947); and in a brilliant introductory essay by Frederick Merk to Simpson's journal for 1824–25, published under the title *Fur Trade and Empire* (Cambridge, Mass.: Harvard University Press, 1968).

John McLoughlin has had more written about him than any other Northwest figure. Burt Brown Barker's *The McLoughlin Empire and Its Rulers* (Glendale, Calif.: Arthur H. Clark Co., 1959) is the most complete. William R. Sampson has an excellent short profile in the Introduction to *John McLoughlin's Business Correspondence, 1847–48* (Seattle: University of Washington Press, 1973). John Work is covered best in the *Dictionary of Canadian Biography.* Gloria Griffen Cline has done a marvellous job of research in *Peter Skene Ogden and the Hudson's Bay Company* (Norman: University of Oklahoma Press, 1974).

The narrative of the McMillan-Work journey is drawn from Work's journal, part of which has been reprinted in vol. 3 of *American Indian Ethnohistory,* edited by David Agee Horr (New York: Garland, 1974).

Tolmie's trip up the Cowlitz comes from his journal, which has been reprinted as *Physician and Fur Trader,* edited by R. G. Large (Vancouver, B.C.: Mitchell Press, 1963). Aubrey L. Haines's history of Mount Rainier, *Mountain Fever* (Portland: Oregon Historical Society, 1962), explains the route followed by Tolmie in his approach to the Mountain.

The Princess Story: A Century and a Half of West Coast Shipping by Norman R. Hocking and W. Kaye Lamb (Vancouver, B.C.: Mitchell Press, 1974) and *Lewis and Dryden's Marine History of the Pacific Northwest,* edited by E. W. Wright (Portland, 1895), supplied the background for the story of Hudson's Bay Company shipping problems. The descriptions of Fort Vancouver are drawn largely from John A. Hussey's detailed *The History of Fort Vancouver and Its Physical Structure* (Tacoma: Washington State Historical Society, 1957).

Ralph R. Martig's "Hudson's Bay Company Claims, 1846–69," *Oregon Historical Quarterly,* 36, no. 1 (March 1935): 60–70, offers an interesting summary of the company's land holdings. The fullest description is in the fourteen-volume *Papers of the British and American Joint Commission for the Final Settlement of the Claims of the Hudson's Bay and Puget's Sound Agricultural Companies* (Washington/Montreal, 1865–69). Volumes 6, 7, 10, 11, and 14 have special reference to the Puget's Sound Agricultural Company.

The Eyes of Empire . . .

The delight in researching this section lay in reading the microfilms of the original journals of the Wilkes expedition, most of which are available through the National Archives. They provide varied impressions of the Oregon Country during the period of joint occupation. Those with the most detail about the Pacific Northwest are Wilkes (Rolls 7–9), George Sinclair (Roll 21), John W. W. Dyes (Roll 11), Joseph P. Sanford (Roll 19), Robert E. Johnson (Roll 15), William Briscoe (Roll 13), and R. P. Robinson (Roll 22).

The most helpful published sources were Wilkes, *Narrative of the United States Exploring Expedition* (Philadelphia, 1845); Wilkes, "Synopsis of the Cruise of the U.S. Exploring Expedition," a paper delivered before the National Institute, and published in Washington, 1842; George M. Colvocoresses, *Four Years in a Government Expedition* (New York, 1852); Charles Erskine, *Twenty Years before the Mast* (Philadelphia, 1896); Jessie Poesch, *Titian Ramsay Peale and His Journals of the Wilkes Expedition,* American Philosophical Society Memoirs, vol. 52 (Philadelphia, 1961); and *1841, Fourth of July, 1906: Commemorative Celebration at Sequalitchew Lake* (Tacoma: Pierce County Pioneer Association, 1906).

William Stanton's *The Great United States Exploring Expedition* (Berkeley and Los Angeles: University of California Press, 1975) is excellent on the scientific background and accomplishments of the voyage. David B. Tyler's *The Wilkes Expedition* (Philadelphia: American Philosophical Society, 1968) offers a good summary of the cruise. Vincent Ponko has an interesting account in chapter 3 of *Ships, Seas, and Scientists* (Annapolis, Md.: Naval Institute Press, 1970); and Susan Schlee discusses the expedition's place in the history of oceanography in *The Edge of an Unfamiliar World* (New York: Dutton, 1973).

The Letters of John McLoughlin from Fort Vancouver to the Governor and Committee, Second Series, 1839–44, edited by E. E. Rich, Hudson's Bay Company Series, vol. 6 (Toronto: Champlain Society, 1943), discuss the presence of the expedition in the Oregon Country (pp. 95–105). Useful articles include Captain G. S. Bryan's "The Purpose, Equipment, and Personnel of the Wilkes Expedition" in *Proceedings of the American Philosophical Society,* 82 (1940): 551–59, and James Dana's "Notes on Upper California" in the *American Journal of Science,* 1849. A version of Wilkes's Oregon diary, edited by Edmond S. Meany, can be found in the *Washington Historical Quarterly,* 16 (1925): 49–61, 137–45, 207–23, 291–301; 17 (1926): 43–65, 129–44, 223–29. *WHQ,* 21 (July 1930): 218–29, has Brackenridge's Oregon journal, edited by O. B. Sperlin, under the title "Our First Official Horticulturist."

The Slacum material is drawn from *Memorial of William A. Slacum,* Senate Ex. Doc. 24, 25th Cong., 2d sess., December 18, 1837. See also "Slacum's Report on Oregon, 1836–37" in the *Oregon Historical Quarterly,* 13 (June 1912): 175–224, and "Slacum of the Pacific, 1832–37: Backgrounds of the Oregon Report" by David T. Leary, *OHQ,* 76, no. 2 (June 1975): 3–67.

H. H. Bancroft's *History of Oregon,* vol. 1, and David Lavender's *Land of Giants: The Drive to the Pacific Northwest, 1750–1950* (Garden City, N.Y.: Doubleday, 1958) have interesting accounts of Slacum, and he is mentioned in Wilkes's *Narrative.*

The politics of the dispute over the boundary is best covered in Frederick Merk's volume of essays, *The Oregon Question* (Cambridge, Mass.: Harvard University Press, 1967), and summarized in chap. 35 ("The Oregon Question") in his posthumous *History of the Westward Movement* (New York: Alfred A. Kropf, 1978).

The odd performance of Captain the Honorable John Gordon is detailed by Barry M. Gough in *The Royal Navy and the Northwest Coast of America, 1810–1914* (Vancouver: University of British Columbia Press, 1971). The "Journal of HMS America," kept by Lieutenant Thomas Dawes, is in the National Maritime Museum, Greenwich, and the log of the same ship is in the Public Records Office, Kew (Adm 53/1946).

The *Oregon Historical Quarterly,* 10, no. 1 (March 1909): 1–24, carried "Documents Relative to Warre and Vavasour's Military Reconnaissance in Oregon, 1845–46," edited by Joseph Schafer. The Northwest Collection of the University of Washington Library has a typescript of the Colonial Office copy of Vavasour's report, and the recommendations of the two agents. Sixteen lithographs of Warre's sketches, and a brief description of his trip (without mention of its secret purpose) were published in London under the title *Sketches in North America and the Oregon Territory.* Peter Skene Ogden's account of their trip to the Columbia is included in chap. 7 of Gloria Cline's biography, *Peter Skene Ogden and the Hudson's Bay Company* (Norman: University of Oklahoma Press, 1974). Father De Smet's impressions of the agents are given in *The Life, Letters, and Travels of Father Pierre-Jean De Smet, S.J., 1801–1873,* edited by H. M. Chittenden and A. T. Richardson (4 vols.; New York: Francis P. Harper, 1905), 2:485. A typescript copy of the "Fort Nisqually Blotter," listing the presence of Warre and Lieutenant Robert Peel on Puget Sound, is in the University of Washington Library. The activities of Peel are covered in "Report of Lieut. Peel on Oregon in 1845–46," edited by Leslie M. Scott, in the *OHQ,* 29 (March 1928): 51–76. Captain Gordon's denigration of Vancouver Island is quoted in the *Biography of Roderick Finlayson* (Victoria, 1891), p. 15, and his comment on Pacific salmon is quoted by John T. Walbran in *British Columbia Coast Names* (1909; reprint ed., Seattle: University of Washington Press, 1972), p. 210.

Material on George Washington Bush and Michael Troutman Simmons is to be found in all standard histories of the area, including those by Bancroft, Snowden, Hunt, Bonney, and Elwood Evans, *Washington Territory: Her Past, Her Present, and the Elements of Wealth Which Ensure Her Future* (Olympia, 1877). Robert Cantwell has a charming account of his ancestor, Simmons, in *The Hidden Northwest* (Philadelphia: Lippincott, 1972), though he errs in describing Bush as a former slave. The most reliable work on Bush is Paul Thomas' 1965 master's thesis, University of Washington. The Bush Papers in the University of Washington Archives contain descriptions of the Bush farm. Bureau of the Census publications touching on the question of Bush's ethnic heritage include *Compendium of the Seventh Cen-*

sus; *Negro Population, 1790–1915; Preliminary Report on the Eighth Census, 1860.*

The Engineer and the Indians

The story of Nicholas Delin and his mill is told in Hunt's *Tacoma,* vol. 1; Bonney's *Pierce County,* vol. 1; William Prosser's *A History of the Puget Sound Country,* vol. 1; and, most fully, in Hans Bergman's *History of Scandinavians in Tacoma and Pierce County* (Tacoma: privately printed, 1926).

For Isaac Ingall Stevens, the basic biography remains that by his son, Hazard, worshipful though it may be. Kent Richards' "Isaac I. Stevens and Federal Military Power in Washington Territory," *Pacific Northwest Quarterly,* 63 (July 1972): 81–86, offers promise that his work-in-progress will provide a more balanced biography. Vol. 12 of *Reports of Explorations and Surveys to Ascertain the Most Practicable and Economic Route for a Railroad from the Mississippi River to the Pacific Ocean* (Government Printing Office, 1855) describes Stevens' survey in detail.

No events in Puget Sound history have given rise to such prolonged and bitter controversy as the negotiation of the Indian treaties by Governor Stevens in 1854 and 1855, especially the Medicine Creek Treaty, the interpretation of which is in 1979 again before the United States Supreme Court.

The best summary of the treaty making is to be found not in a book but, rather, in Judge George H. Boldt's lengthy decision in the case of *United States of America v. State of Washington* filed in U.S. District Court, Western District of Washington at Tacoma, January 11, 1974. The Boldt decision, along with the exhibits by plaintiff and defendant, constitute an exceptionally detailed picture of conditions in Washington Territory shortly after its separation from Oregon.

In addition to Bancroft, *History of Washington . . . ,* Hunt, *Tacoma,* vol. 1, and Bonney, *Pierce County,* vol. 1, books dealing with the treaty period which I consulted include: *Uncommon Controversy: Fishing Rights of the Muckleshoot, Puyallup and Nisqually Indians,* a report prepared for the American Friends Service Committee (Seattle: University of Washington Press, 1970); *Pioneer Reminiscences of Puget Sound: The Tragedy of Leschi,* by Ezra Meeker (Seattle, 1905); *Reminiscences of Seattle, Washington Territory, and of the U.S. Sloop-of-War Decatur during the Indian War of 1855–56,* by Thomas Phelps (reprint ed., Fairfield, Wash.: Ye Galleon Press, 1971); *Messages of the Governors of the Territory of Washington to the Legislative Assembly, 1854–1889,* edited by Charles Gates (Seattle: University of Washington Press, 1940); *Reminiscences of Washington Territory,* by Charles Prosch (Seattle, 1904); *Recollections and Reminiscenses,* by Andrew Jackson Chambers (written 1904; privately printed, Tacoma, 1947); "The Indians' Side of the Story," by Henry Sicade, in *Building a State,* edited by Charles Miles and O. B. Sperlin (Tacoma: Washington State Historical Society, 1940); *The Official History of the Washington National Guard,* vol. 2: *Washington Territorial Militia in the Indians Wars of 1855–56* (Camp Murray, Wash., n.d.); "Puyallup Indian War: The Stevens-Wool Letters," bound file, Tacoma Public Library; *Indian Wars of the Pacific Northwest,* by Ray H. Glassley (Portland: Binford and Mort, 1972); "A Documentary History of Fort Steilacoom," by Gary Fuller Reese, typescript, Tacoma Public Library, 1978; *Records of the Proceedings of the Commission to hold treaties with the Indian tribes in Washington Territory and the Blackfoot Country* (National Archives, no. 1391, Medicine Creek Treaty).

The Washington State Historical Society has a clipping file of stories about the Medicine Creek Treaty written by Ezra Meeker, Benjamin Franklin Shaw, Edward Huggins, and Hazard Stevens between 1892 and 1904, in which they argued such issues as whether Leschi signed the treaty.

Cecelia Svinth Carpenter, the Nisqually tribal historian, has written the most reliable short biography of Leschi, which appeared in *Pacific Northwest Forum,* 1, no. 1 (January 1976): 4–11, under the title "Leschi: Last Chief of the Nisquallies." Mrs. Carpenter has also written a master's thesis, "Troubled Waters of Medicine Creek" (Pacific Lutheran University, 1971), and *They Walked Before: The Indians of Washington State* (Tacoma: Washington State Historical Society, 1977).

Leschi's first trial is covered in *Pioneer Reminiscences* by Ezra Meeker, a member of the jury. The second trial is summarized in *Territory of Washington vs. Leschi (an Indian): Transcript of Court Proceedings of the Trial of Leschi in the District Court for the Second Judicial District, W.T.* Other views of the trial are to be found in chap. 2 of the biography *Gen. August V. Kautz and the Southwestern Frontier* by Andrew Wallace (Tucson: privately printed, 1967); in a letter from Col. Granville O. Haller to the Seattle *Post-Intelligencer,* August 11, 1895, headlined "The Tragedy of Leschi"; and in Martin Schmitt's "The Execution of Chief Leschi and the 'Truth Teller,' " *Oregon Historical Quarterly,* 50 (March 1949): 9–39.

"The Martial Law Controversy in Washington Territory, 1856," by Roy N. Lokken, *Pacific Northwest Quarterly,* 43 (April 1952): 91–119, is the best summary of Stevens' attempts to prosecute the Muck Creek settlers. Other sources include the *Journal of the Council of the Territory of Washington . . . Session of 1857;* files of the Olympia *Pioneer and Democrat,* 1855–57; *Puget Sound Courier,* 1855–56; *Brief Notice of the Recent Outrages Committed by Isaac I. Stevens, Governor of Washington Territory,* by William H. Wallace and others (Olympia, 1856); *Proceedings of the Meeting of the Bar, Third Judicial District, Washington Territory, on the Arrest of the Hon. Edward Landers, Chief Justice of Said Territory . . . by an Armed Force, under Orders of Governor Isaac I. Stevens, together with the Proceedings of a Mass Meeting of Citizens of Pierce Co., W.T.* (Steilacoom, May 7, 1856); and *Vindication of Governor Stevens, for Proclaiming and Enforcing Martial Law in Pierce County, W.T.,* by Isaac I. Stevens, (Olympia, May 10, 1856); "Martial Law in Washington Territory," by Captain Samuel F. Cohn, *Pacific Northwest Quarterly,* 27 (July 1936): 195–218; and "Governor Stevens' Famous Pardon of Himself," edited by Edmond S. Meany, *Washington Historical Quarterly,* 25 (July 1934): 229–30.

The Quaker, the Boomer, and the Railroad

I am indebted to Rick and Francie Carr of Tacoma for making available the diaries of Howard and Anthony Carr, Job Carr's sons, as well as Carr family letters, documents, and scrapbooks.

For material on McCarver I relied primarily on *McCarver and Tacoma* (Seattle, 1906), making allowances for the fact that McCarver's biographer, Thomas Prosch, was also his son-in-law. Other McCarver material can be found in Bancroft, *History of Washington . . . ;* Hunt, *Tacoma,* vol. 1; Bonney, *Pierce County,* vol. 1; Clinton A. Snowden, *History of Washington,* vol. 2; and Charles H. Carey, *General History of Oregon* (3d ed.; Portland: Binford and Mort, 1971).

Thomas R. Cox's *Mills and Markets: A History of the Pacific Coast Lumber Industry to 1900* (Seattle: University of Washington Press, 1974) tells the story of Hanson, Ackerson, and Co.

The best single source for the story of the transcontinental railroads and the cities of the Northwest is *They Built the West* by Glenn Chesney Quiett. Quiett's 38-page chapter on Tacoma is the best sketch yet written about the city. David Lavender has a brilliant section on the railroads "Extravaganza," in *Land of Giants: The Drive to the Pacific Northwest, 1750–1950* (Garden City, N.Y.: 1958), and Stewart Holbrook has numerous entertaining portraits of the empire builders and grabbers in *The Age of the Moguls* (Garden City, N.Y.: Doubleday, 1953).

William Canfield's quotation about enlisting William Butler Ogden's support is from Hunt, *Tacoma,* vol. 1. Mrs. James B. Montgomery tells the story of her husband's work on the Kalama-to-Tacoma spur, "The First Railroad," in *Building a State,* edited by Charles Miles and O. B. Sperlin (Tacoma: Washington State Historical Society, 1940). James Swan's railroad survey is covered in *Swan among the Indians* by Lucile McDonald (Portland: Binford and Mort, 1972). Henrietta M. Larson gives a favorable view of Jay Cooke in *Jay Cooke, Private Banker* (Cambridge, Mass.: Harvard University Press, 1936); and Matthew Josephson an unfavorable one in *The Robber Barons: The Great American Capitalists, 1861–1901* (New York: Harcourt, Brace and Co., 1934).

The most complete work on the construction of the Northern Pacific main line is to be found in Eugene V. Smalley, *History of the Northern Pacific Railroad* (New York: 1883). *"He Built Seattle": A Biography of Judge Thomas Burke* by Robert C. Nesbit (Seattle: University of Washington Press, 1961) is excellent on Seattle's reaction to Tacoma's selection as terminus. Articles include "The Northern Pacific Railroad and Some of Its History" by H. W. Fairweather, *Washington Historical Quarterly,* 10 (April 1919): 95–100; and "A History of the Railroads in Washington" by Sol H. Lewis, *WHQ,* 3 (July 1912): 186–97. There is more material than can easily be absorbed in *Investigation of the Northern Pacific Railroad* by United States Congress Joint Committee (Washington, D.C.: Government Printing Office, 1925–28).

Samuel Wilkeson gives a promoter's view of the terminal area in *Notes on Puget Sound,* a 47-page pamphlet published in 1870.

The best account of the decision to make Tacoma the terminus is to be found in a master's thesis by Robert Dean Palmer, "The Northern Pacific Railroad and Its Choice of a Western Terminus" (University of Washington, 1968).

The Gap Is Closed

Charles B. Wright is the subject of an admiring, privately printed biography by his grandson-in-law, Thomas Porter Harney: *Charles Barstow Wright, 1822–1898, a Builder of the Northern Pacific Railroad and of the City of Tacoma* (1926). His career to 1883 is summarized by Eugene V. Smalley, *History of the Northern Pacific Railroad* (New York, 1883).

Papers of the Tacoma Land Company are to be found at the Tacoma Public Library and in the St. Paul and Tacoma Lumber Company collection, University of Washington Manuscript Collection.

There is an abundant literature on Frederick Law Olmsted but the books contain nothing about his aborted plan for Tacoma. It is treated superficially in Hunt, *Tacoma,* vol. 1, but is well reported by Norman J. Johnston, professor of architecture and urban planning at the University of Washington, in "The Frederick Law Olmsted Plan for Tacoma," *Pacific Northwest Quarterly,* 66 (July 1975): 97–104.

William Blackwell appears in Hunt, *Tacoma,* vol. 3; in Thomas Ripley's *Green Timber* (Tacoma: Washington State Historical Society, 1968); and in Charles Prosch's *Reminiscences of Washington Territory: Scenes, Incidents, and Reflections of the Pioneer Period on Puget Sound* (1904; reprint ed., Fairfield, Wash.: Ye Galleon Press, 1969). I have also drawn on a 5-page typescript of "Pioneer Hotels," by William B. Blackwell, which is in the Tacoma Community College Library.

For Henry Villard I found the best sources to be *Henry Villard and the Railways of the Northwest* by James Blaine Hedges (New Haven, Conn.: Yale University Press, 1930), and *The Early History of Transportation in Oregon* by Henry Villard (edited by Oswald Garrison Villard) (Eugene: University of Oregon Press, 1944). There is also the *Memoirs of Henry Villard, Journalist and Financier, 1835–1900* (2 vols.; Boston: Houghton Mifflin, 1904), a stately apologia but with some valuable material on the Pacific Northwest in its second volume.

The description of travel between Tacoma and Portland prior to the railroad is based on an article in the Tacoma *Ledger,* January 4, 1884.

A useful source for railroad information is "The Development of Railroads in the State of Washington, 1860 to 1948, Parts 1 and 2," a master's thesis by Bruce Bissell Cheever (Western Washington College of Education, 1949).

"Bore, Bennett, Bore"

Virgil Bogue told the story of his discovery of Stampede Pass in the *Bulletin of the American Geographical Society.* It was reprinted in the Seattle *Post-Intelligencer,* October 27, 1895. The account of the naming of the pass is taken from an address by W. P. Bonney, secretary of the Washington State Historical Society, at the Twenty-ninth Annual Farmers' Picnic in Enumclaw on August 6, 1921, during which he quoted from a letter written to him by Bogue. Information on Bogue's later career can be found in *Seattle: Past to Present* by Roger Sale (Seattle: University of Washington Press, 1976).

Robert C. Nesbit's *"He Built Seattle": A Biography of Judge Thomas Burke* (Seattle: University of Washington Press, 1961) is excellent on the politics of the proposed land grant forfeiture, which led to the construction of the Cascade Division.

Nelson Bennett is profiled in Hunt, *Tacoma*, vol. 3, and other subscription histories. The narrative of the Stampede Tunnel is taken from "The Cascade Tunnel" in *The Magazine of Western History*, March 1891. Stewart Holbrook drew from the same source in "The Saga of Stampede Pass," chapter 17 of *The Story of American Railroads* (New York: Crown, 1947). My version is supplemented with stories from the Tacoma *News*, Tacoma *Ledger*, Seattle *Post-Intelligencer*, and the typescript of the R. F. Radebaugh memoirs, Tacoma Public Library.

"The Chinese Must Go"

The Tacoma Community College Library has assembled three filing drawers of documents on the Chinese in the Pacific Northwest. The collection, supervised by Lorraine Barker Hildebrand (the author of *Straw Hats, Sandals, and Steel: The Chinese in Washington State* [Tacoma: Washington State–American Revolution Bicentennial Commission, 1977]), includes reproductions of all news stories in the Tacoma *Ledger* about the Chinese expulsion.

Affidavits from the Chinese concerning the Tacoma expulsion were located, unexpectedly, in Miscellaneous Letters of the Department of State, 1789–1906, National Archives, Microfilm Pub. no. M-179, Roll 707, July 17–31, 1886.

The United States district attorney's reports on the Squak Valley murders and the Tacoma expulsion are in U.S. Congress, 2d sess., House Executive Documents, 1886–1887, vol. 9 (Government Printing Office, 1887); and in U.S. Department of the Interior, *Report of the Secretary of the Interior, 1886* (Government Printing Office, 1886).

General Records of the Department of State, Record Group 59, *Despatches from U.S. Ministers to China* in the National Archives (Microfilm Pub. no. M-92, rolls 74–79, 1885–86) contain material bearing on the question of reparations by the United States for the assaults on the Chinese. No breakdown of the distribution of the $276,619.75 "to the Chinese Government as full indemnity for all losses and injuries sustained by Chinese Subjects within the United States at the hands of residents thereof" has been located.

Public Records Office files at Kew contain the reports of the British consul at San Francisco and the subconsul at Port Townsend on anti-Chinese agitation, but no reference to British subjects of Chinese extraction whom newspaper accounts say were expelled from Tacoma.

The Tacoma Public Library has the unpublished manuscript of David

LeSourd's "Sketches of an Itinerant's Career," which has valuable material on the agitation in Seattle. The papers used by Herbert Hunt in compiling his *History of Tacoma* are at the Washington State Historical Society, and are rich in anti-Chinese detail. WSHS also has the original copy of "Sentiments of the Ministerial Union of Tacoma respecting the Present anti-Chinese Question," adopted October 26, 1885. The "Journal of the Proceedings of the Common Council of the City of Tacoma" during the period of hysteria is in the Tacoma Public Library.

Robert E. Mack's bachelor's thesis in history, Harvard College, 1972, "The Seattle and Tacoma anti-Chinese Riots of 1885 and 1886," is in the Tacoma Community College Library. Robert E. Wynne's doctoral thesis, "Reaction to the Chinese in the Pacific Northwest and British Columbia, 1850–1910," University of Washington, 1964, is available in reprint: Ann Arbor, Mich., University Microfilms, 1972.

"The Anti-Chinese Outbreak in Tacoma, 1885," by Jules Alexander Karlin, appeared in *Pacific Northwest Quarterly,* 39, no. 2 (April 1948): 103–30. The apologia for the expulsion, "The Tacoma Method," by one of the participants, George Dudley Lawson, first appeared in the *Overland Monthly,* 2 (1886): 239–40. Ronald DeLorme gives the background for reports of illegal Chinese immigration in "The United States Bureau of Customs, and Smuggling on Puget Sound, 1851–1913" in *Prologue: The Journal of the National Archives,* 5, no. 2 (Summer 1973): 77–88.

Alexander Saxton's *The Indispensable Enemy: Labor and the Anti-Chinese Movement in California* (Berkeley: University of California Press, 1971) is the indispensable book for understanding the use made of prejudice by labor organizers and other groups usually thought of as liberal or progressive. Saxton is rewarding, too, in his study of national attitudes, and his book is the source of most of my quotations demonstrating Sinophobia in high places.

Thomas Ripley's *Green Timber* (Tacoma: Washington State Historical Society, 1968) reflects the Tacoma hysteria as recalled long afterwards by a man who was young at the time. Ruby Chapin Blackwell's *A Girl in Washington Territory* (Tacoma: Washington State Historical Society, 1972) expresses the attitude of the antiexpulsion element. The Tacoma *News* and Tacoma *Ledger* were models of bias in their reporting of the question.

There is a short biography of Watson Squire in *Messages of the Governors of the Territory of Washington to the Legislative Assembly, 1854–89,* edited by Charles M. Gates (Seattle: University of Washington Press, 1940), and in *Meet the Governors* by Louis A. Magrini (Tacoma: Washington State Historical Society, 1946).

I am indebted to the Kansas Historical Society for biographic information of Jacob Robert Weisbach.

Instant Tacoma

The best accounts of this period are in Thomas Ripley's *Green Timber* (Tacoma: Washington State Historical Society, 1968) and the Tacoma chapter of Quiett's *They Built the West.* The authorized biographies in Hunt's *Ta-*

coma, vols. 2 and 3, are rich in unexpected detail though shy of much criticism of their subjects. Tacoma as boom-town is covered interestingly in *The Pacific Scenic Tour* by Henry L. Finck (New York, 1891), pp. 217–25.

My sketch on Allen C. Mason is drawn largely from Hunt, Quiett, the R. F. Radebaugh memoirs (typescript at Tacoma Public Library), and the Mason file at the Washington State Historical Society. The files of the major Tacoma papers of the 1880s–the *Ledger, News, Globe,* and *Herald*—were useful on Mason and on much else in this chapter. Mason's real estate activities are covered in *Real Estate Journal.* The Tacoma Public Library has a bound collection of newspapers stories, "Tacoma Street Car Lines," which describe some of his transportation activities, as does the typescript "The Early History of Street Cars in Tacoma," by Clinton Reynolds, and two papers prepared for my history of Tacoma class, "Tacoma Transit Then and Now" by Richard E. Septon, and "Tacoma Street Railways and Related Lines" by Jean C. Gobel, copies of which are on file in the Tacoma Community College Library.

Mills and Markets by Thomas R. Cox (Seattle: University of Washington Press, 1974) is especially good on the growth of the lumber industry and the expansion of markets around the Pacific Rim in the 1880s. *The Lumber Industry in Washington,* edited by Roy Melton, and published by the Washington Secretary of State, 1941, is an excellent source of information on early lumbering. Chauncey Griggs, Henry Hewitt, Jr., Charles H. Jones, and A. G. Foster, the founding fathers of the St. Paul and Tacoma Lumber Company, appear in all of the subscription histories of the period. An authorized history of the St. Paul and Tacoma, exceptionally well illustrated, was carried as an advertising supplement in *American Lumberman,* May 21, 1921.

My version of the founding of Foss Launch and Tug Company comes from interviews with Henry and Andrew Foss, two of the sons of Thea and Andrew Foss, and from company records at the Tacoma and Seattle offices.

The account of the founding of the Tacoma Smelter is drawn from Hunt, *Tacoma,* vol. 2, and the newspapers of the period.

The adventures and misadventures of Harry Morgan in Tacoma are chronicled extensively and with unabashed bias in the Tacoma *Ledger,* starting in February 1884 and ending with his obituary on April 26, 1890. Other obituary notices were carried by the Tacoma *Morning Globe,* April 27 and 29; and the Tacoma *News* (reprinted from the Fairview *Herald*), April 30. The locations of Morgan's various billiard parlors, box-houses, gambling joints, and theaters were traced through the *Polk City Directories,* 1885–91, and the public aspect of his relations with city officials in "Journals of the Proceedings of the Common Council" in the Tacoma Public Library. Records of the probate of the estate of Henry S. "Harry" Morgan are in Will Probate File 809, Pierce County Clerk's office.

C. P. Ferry's successes are chronicled by Hunt, *Tacoma,* vol. 3; his second honeymoon, in considerable detail, in the Tacoma *Ledger.* Kipling's account of his visit to Tacoma appeared in *From Sea to Sea* (New York, 1899).

The Uses of Adversity

Howard Preston's chapter, "Banking and Finance," in *Building a State*, edited by Charles Miles and O. B. Sperlin (Tacoma: Washington State Historical Society, 1940), gives background on the Panic of 1893 in Washington. Hunt, *Tacoma*, vol. 2, and Quiett, *They Built the West*, detail the effect of the collapse on Tacoma. "Building the Good Life," chap. 3 of Norman H. Clark's bicentennial history, *Washington* (New York: W. W. Norton, 1976), brilliantly portrays the period.

The story of William and Alice Blackwell during the Panic period is drawn largely from Ruby Chapin Blackwell's *A Girl in Washington Territory* (Tacoma: Washington State Historical Society, 1972); the Blackwell Papers at the Washington State Historical Society; "The Tacoma Hotel," a collection of newspaper clippings at the Tacoma Public Library; and obituary notices on William Blackwell.

The rise of Paul Schulze is described in Hunt, *Tacoma*, vol. 2, and in Eugene V. Smalley, *History of the Northern Pacific* (New York, 1883). Details of his fall are to be found in the daily press of his time.

Coxey's Army: A Study of the Industrial Army Movement of 1894 by Donald L. McMurry (1929; reprint ed., Seattle: University of Washington Press, 1961) is good for the national background on the activities of the unemployed during that depression. *The Story of the Commonweal* by Henry Vincent (Chicago, 1894) is the official account of the Coxey movement. Firsthand accounts of the march are found in W. T. Stead, "Coxeyism: A Character Sketch" and "Marching Itinerary of the Industrials," both in *American Review of Reviews,* July 1894, pp. 47–56; in "A Jack London Diary: Tramping with Kelly through Iowa," *Palimpset,* 7 (May 1926): 129–58; and in London's "The March of Kelly's Army: The Story of an Extraordinary Migration," *Cosmopolitan,* 43 (October 1907): 643–48.

Accounts of Frank and Charlotta Cantwell and of the march of the Tacoma and Seattle armies are drawn from the Seattle *Post-Intelligencer,* Seattle *Call,* Seattle *Press-Times,* Tacoma *Daily Ledger,* Tacoma *Daily News,* Tacoma *Daily Union,* the Kittitas *Equalizer,* and the Spokane *Spokesman-Review.*

Mount Rainier, a Record of Exploration by Edmond S. Meany (New York, 1916), and *Mountain Fever: Historical Conquests of Rainier* by Aubrey L. Haines (Portland: Oregon Historical Society, 1962) have considerable material on the controversy over the name of the Mountain. The Washington State Historical Society is the repository for the extensive collection compiled by the "Justice to the Mountain Committee." C. T. Conover's "Mount Rainier and the Facts of History" in *The Great Myth: Mount Tacoma* (Olympia: privately printed, 1924) is the most vehement assault on the idea that the Mountain ever was called *Tacoma.*

For a statement of the theory that Seattle's exploitation of the Klondike-Alaska gold rush was the decisive factor in the Seattle-Tacoma rivalry, see Murray Morgan, *Skid Road* (rev. ed., New York: Viking Press, 1960). Roger Sale in *Seattle, Past to Present* (Seattle: University of Washington Press, 1976), takes the position that Seattle's success was already assured.

Quiett, *They Built the West,* is excellent on the boost that Jim Hill's Great Northern gave the Seattle economy. The Tacoma daily papers, and Hunt, *Tacoma,* vol. 2, record Tacoma's disorganized response to the opportunity of the gold rush. "A History of Early Waterfront Organizations in Tacoma," a typescript at the Tacoma Public Library, reflects the situation in its only entry for 1897. The Chauncey Griggs Letterbook in the St. Paul and Tacoma File, University of Washington Manuscripts Collection, reflects the impact of the gold rush on the economy.

Population figures for Tacoma and Seattle were drawn from federal census reports, the *Polk City Directories,* and *Fifty Years of Population Growth in Washington, 1890–1940,* by Paul H. Landis (Pullman: Washington State University, 1942).

Absentees and Hometowners

For the Weyerhaeusers, the basic book remains *Timber and Men: The Weyerhaeuser Story,* by Ralph W. Hidy, Frank Ernest Hill, and Allen Nevins (New York: Macmillan, 1963), authorized though it may be. The James Hill–Frederick Weyerhaeuser connection is covered in lively fashion by Stewart Holbrook in *James J. Hill: A Great Life in Brief* (New York: Random House, 1955), and at greater length by Albro Martin in *James J. Hill and the Opening of the Northwest* (New York: Oxford University Press, 1976).

Holbrook's *The Age of the Moguls* (Garden City, N.Y.: Doubleday, 1953) encapsulates the creation of the American Smelting and Refining Company in part 5, "Dynastic Succession." A fuller treatment is given in *Metal Magic: The Story of the American Smelting and Refining Company* by Isaac F. Marcosson (New York: Farrar, Straus, 1949). The company, its founders, and its heirs are studied in *The Guggenheims and the American Dream* by Edwin P. Hoyt (New York: Funk and Wagnall, 1967). Hunt, *Tacoma,* vol. 2, gives some details of the Guggenheims' purchase of the Tacoma Smelter from William Rust and associates. Margaret L. Coit has a fuller account in the "Easy Money" chapter of *Mr. Baruch* (Boston: Houghton Mifflin, 1957), and Bernard Baruch tells his own version of the way he earned his million-dollar fee in *My Own Story* (New York: Holt, Rinehart and Winston, 1957).

David Lavender, *Land of Giants: The Drive to the Pacific Northwest, 1750–1950* (Garden City, N.Y.: Doubleday, 1958), and Glenn Chesney Quiett, *They Built the West,* each give good summaries of the complex railroad maneuverings involving James J. Hill and Edward Harriman that followed the Supreme Court decision in 1904 on the Northern Securities case. Reports in the Tacoma papers of the day only add confusion.

The struggle over the Tacoma Light and Water Company purchase by the City of Tacoma is covered in Hunt's *Tacoma,* vol. 2, Bonney's *Pierce County,* vol. 2, and in Thomas Porter Harney's *Charles Barstow Wright, 1822–1898* (Tacoma: privately printed, 1956), but the best source is the Washington Supreme Court transcript of *City of Tacoma, Respondent, versus Tacoma Light and Water Company, Appellant* (1897). Biographical material on James Wickersham during his Tacoma phase is to be found in Hunt, *Tacoma,* vol. 2; in the Wickersham folder at the Washington State

Historical Society; in the Bagley Scrapbook, vol. 5, in the University of Washington's Northwest Room, and in various issues of the Washington Legislative Manual between 1888 and 1895. Valuable data bearing on the purchase are found in graphs and charts in "A Financial History of the City of Tacoma, Washington from 1890 to 1948," by Samuel Leonard Heritage, a (master's thesis, University of Puget Sound, 1949).

Angelo Fawcett is subject of a somewhat hostile biographic sketch in Hunt, *Tacoma*, vol. 2, of innumerable editorial appraisals in the Tacoma papers over a forty-year period, and of a scholarly study by George W. Walk, "Fighting Fawcett: A Political Biography" (master's thesis, Western Washington University, 1976).

Tacoma's campaign to capture a military post payroll is covered in *Camp Murray Story: The Command Post* by Virgil Field (Tacoma: Washington State Historical Society, 1959); "Camp Lewis: Promotion and Construction" by Bernard L. Boyland, in *Pacific Northwest Quarterly*, 58 (October 1967): 188–95; *Camp Lewis* by Belmore Browne (Tacoma: Washington State Historical Society, 1918); "Camp Lewis" by Carl F. Pilat, in *Architectural Record*, 43 (1918): 52–64; and *Completion Report of Camp Lewis, Washington*, compiled by Lieutenant Colonel David Stone, Records of the Quartermaster General's Office, Record Group 92, June 1917–February 1919.

Index

Leschi of the Nisqually: denounces Medicine Creek Treaty terms, 94-98, 113-15, 120, 130, 134; pursued by Rangers, 101, 102; efforts for new treaty, 114-15; offers to lay down arms, 120; demands met in revised treaty, 130; offers surrender, 131; captured, 132; first trial, 132-33; second trial, 133-34; statement translated, 134; hanging, 135; reburial, 135
Lister Foundry, 270
Livensparger, J. C., 264-65
Long, George S., 304-5
Longmire, James, 81
Loriot, 42, 43
Lum May, 238

McAllister, James: member of Bush-Simmons party, 70, 74; warns of Indian rising, 100; joins Puget Sound Rangers, 101; death of, 101-2
McAllister, John, 195, 204
McCallum, David, 280
McCarver, Morton Matthew: early career, 144-47; buys Carr claim, 148; promotes townsite, 151; prospects for coal, 151; changes townsite name, 152-53; helps Hanson buy mill site, 154; brings family to Tacoma, 155; lines up property for NP, 164; helps drive last spike for Kalama-to-Tacoma spur, 167
McCaw, Sam, 80
McChord Air Field, 330
McClellan, Captain George B., 84-85, 86
McCormick, Robert Laird, 305
McDonald, Archibald, 29, 30
McFarland, Rev. W. D., 231, 239-40
McGraw, John M.: King County sheriff, 244-45; Washington governor, 286-87
McKenzie, Alexander, 26
McKnight, S. T., 303
McLeod, John, 120
McLoughlin, Dr. John: character, 24-25; punishes Clallam Indians, 26-28; proposes cattle ranch, 38-39; appointed to manage Puget's Sound Agricultural Company affairs, 39; entertains Slacum, 42; visited by Wilkes, 56; authorizes Tolmie to sell supplies to Bush-Simmons party, 74
McMillan, James, 20-24 passim
McMillan-Work brigade, 20-24
McNeil Island, 54
McNeill, Henry, 49, 54
McPhail, John, 122
Macready, Alex, 229
Madigan Army Hospital, 330
Mahncke, Henry, 277
Malaria, 31

Maloney, Capt. Maurice, 100, 106, 110, 114
Manning, Lucius R., 311
Manypenny, George, 130
Mark Ten Sui, 222
Marshall, James Wilson, 77-78
Martial law. *See* Indian War
Mashel River, 122
Mason, Allen, 254-55, 270
Mason, Charles, 88, 92, 99
Mason, Libbie (Mrs. Allen), 254-55
Mattice, Henry, 98
Maury, Lt. William, 54
Maury Island, 54
Maxon, Hamilton J. C., 122
Medicine Creek (She-nah-nam), 90
Medicine Creek Treaty: Stevens summons Indians to parlay, 90-91; members of U.S. delegation, 91-92; terms of, 93-94; Chinook Jargon used in translation, 95; Leschi's objections, 96; Leschi's name on treaty, 96; Indians ask revision, 97; Wickersham's evaluation of treaty, 97; treaty revised, 130. *See also* Indian War
Meeker, Ezra: juror in Leschi trial, 132-33; takes claim at Kalama, 160; opposes Chinese expulsion, 232-33; joins stampede to Klondike, 301
Meeker, John, 142-43
Meller, Gertrude, 82
Menzies, Archibald, 6, 17
Merchants National Bank, 276
Miiki Maru, 298
Miles, Joseph, 106-7, 132-34
Mills, Darius Ogden, 306-7
Minter Creek (Alarm Cove?), 11-12
Minto, John, 72
Mitchell, John H., 184
Mogul, 261
Montgomery, James: contracts to build spur from Kalama, 160-61, 165
Montgomery, Mary, 161, 165
Moore, Governor Marshall, 150
Morgan, Dora Charlotta. *See* Cantwell, Charlotta Morgan
Morgan, Harry, 263-67
Morgan, J. P., 187, 309
Morgan's Theater Comique, 265-66
Moses, A. Benton, 106-7, 132-34
Mosquito fleet, 261
Mount Rainier. *See* Rainier, Mount
Mount Rainier National Park, 296
Mount Tacoma. *See* Rainier, Mount
Municipal ownership: in Tacoma, 317, 320-24 passim
Murray, Henry, 79

Naches Pass, 55, 81, 85
Narrows, 8

terminus of Puget Sound spur, 160; elected mayor, 220; reassures Tacoma Chinese, 230; reports to Squire, 235

Squak Valley (Issaquah): massacre of Chinese, 226-27; participants acquitted, 236

Squire, Watson: character, 233-34; urges officials to protect Chinese, 235; takes no action, 243; warns against lawlessness, 245

Stahi (Nisqually Indian), 97

Stallcup, Judge John C., 317-18

Stampede Pass, 199, 200

Stampede Tunnel: contract awarded, 203; Bennetts drill tunnel, 203-11; Commonwealers walk through, 289

Starr, Lewis, 149, 178

State Savings Bank, 276

Steele, H. N., 154

Steele, Janet Elder, 154

Stevens, Hazard, 91, 165

Stevens, Isaac: appointed territorial governor, superintendent of Indian Affairs, commander of northern railroad survey, 84; conducts survey, 85-87; organizes territorial government, 88-89; negotiates Indian treaties, 90-98; returns to Olympia as war leader, 116-18; orders arrest of Muck Creek settlers, 122; declares martial law, 123-27; lifts martial law, 128; censured, 128; elected delegate to Congress, 136; killed in battle at Chantilly, 137

Stevens, John F., 311

Stewart, A. Williamson, 140

Stewart, James, 155

Stone and Webster, 320

Sun Chong, 230

Swan, James, 161-62

Swan, John: first commercial fisherman in Tacoma, 82; at Medicine Creek, 92; supervises nonhostile Indians on Fox Island, 113-15; visits Leschi camp, 120; sells McNeil Island claim, 137

Sylvester, Edmund, 77, 78-79, 140

Tacoma, aroma of, 328

Tacoma, City of: New and Old merge, 219; census statistics, 1870-1900, 273-74; bond payments suspended, 276; without funds, 278; commission form of government adopted, 330; city manager character adopted, 331; All-American City, 331

Tacoma, "City of Destiny," 332

Tacoma and Southeastern Railroad, 270

Tacoma Anti-Chinese League, 225

Tacoma ASARCO Smelter: profits, 309; reverberatory process, 310. *See also*

Baruch, Bernard; Guggenheim brothers; Rust, William; Ryan, Dennis

Tacoma City, 178

Tacoma City Light: cheap power lures industry, 320, 328-29, 330

Tacoma Hotel, 253, 276

Tacoma Land Company: 169, 173-74, 182

Tacoma Law and Order League, 224-25

Tacoma Light and Water Co., 313, 316, 317, 319

Tacoma Milling and Smelting Co., 262

Tacoma National Bank, 276

Tacoma Public Market, 324

Tacoma Smelting and Refining Co., 263

Tacoma Street Railway, 255

Tacoma Theater, 255, 269

Tallentine claim, 107

Thompson, J. B., 223, 224

Tidd, William, 104, 106

Tideflats, Tacoma, 259

Tidende, 269

Tilton, James: territorial adjutant general, 126-27, 131; plat for Tacoma, 169-70

Tobasket (Puyallup Indian), 130

Tolmie, William Fraser: arrives at Fort Vancouver, 30; travels overland to Fort Nisqually, 30-32; saves injured man's foot, 33; first recorded approach to Mount Rainier, 34-36; calls mountain *Tuchoma,* 36; sells Bush-Simmons party supplies on credit, 74; supports Leschi, 134

Totten, Lt. George M., 53

Totten Inlet, 53

Tourist Hotel (Stadium High School), 276

Tower, Charlemagne, 169

Trafton, Cynthia (Mrs. C. P. Ferry), 267-68

Train, George Francis, 328

Tribunen, 264

Tule Lake, 314

Tunnels, in Tacoma, 312

Um Gow, 222

Union depot, 327

Union Pacific Railroad, 270, 310-13. *See also* Harriman, Edward H.

U.S. Naval Exploring Expedition. *See* Wilkes Expedition

Vancouver, George: commands HMS *Discovery,* 3; receives orders for voyage to Northwest America, 4; assigns Puget to chart southern Sound, 5; explores southern Sound from east shore, 14-16; describes Commencement Bay, 15-16; impressions of Puget Sound, 16-17

Vashon Island, 52-53, 54

Vavasour, Lt. Merwin, 64-67
Vendovi (Fiji chief), 46, 57
Vendovi Island, 54
Villard, Henry: early career, 183-84; represents German investors, 184; takes control of Holladay transportation interests, 185; buys Oregon Steam Navigation Co., 185; organizes Oregon Improvement Co., 186; wins control of NP through "blind pool," 187-88; visits Tacoma, 188-91; finishes transcontinental, 191-93; loses power, 193-94; regains control of NP, 270; buys Tacoma Street Railway Co., 270; role in Mount Tacoma–Mount Rainier controversy, 293, 295
Vincennes: Wilkes's flagship, 45; in danger off Point Grenville, 47-48
Visscher, Col. William Lightfoot, 266-67
Viti Rocks (San Juans), 54
Voorhees, Charles, 202, 227-28

Wacht Am Sunde, 267
Wallace, Hugh, 300
Wallace, William H.; martial law dispute, 123-24; defense attorney for Leschi, 132, 133
Walla Walla Council, 97-98
Ward, Rev. J. A. 223, 224
Washington Territory: first census, 88
Water systems, Tacoma: early, 313, 315; Green River, 322-23, 330
Weisbach, Jacob Robert: early career, 218-19; elected alderman, 219-20; elected mayor, 220; organizes anti-Chinese movement, 222-24; president of Tacoma Anti-Chinese League, 225-26; attends Knights of Labor investiture, 227; elected president of Puget Sound Anti-Chinese Congress, 228-29; criticized by Meeker, 233; observes expulsion, 237-45 passim; indicted, 246; arrested, 247; honored at civic banquet, 248-49; indictment quashed, 251
West Coast Grocery, 300
West Coast Lumberman, 269
West Coast Newsprint, 328
Westra Posten, 269
Weyerhaeuser, Frederick, 302-4
Weyerhaeuser, George, 329
Weyerhaeuser Timber Company: purchases land grant timber, 303; increases holdings, 304-5; Tacoma becomes headquarters, 305; becomes world's largest timber operation, 305-6
Whidbey, Joseph, 6, 17
White, Stanford: designs Tacoma Hotel, 253
Whitehorn, Daniel, 59-60

White River massacre, 102-4
Wickersham, James: on Medicine Creek Treaty, 97; participates in Chinese expulsion, 239; elected probate judge, 318; convicted of seduction, 318; appointed city attorney, 318; wins damage suit for Tacoma against Tacoma Light and Water Co., 318-19
Wiley, J. W., 102
Wilkes, Charles: given command of U.S. Naval Exploring Expedition of 1838-42, 44; character of, 44, 45; guest of HBC, 48-49; visits Columbia and Willamette settlements, 55-56; stages Fourth of July celebration, 57-60; charts Columbia River, 62; describes Puget Sound, 62-63. *See also* Wilkes Expedition
Wilkes Expedition: in Antarctic, 45-46; in South Pacific, 46; approaches Oregon Coast, 46-47; anchors in Discovery Bay, 48; *Porpoise* explores north of Narrows, 51-53; places named for members of, 52-55 passim; *Vincennes* explores south of Narrows, 53-54; Johnson leads inland expeditions, 55-56, 60-62; Wilkes explores Cowlitz and Columbia, 56-57
Wilkeson coal fields, 200
Willamette Cattle Co., 43
Willapa Harbor, 20, 21
Williams, George, 134
Willson, William Holden, 58
Wintermute, Horace, 212
Winthrop, Theodore: influence on naming of Tacoma, 152, 293
Wollochet Bay, 9
Wood, J. M., 269
Wool, Gen. John, 116-18
Work, John, 20-24 passim
World War II: payrolls in Tacoma, 329-30
Wren, Charles, 122
Wright, Charles: early career, 168; favors Tacoma as terminus, 169; appointed president of Tacoma Land Co., 170; hires Olmsted to plan Tacoma, 170-72; becomes president of NP, 181; donates land and cash for church, schools, park, 181-82; finances railroad to coal fields, 182; organizes Tacoma Light and Water Co., 182, 313, 314; retires as president of NP, 183; presses for construction of Cascade Division, 182, 194; estate pays damages to Tacoma, 319

Yesler, Henry, 228, 244
Young, Mrs. Byron, 239
Young, Ewing, 43